LIBRARY OF SECOND TEMPLE STUDIES

96

Formerly Journal for the Study of the Pseudepigrapha Supplement Series

THE MATRIARCHS IN *GENESIS RABBAH*

Katie J. Woolstenhulme

t&tclark

LONDON • NEW YORK • OXFORD • NEW DELHI • SYDNEY

T&T CLARK

Bloomsbury Publishing Plc

50 Bedford Square, London, WC1B 3DP, UK

1385 Broadway, New York, NY 10018, USA

29 Earlsfort Terrace, Dublin 2, Ireland

BLOOMSBURY, T&T CLARK and the T&T Clark logo
are trademarks of Bloomsbury Publishing Plc

First published in Great Britain 2021
This paperback edition published in 2022

Copyright © Katie J. Woolstenhulme, 2021

A catalogue record for this book is available from the British Library.

Library of Congress Cataloging-in-Publication Data

Names: Woolstenhulme, Katherine, author. Title: The Matriarchs in Genesis rabbah / Katherine
Woolstenhulme. Description: London ; New York ; Oxford ; New Dehli ; Sydney : T&T Clark, [2021] |
Series: Library of Second Temple studies ; volume 96 | Revised version of the author's doctoral
dissertation submitted to Durham University, Durham, England, 2017. | Includes bibliographical
references and index. | Summary: "Katie J. Woolstenhulme considers the pertinent question: Who were
'the matriarchs', and what did the rabbis think about them? Whilst scholarship on the role of women
in the Bible and rabbinic Judaism has greatly increased, the authoritative group of women known as
'the matriarchs' has been neglected. This volume consequently focuses on the role and status of the
biblical matriarchs in Genesis Rabbah, the fifth century CE rabbinic Jewish commentary on Genesis.
Woolstenhulme begins by exploring definitions in Genesis Rabbah, such as the nature of midrash, the
nature of the term 'matriarchs', the development of the term throughout early exegetical literature, and the
two definitions that have emerged - the legitimate wives of Israel's patriarchs, and a reference to Jacob's
four wives, who bore Israel's tribal ancestors. She then moves to discuss 'the matriarchal cycle' in Genesis
Rabbah, and its three stages: barrenness; motherhood; and succession. Finally Woolstenhulme considers
Genesis Rabbah's portrayal of the matriarchs as representatives of the female sex, exploring the positive
and negative rabbinic attitudes towards women such as piety, prayer, praise, beauty and sexuality, and how
the matriarchs occasionally exemplify stereotypical, negative female traits. This volume concludes that for
the ancient rabbis, the matriarchs were the historical mothers of Israel, bearing covenant sons, but also the
present mothers of Israel, continuing to influence Jewish identity"-- Provided by publisher.
Identifiers: LCCN 2020033869 (print) | LCCN 2020033870 (ebook) | ISBN 9780567695734 (hardback) |
ISBN 9780567696847 (paperback) | ISBN 9780567695741 (pdf) | ISBN 9780567695765 (epub)
Subjects: LCSH: Women in rabbinical literature. | Matriarchs (Bible) | Midrash rabbah. Genesis--
Criticism, interpretation, etc. | Bible. Genesis--Criticism, interpretation, etc. | Women in the Bible.
Classification: LCC BM518.W7 W66 2021 (print) | LCC BM518.W7 (ebook) | DDC 296.1/4--dc23
LC record available at https://lccn.loc.gov/2020033869
LC ebook record available at https://lccn.loc.gov/2020033870

ISBN:	HB:	978-0-5676-9573-4
	PB:	978-0-5676-9684-7
	ePDF:	978-0-5676-9574-1
	ePUB:	978-0-5676-9576-5

Series: The Library of Second Temple Studies, ISSN 2515-666X, volume 96

To find out more about our authors and books visit www.bloomsbury.com
and sign up for our newsletters.

For my parents

Look to the rock from which you were hewn,
and to the quarry from which you were dug.
Isa 51:1 NRSV

Contents

Part II
'THE MATRIARCHAL CYCLE':
THE PORTRAYAL OF THE MATRIARCHS IN *GENESIS RABBAH*

Chapter 4
PREFACE TO PART II:
'THE MATRIARCHAL CYCLE'

Chapter 5
BARRENNESS

ACKNOWLEDGEMENTS

An earlier version of this work was submitted as my PhD thesis in the Department of Theology and Religion at Durham University. There are so many people that I want to thank for their support in its completion.

First of all, my thanks go to everyone in the Department of Theology and Religion who nurtured me from my first days as an Undergraduate through to the doctorate. I learned so much from so many of you and I would not be where I am today without you. The conversations we had; the time and support offered; and the encouragement provided mean so much to me and were fundamental in my development as a scholar. I am also very grateful to the AHRC for providing me with a doctoral scholarship, which allowed me to complete my PhD work. Dr Matthew Collins's support and encouragement between thesis submission and publication has also been so much appreciated.

To my Durham officemates—Katy, Katie, John, James, Martin, Rachel, Siiri—I loved working alongside all of you and you made days staring at a screen much more bearable!

I am grateful to the staff and students at St John's College, Durham. I was lucky enough to call John's my home for seven years and I am grateful for all of the friendships I made and the opportunities I had there. I want to thank Susie Thorp in particular for giving me her time and providing a listening ear.

I could not have done this without my amazing friends. Thank you to Rich, Zoë, Madison, Ellie, Maddy, Lucy, Sarah, Sarah, Andy, Lizzie, and my 'Durham girls'—Hannah, Chloe, Rachael, Alice, and Sorcha. You are the best friends I could wish for and I am so lucky to have you all.

Finally, thank you to my family, especially my parents, Hellen and Nigel. Doing a PhD has always been my dream and you have always encouraged me; believed in me; and kept me going through it all. You never doubted that I could do this and for that I am so grateful. You taught me to work hard and never give up. I love you more than I can say. And to Phoenix, Dizzy, Fudge, and Archie—thank you for providing the kind of love that no human can.

NOTE ON TEXTS AND TRANSLATIONS

Key Primary Texts

Theodor-Albeck J. Theodor and Chaim Albeck, eds. *Bereschit Rabba mit kritischem Apparat und Commentar*. 2 vols. Veröffentlichungen der Akademie für die Wissenschaft des Judentums. Berlin, 1912–29; repr. in 3 vols., Jerusalem, 1965.

BHS K. Elliger and W. Rudolph, eds. *Biblia Hebraica Stuttgartensia*. 5th rev. ed. Stuttgart, 1997

Primary Text Translations

NRSV New Revised Standard Version

JPS Jewish Publication Society *Tanakh*

Freedman H. Freedman, trans. *Midrash Rabbah Genesis*. 2 vols. London, 1951

Neusner Jacob Neusner, trans. *Genesis Rabbah: A New American Translation*. 3 vols. Atlanta, GA, 1985

Danby Herbert Danby, trans. *The Mishnah*. Oxford, 1964, repr. from 1933 ed.

Soncino Isidore Epstein, ed. *The Babylonian Talmud*. 18 vols. London, 1936–52

Jacobson Howard Jacobson, *A Commentary on Psuedo-Philo's* Liber Antiquitatum Biblicarum. 2 vols. Leiden, 1996

Lauterbach Jacob Z. Lauterbach, trans. *Mekilta de-Rabbi Ishmael*. 2 vols. Philadelphia, 1993

VanderKam James C. VanderKam, trans. *The Book of Jubilees*. Leuven, 1989

Primary Text Abbreviations Used in Freedman

cur. edd. current editions of *Genesis Rabbah*

MS(S) manuscript(s)

NV New Version: *New Version of Bereshith Rabah on the Blessings of the Patriarch Jacob*, in משפטי שבועות of R. Hai Gaon (Venice, 1601; Hamburg, 1781; cur. Vilna ed.): Contains a midrash on Jacob's blessings in Gen 49–50, which most MSS include

MSV Vatican Manuscript 30: Freedman notes that chs. 95–97 of MSV, dealing with Gen 46–48, replace cur. edd. chs. 95–96

Reference Works

BDB	F. Brown, S. Driver, and C. Briggs, *The Brown-Driver-Briggs Hebrew and English Lexicon*. Peabody, MA, 2008, repr. from 1906 ed.
Jastrow	Marcus Jastrow, *Dictionary of the Targumim, Talmud Bavli, Talmud Yerushalmi* and *Midrashic Literature*. 2d ed. 1903; repr. New York, 2004
GKC	*Gesenius' Hebrew Grammar*, ed. E. Kautzsch, trans. A. E. Cowley. 2d. Eng. ed., Oxford, 1910

Transliteration

Transliteration style generally follows *The SBL Handbook of Style for Ancient Near Eastern, Biblical, and Early Christian Studies* (Peabody, MA, 1999).

ABBREVIATIONS

Rabbinic Texts

m.	Mishnah
y.	*Yerushalmi*/Jerusalem Talmud
b.	*Bavli*/Babylonian Talmud
Gen. Rab.	*Genesis Rabbah*
'Abot	*'Abot*
B. Bat.	*Baba Batra*
Bek.	*Bekorot*
Ber.	*Berakot*
'Erub.	*'Erubin*
Ketub.	*Ketubbot*
Meg.	*Megillah*
Mo'ed Qaṭ.	*Mo'ed Qaṭan*
Naš.	*Našim*
Naz.	*Nazir*
Nid.	*Niddah*
Pesaḥ.	*Pesaḥim*
Qidd.	*Qiddušin*
Roš. Haš.	*Rošh Haššanah*
Sanh.	*Sanhedrin*
Šabb.	*Šabbat*
Sipre	*Sipre*
Soṭah	*Soṭah*
Ta'an.	*Ta'anit*
Yebam.	*Yebamot*
'Abot R. Nat.	*'Abot. de Rabbi Nathan*
Cant. Rab.	*Canticles Rabbah*
Lam. Rab.	*Lamentations Rabbah*
Mek. R. Ish.	*Mekilta de Rabbi Ishmael*
Pirqe R. El.	*Pirqe Rabbi Eliezer*
Pesiq. Rab Kah.	*Pesiqta de Rab Kahana*
Tanḥ	*Midrash Tanḥuma*
Tg.	*Targum*
Tg. Neof.	*Targum Neofiti*
Tg. Ps.-J.	*Targum Pseudo-Jonathan*
T. Naph.	*Testament of Naphtali*

Other Primary Text Abbreviations

1Qap Gen	*Genesis Apocryphon* (Qumran Cave 1)
1QS	*Serek hayaḥad* or *Rule of the Community* (Qumran Cave 1)
4Q270	Qumran Cave 4 *Damascus Document* Manuscript
Bar.	Baruch
CD	Cairo Geniza *Damascus Document*
D	*Damascus Document*
Jub.	*Jubilees*
L.A.B.	*Liber antiqitatum biblicarum*
LXX	Greek Septuagint
MT	Masoretic Text (of the Hebrew Bible)
OT	Old Testament
Q	Qumran
Sam.	Samaritan
ShirShabb	*Shirot 'Olat Hashabbat* or *Songs of the Sabbath Sacrifice*
Syr.	Syriac

Secondary Source Abbreviations

ABD	*Anchor Bible Dictionary*. Edited by David Noel Freedman. 6 vols. New York, 1992
DJD	Discoveries in the Judaean Desert
EDB	*Eerdmans Dictionary of the Bible*. Edited by David Noel Freedman. Grand Rapids, 2000
EncJud	*Encyclopaedia Judaica*. Edited by Michael Berenbaum and Fred Skolnik. 22 vols. 2nd ed. Detroit, 2007
JSOT	*Journal for the Study of the Old Testament*
Judaism	*Judaism*
Semeia	*Semeia*
Shofar	*Shofar*
SBL	Society of Biblical Literature
SC	Sources chrétiennes. Paris, 1943–

Technical Abbreviations

BCE	Before Common Era
ca.	circa
CE	Common Era
cf.	*confer*, compare
ed.	edition
ed(s).	editor(s)
e.g.	*exempli gratia*, for example
esp.	especially
ET	English Translation
et passim	and here and there

f(f).	and the following one(s)
frg.	fragment
i.e.	*id est*, that is
loc. cit.	*loco citato*, in the place cited
lit.	literally
n.	note
repr.	reprinted
rev.	revised
sic	so, thus, in this manner
sg.	singular
trans.	translator; translated by
v(v).	verse(s)

Chapter 1

INTRODUCTION

Who are 'the matriarchs' (האימהות) and what did the rabbis think about them? These questions form the basis of this study of the role and status of the biblical matriarchs in *Genesis Rabbah*. The title 'matriarch' (אם) is not found in the Hebrew Bible, but it is a category that has been applied to a number of significant biblical women throughout the history of interpretation. It appears numerous times in rabbinic literature, yet little attention has been paid to the meaning of this title, a surprising fact given its widespread use by scholars and interpreters of the Bible. Moreover, increased attention to the role of women in the biblical texts and in Israelite and Jewish societies makes this a particularly pertinent time to turn to 'the matriarchs', considering their identity and characteristics in greater detail.

This study will focus on the portrayal of the biblical matriarchs in *Genesis Rabbah*, the fifth-century CE rabbinic Jewish commentary on the biblical book of Genesis. If the matriarchs are significant female figures from Israel's history, Genesis is the obvious place to begin any inquiry into them. This biblical book describes the earliest history of humankind, beginning with creation, and most importantly, it describes the earliest history of the nation Israel. Genesis 11–50 narrates the lives of Israel's earliest ancestors, beginning with Abram and his wife, Sarai, and ending with Jacob, his wives and his twelve sons, who founded the twelve tribes of Israel. As the classical midrashic commentary on Genesis, *Genesis Rabbah* offers invaluable insights into rabbinic interpretations of this book. It uses the title 'matriarch(s)' (אם/אימהות) a number of times in relation to the women from Genesis and expands on the biblical characterisation of these figures. There has been no systematic analysis of the matriarchs in *Genesis Rabbah*. In fact, there is only limited discussion of this text and its views on women in existing secondary literature. *Genesis*

Rabbah provides a reliable source for the rabbis' views on the matriarchs and this study will offer a critical account of those traditions.[1]

In discussing *Genesis Rabbah*, I will keep a close eye on Genesis, noting how the rabbis have interpreted the biblical text. The issues addressed in this monograph form part of the reception history of the Hebrew Bible.[2] As such, historical-critical analysis of Genesis will be avoided, as the rabbis were working with a received tradition that they regarded as authoritative.

This monograph thus seeks to understand who 'the matriarchs' are and whether or not the title represents a fixed group. It will look at the individual characterisation of the women regarded as 'the matriarchs' and will consider how their individual portrayals contribute to their group identity. I will impose no particular perspective or preconceptions on the material found in *Genesis Rabbah*. Careful analysis will guide the discussion, with attention paid to language, literary features, and cultural and historical contexts. Focusing on *Genesis Rabbah* will allow a detailed study of these important figures to be conducted within the clear parameters of one rabbinic text. Where necessary, other rabbinic literature will be mentioned to complement what is found in *Genesis Rabbah*.

On the question of feminism and gender studies, I align myself with the approach adopted by Betsy Halpern-Amaru in her monograph on the portrayal of women in *Jubilees*:

> The intent of the title is not to suggest a conceptual framework rooted in feminist theory, but rather to direct attention to an interest in women characters and a highly unusual elevation of their roles in an ancient interpretive reworking of the biblical book of Genesis and early chapters of Exodus.[3]

Like Halpern-Amaru, I remain acutely aware of the patriarchal context within which authors and compilers of previous ages were living, working and writing.[4] I do not wish for this to cloud the evidence provided by the text. I will discuss many rabbinic traditions about the matriarchs, both

---

1. For an introduction to the midrash, see §2.5, '*Genesis Rabbah*'; §2.6, 'A Note on the Text of *Genesis Rabbah*'.

2. Unless otherwise stated, biblical quotations will be from the NRSV. Within the NRSV quotations, round brackets indicate my own translation/explanations. Where individual words or short phrases are discussed, translations are sometimes my own.

3. Betsy Halpern-Amaru, *The Empowerment of Women in the Book of Jubilees*, Supplements to the Journal for the Study of Judaism 60 (Leiden: Brill, 1999), 1.

4. Ibid.

positive and negative. Whilst some views held by the rabbis about women are demeaning and repressive, there are numerous traditions that oppose this view and all must be considered equally.

1.1. *Literature Review*

The fields of biblical and Jewish studies are becoming increasingly populated with works considering the presentation of women in biblical and rabbinic texts, as well as women's roles in Israelite and Jewish society more generally. Whilst some of these works openly identify themselves as feminist, others avoid this label and simply express their interest in learning more about women, their lives and the assumptions made about them throughout history.

The last forty years have seen an explosion in works dealing with the role of women in the Hebrew Bible. The biblical text of Genesis has been subjected to numerous studies of this kind. Perhaps the earliest example is Phyllis Trible's 1973 article, 'Depatriarchalizing in Biblical Interpretation'.[5] Trible argues that whilst the Bible is undeniably patriarchal, it contains themes that counteract sexism. She argues:

> Believing that the text affirms male dominance and female subordination, commentators find evidence for that view. Let us read with the opposing concern: Does the narrative break with patriarchy?[6] By asking this question, we may discover a different understanding.[7]

For example, God transcends sexuality and is often described in feminine terms (e.g. Isa 42:14); the exodus speaks of liberation from oppression, a theme that coheres with the aims of the Women's Liberation Movement; and women also played an active role in that event (see Moses' mother and sister, and the midwives in Exod 1–2). Trible then turns to two biblical texts, Gen 1–3 and the Song of Songs. Her rereading of these narratives uncovers an equality of the sexes that is often overlooked by modern

---

5. Phyllis Trible, 'Depatriarchalizing in Biblical Interpretation', *Journal of the American Academy of Religion* 41 (1973): 30–48. Cf. John W. Miller, 'Depatriarchalizing God in Biblical Interpretation: A Critique', *The Catholic Biblical Quarterly* 48 (1986): 609–16.

6. 'Patriarchy' is, according to Alice Laffey (*An Introduction to the Old Testament: A Feminist Perspective* [Philadelphia: Fortress, 1988], 2), 'a way of ordering reality whereby one group, in this case the male sex, is understood to be superior to the other, the female sex'.

7. Trible, 'Depatriarchalizing', 35.

interpreters, who instead see women demeaned in comparison to men. In suggesting that 'Depatriarchalizing…is a hermeneutic operating within Scripture itself', Trible's work opened up new avenues for discussion of biblical texts.[8] According to Trible, 'we [must not] permit our interpretations to freeze in a patriarchal box of our own construction'.[9]

Danna Nolan Fewell and David M. Gunn's *Gender, Power, & Promise: The Subject of the Bible's First Story* (1993) provides a feminist interpretation of the biblical books of Genesis through to Kings.[10] Fewell and Gunn's reading focuses on the women who are mentioned in those early biblical narratives, but who never take centre stage. They are critical of the patriarchal order, which subsumes the voices and rights of women under male domination. In particular, Abraham is reprimanded for his continued maltreatment of Sarah, as he puts her in danger to protect his own life and refuses to relay God's covenant promises to her. Moreover, these scholars highlight 'the poignant trap of patriarchal motherhood: women face social death without children and physical death to bear children. The risks and the sorrows, the ambiguities and the ironies, are all but passed over in the rush to tell a man's story'.[11] Gunn and Fewell offer a sobering interpretation of the biblical narrative and their conclusions are largely negative.

More recently, and most relevant for my own study, is Tammi J. Schneider's monograph, *Mothers of Promise: Women in the Book of Genesis* (2008).[12] Schneider deals with the portrayal of every woman in Genesis, from central figures like Sarah and Rebekah, to those receiving only brief mention, like Esau's wives. Schneider's study has two major strengths. First, her work offers comprehensive coverage of all female characters in Genesis. Schneider looks at their characterisation within the text, through descriptions given of them; their use as subject or object in the narratives; and their relationships with other figures. Secondly, based on shared characteristics, she groups the females in Genesis together. She argues that in Genesis, women 'determine who receives the promise from the Israelite Deity'.[13] She takes different groups of mothers as the basic structure for her work: matriarchs; mothers of potential heirs; mothers

---

8. Ibid., 48.

9. Ibid.

10. Danna Nolan Fewell and David M. Gunn, *Gender, Power, & Promise: The Subject of the Bible's First Story* (Nashville: Abingdon, 1993).

11. Ibid., 79.

12. Tammi J. Schneider, *Mothers of Promise: Women in the Book of Genesis* (Grand Rapids: Baker Academic, 2008).

13. Ibid., 11.

who predate the promise; and women who do not bear.[14] Schneider allows the characters within a particular group, but also between groups, to be compared and contrasted, drawing attention to nuances in the characterisation of individual females. Schneider concludes that in Genesis, a woman's most important role is as a physical mother through childbearing and that the background of the mother affects the status of her children. *Mothers of Promise* provides sound analysis of the female characters in Genesis and is a useful resource for any further work on these figures.

Finally on the biblical material, it is important to note Athalya Brenner-Idan's *The Israelite Woman: Social Role and Literary Type in Biblical Narrative*, first published in 1985, with a second edition following in 2015.[15] The first half of the monograph is devoted to the particular professions and social institutions assumed by women, including the roles of queens and female prostitution. The second half explores literary paradigms used in the Bible, such as mothers of great men, and foreign women.

This study provides good character analysis of women from the Bible, considering how they are portrayed in the biblical text, and why. This is used as evidence and as source material for the roles of women in ancient Israelite society. Importantly, Brenner-Idan focuses on narrative material from the Hebrew Bible. Though often shaped by an author's ideology, narrative offers a more realistic, 'independent' view of reality than the idealised vision of legal material.[16] *The Israelite Woman* highlights both the range of roles that women performed in ancient Israel and the particular literary archetypes shaping how certain biblical women were portrayed. Brenner-Idan argues that whilst biblical texts are largely composed and edited by men, this does not necessarily make them biased.[17] Yet, she concludes that women are regarded as inferior to men in biblical society; they were to remain within the domestic sphere, ensuring society's successful continuation through childbearing, and preventing them from behaving unacceptably in public.[18] Like Brenner-Idan, I will

---

14. Matriarchs (Sarah, Rebekah, Leah, Rachel); mothers of potential heirs (Hagar, Esau's wives, Zilpah, Bilhah, Dinah, Mrs Judah, Tamar, Asenath); mothers who predate the promise (Eve, Adah and Zillah, Milcah, Mrs Lot, Lot's daughters); and women who do not bear (the woman in the garden, Deborah, Mrs Potiphar).

15. Athalya Brenner-Idan, *The Israelite Woman: Social Role and Literary Type in Biblical Narrative*, Cornerstones (London: Bloomsbury, 2015).

16. Ibid., xvii.

17. E.g. ibid., xvi, 89.

18. E.g. ibid., 132–3.

consider the individual characterisation of certain female figures, namely the Genesis matriarchs, and explore how their individual identities relate to their membership of the wider group entitled 'the matriarchs'.

The role of women in the Hebrew Bible remains a popular area of research. It highlights the value of paying greater attention to women as portrayed in the biblical text, offering a window onto the status of females in ancient society, and the assumptions and prejudices evinced by males, represented largely by the biblical authors, towards them.

Work on women in Judaism has taken longer to emerge.[19] Judith Plaskow's *Standing Again at Sinai: Judaism from a Feminist Perspective* (1991) seeks to form a feminist Jewish theology, paying greater attention to women; recognising the androcentrism of biblical texts and religious traditions; and allowing female voices finally to be heard.[20] Work such as this opened the way for other scholars to begin exploring the role of women in classical Judaism.

Halakhah is the term used to describe Jewish legal traditions, which are recorded in the Mishnah, a second-century CE rabbinic compilation, and in the Palestinian and Babylonian Talmuds (fifth–sixth century CE).[21] Judith Romney Wegner and Rachel Biale have each conducted comprehensive studies of the role of women in halakhah. Wegner's *Chattel or Person? The Status of Women in the Mishnah* (1988) asks whether Jewish law views women merely as property or whether it attributes to them personhood.[22] She concludes that Jewish law regards women as persons, with legal rights and responsibilities, unless their sexuality is at issue, in which case they are treated as property (chattel). Women's sexuality is controlled by men: daughters' sexuality by their fathers and wives' sexuality by their husbands. The levirate widow's sexuality is subject to her deceased husband's brother, who is required by Jewish law to marry the childless widow in order to continue his brother's name. Where sexuality is not at issue, or in the case of women who control their own sexuality

---

19. See Rachel Biale, *Women and Jewish Law: The Essential Texts, Their History, & Their Relevance for Today: With a New Foreword by the Author* (New York: Schocken, 1995), x–xi; Judith Romney Wegner, *Chattel or Person? The Status of Women in the Mishnah* (New York: Oxford University Press, 1988), 4–9, 182–98; Judith R. Baskin, *Midrashic Women: Formations of the Feminine in Rabbinic Literature*, Brandeis Series on Jewish Women (Hanover: Brandeis University Press, 2002), 6–8.

20. Judith Plaskow, *Standing Again at Sinai: Judaism from a Feminist Perspective* (San Francisco: HarperCollins, 1991).

21. See §2.4, 'Rabbinic Texts'.

22. Wegner, *Chattel or Person?*

having been freed from male control, namely the emancipated daughter, the divorcée and the widow, the law treats women as persons.

Wegner's study highlights the tension present in rabbinic views of women's status: 'the Mishnah treats women as chattel *only* when her biological function belongs to a specified man *and* the case poses a threat to his control of that function'.[23] As the determining factor for deciding the woman's status in each situation, sexuality constitutes the fundamental difference between men and women.[24] Wegner suggests that:

> My analysis of the status of women in the mishnaic system may convince Jewish feminists that their best strategy is not to campaign aggressively for rights that were systematically denied to women but rather to argue for the restoration of women's personhood in Jewish law in accordance with basic mishnaic conceptions.

She argues that 'the sages departed from their own view of woman as person only when their social system needed to reinforce male claims on woman's reproductive system or to allay male fears of women's sexuality'.[25]

Rachel Biale's *Women and Jewish Law: The Essential Texts, Their History, & Their Relevance for Today* (1984, reprinted in 1995) addresses areas of halakhah pertaining to women, beginning with biblical injunctions and tracing these through into the Mishnah and Talmuds, as well as medieval and modern commentators.[26] Contrasting her own work with other studies on women in Jewish law, Biale aims to present, without bias, Jewish legal rulings on issues such as marriage, divorce, levirate widowhood and sexuality. Biale wills modern Jewish women to learn more about halakhah so they may fruitfully contribute to present discussions of women's roles in Judaism. Biale presents numerous classical rabbinic texts and opinions on central halakhic issues concerning women. In turn, her objective presentation of such material unearths various assumptions, biases and inequalities present in those texts, particularly the secondary status of women, whose marriages, divorces and sexual relations are determined by men.[27] The topic of women in halakhah has

---

23. Ibid., vi. Emphasis original.
24. Ibid., esp. 165–81.
25. Ibid., vii.
26. Biale, *Women and Jewish Law*.
27. Judith Hauptman offers a similar study. She concludes that the rabbis gave women more rights and responsibilities than the Bible had done. See Judith Hauptman, *Rereading the Rabbis* (Boulder: Westview, 1998).

received reasonable attention in scholarship, as the studies of Biale and Wegner highlight. This may be explained by the continued relevance of halakhah in present-day Judaism, as these rulings continue to shape Jewish life and identity. As Biale concisely concludes, even for those Jews who do not adhere to halakhah, 'it is the framework and vocabulary of Jewish life'.[28] The work of Biale and Wegner provides important information about the context in which the rabbis were living and working.

Aggadah describes non-legal rabbinic material.[29] Judith R. Baskin's *Midrashic Women: Formations of the Feminine in Rabbinic Literature* (2002) is the most comprehensive study to date on the portrayal of women in aggadah.[30] Baskin argues that women are regarded as secondary beings, inferior to men in every way. For Baskin, rabbinic literature shows an awareness of women's disadvantages and even sympathises with them, but ultimately the rabbis seek to justify the secondary status of women by linking this right back to their creation after man in Gen 2. Baskin's work highlights the prejudices that abounded in rabbinic society, although she does not deny that the rabbis also valued women within their domestic roles, especially in so far as they aided men as wives and mothers. Baskin's work is nuanced and, like Wegner, draws attention to the tensions concerning females that are present in rabbinic literature. As Baskin is convinced that the rabbis' overall understanding of women is demeaning, she continuously returns to this point, even after presenting positive rabbinic traditions.

An equally noteworthy contribution to the role of women in aggadah is Leila Leah Bronner's *From Eve to Esther: Rabbinic Reconstructions of Biblical Women* (1994).[31] Like Biale, Bronner refuses to retroject particular modern opinions back onto rabbinic texts; they must speak for themselves. Bronner's monograph specifically concerns the portrayal of biblical females in aggadah. She considers various women, including Hannah and her prayer; Deborah; prophetesses; and biblical daughters, like Dinah and the daughters of Zelophehad. Bronner concludes that:

---

28. Biale, *Women and Jewish Law*, 266; cf. 10. See also Wegner, *Chattel or Person?*, 4–6. Wegner notes that Judaism is: 'a tradition in which religion and law are virtually inseparable and in which practice takes on greater prominence than doctrine' (p. 183).

29. See §2.4, 'Rabbinic Texts'.

30. Baskin, *Midrashic Women*.

31. Leila Leah Bronner, *From Eve to Esther: Rabbinic Reconstructions of Biblical Women*, Gender and the Biblical Tradition (Louisville: Westminster John Knox, 1994).

although these bodies of rabbinic exegesis are rife with stereotypes of feminine qualities, the sages were also ready to appreciate admirable and even heroic qualities in female characters, sometimes even when such characteristics are not plainly evident in the biblical account.[32]

In addition, Bronner suggests that modesty is central to the rabbis' understanding of women. The insistence upon female modesty is regarded as a necessary measure to regulate female action. It prevents unacceptable sexual temptation and behaviour and enables women to successfully fulfil their roles as wives and mothers within the home.

Bronner usefully examines biblical women in aggadah, noting the tension between rabbinic views of the female sex and portrayals of strong women in the Bible. Her recognition that both positive and negative traditions about women exist in aggadah 'present[s] a more balanced picture than one might have anticipated'.[33] Bronner agrees with Baskin that the rabbis showed various prejudices towards women. Yet her argument focuses on an accurate representation of the rabbinic material, both positive and negative. Although Bronner deals with biblical women, she hardly touches on the central female figures from Genesis.

Sing, O Barren One: A Study in Comparative Midrash (1986) by Mary Callaway has been the most important scholarly influence on this study of the matriarchs in *Genesis Rabbah*.[34] Callaway's monograph deals in detail with the development of the barren matriarch tradition, from its biblical origins in Genesis to its interpretation in rabbinic midrash. Callaway employs the method of 'comparative midrash', which 'asks how a given tradition was adapted in different communities which all shared the conviction that the Scriptures would teach them how to live as the people of God in their own times'.[35] Callaway's major concern is to consider the use of the barren matriarch tradition in various historical contexts: in the biblical, intertestamental, Second Temple and classical rabbinic periods.

Callaway presents the most focused study to date on the portrayal of (barren) matriarchs. As such, the content of her work is of direct relevance to my own, providing useful and detailed analysis of the female biblical figures that I will be concerned with. She compares the biblical portrayal of these women with later interpretations of their roles in a range of literature, including the rabbinic midrashim. Moreover, because Callaway

32. Ibid., xx.
33. Ibid., 185.
34. Mary Callaway, *Sing, O Barren One: A Study in Comparative Midrash*, SBL Dissertation Series 91 (Atlanta: Scholars Press, 1986).
35. Ibid., 10.

deals with the development of the barren matriarch tradition from Bible to Midrash, her work provides important observations about the ways in which the tradition was taken up and used in different contexts.

For all of its strengths, Callaway's monograph remains limited. As Callaway offers a survey of traditions about the barren matriarchs from a variety of sources, she is unable to deal at length with any one source. Notably, Callaway's study offers limited engagement with *Genesis Rabbah*, discussing only a few passages. Genesis depicts a number of barren matriarchs and, thus, *Genesis Rabbah* is a central source for understanding rabbinic attitudes to these women. Callaway deals with barrenness as a key characteristic of the matriarchs. Yet, barrenness cannot be considered in isolation from their other central traits. Lastly, Callaway does not really engage with negative traditions about the matriarchs. Such traditions do exist and must be dealt with alongside positive passages. The multivocality of rabbinic texts enables a more accurate judgment about the rabbis' views on women to be attained.

Finally, two of Michael Satlow's works, *Tasting the Dish: Rabbinic Rhetorics of Sexuality* (1995) and *Jewish Marriage in Antiquity* (2001) must be mentioned.[36] These two studies discuss rabbinic views of sexuality. Sexuality was a fundamental part of the rabbis' understanding of women and, thus, studies such as these are able to shed valuable light on the rabbis' socio-cultural context.

This literature review shows that whilst scholarship on the role of women in Rabbinic Judaism is increasing, there is still work to be done. Most studies thus far have focused on the role of women in rabbinic halakhah and aggadah with a view to understanding the status of Jewish women in the present. Whilst this is a noble cause, it is important to allow the texts to speak for themselves, from within their own context. Previous scholarship has also tended to focus on either general or more negative rabbinic views on women.

'The matriarchs' are central figures from the Hebrew Bible, but they have largely been neglected by modern scholars. Given the appearance of the title 'the matriarchs' (האימהות) in rabbinic texts and the widespread usage of this category in modern scholarship, it is necessary to finally afford these women the attention they deserve. This study will move beyond previous work by offering a detailed and comprehensive study of *Genesis Rabbah*'s views of 'the matriarchs', as individuals and as a group.

---

36. Michael L. Satlow, *Tasting the Dish: Rabbinic Rhetorics of Sexuality*, Brown Judaic Studies 303 (Atlanta: Scholars Press, 1995), and *Jewish Marriage in Antiquity* (Princeton: Princeton University Press, 2001).

1.2. *Content Outline*

This monograph is divided into three parts. Part I, entitled '"The Matriarchs" in *Genesis Rabbah*', may essentially be regarded as an extension of the Introduction. The terms and concepts that are central to this work will be explored in the two chapters making up Part I. The first will discuss midrash, rabbinic biblical exegesis. A definition will be offered and the rabbinic worldview and common midrashic techniques will be explored. Finally, an overview of different rabbinic texts will be provided, before *Genesis Rabbah* is introduced. The second chapter will then focus on 'the matriarchs'. Whilst this title is used often in both ancient and modern literature, it is rarely defined. This chapter will trace the origins and development of the term and will then explore its use in *Genesis Rabbah*. Two common definitions of the term will emerge: first and foremost, as the wives of the patriarchs, but secondarily also as the mothers of Israel's tribal ancestors. In making clear how I will use these key terms, the reader will have a clearer sense of what it means to speak about 'the matriarchs in *Genesis Rabbah*'. This is especially important in the field of rabbinic literature, where the same terminology is often used in a variety of ways.

Part II will form the central tenet of the study. Coining language from Lieve Teugels, I have discerned a 'matriarchal cycle' at work in *Genesis Rabbah*. I use this phrase to describe the transformation of each wife of the patriarchs from a barren woman to a mother of covenant sons. Repeated in each generation, this cycle is central to the rabbinic portrayal of the matriarchs and helps to maintain continuity through the patriarchal era, as the nation Israel emerges from one ancestral family. Part II begins with a necessary preface, which introduces and explains what 'the matriarchal cycle' is and how it developed. The biblical barrenness tradition and the viewpoints of modern scholars will be considered within this chapter. This preface leads into a detailed study of the cycle itself, which is made up of three stages: barrenness, motherhood, and legitimacy and succession. Most importantly, 'the matriarchal cycle' shows the great respect that the rabbis had for the mothers of Israel, who bore and protected the covenant sons. Sarah, Rebekah, Leah and Rachel are each shown to be worthy of taking on the matriarchal role and *Genesis Rabbah* emphasises their enduring maternity through 'the matriarchal cycle'.

Finally, Part III will consider the characterisation of the matriarchs as women. Alongside their portrayal within 'the matriarchal cycle', *Genesis Rabbah* also sees the matriarchs as exemplars of stereotypically female virtues and vices. This chapter will discuss, for example, positive and negative interpretations of female beauty and of actions usually associated with women. This will provide an important balance to the preceding discussion of 'the matriarchal cycle'. As well as belonging to the authoritative group of Israel's ancestresses, these characters are also ordinary women. The ways in which the rabbis reconciled these two statuses within the characterisation of each female figure are significant.

Overall, this study will demonstrate that the rabbis revered the founding ancestresses of Israel, who are presented in Genesis. In *Genesis Rabbah*, the rabbis were able to develop their characterisation of the matriarchs through the 'matriarchal cycle'. This 'matriarchal cycle' emphasised the importance of motherhood for defining these women, who bore Israel's earliest ancestors. For the rabbis, the matriarchs were not simply the historical mothers of Israel; they were the present mothers of Israel, whose lives and experiences continued to shape Jewish identity. When portraying the matriarchs as women, they were sometimes portrayed negatively, exhibiting weaknesses that the rabbis believed women in general to possess. Such biases reflect the patriarchal context within which the rabbis were compiling their works. This context must never be ignored, and it should not be justified, but it does help us to understand more clearly the complex characterisation of these biblical women in *Genesis Rabbah*.

Part I

'THE MATRIARCHS' IN *GENESIS RABBAH*

Chapter 2

RABBINIC MIDRASH: AN INTRODUCTION

'The Matriarchs' and 'Genesis Rabbah' are key terms that appear throughout this study and they must be appropriately defined from the beginning. This chapter will offer an introduction to midrash, the term used to describe rabbinic biblical exegesis. After discussing the nature of midrash and the common techniques used within this genre to interpret the Hebrew Bible, *Genesis Rabbah* will be introduced. The next chapter will then present an analysis of the title 'the Matriarchs'. By the end of Part I, the reader will have a clearer understanding of what it means to speak about and explore the role of 'the matriarchs in *Genesis Rabbah*'.

2.1. *Midrash (מדרש)*

Midrash is the term used to describe rabbinic exegesis of the Hebrew Bible.[1] The noun midrash (מדרש) derives from the Hebrew verbal root

1. For all that follows, see: Jacob Neusner, *Rabbinic Literature: The Essential Guide*, Abingdon Essential Guides (Nashville: Abingdon, 2005); H. L. Strack and Günter Stemberger, *Introduction to the Talmud and Midrash*, trans. Markus Bockmuehl (Minneapolis: Fortress, 1996); Eyal Ben-Eliyahu, Yehudah Cohn and Fergus Millar, *Handbook of Jewish Literature from Late Antiquity, 135–700 CE* (Oxford: Published for The British Academy by Oxford University Press, 2012); R. S. Sarason, 'Midrash', in *Dictionary of Biblical Interpretation, K–Z*, ed. John H. Hayes (Nashville: Abingdon, 1999), 155–7; Philip S. Alexander, 'Midrash', in *A Dictionary of Biblical Interpretation*, ed. R. J. Coggins and J. L. Houlden (London: SCM; Philadelphia: Trinity Press International, 1990), 452–9; Carol Bakhos, ed., *Current Trends in the Study of Midrash*, Supplements to the Journal for the Study of Judaism 106 (Leiden: Brill, 2006); Daniel Boyarin, *Intertextuality and the Reading of Midrash* (Bloomington: Indiana University Press, 1990); Geoffrey H. Hartman and Sanford Budick, eds., *Midrash and Literature* (New Haven: Yale University Press, 1986);

דרשׁ, meaning 'to search' or 'seek out'.[2] The verb appears many times in the Hebrew Bible, often connoting human enquiry of God.[3] The noun may be found in 2 Chr 13:22 and 24:27, used as the title of two works, each of which clearly studies or elucidates another text.[4]

Midrash (מדרשׁ) became the standard term for both the process and product of rabbinic biblical interpretation.[5] It describes the classical Jewish rabbis' approach to Torah, including their hermeneutical framework and the techniques used to expound and expand upon Scripture. Kugel suggests that the term:

> might be best translated as 'research', a translation that incorporates the word's root meaning of 'search out, inquire' and perhaps as well suggests that the results of that research are almost by definition recherché, that is, not obvious, out-of-the-way, sometimes far-fetched.[6]

Midrash also refers to the texts produced by this process: an entire work may be named a 'midrash'; but each individual pericope comprising that work is also called a 'midrash'. Midrashic texts are structured in various ways and derive from different eras, but they all share the common aim of attempting to explain the meanings of Torah.

Midrash is a difficult word to define, not least because it can mean different things to different scholars. As Philip Alexander explains, the term midrash may be used to refer to all ancient Jewish biblical interpretation, rabbinic or not, or it may be used to refer exclusively to rabbinic

---

Michael Fishbane, *The Exegetical Imagination: On Jewish Thought and Theology* (Cambridge, MA: Harvard University Press, 1998); Irving Jacobs, *The Midrashic Process* (Cambridge: Cambridge University Press, 1995); Callaway, *Sing, O Barren One*, 1–12.

2. BDB, 205; Jastrow, 325.

3. For דרשׁ as enquiring of God, see e.g. Gen 25:22; Exod 18:15; 1 Kgs 22:5; Ezek 14:7. For other uses of דרשׁ, see Lev 10:16; 1 Kgs 14:5.

4. 'The midrash of the prophet Iddo' (2 Chr 13:22) and 'the midrash of the book of the Kings' (24:27). BDB, 205. Cf. Jastrow, 735.

5. James L. Kugel ('Two Introductions to Midrash', in Hartman and Budick, eds., *Midrash and Literature*, 91) says that midrash 'is both the activity of interpretation and the fruits of that activity'; Alexander ('Midrash', 453) sees it 'as a process and as an artefact'. See also Sarason, 'Midrash', 155–6; Strack and Stemberger, *Introduction*, 234–5. Fishbane (*Exegetical Imagination*, ix) argues that detailed analysis of midrash allows us 'to retrieve the inner texture of classical Jewish thinking as an ongoing exegetical process. This process is not found in any given text or complex, but in the unfolding of ideas around key biblical texts over the course of millennia.'

6. Kugel, 'Introductions', 91.

exegesis.[7] In his article introducing midrash, Kugel takes the former stance, claiming: 'At bottom midrash is not a genre of interpretation but an interpretative stance, a way of reading the sacred text, and we shall use it in this broad sense'.[8] Midrash does indeed represent an approach to the biblical text; but its nuances are lost when used as a general term for all early biblical exegesis. In this study, midrash will refer only to rabbinic biblical interpretation. This is the most accurate use of the term and avoids confusion with other literature, such as that produced by the Dead Sea sect at Qumran, whose approach to the Bible is often very different from the rabbis' own.[9]

2.2. *The Theory of Midrash: The Rabbinic Worldview*

To understand the aims and purpose of midrash, rabbinic views on the nature of Scripture must be considered.[10] For the rabbis, there are two Torahs: the Written Torah and the Oral Torah.[11] The Written Torah is the text of the Hebrew Bible, whilst Oral Torah describes accompanying oral traditions also relayed to Moses on Mount Sinai and conveyed orally from teacher to student down to the rabbis' own day. Oral Torah is recorded in the various written texts which emanate from the rabbis, including the Mishnah (second century CE) and midrashim.[12] The Written and Oral Torah are equally authoritative for the Jewish people and rabbinic works function alongside Scripture as the central texts of Judaism. In fact, many Jewish practices throughout history, such as prayer rituals, are laid down in rabbinic texts and continue to be authoritative even in modern Judaism.[13]

7. Alexander, 'Midrash', 452–3.

8. Kugel, 'Introductions', 91. Kugel includes *Genesis Apocryphon* and *Targumim* alongside the rabbinic midrashim in this category (ibid., 91–2). On 'Rewritten Bible' compared with midrash, see Steven Fraade, 'Rewritten Bible and Rabbinic Midrash as Commentary', in Bakhos, ed., *Current Trends in the Study of Midrash*, 59–78.

9. See Geza Vermes, *The Complete Dead Sea Scrolls in English* (London: Penguin, 2004).

10. Fishbane's work has shaped what follows, especially Scripture as God's word; see Fishbane, *Exegetical Imagination*, esp. 2, 9–21.

11. On Dual Torah, see Alexander, 'Midrash', 458; David Stern, *Midrash and Theory: Ancient Jewish Exegesis and Contemporary Literary Studies*, Rethinking Theory (Evanston: Northwestern University Press, 1996), 26–7; Neusner, *Essential Guide*, 2; Ephraim E. Urbach, *The Sages: Their Concepts and Beliefs*, trans. Israel Abrahams (Jerusalem: Magnes, The Hebrew University, 1975), 286–314.

12. See Strack and Stemberger, *Introduction*, 31–44.

13. On prayer ritual, see Reuven Kimelman, 'Rabbinic Prayer in Late Antiquity', in *Cambridge History of Judaism. Vol. 4, The Late Roman-Rabbinic Period*, ed.

As Alexander summarises:

> The idea of the Oral Torah introduces flexibility into the doctrine of Torah. The written Torah is a closed, canonic text, fixed and inviolable. The Oral Torah is open-ended, ever developing. It is able to demonstrate the relevance of the written Torah to changing historical circumstances. At the same time the Oral Torah imposes limits on the interpretation. The *darshan* does not stand before the text of scripture with absolute freedom. He must work within the tradition.[14]

Most importantly, the rabbis believed that Torah is the Word of God.[15] As such, it is infinitely greater than human language and cannot be contained within it. This means that Scripture can be interpreted in multiple ways, revealing different facets of its divine language. Rabbinic midrash complements the text of the Hebrew Bible, aiding human understanding of God's law by acknowledging that every word, even every letter, of Scripture is meaningful.[16] This approach is encapsulated in the oft-cited expression: 'Turn it and turn it again for everything is in it' (*m. 'Abot* 5:22).

The rabbis' understanding of Scripture provided opportunities for interpreting biblical verses in numerous ways. Rabbinic literature is characterised by its dialogical and multivocal approach to biblical texts. Multiple, even contradictory, interpretations of a biblical verse are often presented next to one another and without adjudication, even within the same midrash.[17] This highlights once more the complexity of scriptural

---

Steven T. Katz (Cambridge: Cambridge University Press, 2006), 573–611; Ismar Elbogen, *Der jüdische Gottesdienst in seiner geschichtlichen Entwicklung*, Schriften / hrsg. von der Gesellschaft zur Förderung der Wissenschaft des Judentums Grundriss der Gesamtwissenschaft des Judentums (Frankfurt: Kaufmann, 1931); Stefan C. Reif, *Judaism and Hebrew Prayer: New Perspectives on Jewish Liturgical History* (Cambridge: Cambridge University Press, 1995); Israel Abrahams, 'Prayer', *EncJud*, XVI:458–9.

14. Alexander, 'Midrash', 458. Cf. Fishbane, *Exegetical Imagination*, 12; Strack and Stemberger, *Introduction*, 15–16.

15. See Fishbane, *Exegetical Imagination*, 9–20.

16. See Alexander, 'Midrash', 457–8; Joseph Heinemann, 'The Nature of the Aggadah', in Hartman and Budick, eds., *Midrash and Literature*, 48; Kugel, 'Introductions', 96; Fishbane, *Exegetical Imagination*, 12, 18; Stern, *Midrash and Theory*, 31–2, 60.

17. See Kugel, 'Introductions', 94; Sarason, 'Midrash', 156; Jerry Rabow, *The Lost Matriarch: Finding Leah in the Bible and Midrash* (Philadelphia: The Jewish Publication Society, 2014), 10; Baskin, *Midrashic Women*, 5, 11; Hauptman, *Rereading*, 9; Alexander, 'Midrash', 454–7. Alexander also notes the anonymity of

language and may also relate to the historical context within which the midrashim were produced. Debates habitually took place within study houses (בית המדרש) in Palestine and Babylonia, the two main centres of rabbinic Judaism, and midrashic texts appear to record these kinds of discussions.[18]

In *The Exegetical Imagination*, Michael Fishbane describes rabbinic biblical exegesis as a 'textualisation of the world', where 'the world of the text serves as the basis for the textualisation of the world – and its meaning'.[19] Furthermore, he states: 'This rabbinisation of Torah is thus one side of a double mirror; the other is the biblicisation of Judaism'.[20] Fishbane's work highlights the interconnectedness of the rabbis' world-view, as their approaches to Scripture and human life are combined. Modern readers must subsume themselves within this all-encompassing rabbinic worldview. Without total immersion in their reality, it is impossible to understand how the rabbis conceived of their world and what they hoped to achieve through their biblical exegesis.[21]

2.3. *Common Midrashic Exegetical Techniques*

Midrash employs a wide range of exegetical techniques as it interprets biblical texts.[22] These techniques are intended to fill scriptural gaps,[23]

the midrashim, which include different rabbis' views (Alexander, 'Midrash', 454–5). When the midrash attributes a view to 'the rabbis', it seems to represent a particularly authoritative position, endorsed by a group of sages.

18. Alexander, 'Midrash', 454–5.

19. Fishbane, *Exegetical Imagination*, 4. Fishbane's 'textualization' language is based on/echoes Thomas Mann's notion of '*zitathaftes Leben*' (ibid., 1).

20. Ibid., 5.

21. See ibid.

22. See Alexander, 'Midrash', 457–8; Sarason, 'Midrash', 156. A strong scholarly trend reads midrash as literature. This approach has heavily influenced the present study and its approach to *Genesis Rabbah*. For midrash as literature, see eds. Hartman, and Budick, *Midrash and Literature*; Fishbane, *Exegetical Imagination*; Stern, *Midrash and Theory*; Kugel, 'Introductions', 77–103; Joshua Levinson, 'Literary Approaches to Midrash', in Bakhos, ed., *Current Trends in the Study of Midrash*, 189–226; Boyarin, *Intertextuality*. For current scholarly approaches to midrash, see the essays in Bakhos, ed., *Current Trends in the Study of Midrash*; Moshe Lavee, 'Rabbinic Literature and the History of Judaism in Late Antiquity: Challenges, Methodologies and New Approaches', in *Rabbinic Texts and the History of Late Roman Palestine*, ed. Martin Goodman and Philip Alexander, Proceedings of the British Academy 165 (Oxford: Published for The British Academy by Oxford University Press, 2010), 319–51.

23. Or 'surface irregularities' (Kugel, 'Introductions', 92).

and to elucidate, explain, expand and comment upon Scripture to allow greater understanding of its contents. For the rabbis, Scripture is a unity and so texts from one part of the Torah may be used to comment upon a verse from elsewhere in the written tradition.[24] Moreover, this concept of unity negates the existence of contradictions between biblical texts or rulings. If one ruling appears to contradict another, this is because human understanding of divine language is limited. Were we to fully understand Scripture, these 'contradictions' would disappear.[25]

Whilst it would be impossible to list here all of the exegetical techniques found in rabbinic midrash, four of the most prominent—wordplay, *gezerah shawah, gematria* and proems—will be outlined briefly.[26] These examples offer valuable insight into the rabbis' approach to biblical exegesis and each will be referred to in this study as specific traditions from *Genesis Rabbah* are explored.

The rather broad category of wordplay enables the rabbis to uncover additional meanings hidden within the language of the biblical text.[27] One example of this may be seen in *Gen. Rab.* 71:2, where the Hebrew term used to describe Rachel as 'barren' (עקר) is reinterpreted as 'chief' (עיקר). The trait marking Rachel's weakness in the biblical text, as she is unable to bear children for her husband, becomes a symbol of her authority in the rabbinic interpretation of this verse.[28] Wordplay thus allows the rabbis to demonstrate the richness of Scripture.

Gezerah shawah ('equal ordinance'; 'statute') is another popular midrashic technique.[29] It creates connections between two disparate biblical verses based on the use of an identical word in each. Thus, if the use of a word in a particular biblical verse is unclear, the use of that same word in another verse elsewhere in Scripture may be able to elucidate its meaning. One such example is *Gen. Rab.* 53:8, where the use of the verb עשה, 'to make', in Gen 21:6 is explained through its usage in Est 2:18.[30]

---

24. Strack and Stemberger, *Introduction*, 237; Fishbane, *Exegetical Imagination*, 12–13.

25. Alexander, 'Midrash', 457–8.

26. Rabbinic literature provides several lists of midrashic exegetical techniques; none are exhaustive. See Alexander, 'Midrash', 458; Strack and Stemberger, *Introduction*, 15–30; Philip S. Alexander, 'The Rabbinic Hermeneutical Rules and the Problem of the Definition of Midrash', *Proceedings of the Irish Biblical Association* 8 (1984): 97–125.

27. Cf. Rabow, *Lost Matriarch*, xiii.

28. See §5.4, 'Matriarchs as Representatives: Of the National Identity'; §6.5.4, 'Leah and Rachel: The Mothers of Tribal Ancestors'.

29. See Strack and Stemberger, *Introduction*, 17–18.

30. See §5.3.2, 'The Reversal of Barrenness and Its Consequences'.

Gezerah shawah may only be transmitted from teacher to pupil because it is not necessarily the case that any two verses containing a particular word may be used to explain one another.[31]

In *gematria*, each letter of the Hebrew alphabet is provided with a numerical equivalent (א is 1; ב is 2; etc).[32] This allows the rabbis to see hidden meanings within certain words that they interpret. For example, זה, 'this', forms part of Rebekah's complaint about her pregnancy in Gen 25:22. The numerical values of these two letters, seven and five respectively, add up to twelve and thus conceal reference to the tribes of Israel.[33]

Finally, the proem is a homiletical technique that finds its way into written midrash.[34] A midrash may open with (hence its alternate name, *petiḥah*, is derived from the verb פתח, 'to open')[35] one verse of Scripture, and by the end of the pericope this seemingly unconnected verse will be shown to comment directly upon the verse being expounded.[36] The technique is believed to have originated in the synagogue, where a preacher hoped to maintain his audience's attention throughout his sermon by creating an element of intrigue about how two disparate biblical verses actually connect.[37] Again, this highlights the ultimate unity of Scripture.[38]

Rabbinic midrash offers an exciting and intellectually challenging approach to the Torah, which continuously encourages its audience to ask deeper questions of the scriptural text.

---

31. Strack and Stemberger, *Introduction*, 18.

32. See Strack and Stemberger, *Introduction*, 29; David Derovan, Gershom Scholem and Moshe Idel, 'Gematria', *EncJud*, VII:424–7.

33. See §6.5.3, 'Rebekah: The Mother of Two Nations'.

34. On the proem and what follows here, see Alexander, 'Midrash', 457; Strack and Stemberger, *Introduction*, 244–5; Joseph Heinemann, 'The Proem in the Aggadic Midrashim—A Form-Critical Study', in *Studies in Aggadah and Folk-Literature*, ed. Joseph Heinemann and Dov Noy, Scripta Hierosolymitana (Jerusalem: Magnes, 1971), 100–122; Martin S. Jaffee, 'The "Midrashic" Proem: Towards the Description of Rabbinic Exegesis', in *Studies in Liturgy, Exegesis, and Talmudic Narrative*, ed. William Scott Green, Approaches to Ancient Judaism 4 (Chico: Scholars Press, 1983), 95–112; Richard S. Sarason, 'The Peiḥtot in Leviticus Rabba: "Oral Homilies" or Redactional Constructions?', *Journal of Jewish Studies* 33, no. 1–2 (1982): 557–67; Stern, *Midrash and Theory*, 19, 57–8; Jacobs, *Midrashic Process*, 2, 13–14, 17, 79–94.

35. See Jastrow, 1252–3.

36. Cf. Kugel, 'Introductions', 93; Fishbane, *Exegetical Imagination*, 94–5; Strack and Stemberger, *Introduction*, 237.

37. Heinemann, 'Aggadah', 47, 49; Alexander, 'Midrash', 455; Kugel, 'Introductions', 95.

38. Jacobs, *Midrashic Process*, 17.

2.4. *Rabbinic Texts*

Classical rabbinic Judaism produced a number of authoritative texts. These texts are written in Hebrew or Aramaic, often a mixture of both. Whilst tentative dates may be offered for the final redaction of each text, traditions contained within these compilatory works may date much earlier.[39]

Rabbinic texts contain two types of material. Halakhah describes Jewish legal material, relating to the laws that govern Israel's life within the covenant. Aggadah is a wide-ranging term, including all non-legal material transmitted by the rabbis. Examples of aggadic material would be the use of narratives, parables, or wordplay to convey something about how Jews should or should not live their lives.[40]

The Mishnah, dating to around 200 CE, is the earliest extant rabbinic text.[41] As the main collection of rabbinic legal rulings (halakhah), it is central to rabbinic Jewish life. There are two rabbinic commentaries on the Mishnah: the Palestinian Talmud (Yerushalmi, around 400 CE)[42] and the Babylonian Talmud (Bavli, around 600 CE).[43] The Bavli became the more well-known of the two Talmudim because Babylonia remained the centre of rabbinic Judaism until the Middle Ages.[44]

---

39. See Alexander, 'Midrash', 455–6.

40. On halakhah and aggadah, see Sarason, 'Midrash', 156; Ben-Eliyahu, Cohn and Millar, *Handbook*, 78; Strack and Stemberger, *Introduction*, 16, 50–5, 238–40; Neusner, *Essential Guide*, 19, 122; Baskin, *Midrashic Women*, 4–7. Heinemann's discussion of aggadah emphasises its diverse nature and didactic qualities (Heinemann, 'Aggadah', 41–55). For the relationship between halakhah and aggadah, see Heinemann, 'Aggadah', 50–4.

41. See Ben-Eliyahu, Cohn and Millar, *Handbook*, 23–6; Strack and Stemberger, *Introduction*, 108–48; Neusner, *Essential Guide*, 3. Translations of the Mishnah will be from Danby.

42. See Ben-Eliyahu, Cohn and Millar, *Handbook*, 29–32; Strack and Stemberger, *Introduction*, 164–89. It is notable that the Yerushalmi 'often evinces parallels to texts in *Genesis Rabbah, Leviticus Rabbah,* and *Pesiqta DeRav Kahana*' (Ben-Eliyahu, Cohn and Millar, *Handbook*, 29).

43. See Ben-Eliyahu, Cohn and Millar, *Handbook*, 32–7; Strack and Stemberger, *Introduction*, 224. Translations of the Babylonian Talmud will be from Soncino.

44. See Isaiah M. Gafni, 'The Political, Social, and Economic History of Babylonian Jewry, 224–638 CE', 792–820; Richard Kalmin, 'The Formation and Character of the Babylonian Talmud', 840–76; and David Goodblatt, 'The History of the Babylonian Academies', 821–39, all in Katz, ed., *The Late Roman-Rabbinic Period*.

The other major literary outputs of rabbinic Judaism are the midrashim. Modern scholars have devised various categories by which to identify these texts.[45] The halakhic (tannaitic) midrashim were produced by the earliest generation of rabbis (the tannaim)[46] and deal primarily with Jewish legal material from the Pentateuch.[47] The aggadic midrashim were produced between the fifth century CE and the medieval period.[48] They include the exegetical midrashim, which interpret an entire biblical book verse-by-verse,[49] and the homiletical midrashim, interpreting portions of Torah that are read as part of synagogue liturgy.[50]

Whilst *Genesis Rabbah* will remain the focus of this study, other rabbinic texts will be consulted when they shed light on the traditions contained there.

2.5. Genesis Rabbah

Genesis Rabbah is a Palestinian exegetical midrash, written in Hebrew and Aramaic. It dates, in its final redacted form, to the fifth century CE, though many of its traditions originated much earlier.[51]

Genesis Rabbah interprets each verse in the biblical book of Genesis in turn, often providing multiple interpretations of verses. Only a few verses are omitted, most notably Abraham's servant's account of meeting Rebekah at the well (Gen 24:34-49). *Genesis Rabbah* employs many midrashic exegetical techniques as it interprets Genesis. Regarding its structure, Alexander comments:

45. See Alexander, 'Midrash', 453–4; Sarason, 'Midrash', 156–7; Strack and Stemberger, *Introduction*, 239–40.

46. Rabbis: first generation—tannaim; second generation—amoraim; later rabbis—saboraim, geonim. See Alexander, 'Midrash', 453; Strack and Stemberger, *Introduction*, 7.

47. E.g. *Mek. R. Ish.* (third century CE), interpreting Exodus from ch. 12 onwards. On halakhic midrashim, see Ben-Eliyahu, Cohn and Millar, *Handbook*, 61–78; Strack and Stemberger, *Introduction*, 247–75.

48. See Ben-Eliyahu, Cohn and Millar, *Handbook*, 78–95; Strack and Stemberger, *Introduction*, 239–40, 276–325.

49. E.g. *Genesis Rabbah*. On exegetical midrashim, see Ben-Eliyahu, Cohn and Millar, *Handbook*, 79; Strack and Stemberger, *Introduction*, 240, 276–87, 322–5.

50. E.g. *Leviticus Rabbah* (fifth century CE). On homiletical midrashim, see Strack and Stemberger, *Introduction*, 240, 288–314; Ben-Eliyahu, Cohn and Millar, *Handbook*, 79; Jacobs, *Midrashic Process*, 18.

51. See Ben-Eliyahu, Cohn and Millar, *Handbook*, 81–3; Strack and Stemberger, *Introduction*, 276–83; Jacobs, *Midrashic Process*, 16–18; Neusner, *Essential Guide*, 74–7.

It is divided into *parashiyyot* ('sections') which number between 97 and
101, depending on the manuscript.[52] The basis of these *parashiyyot* remains
obscure: they do not correlate in any obvious way with the sections of
either the three- or the one-year lectionary cycle. Each *parashah* falls into
two parts: it begins with a *petiḥah* or a series of *petiḥot* which have the first
verse of the *parashah* as the base verse; then follows a detailed running
commentary on the biblical text.[53]

The text abounds in narratives, wordplay, rabbinic anecdotes and playful
comparisons. In this way, it is a midrash par excellence.

The text of *Genesis Rabbah* forms the foundation of my study for a
number of reasons. The biblical text of Genesis describes the lives of
Israel's earliest ancestors, including the women who married patriarchs
and bore central covenant sons. This is a 'family saga', but more than this,
'historical context does not only look backward; the lives of these heroes
are also illuminated by what will happen to their descendants'.[54] The title
'matriarch' (אם) is found in *Genesis Rabbah* and this makes it a suitable
starting point for a scholarly consideration of rabbinic views of Israel's
ancestresses. Moreover, as the earliest exegetical midrash, produced
within the Holy Land and employing the common characteristics of
rabbinic midrash, *Genesis Rabbah* represents the very heart of Rabbinic
Judaism. It is therefore an extremely important text for understanding
how the rabbis conceived of both the world they lived in and the history
bequeathed to them by their biblical and historical forebears.

2.6. *A Note on the Text of* Genesis Rabbah

Theodor-Albeck is the modern critical edition of *Bereshit Rabba.* This
text uses the London Manuscript as its basis, but references and incorpo-
rates material from other manuscripts, such as the Vienna Manuscript.[55]
This study is interested in the final form and coherency of *Genesis Rabbah*
and will not therefore engage in discussions of text criticism or redaction.

---

52. MS Vatican 30 is divided into 101 sections. See Ben-Eliyahu, Cohn and
Millar, *Handbook*, 81.
53. Alexander, 'Midrash', 453.
54. Rabow, *Lost Matriarch*, 4. Cf. Baskin, *Midrashic Women*, 3.
55. For a text profile of *Genesis Rabbah*, see Alexander Samely, in collaboration
with Philip Alexander, Rocco Bernasconi and Robert Hayward, *Profiling Jewish
Literature in Antiquity: An Inventory from Second Temple Texts to the Talmuds*
(Oxford: Oxford University Press, 2013), 409–25.

Even so, these issues must be recognised, as they have shaped discussions about *Genesis Rabbah* over the last few decades, especially in the work of Peter Schäfer and Chaim Milikowsky. The manuscripts of *Genesis Rabbah* differ from one another in a number of places, particularly towards the end of the text. Schäfer and Milikowsky's ongoing dispute centres on these issues and asks whether we may even speak of a single text, '*Genesis Rabbah*'.[56] This study will be mindful of such textual differences and, where relevant, will note and discuss them.

H. Freedman and Jacob Neusner have each produced English translations of *Genesis Rabbah*, based on Theodor-Albeck's text.[57] Quotations from *Genesis Rabbah* will be taken from Freedman's Soncino translation.[58] This translation has been adopted for practical reasons, as it is a well-known and respected rendering of the original text. Every translation contains flaws and inaccuracies, especially where there is a plethora of manuscript variations to attend to, as in *Genesis Rabbah*. I have checked Freedman's translation carefully against the Theodor-Albeck critical edition. On certain occasions, my own translation of the original text will be offered, where I believe that the Hebrew/Aramaic may be rendered more accurately in English than in Freedman's translation. My own translations will be clearly identified or, if occurring within a quotation from Freedman, will be indicated by round brackets.[59]

---

56. E.g. Peter Schäfer, 'Research into Rabbinic Literature: An Attempt to Define the *Status Quaestionis*', *Journal of Jewish Studies* 37, no. 2 (1986): 139–52; Chaim Milikowsky, 'The *Status Quaestionis* of Research in Rabbinic Literature', *Journal of Jewish Studies* 39, no. 2 (1989): 201–11. These articles were reprinted concurrently in Goodman and Alexander, eds., *Rabbinic Texts and the History of Late-Roman Palestine*, 51–78, and followed in the same volume by an article co-authored by Schäfer and Milikowsky, where they updated responses to one another's arguments (Peter Schäfer and Chaim Milikowsky, 'Current Views on the Editing of the Rabbinic Texts of Late Antiquity: Reflections of a Debate After Twenty Years', 79–88).

57. H. Freedman, trans., *Midrash Rabbah Genesis*, 2 vols., vols. 1–2 of *Midrash Rabbah translated into English with Notes, Glossary and Indices Under the Editorship of H. Freedman and Maurice Simon Complete in 10 Volumes* (London: Soncino, 1951); Jacob Neusner, trans., *Genesis Rabbah: The Judaic Commentary to the Book of Genesis: A New American Translation*, 3 vols., Brown Judaic Studies 104–6 (Atlanta: Scholars Press, 1985).

58. Where Neusner's translation is used, this will be indicated.

59. Hebrew roots/words will often be added to Freedman's translation to aid interpretation of passages.

2.7. *Conclusions*

This chapter has provided an outline of the nature and purpose of rabbinic midrash. Midrash (מדרש) is the term used to describe rabbinic biblical interpretation and the works produced as a result of this. Rabbinic texts record Oral Torah, oral traditions relayed to Moses on Mount Sinai and then passed down from teacher to student until the rabbis' own day. Thus, whilst the rabbis use manifold, often highly creative, strategies to interpret Scripture, the status of these interpretations as Oral Torah makes them just as authoritative as the written text of the Bible itself. Four key interpretive techniques—wordplay, *gezerah shawah*, *gematria* and proems—were then explored.

Genesis Rabbah is a Palestinian exegetical midrash on Genesis and is written in Hebrew and Aramaic. Compiled in the fifth century CE, it also contains traditions that date much earlier. *Genesis Rabbah* interprets the biblical text of Genesis, often offering several interpretations of each verse. It deals with the biblical narratives concerning Israel's earliest ancestors and uses the term 'matriarch' (אם) in several places. *Genesis Rabbah* is therefore a significant source to consider when seeking to understand who the matriarchs are and their importance for Judaism. Having explored these issues, it is now apt to consider the meaning of the other key term used throughout this study: 'the matriarchs'.

Chapter 3

'THE MATRIARCHS' (האימהות)

The term 'the matriarchs' (האימהות) does not appear in the Hebrew Bible; yet, by the second century CE, it has become an authoritative title used in rabbinic literature. This chapter will explore the origins and development of 'the matriarchs' in order to gain a clearer understanding of what the title means and to whom it refers. Beginning with the Hebrew Bible and moving through ancient Jewish literature into early rabbinic midrash, increased attention is paid to the mothers of Israel's covenant sons. This accentuates and develops details found in the biblical text of Genesis and is also influenced by the contextual, historical factor of the matrilineal principle in Judaism, whereby offspring inherit Jewishness from their mothers. In the latter part of this chapter, the use of the title 'the matriarchs' in passages from *Genesis Rabbah* will be considered.[1] *Genesis Rabbah* utilises the term in two different ways. It primarily refers to the wives of the patriarchs: Sarah, Rebekah, Leah and Rachel; but in certain specific contexts, the title may also be used to describe Jacob's wives: Leah, Rachel, Bilhah and Zilpah, those women who bore the eponymous ancestors of Israel's twelve tribes.

3.1. *Modern Scholarly Understandings of the Term 'Matriarch'*

Interpreters of the Hebrew Bible have been referring to 'the matriarchs' as an authoritative group for centuries. It is necessary to explore which biblical women constitute the group and why the title is used at all. Modern scholars often display complacency in this regard, referring to 'the matriarchs' without identifying them. The most common referents appear to be Sarah, Rebekah, Leah and Rachel, the legitimate wives

---

1. See *Gen. Rab.* 39:11; 45:4; 48:15; 53:8; 58:4; 63:6; 67:9; 68:5; 70:7; 71:4; 72:6; 73:3. These passages will be discussed later in this chapter.

of Israel's three great patriarchs, Abraham, Isaac and Jacob; however, this is usually implied rather than stated and justified. A brief survey of secondary literature will highlight some of the diverse ways that modern scholars approach this topic.[2]

Fewell and Gunn interpret Genesis from a gendered perspective.[3] When introducing Gen 12–50, they explain that these chapters are designated 'the patriarchal narratives' because they portray 'the history of the "patriarchs", Abraham, Isaac and Jacob'.[4] The term 'matriarch(s)' appears nowhere in this study and yet the authors seem to assume the existence of a group of 'matriarchs', corresponding to the male 'patriarchs'. They claim that in Gen 24: 'The patriarch's heir Isaac must be matched by a *matriarchal* successor. Enter Rebekah.'[5] Gunn and Fewell do not discuss the title 'matriarch', though they assume that it is known and understood by their readers.

Mary Callaway never defines the term 'matriarch', although barrenness is given as a central trait of the women she discusses.[6] Her chapter entitled 'The Matriarchs in Genesis' discusses the four wives of the patriarchs, but still offers no clear definition of the term.[7] Judith Baskin's *Midrashic Women* contains a chapter entitled: 'Why Were the Matriarchs Barren?'[8] This is actually a quotation from rabbinic midrash, though Baskin does not once clarify who 'the matriarchs' are. Some of the midrashic passages that she discusses include the wives of the patriarchs, but other biblical females are often mentioned as well. Both Callaway and Baskin discuss 'the matriarchs' in relation to barrenness, thus narrowing the list of biblical women to whom they refer. However, it is unclear exactly which of these women they understand to be 'matriarchs'.[9] This difficulty could have been eliminated if a simple explanation of the term had been offered.

A handful of modern scholars deal more specifically with the meaning of the title 'matriarch(s)'. In *Mothers of Promise*, Schneider argues that because the title 'patriarchs' is well attested in ancient Jewish literature

2. See also §1.1, 'Research Context'.
3. Fewell and Gunn, *Gender, Power, & Promise*.
4. Ibid., 68.
5. Ibid., 72. Emphasis mine.
6. Callaway, *Sing, O Barren One*.
7. Ibid., 13–33.
8. Baskin, *Midrashic Women*, 119–40.
9. The full list of biblically barren women is: Sarah, Rebekah, Rachel, the wife of Manoah (Judg 13), Hannah (1 Sam 1–2) and the Shunammite woman (2 Kgs 4:8-37). Zion is also depicted as barren in Isa 54:1. Leah is made barren in the midrash. For more information, see Part II of this study, 'The Matriarchal Cycle'.

and in modern scholarship on Genesis, '"matriarchs" appears to be an appropriate category'.[10] She identifies 'the matriarchs' as the four wives of the patriarchs—Sarah, Rebekah, Leah and Rachel—and notes various commonalities in their stories, including bearing Israel's covenantal sons, having a positive relationship with God and legitimate heritage.[11] Most importantly, Schneider argues that these women 'form the basis of the thesis that the primary role of women in Genesis is to determine who will inherit the promise from the Israelite Deity'.[12]

Despite using the category 'matriarchs' in her work, Schneider admits that she has 'doubts about its veracity'.[13] She notes various problems with the title, including its absence from biblical and early exegetical texts, and the fact that in modern scholarship, 'the term does not appear frequently or with consistent meaning'.[14] In her concluding chapter, Schneider claims: 'Some issues cannot be resolved only with this study... How clear-cut is the category of matriarchs? If there is such a category as matriarchs, what elements define it?'[15] For Schneider, the title is a useful starting point for discussing the women portrayed in Genesis, especially as it allows the wives of the patriarchs to be grouped together by their common purpose of bearing covenant sons. Schneider is, however, reluctant to offer a clear definition of the term 'matriarch' as this would simplify the issues, suggesting that there is an accepted understanding of who these women are. Schneider grapples with key questions about the matriarchs, even if she does not answer them fully herself.

In *The Lost Matriarch: Finding Leah in the Bible and Midrash*,[16] Jerry Rabow suggests that whilst 'Leah is a member of the exclusive club of biblical heroines whom we remember as our Matriarchs', she has been neglected by the Bible and many of its interpreters.[17] He offers what may be regarded as a definition of the term 'matriarch': 'Those other Matriarchs [aside from Leah] are shown living brave and memorable lives of action and initiative, performing acts that change their families

---

10. Schneider, *Mothers of Promise*, 15–16.

11. Ibid., 15–17.

12. Ibid., 16.

13. Ibid., 13.

14. Ibid., 16–17.

15. Ibid., 218.

16. Rabow, *Lost Matriarch*.

17. Ibid., ix. Cf. Eina Ramon, 'The Matriarchs and the Torah of Hesed (Loving-Kindness)', *Nashim: A Journal of Jewish Women's Studies & Gender Issues* 10, no. 2 (2005): 167.

as well as the destiny of the Jewish people'.[18] Sarah, Rebekah and Rachel act to ensure that they bear and promote Israel's covenant sons. In his first chapter, Rabow confirms that 'Leah is one of the four Matriarchs of the Bible', who bears tribal ancestors, is married to the patriarch Jacob and has a personal relationship with God.[19] For Rabow, the matriarchs are a specific group of biblical women, whose personal lives had a profound effect on Israel's national development. These women deserve respect and, because of this, their characters are developed in midrash. For both Rabow and Schneider, the matriarchs are the legitimate wives of the patriarchs, whose importance derives from bearing Israel's covenant sons.

Alvan Kaunfer's article, 'Who Knows Four? The *imahot* in Rabbinic Judaism', best addresses the questions and issues surrounding a definition of this title.[20] Noting the lack of scholarly engagement with '"the Matriarchs" as a concept and rubric', Kaunfer offers a study of 'the matriarchs' in rabbinic literature.[21] According to Kaunfer, gender equality has been used to explain the more recent inclusion of Sarah, Rebekah, Leah and Rachel alongside the patriarchs in certain Jewish prayers. However, he seeks to demonstrate that 'the matriarchs' has been a popular and revered category in Jewish thought for centuries.[22] He notes that the title 'patriarchs' (אבות) appears numerous times in the Hebrew Bible and often in rabbinic literature. The title 'matriarchs' (אימהות) appears around seventy-six times in talmudic and midrashic sources, and fifteen occurrences name the individual matriarchs. Kaunfer concludes that: 'at least to some rabbinic sages, the Matriarchs were deemed worthy of mention as founders of Judaism, along with their male counterparts'.[23]

Kaunfer next discusses the attributes ascribed to the matriarchs in midrash.[24] The 'merit of the mothers' parallels the 'merit of the fathers' as a source of blessing for Israel. The rabbis regard the matriarchs as

18. Rabow, *Lost Matriarch*, ix.

19. Ibid., 1–2.

20. Alvan Kaunfer, 'Who Knows Four? The *imahot* in Rabbinic Judaism', *Judaism* 44 (1995): 94–103.

21. Ibid., 94.

22. Ibid. Cf. Callaway, *Sing, O Barren One*, 117: 'The remarkable creativity of the rabbis and the opportunities which preaching posed for interpreting the ancient texts anew resulted in a rich tradition of the barren matriarchs as beloved figures in popular piety'. For 'the matriarchs' in the *Amidah* prayer, see Ramon, 'Torah of Hesed'; Biale, *Women and Jewish Law*, x. Ramon deals with a number of issues similar to Kaunfer (Ramon, 'Torah of Hesed').

23. Kaunfer, 'Who Knows Four?', 94–5 (quote p. 95).

24. For what follows, see ibid., 95–9.

prophetesses, with Rebekah used as the primary example of this.[25] The matriarchs' barrenness ensures that God receives prayers; and their symbolic significance is discussed, for example, the link that is established between the four matriarchs and the four mentions of blessings on Abraham in Gen 12:2-3.[26] Kaunfer also argues that whilst the title 'matriarchs' largely refers to the four wives of the patriarchs, 'some rabbinic traditions recognise that Bilhah and Zilpah were also mothers of the Tribes of Israel and thus deserve the status of "Matriarchs"'. Hence, certain midrashic passages speak of six matriarchs, rather than the usually assumed four.[27] Kaunfer thus concludes that 'the matriarchs' have long been a revered group within Jewish thought. The title usually refers to Sarah, Rebekah, Leah and Rachel, who were 'partners in the development of Judaism and thus are worthy of recognition'.[28]

Kaunfer offers a useful overview of the concept of 'the matriarchs', dealing with the major themes and characteristics associated with these women. His findings largely correspond to my own analysis of the matriarchs as portrayed in *Genesis Rabbah*, particularly in recognising that whilst the term 'the matriarchs' usually refers to the four wives of the patriarchs, it may sometimes include Bilhah and Zilpah. Kaunfer's analysis is, however, often limited. He mentions barrenness only briefly, thus neglecting the multifaceted nature of this theme and its central importance for the midrashic portrayal of 'the matriarchs'.[29] Moreover, Kaunfer barely addresses motherhood, even though this is the defining characteristic of Israel's 'matriarchs'. Kaunfer's work provides important groundwork for further investigation and he demonstrates the fruitfulness of deeper reflection on this category's place within Jewish literature and thought.

3.1.1. *Summary*

Whilst a number of modern scholars use the term 'matriarch(s)' in their work, they often fail to define exactly which biblical women it refers to. This prohibits fruitful discussion of the category 'the matriarchs' as there is no clear consensus about the meaning of the term or the significance of those women who bear the title. The scholars mentioned here largely use the term 'the matriarchs' to refer to Sarah, Rebekah, Leah and Rachel.

25. E.g. *Gen. Rab.* 67:9; 72:6.
26. See *Gen. Rab.* 39:11. See also §3.6.1.1, 'The Title "the Matriarchs" (האימהות) Paralleled with a Male Equivalent'.
27. Kaunfer, 'Who Knows Four?', 99.
28. Ibid., 101.
29. Ibid., 98.

Kaunfer notes that, at times, Jacob's other wives, Bilhah and Zilpah, may be included in the group, as they bore some of Israel's tribal ancestors alongside Leah and Rachel. The paucity of scholarly discussions about 'the matriarchs' necessitates a return to the primary texts, of the Hebrew Bible and classical Jewish literature, to trace the development of the category of 'the matriarchs' and to understand exactly who and what is meant by it.

3.2. *A Note on the Titles 'Matriarch' (*אם*) and 'Patriarch' (*אב*)*

In the Hebrew Bible, the biological term אב, 'father', becomes an authoritative title for Israel's founding fathers: Abraham, Isaac and Jacob. These 'patriarchs' (אבות) continue the covenant between God and Israel. Various biblical passages mention 'the God of my/your father' (אלהי אבי/ אביך) before listing one or all three men; and in 1 Chr 29:18, King David appeals to the 'LORD, the God of Abraham, Isaac and Israel [meaning Jacob], our ancestors ("our fathers", אבתינו)'. Abraham, Isaac and Jacob are commonly known in Jewish tradition as 'the patriarchs' (האבות) and the biblical text provides the earliest examples of that title.[30]

The existence of a group identity for Israel's key male ancestors antici-pates the emergence of a comparable female category in the postbiblical era.[31] The noun אם, 'mother', and its plural, אימהות, becomes a title denoting those women who bore key covenant sons and became ances-tresses of the nation. The biological origins of this title indicate the significance of maternity as a characteristic of these women.[32]

3.3. *The Matriarchs: Biblical Beginnings*

3.3.1. *The Matriarchs in the Hebrew Bible*

Any enquiry into 'the matriarchs' must begin with the Hebrew Bible, particularly the book of Genesis. Genesis introduces the first three genera-tions of Israel's ancestral family—Abraham, Isaac, Jacob, their wives and

---

30. E.g. Exod 3:6; Lev 26:42; 1 Kgs 18:36; 1 Chr 29:18.

31. Cf. Deborah is called 'a mother in Israel' (אם בישראל) in Judg 5:7. See Cheryl Anne Brown, *No Longer Be Silent: First Century Jewish Portraits of Biblical Women. Studies in Pseudo-Philo's* Biblical Antiquities *and Josephus's* Jewish Antiquities, Gender and the Biblical Tradition (Louisville: Westminster John Knox, 1992), 69; cf. 71. See also Jack M. Sasson, *Judges 1–12*, Anchor Bible / Anchor Yale Bible 6D (New Haven: Yale University Press, 2014), 289–90, 322–3.

32. Context is important for deciding whether the biological or titular usage of the term is intended in each case.

their children—culminating in the emergence of the twelve tribes of Israel from Jacob's twelve sons. Details provided in the biblical narrative help to shape the later category of 'the matriarchs'.

Of all the women in Genesis, Sarah, Rebekah, Leah and Rachel receive the most narrative attention. They each bear sons for their patriarchal husbands, who will uphold God's covenant with Israel. Various characteristics connect various women in Genesis. All of the matriarchs descend from the family line of Terah, Abraham's father (Gen 11:26). Rebekah is the daughter of Bethuel, whose father Nahor is Abraham's brother (Gen 22:23). Rebekah has a brother, Laban, who fathers Rachel and Leah. Sarah may even descend from Terah's line, if Abraham's comment that 'she is the daughter of my father but not the daughter of my mother' (Gen 20:12) is true.[33] Israel's identity depends on familial lineage and thus, correct ancestry is of great importance.[34]

Only in the case of Sarah and Rebekah is a direct link established between the roles of individual female characters. The genealogy of Gen 22:20-24 notes that: 'Bethuel became the father of Rebekah' (Gen 22:23). Following the near-sacrifice of Isaac in the Akedah episode (Gen 22:1-19) and immediately prior to the announcement of Sarah's death in Gen 23:1-2, this prepares readers for the transition into the next generation of Israelite ancestors.[35] As Schneider suggests, 'The role of this passage here highlights not only the importance of Rebekah, but also the roles that Rebekah and Sarah fulfil as matriarchs in the story'.[36]

33. See Satlow, *Tasting the Dish*, 68–70.

34. On descent from Terah, see Schneider, *Mothers of Promise*, 96; Cynthia R. Chapman, '"Oh That You Were Like a Brother to Me, One Who Had Nursed at My Mother's Breasts": Breast Milk as a Kinship-Forging Substance', *Journal of Hebrew Scriptures* 12 (2012): 27; Naomi Steinberg, 'Alliance or Descent? The Function of Marriage in Genesis', *Journal for the Study of the Old Testament* 51 (1991): 45–55; David L. Petersen, 'Genesis and Family Values', *Journal of Biblical Literature* 124 (2005): 14–22; Louis M. Epstein, *Marriage Laws in the Bible and the Talmud*, Harvard Semitic Series XII (Cambridge, MA: Harvard University Press, 1942), 146–8.

35. Lieve M. Teugels, *Bible and Midrash: The Story of 'the Wooing of Rebekah' (Gen. 24)*, Contributions to Biblical Exegesis and Theology (Leuven: Peeters, 2004), 59–67; Teugels, 'A Matriarchal Cycle?', *Bijdragen: International Journal for Philosophy and Theology* 56 (1995), 65; Tammi J. Schneider, *Sarah: Mother of Nations* (New York: Continuum, 2004), 112–13, 121; Schneider, *Mothers of Promise*, 42–3, 181; Gordon Wenham, *Genesis 16–50*, Word Biblical Commentary 2 (Dallas: Word, 1994), 121.

36. Schneider, *Sarah*, 113. Teugels follows Benno Jacob in asserting a similar connection between Sarah and Rebekah; see Teugels, *'The Wooing of Rebekah' (Gen. 24)*, 66–7; Teugels, 'A Matriarchal Cycle?', 65.

Confirmation of the succession from Sarah to Rebekah occurs in Gen 24:67. This verse follows a long betrothal scene, which ends when Rebekah leaves her homeland to become Isaac's wife. Genesis 24:67 reads: 'Then Isaac brought her into his mother Sarah's tent. He took Rebekah, and she became his wife; and he loved her. So Isaac was comforted after his mother's death.' Here, Isaac and Rebekah's marriage becomes official and Rebekah replaces Sarah as the female head of the family, assuming the role previously performed by her mother-in-law.[37] Isaac effects the transition from his mother, Sarah, to his wife, Rebekah, a particularly noteworthy action performed by this otherwise rather passive patriarch.[38] The second patriarchal generation and the continuing development of the nation are secured, as the correct father (Isaac) and mother (Rebekah) are once again in place.[39] Genesis 24:67 may be said to provide a biblical basis for bringing women from Genesis together under a single title, 'the matriarchs'.[40]

3.3.2. *Marriages between Patriarchs and Handmaids*

When struggling to bear children for their patriarchal husbands, the Genesis matriarchs provide their handmaids, Hagar, Bilhah and Zilpah, as alternate wives and concubines.[41] Schneider labels these women, 'Mothers of Potential Heirs': 'All of these women are in a relationship with a man that could lead to the inclusion of their child in the inheritance of the promise'. Thus, '[w]hat unites these women is the threat their

---

37. Wenham, *Genesis 16–50*, 151–2; Schneider, *Sarah*, 120–1; Teugels, 'The Wooing of Rebekah' (Gen. 24), 66–7; Phyllis Trible, 'Ominous Beginnings for a Promise of Blessings', in *Hagar, Sarah, and Their Children: Jewish, Christian, and Muslim Perspectives*, ed. Phyllis Trible and Letty M. Russell (Louisville: Westminster John Knox, 2006), 60; Nahum M. Sarna, *The JPS Torah Commentary: Genesis: The Traditional Hebrew Text with the New JPS Translation Commentary* (Philadelphia: The Jewish Publication Society, 1989), 170. See *Gen. Rab.* 60:16. See also §8.1.2, 'Piety'.

38. E.g. Isaac's passivity is demonstrated when Abraham's servant finds him a wife (Gen 24). On Isaac's lack of action compared with Abraham and Jacob, and the implications of this for Rebekah's role, see Teugels, *'The Wooing of Rebekah' (Gen. 24)*, 119–9; Wenham, *Genesis 16–50*, 174, 188, 194.

39. Sarna, *JPS: Genesis*, 161, 170.

40. Cf. Halpern-Amaru, *Women in the Book of Jubilees*, 80–1.

41. Sarah and Rachel are barren. Zilpah is to produce more children for Jacob on Leah's behalf as she seeks to earn his love and outrank her sister. On concubines and polygamy, see Epstein, *Marriage Laws*, 3–76; Biale, *Women and Jewish Law*, 49–50.

children pose to those who inherit'.[42] Hagar, Bilhah and Zilpah are not usually included among Israel's 'matriarchs'. They therefore demonstrate that union with a patriarch, resulting in offspring, does not automatically garner matriarchal status; neither does bearing several of Israel's tribal ancestors.[43] Understanding more about these women, their roles in the Genesis narrative and their interaction with the patriarchs and their wives, helps to define the boundaries of the category 'matriarch'.

Hagar is Sarah's Egyptian handmaid, given to Abraham by his barren wife in the hope that she will bear children for him (Gen 16).[44] Hagar conceives immediately and views Sarah with less respect as a result.[45] Though Abraham tries to promote Ishmael as his heir (Gen 17:18), God insists that it is Sarah who will bear the covenant son. Sarah finally gives birth to Isaac in Gen 21 and upon seeing Ishmael 'playing', she insists that Hagar and her son be banished from the patriarchal household. Sarah

---

42. Schneider, *Mothers of Promise*, 101–2. Schneider also includes Dinah, Tamar, and Aseneth in this category (ibid., 101, 166). These women are all related, sexually or biologically, to a patriarchal figure.

43. Bilhah and Zilpah are sometimes included in the rabbinic category 'the matriarchs' (Kaunfer, 'Who Knows Four?', 99). See §3.6.4.1, 'The Matriarchs as "Mothers of the Tribal Ancestors"', in Reference to their Children'.

44. See Wenham, *Genesis 16–50*, 7; Phyllis Trible, *Texts of Terror: Literary-Feminist Readings of Biblical Narratives*, SCM Classics (London: SCM, 2002), 15; Katheryn Pfisterer Darr, *Far More Precious than Jewels: Perspectives on Biblical Women*, Gender and the Biblical Tradition (Louisville: Westminster John Knox, 1991), 98; John Van Seters, 'The Problem of Childlessness in Near Eastern Law and the Patriarchs of Israel', *Journal of Biblical Literature* 87, no. 4 (1968): 401–8; Trible, *Texts of Terror*, 6–7. For treatments of Hagar, see ibid., 5–24; Schneider, *Mothers of Promise*, 103–19; Tikva Frymer-Kensky, 'Hagar', in *Women in Scripture: A Dictionary of Named and Unnamed Women in the Hebrew Bible, the Apocryphal/ Deuterocanonical Books, and the New Testament*, ed. Carol Meyers (Grand Rapids: Eerdmans, 2001), 86–7; Darr, *Far More Precious*, 132–63; David J. Zucker and Rebecca Gates Brinton, '"The Other Woman": A Collaborative Jewish-Christian Study of Hagar', in *'Perspectives on Our Father Abraham': Essays in Honour of Marvin R. Wilson*, ed. Steven A. Hunt (Grand Rapids: Eerdmans, 2010), 339–83.

45. Trible, *Texts of Terror*, 6–8; Wenham, *Genesis 16–50*, 12; Fewell and Gunn, *Gender, Power, & Promise*, 46. The Code of Hammurabi states that a mistress can treat her pregnant handmaid as a normal slave, preventing the handmaid from seeing herself as equal to the mistress (Frymer-Kensky, 'Hagar', 86). See also John Byron, 'EGLBS Presidential Address Childlessness and Ambiguity in the Ancient World', *Proceedings of the Eastern Great Lakes Biblical Society and Midwest Region of the Society of Biblical Literature* XXX (2010): 35–9.

recognises that without banishment, Ishmael and not her son, would inherit from Abraham.[46] God agrees with her plan but promises that Ishmael will become a great nation (Gen 17:20; 21:13, 18). Hagar's final action in the narrative is to find an Egyptian wife for her son.[47]

Trible highlights the importance of Hagar's character:[48] she is the only woman to receive promises of progeny like the patriarchs (Gen 16; 21:18); she receives the first divine annunciation and speaks to God twice (Gen 16; 21), privileges not afforded to Sarah;[49] she bears the first son of the patriarchal narratives (Gen 12–50; esp. Gen 16); and she is the first figure to name God in the Hebrew Bible (Gen 16:13).[50] Schneider further explains that Hagar is associated with motherhood from her first mention in Genesis (Gen 16) to her last (21:21).[51] Though her son does not inherit God's promises to Abraham and Israel, he founds a nation and thus, Hagar is also the ancestress of a people.[52] In spite of these qualities, Hagar is never conceived of as a 'matriarch' in either the Bible or midrash.

Hagar's Egyptian heritage is her defining characteristic. She maintains this identity throughout, from her introduction in the narrative to choosing an Egyptian wife for Ishmael.[53] Hagar is a clear outsider, who threatens the covenantal line early on by bearing a son before Sarah. Such foreign influence must be eliminated to ensure the genealogical purity of Israel.[54] Moreover, the Sarah–Hagar conflict seems to reflect the archetypal tension between Israel and Egypt, centring on Israel's enslavement in Egypt and their subsequent exodus (Exodus). The portrayal of an Egyptian handmaid ousted by her Israelite mistress exemplifies Israel's

46. Cf. Schneider, *Mothers of Promise*, 166.

47. Trible, *Texts of Terror*, 22–3; Schneider, *Mothers of Promise*, 108; Wenham, *Genesis 16–50*, 86; Savina J. Teubal, *Sarah the Priestess: The First Matriarch of Genesis* (Athens: Swallow, 1984), 41; Jo Ann Davidson, 'Genesis Matriarchs Engage Feminism', *Andrews University Seminary Studies* 40, no. 2 (2002): 172–3.

48. Trible, *Texts of Terror*, 12, 13, 15, 23–4. Cf. Schneider, *Mothers of Promise*, 103.

49. Sarah is rebuked by the Lord (Gen 18:15) (Trible, *Texts of Terror*, 15). Hagar does not speak with any human characters in the narrative (Schneider, *Mothers of Promise*, 110). Frymer-Kensky notes that the annunciation links Hagar to Hannah, Samson's mother, and in the New Testament, Mary (Frymer-Kensky, 'Hagar', 87).

50. See also Schneider, *Mothers of Promise*, 110.

51. Ibid., 119. 'Most of Hagar's actions are similar to those of the matriarchs and concern procreation' (ibid., 108).

52. Cf. Trible, *Texts of Terror*, 17; Schneider, *Mothers of Promise*, 108; Frymer-Kensky, 'Hagar', 87.

53. Schneider, *Mothers of Promise*, 105–6.

54. Cf. ibid., 113.

triumph over her oppressors.[55] As Trible remarks, 'In the hand of Sarai, with the consent of Abram, Hagar becomes the suffering servant, the precursor of Israel's plight under Pharaoh'.[56] Trible notes further inversions of the exodus account: Sarah uses the same verb, גרש, to demand Hagar and Ishmael's expulsion (Gen 21:10) as is used to describe Israel being 'driven out' of Egypt in Exod 12:39; and Hagar twice flees into the wilderness (Gen 16; 21), just as Israel wandered in the desert following the exodus.[57] Additionally, Frymer-Kensky draws parallels between the angel's speech to Hagar in Gen 16 and the Lord's prediction of Israel's slavery in Gen 15:13.[58]

Schneider offers a more personal explanation of Sarah's maltreatment of Hagar: the handmaid's Egyptian heritage reminds Sarah of her earlier ordeal in Egypt, when she was taken into Pharaoh's household (Gen 12:10-20).[59] Whether Hagar harks back to Sarah's experience in Gen 12, or anticipates Israel's enslavement in Egypt, the biblical text makes clear that, as an Egyptian, Hagar is unworthy of becoming an ancestress of Israel.

Bilhah and Zilpah are given to Rachel and Leah respectively by their father, Laban, when they marry Jacob (Gen 29:24, 29).[60] In Gen 30:9, Leah gives Zilpah to Jacob because she is no longer bearing children. The maid then bears two sons for Jacob (Gen 30:10, 12). Schneider describes Zilpah as 'a flat character' because so little information is provided about her.[61] Bilhah plays a greater role in the Genesis narrative.[62] The barren

---

55. Drawing on Boyarin, Levinson argues that here the Jews fantasise about a reversal of reality, where dominant people become the subservient, and vice versa. This affirms and strengthens Jewish identity. Joshua Levinson, 'Bodies and Bo(a)rders: Emerging Fictions of Identity in Late Antiquity', *Harvard Theological Review* 93, no. 4 (2000): 348–52. See also Levinson, 'Literary Approaches', 209–12.

56. Trible, *Texts of Terror*, 9. See also ibid., 24 n. 16, 87.

57. Ibid., 16. Trible notes that, unlike the exodus, God sends Hagar back to those who have wronged her (ibid., 18). Cf. Sarna, *JPS: Genesis*, 120; Wenham, *Genesis 16–50*, 81.

58. Frymer-Kensky, 'Hagar', 87. Cf. Wenham, *Genesis 16–50*, 9.

59. Schneider, *Mothers of Promise*, 105–6.

60. See Wenham, *Genesis 16–50*, 6. For Bilhah and Zilpah's biblical portrayal, see Schneider, *Mothers of Promise*, 126–37; Tikva Frymer-Kensky, 'Bilhah', in Meyers, ed., *Women in Scripture*, 61–2, and, in the same volume, Naomi Steinberg, 'Zilpah', 169–70. For Bilhah and Zilpah's status, see Rabow, *Lost Matriarch*, 90–2. Rabow also discusses Leah and Rachel offering Bilhah and Zilpah to Jacob, and the children they bear for him (pp. 92–8).

61. Schneider, *Mothers of Promise*, 130; cf. 124.

62. See ibid., 131, 134.

Rachel offers her maidservant to Jacob so that she may bear the children that Rachel cannot (Gen 30:3), and Bilhah subsequently bears two sons (Gen 30:5, 7). Like Sarah, Rachel hopes to overcome her barrenness by claiming her handmaid's children as her own. Unlike Hagar, Bilhah does not lose respect for her mistress as a result of her pregnancies.

Genesis 35:22 reports that 'Reuben went and lay with Bilhah his father's concubine'. No further information is provided about this incident, although Jacob finds out and refers to it in his deathbed blessing on Reuben (Gen 49:4). The incident further highlights the vulnerability of this woman.[63] Bilhah and Zilpah are given little attention in the biblical narrative and yet they are genealogically significant, bearing tribal ancestors and thus standing at the head of Israel with the patriarchs and their legitimate wives.

In contrast to Hagar, Bilhah and Zilpah are not forced away from Jacob's household after they bear children. As Steinberg notes, there is 'a shift in the generation of Jacob's offspring from a vertical genealogy to a horizontal one' as all of his sons, including Bilhah and Zilpah's offspring, inherit the covenant promises.[64] Bilhah and Zilpah's sons are in some sense regarded as belonging to Leah and Rachel, something suggested when those women name their handmaids' offspring.[65] Yet, Bilhah and Zilpah's children also seem to be affected by their mothers' status as handmaids. When meeting Esau in Gen 33, Jacob sends the handmaids and their sons ahead of Leah, Rachel and their children, suggesting that they are more dispensable and less worthy of protection from the brother he assumes still abhors him.[66] Legitimacy is an important theme present from the earliest parts of Israel's history. Schneider suggests: 'Zilpah and

63. Ibid., 133–7; Frymer-Kensky, 'Bilhah', 62; Sarna, *JPS: Genesis*, 244–5; Wenham, *Genesis 16–50*, 327–8.

64. Steinberg, 'Zilpah', 170.

65. For Frymer-Kensky, this indicates 'maternal authority' (Frymer-Kensky, 'Bilhah', 61). See also Steinberg, 'Zilpah', 170; J. Cheryl Exum, *Fragmented Women: Feminist (Sub)versions of Biblical Narratives*, Journal for the Study of the Old Testament Supplement Series 163 (Sheffield: Sheffield Academic, 1993), 131; Sharon Pace Jeansonne, *The Women of Genesis: From Sarah to Potiphar's Wife* (Minneapolis: Fortress, 1990), 19–20, 76 n. 22, 135; Teubal, *Sarah the Priestess*, 94; Byron, 'Childlessness and Ambiguity', 35–9. Ilana Pardes, *Countertraditions in the Bible: A Feminist Approach* [Cambridge, MA: Harvard University Press, 1992], 65) suggests that naming their handmaids' children 'is more the delusion of a desperate woman, trying to find comfort in the offspring of her maid'.

66. Frymer-Kensky, 'Bilhah', 62; Jeansonne, *Women of Genesis*, 89; Rabow, *Lost Matriarch*, 137–43; Exum, *Fragmented Women*, 146, 131; cf. 104–12.

Bilhah emphasise that the status of the women, free or servile, is not as much an issue as their background'.[67] Bilhah and Zilpah's heritage is not specified by the biblical text but Schneider assumes that they come from Haran, just like Leah and Rachel.[68] If this is inferred from the biblical text, it may explain why Bilhah and Zilpah's sons are deemed worthy to become tribal ancestors of Israel when Hagar the Egyptian's son is excluded from the covenant promises.

3.3.3. Summary

The portrayal of female characters in Genesis is important for under-standing the development of the title 'matriarch(s)'. The four legitimate wives of the patriarchs, Sarah, Rebekah, Leah and Rachel, have the correct genealogical heritage for bearing covenant sons, and Genesis models a pattern of succession that enables one female figure to take on the matriarchal role held by her predecessor (Gen 24:67). The portrayal of the handmaidens Hagar, Bilhah and Zilpah helps to define the category of 'the matriarchs' more clearly, as they lack characteristics necessary to earn this title. Although the category of 'the matriarchs' does not emerge in Genesis, it establishes the roots of the concept.

3.4. The Matriarchs in Ancient Jewish Sources

3.4.1. The Book of Jubilees

The book of *Jubilees* (mid-second century BCE) provides an early exeget-ical treatment of Genesis, retelling the biblical narrative of Gen 1–Exod 12.[69] The work presents itself as the angel of the Lord's word, spoken to

---

67. Schneider, *Mothers of Promise*, 166; Exum, *Fragmented Women*, 131.

68. Schneider, *Mothers of Promise*, 164.

69. For dating of *Jubilees*, see VanderKam, 511:v; James C. VanderKam, *The Book of Jubilees*, Guides to Apocrypha and Pseudepigrapha Sheffield: Sheffield Academic Press, 2001), 17–22; Halpern-Amaru, *Women in the Book of Jubilees*, 2. The extant text of *Jubilees* is written in Ethiopic. The text is believed to have originally been written in Hebrew, with Greek, then Latin and Ethiopic transla-tions following. Various Hebrew *Jubilees* fragments were discovered at Qumran (see VanderKam, 511:vi–xxxiii; VanderKam, *Guide: The Book of Jubilees*, 13–17). VanderKam provides a critical text, translation and commentary of *Jubilees*. I will quote from his translation (brackets in *Jubilees* translations are VanderKam's). Other texts and English translations are by R. H. Charles and O. S Wintermute, the latter using the former's text: R. H. Charles, *The Book of Jubilees or The Little Genesis Translated from the Editor's Ethiopic Text and Edited, with Introduction, Notes, and Indices by R. H. Charles* (London: A. & C. Black, 1902); R. H. Charles, *The Book*

Moses on Mount Sinai as he receives the Law.[70] As Halpern-Amaru notes, *Jubilees* demonstrates 'an interest in women characters and a highly unusual elevation of their role'.[71] *Jubilees* develops the characterisation of the women portrayed in Genesis, providing them with more of a voice and giving them a greater awareness of Israel's covenant. *Jubilees* recognises the significance of these women; but the title 'matriarch' appears nowhere in the text. In spite of this, *Jubilees* represents an important initial stage in the development of the category, 'the matriarchs'.

Jubilees develops the biblical women's characters in various ways. Each matriarch is informed about the covenant. After being told by God that he will father a child (*Jub.* 14:2-3), 'Abram was very happy and told all these things to his wife Sarai' (*Jub.* 14:21). Abraham also tells Rebekah that Jacob will continue the covenant that began with him and was passed to his son, Isaac (*Jub.* 19:15-31). When Jacob persuades Leah and Rachel to leave Laban: 'he told them how he had seen everything in a dream and everything about his statement to him that he would return to his father's house' (*Jub.* 29:3). The wives of the patriarchs learn about the covenant from their husbands, or in Rebekah's case, from her father-in-law. Halpern-Amaru notes that this 'transforms the matriarchal role' as each woman becomes '[a] co-partner with her husband', acting not merely for personal reasons, but in order to protect and further the covenant.[72] This contrasts with the biblical text, where the patriarchs usually neglect to inform their wives of their encounters with the divine. The most obvious example of this is Abraham, who does not tell Sarah of the divine promise that she will bear a son (Gen 17:16-22); she instead overhears

---

of *Jubilees or The Little Genesis Translated from the Ethiopic Text by R. H. Charles with an Introduction by G. H. Box*, Translations of Early Documents (London: Haymarket; New York: Society for Promoting Christian Knowledge/Macmillan, 1917); O. S. Wintermute, 'Jubilees (Second Century B.C.)', in *The Old Testament Pseudepigrapha*. Vol. 2, *Expansions of the 'Old Testament' and Legends, Wisdom and Philosophical Literature, Prayers, Psalms, and Odes, Fragments of Lost Judeo-Hellenistic Works*, ed. James H. Charlesworth (London: Darton, Longman & Todd, 1985), 35–142.

70. On *Jubilees*'s genre and exegetical character, see Halpern-Amaru, *Women in the Book of Jubilees*, 133–46; VanderKam, *Guide: The Book of Jubilees*.

71. Halpern-Amaru, *Women in the Book of Jubilees*, 1. In this study, Halpern-Amaru considers the portrayal of females in *Jubilees*. On *Jubilees* and the matriarchs, see especially ibid., 33–102. See also Betsy Halpern-Amaru, 'The First Woman, Wives, and Mothers in *Jubilees*', *Journal of Biblical Literature* 113, no. 4 (1994): 609–26.

72. Halpern-Amaru, *Women in the Book of Jubilees*, 4–5. Cf. ibid., 34.

the reiteration of that promise in Gen 18:10, when the three angelic men visit Abraham.

In the biblical text of Genesis, Rebekah stands out as a feisty and strong-willed woman. She acts independently, agreeing to travel to a foreign land to marry a man she has never met (Gen 24:58); she complains about her painful pregnancy and receives a divine oracle in return (Gen 25:22-23); and she promotes Jacob above Esau, ensuring that her younger son inherits the covenant promises from Isaac (Gen 27).[73] *Jubilees* develops Rebekah's characterisation and role in the narrative more than the other matriarchs.[74] Most significantly, Abraham bypasses Isaac and instead confides in Rebekah that Jacob will continue the covenant, after seeing that she prefers Jacob to Esau.[75] *Jubilees* 19:17-20 reads:

> He said to her: 'My daughter, take care of my son Jacob because he will occupy my place on the earth and (will prove) a blessing among mankind and the glory of all the descendants of Shem. For I know that the Lord will choose him as his own people (who will be) *special* from all who are on the surface of the earth. My son Isaac now loves Esau more than Jacob, but I see that you rightly love Jacob. Increase your favour to him still more; may your eyes look at him lovingly because he will prove to be a blessing for us on the earth from now and throughout all the history of the earth.'

Abraham's speech continues, echoing covenantal imagery of seed and sand, and recalling great figures such as Shem, Noah, Enoch and Adam, all of whom will be remembered through Jacob (*Jub.* 19:21-25).[76] In *Jubilees*, Rebekah is entrusted with information about covenantal succession and seems to be regarded more highly than her patriarchal husband.

Finally, Leah's portrayal in *Jubilees* is noteworthy.[77] Leah is marginalised in the biblical text because Jacob is tricked into marrying her instead of Rachel.[78] This was problematic for *Jubilees* because Leah bears several tribal ancestors of Israel and thus plays a central role in the emergence of the nation.[79] Upon her death, which is not even noted in Genesis, *Jubilees*

---

73. See Teugels, *'The Wooing of Rebekah' (Gen. 24)*, 92–132.

74. See Halpern-Amaru, *Women in the Book of Jubilees*, 55–64, 80–1; Randall D. Chestnut, 'Revelatory Experiences Attributed to Biblical Women in Early Jewish Literature', in Levine, ed., *'Women Like This'*, 107–25.

75. See Halpern-Amaru, *Women in the Book of Jubilees*, 58, 81–90.

76. E.g. Gen 13:16; 16:10; 22:17; 32:12 all feature seed/sand imagery.

77. See Halpern-Amaru, *Women in the Book of Jubilees*, 43–6, 66–72, 97–102.

78. Rabow, *Lost Matriarch*, 1–11.

79. Cf. ibid., 1.

explains that Jacob and his family mourned Leah together. *Jubilees* 36:23 explains that Jacob:

> loved her very much from the time when her sister Rachel died because she was perfect and right in all her behaviour and honoured Jacob. In all the time that she lived with him he did not hear a harsh word from her mouth because she was gentle and possessed (the virtues of) peace, truthfulness, and honour.

Jacob recognises Leah's virtues after her sister's death and finally loves her. *Jubilees* presents an example of increased attention to Leah's character in postbiblical texts, and this is a feature that reappears in rabbinic literature, where the rabbis were keen to portray Leah as a worthy matriarch, equal to Sarah, Rebekah and Rachel.[80]

Halpern-Amaru remarks that women's roles are still limited to the family in *Jubilees*, '[b]ut since the dynamic of the family and covenant history intersect, the matriarchs have the potential to influence the movement of that history in the direction in which it is intended to go'.[81] *Jubilees* recognises the matriarchs' shared characteristics, especially increased involvement in the covenant.[82] This text is an important stage in the emergence of 'the matriarchs' as an authoritative category of women.[83]

3.4.2. *The* Damascus Document

The title 'the mothers' appears in the *Damascus Document*. This is one of the key sectarian texts found among the Dead Sea Scrolls and probably dates to the second century BCE.[84] The *Damascus Document* begins

80. See Part II of the present study.

81. Halpern-Amaru, *Women in the Book of Jubilees*, 75.

82. Ibid., 34, 100–101. Matriarchal barrenness is played down in *Jubilees*, though it is a key characteristic of the matriarchs in Genesis and *Genesis Rabbah*. See Chapter 5, 'Barrenness'.

83. Jacob refers to Abraham as 'our father' in *Jub.* 25:5. Abraham is Jacob's grandfather, but in later exegetical texts, 'our mother' and 'our father' also become ways of referring to Israel's matriarchs and patriarchs (see e.g. §3.4.3, 'Pseudo-Philo's *Liber antiquitatum biblicarum*'; §3.6.2, 'Uses of the Noun אם as 'Matriarch''). Israel began as a family, and the extension of family titles to national figures is logical.

84. On D, see Joseph M. Baumgarten, on the basis of transcriptions by Józef T. Milik, and with contributions by Stephen Pfann and Ada Yardeni, *Qumran Cave 4 XIII The Damascus Document (4Q266-273)*, Discoveries in the Judaean Desert XVIII (Oxford: Clarendon, 1996) (hereafter *DJD XVIII*); Vermes, *Dead Sea Scrolls in English*, 127–62. On D and gender, see Maxine Grossman, 'Reading for Gender in the Damascus Document', *Dead Sea Discoveries* 11 (2004): 212–39. For women

with an exhortation to community members to live well and describes the origins of the sect, including how they broke away from a faithless Israel. The second half of the document contains rules and regulations that govern those living within the community. Fragments of the *Damascus Document* found in Cave 4 supplement the Penal Code at the end of the text found in the Cairo Geniza and three of Qumran's caves, listing various transgressions and their punishment by penance or exclusion from the community.[85] One of these fragments, 4Q270 frg.7, describes various transgressions and includes among them speaking against two groups described as 'the Fathers' and 'the Mothers':[86]

> [If he has murmured] against the Fathers, he shall leave and shall not return [again... But if he has murmured] against the Mothers, he shall do penance for ten days. For the Mothers have no *rwqmh* (distinction?) within [the Congregation. *vacat*[87]

Baumgarten notes that a number of the transgressions listed in 4Q270 correspond to those found in 1QS VII, 17, with the particular exception of murmuring against the Fathers and Mothers, which only occurs here.[88]

The text does not make clear exactly who the 'Fathers' and 'Mothers' are. Cecilia Wassen argues that: 'The titles Mothers and Fathers suggest that the holders were viewed as fatherly and motherly protectors within the community where they held a high authority, with the authority of the Fathers surpassing that of the Mothers'.[89] Baumgarten argues that the title 'the Mothers' suggests '[t]hat women had some form of corporate status within the community', but he offers no suggestion of who these women may be.[90] The discrepancies in the status of female compared

in the Dead Sea Scrolls, see Moshe J. Bernstein, 'Women and Children in Legal and Liturgical Texts from Qumran', *Dead Sea Discoveries* 11 (2004): 191–211.

85. See Vermes, *Dead Sea Scrolls in English*, 152.

86. Heb. האבות and האמות. Textual uncertainties should, however, be noted here. According to *DJD XVIII*, 163, the letter ת in האבות is probable, whilst in the second אמות, the letter מ is possible, and the letter ו is reconstructed.

87. Vermes, *Dead Sea Scrolls in English*, 154. Cf. 1QS VII (ibid., 107–8). The critical edition is *DJD XVIII*, 163–4.

88. See *DJD XVIII*, 164.

89. Cecilia Wassen, *Women in the Damascus Document*, Society of Biblical Literature: Academia Biblica 21 (Leiden: Brill, 2005), 196; see, more broadly, 184–97.

90. See *DJD XVIII*, 8. Baumgarten mentions the use of 'the Sisters' in 4Q502 and also notes the appearance of female titles suggests a mixed community, in contrast with 1QS's suggestion of only males (ibid.).

with male figures in the community is clear, as muttering against 'the Fathers' leads to permanent exclusion from the community; whilst the same action against 'the Mothers' only requires ten days of penance.[91] 4Q270 frg.7 explains that 'the Mothers have no *rwqmh* (רוקמה)', but it is unclear what this term means.[92] Baumgarten argues that the oft-suggested meaning 'authoritative status' is derived merely from the context of the passage, rather than from its attested meaning as an embroidered garment in 4QShirShabb and 11QShirShabb.[93] Hurowitz suggests simply that: 'We expect a legal term describing something (a right or a status) enjoyed by the "fathers" and denied the "mothers"'.[94] He proposes an alternate definition for the term רוקמה as a form of Akkadian *rgummû*, meaning 'legal claim', and explains: 'It means that the mothers have *a priori* no legal claim on one who complains against them, so one who maligns them is punished less severely'.[95]

Although the exact meaning of רוקמה is unknown, 'the Mothers' clearly had less authority in the community than 'the Fathers'. Nevertheless, 4Q270 frg.7, a text dating from the Second Temple period and emerging from a largely male-oriented sect, does refer to a group of authoritative women whom the community respects.[96]

The scholars mentioned above assume that these groups are particular authorities within the Qumran community. 'The Fathers' and 'the Mothers' are, however, also the terms used to describe Israel's great ancestors and ancestresses; nothing in the *Damascus Document* precludes these titles referring to the biblical figures whose lives are portrayed in Genesis.[97] Earlier in the *Damascus Document*, Abraham, Isaac and Jacob are listed as moral exemplars, exhibiting the same dedication to God's

91. Wassen, *Women in Damascus Document*, 188–9, 197; Grossman, 'Gender in the Damascus Document', 219, 227–8.

92. On this term, see Wassen, *Women in Damascus Document*, 189–96. Wassen concludes that it refers to a garment 'worn by the Fathers to indicate their authority as mystical mediators between the heavenly host and the earthly community' (ibid., 196).

93. See *DJD XVIII*, 166. See also Bernstein, 'Women and Children', 204–5.

94. Victor Avigdor Hurowitz, 'רוקמה in Damascus Document (4Q270) 7 i 14', *Dead Sea Discoveries* 9 (2002): 34.

95. Ibid., 34–7 (quote p. 35).

96. Cf. Grossman, 'Gender in the Damascus Document', 227–8.

97. Cf. Wassen notes that the title 'Fathers' is used in the Dead Sea Scrolls to refer to Israel's ancestors, and 'Mother' is used as a title for Israel's ancestresses in texts outside the Dead Sea Scrolls (Wassen, *Women in Damascus Document*, 186–7).

commandments that the Qumranites should aspire to.[98] Though the text does not explicitly label these three men 'the patriarchs' (אבות), they are connected through their shared uprightness and this implies some kind of shared or group identity. The *Damascus Document* also makes several references to 'the forefathers' (ראשנים), thus maintaining a clear link to the past by mentioning an ancestral group.[99] Given the document's prior acknowledgment of great figures in Israel's past, a convincing case can be made for 'the Fathers' in 4Q270 frg.7 being Israel's patriarchs. The category was already in existence, as the biblical text itself uses the title 'fathers' (אבות), it need not be seen as a Qumran initiative. If this were the case, 'the Mothers', paralleled with the male category, would most likely refer to the patriarchs' wives.[100] This would then become the first attested reference in Jewish literature to the biblical matriarchs.

3.4.3. *Pseudo-Philo's* Liber antiquitatum biblicarum

Pseudo-Philo's *Liber antiquitatum biblicarum* (*L.A.B.*) retells the events of Israel's earliest history, from Adam to Saul's death (Genesis to 2 Samuel).[101] The text is usually dated between 50 and 100 CE, with

98. According to *CD*. See S. Schechter, and Prolegomenon by Joseph A. Fitzmyer, *Documents of Jewish Sectaries*. Vol. 1, *Fragments of a Zadokite Work: Edited from Hebrew Manuscripts in the Cairo Genizah Collection Now in Possession of the University Library, Cambridge and Provided With an English Translation, Introduction and Notes*, The Library of Biblical Studies (New York: Ktav, 1970), 65, 116.

99. See Lev 26:45; Schechter and Fitzmyer, *Fragments of a Zadokite Work*, 63, 64, 67, 70.

100. Women barely feature in D. The lack of references to biblical women does not disprove the suggestion that 'mothers' (אמות) may refer to the biblical matriarchs.

101. The text is in Latin, but scholars suggest a Hebrew original and a Greek translation preceded this (see Jacobson, 1:215–24). Howard Jacobson provides the modern critical edition of *L.A.B.*, with translation and commentary (Jacobson, vols. 1 and 2). Quotations of *L.A.B.* will be from Jacobson. Further English translations are found in: D. J. Harrington, 'Pseudo-Philo (First Century A.D.)', in Charlesworth, ed., *Old Testament Pseudepigrapha*, 2:297–84; M. R. James, *The Biblical Antiquities of Philo Now First Translated from the Old Latin Version by M. R. James. Prolegomenon by Louis H. Feldman*, The Library of Biblical Studies (New York: Ktav, 1971). Harrington bases his translation on the SC Latin text; Jacobson makes frequent reference to this work (D. J. Harrington, J. Cazeaux, C, Perrot and P.-M. Bogaert, *Pseudo-Philon, Les Antiquités Bibliques*, Sources chrétiennes 229–30 [Paris: Editions du Cerf, 1976]).

scholars such as Jacobson arguing for a date post-70 CE.[102] The text moves quickly through the primordial history and the patriarchal narratives, prior to Israel's inception as a nation. Events in Genesis are treated rather superficially, largely through genealogies and short synopses of biblical episodes.[103] To cite one example, *L.A.B.* reduces the complexities of Gen 16 to one short sentence: 'Since Sarai was sterile and had borne no children, Abram then took Hagar his maid and she bore him Ishmael' (*L.A.B.* 8:1).[104] Gone is Sarah's insistence that Abram use her Egyptian maid, Hagar, to provide the children that she cannot. The action is Abram's and *L.A.B.* even refers to Hagar as 'his' maid, rather than Sarai's, which Jacobson suggests, if deliberate, may be intended 'to obliterate all traces of the biblical episode'.[105] Little detail is given about any of the matriarchs (or patriarchs) and, notably, Rebekah's role is diminished: 'Isaac took for himself a wife from Mesopotamia, the daughter of Bethuel, who conceived and bore to him Esau and Jacob' (*L.A.B.* 8:4). The Bible's most developed female matriarch, who plays a central role also in *Jubilees*, is described here simply as bearing her husband's two children. Her name is not even given.[106]

L.A.B. later returns to key episodes from Genesis, interrupting the narrative flow of the nation's history to illustrate the ways in which events from the patriarchal period shaped later Israel's identity. For example, the Aqedah of Gen 22 is recalled in *L.A.B.*'s reworked version of Deborah's song from Judg 5 (*L.A.B.* 32).[107] Women also receive a great deal of attention throughout *L.A.B.* As Brown comments, 'Pseudo-Philo is clearly sympathetic to women, often introducing feminine imagery and significantly upgrading women's status and role vis-a-vis the biblical

102. See Jacobson, 1:199–209; Brown, *No Longer Be Silent*, 21, 216. Jacobson suggests mid-second century CE as the latest date (Jacobson, 1:209).

103. See Howard Jacobson, 'Biblical Quotation and Editorial Function in Pseudo-Philo's *Liber Antiquitatum Biblicarum*', *Journal for the Study of the Pseudepigrapha* 5 (1989): 47–64.

104. *L.A.B.* 23:5 also mentions Sarah's barrenness.

105. Jacobson, 1:386. He notes this may be a grammatical ambiguity and mean 'her maid', as James interpreted it.

106. Betsy Halpern-Amaru, 'Portraits of Women in Pseudo-Philo's *Biblical Antiquities*', in Levine, ed., *'Women Like This'*, 89; Pieter Willem van der Horst, 'Portraits of Biblical Women in Pseudo-Philo's Liber Antiquitatum Biblicarum', *Journal for the Study of the Pseudepigrapha* 5 (1989): 30. The following scholars discuss women in *L.A.B.*: Halpern-Amaru, 'Women in Pseudo-Philo', 83–106; van der Horst, 'Portraits of Women in L.A.B.', 29–46.

107. Deborah's song in *L.A.B.* is very different to its biblical counterpart. See Jacobson, 2:859; Brown, *No Longer Be Silent*, 56–63.

accounts'.[108] This is evident in the detailed retelling of Hannah's narrative of barrenness and motherhood (1 Sam 1–3), where *L.A.B.* highlights this woman's piety (*L.A.B.* 49–51).[109] It is also clear in this text's retelling of Josh 24 (*L.A.B.* 23), which recalls events early in Israel's history and encourages the Israelites to be faithful to God:

> Joshua rose up in the morning and gathered all the people and said to them, 'So says the Lord: "There was one rock from which I hewed out your father. The hewing-out of that rock bore two men whose names are Abraham and Nahor, and out of the hollowed-out place were born two women whose names are Sarah and Melcha, and they lived together across the river. And Abraham took Sarah, and Nahor took Melcha."' (*L.A.B.* 23:4)

Using imagery reminiscent of Isa 51:1-2, the author of *L.A.B.* describes the origins of the people Israel.[110] Although little is said about Sarah and Melcha, their presence is notable, as the biblical text of Josh 24 mentions only the three patriarchs: Abraham, Isaac and Jacob.

L.A.B. uses 'mother' as a title in relation to three biblical women: Tamar (Gen 38); Deborah (Judg 3–5); and Jephthah's daughter (Judg 11). In Gen 38, Tamar tricks her father-in-law, Judah, into having sexual relations with her after he neglects to marry her to his youngest son after his two eldest sons die.[111] Tamar becomes pregnant by Judah and bears twins, one of whom, Perez, is an ancestor of King David.[112] *L.A.B.* recalls

108. Brown, *No Longer Be Silent*, 12. See also ibid., 212–14, 218–19.

109. See Jacobson, 2:1082–1109; Brown, *No Longer Be Silent*, 141–63; Halpern-Amaru, 'Women in Pseudo-Philo', 96–8. Cf. *L.A.B.*'s retelling of Judg 13, the wife of Manoah's barrenness and pregnancy (*L.A.B.* 42).

110. See Jacobson, 2:713–17.

111. On the plight of the childless widow in antiquity, see Byron, 'Childlessness and Ambiguity', 39–44.

112. On Gen 38, see Mieke Bal, *Lethal Love: Feminist Literary Readings of Biblical Love Stories* (Bloomington: Indiana University Press, 1987), 101; David Biale, *Eros and the Jews: From Biblical Israel to Contemporary America* (Berkeley: University of California Press, 1997), 18–19; Bronner, *From Eve to Esther*, 148, 153–6; Calum M. Carmichael, *Women, Law, and the Genesis Traditions* (Edinburgh: Edinburgh University Press, 1979), 8–9, 57–73; Epstein, *Marriage Laws*, 80–1, 224–5, 242; Fokkelein van Dijk-Hemmes, 'Tamar and the Limits of Patriarchy: Between Rape and Seduction', in *Anti-Covenant: Counter-Reading Women's Lives in the Hebrew Bible*, ed. Mieke Bal, JSOT Supplement Series 81; Bible and Literature Series 22 (Sheffield: Almond, 1989), 135–56; Fewell and Gunn, *Gender, Power, & Promise*, 86–90; Laffey, *An Introduction to the Old Testament*, 44–6; Schneider, *Mothers of Promise*, 101–2, 151–60; Susan Niditch, 'The Wronged Woman Righted:

this episode in its retelling of Exod 1–2 (*L.A.B.* 9). According to *L.A.B.*, Pharaoh decrees that all male Hebrew babies be killed (Exod 1:16, 22); but the Egyptians also decide that any Hebrew daughters shall be married to Egyptian slaves so they may produce more slaves (*L.A.B.* 9:1). The Israelite leaders ask them to refrain from sexual intercourse to prevent their daughters becoming idolaters (*L.A.B.* 9:2). Amram objects and as a result, Moses is born:

> I will go in and take my wife and produce children so that we will multiply upon the earth. For God will not continue in his anger, nor will he forget his people forever, nor will he cast forth the race of Israel into nothingness upon the earth; nor did he emptily establish a covenant with our fathers. (*L.A.B.* 9:4)

L.A.B. thus explains why Exod 2:1 narrates the marriage of a Levite and the daughter of a Levite immediately after Pharaoh's plans to exterminate Israelite children are revealed in Exod 1.[113] Amram 'stands apart from the group by virtue of his absolute, unyielding and uncompromising confidence in God. Because of this he refuses to take part in the plan.'[114] He justifies his actions on a national and covenantal scale, even making reference to 'our fathers', the patriarchs.[115]

Amram then evokes Tamar:

An Analysis of Genesis 38', *Harvard Theological Review* 72, no. 1/2 (1979): 143–9; Nelly Furman, 'His Story Versus Her Story: Male Genealogy and Female Strategy in the Jacob Cycle', *Semeia* 46 (1989): 144–8; Wenham, *Genesis 16–50*, 365–9; Sarna, *JPS: Genesis*, 264–333; Claus Westermann, *Genesis 37–50: A Commentary*, trans. John J. Scullion SJ from the German 1982 published by Neukirchener Verlag (Minneapolis: Augsburg, 1986), 49–56. On Gen 38 in ancient Jewish sources, see Esther Marie Menn, *Judah and Tamar (Genesis 38) in Ancient Jewish Exegesis*, Supplements to the Journal for the Study of Judaism (Leiden: Brill, 1997); Moshe Reiss and David J. Zucker, 'Co-opting the Secondary Matriarchs: Bilhah, Zilpah, Tamar, and Aseneth', *Biblical Interpretation* 22 (2014): 307–24, esp. 312–14; Mordechai A. Friedman, 'Tamar, a Symbol of Life: The "Killer Wife" Superstition in the Bible and Jewish Tradition', *AJS Review* 15 (1990): 23–61. On Gen 38 in early rabbinic exegesis, see Stephen C. Reif, 'Early Rabbinic Exegesis of Genesis 38', in *The Exegetical Encounter Between Jews and Christians in Late Antiquity*, ed. E. Grypeou and H. Spurling, Jewish and Christian Perspectives Series 18 (Leiden: Brill, 2009), 221–44. On levirate marriage, see Wegner, *Chattel or Person?*, 97–113.

113. Jacobson, 1:404.
114. Ibid. Cf. Brown, *No Longer Be Silent*, 22.
115. See Jacobson, 1:404.

For when our wives conceive, they will not be recognised as pregnant until three months have passed, as also our mother Tamar did. For her intention was not to commit fornication, but being unwilling to separate from the sons of Israel she so reflected and said, 'It is better for me to have intercourse with my father-in-law and die than to have intercourse with gentiles'. And she hid the fruit of her womb until the third month. For then she was recognised. (L.A.B. 9:5)

Tamar's refusal to have sexual relations with a non-Jew offers further justification for Amram's continued relations with his wife.[116] Jacobson remarks that, 'LAB illuminated the Exodus story through the Genesis one, and then (as SC notes) reports the Genesis tale in language borrowed from the Exodus one (2:2)'.[117] Although he suggests that the mention of a three-month period is neither explained nor given context in L.A.B., it seems likely that the authors perceived a connection between the events narrated in Gen 38, where Tamar's pregnancy is hidden from Judah for around three months (Gen 38:24) and the fact that in Exod 2:2, Moses's mother hides him for three months after he is born.[118]

Amram refers to Tamar as 'our mother Tamar'. He claims her as an ancestress of Israel whose influence endures, continuing to shape the identity of those descending from her, including Amram. The use of 'our mother' as an authoritative title is further supported by L.A.B.'s employment of the equivalent male term: 'our father Jacob' (L.A.B. 21:5) and 'our fathers' in relation to the covenant (L.A.B. 9:4). L.A.B. appears to view Tamar as belonging to an authoritative ancestral group. Halpern-Amaru argues: 'Tamar is given the role of a male hero. She assumes and asserts full responsibility for the nature of the seed which she will produce. In so doing, she becomes, like Abraham and like her spokesman, Amram, a model of fidelity to the covenant'.[119] The term 'our mother' appears in rabbinic literature to designate various matriarchal figures and it is

---

116. On Tamar in L.A.B., see Halpern-Amaru, 'Women in Pseudo-Philo', 92–4; Donald C. Polaski, 'On Taming Tamar: Amram's Rhetoric and Women's Roles in Pseudo-Philo's Liber Antiquitatum Biblicarum 9', Journal for the Study of the Pseudepigrapha 13 (1995): 79–99; Jacobson, 1:409–11.

117. Jacobson, 1:410. SC refers to Harrington, Pseudo-Philon, Les Antiquités Bibliques.

118. See Jacobson, 1:408–9, 422; Polaski, 'Taming Tamar', 85. This is similar to gezerah shawah, where the language used in one biblical context explains its usage in another (see §2.3, 'Common Midrashic Exegetical Techniques').

119. Halpern-Amaru, 'Women in Pseudo-Philo', 92. Cf. van der Horst, 'Portraits of Women in L.A.B.', 31–3.

thus significant to find a pre-rabbinic use of the term here.[120] Moreover, as Jacobson notes, this is a 'remarkable characterisation of Thamar', as rabbinic sources usually limit the title to the wives of the patriarchs.[121]

In Judg 5:7, Deborah is referred to as 'a mother in Israel' (אם בישראל). *L.A.B.* regards Deborah as a pious individual, worthy of this title.[122] In *L.A.B.* 33:1, Deborah exhorts the people to 'Heed me like your mother', drawing on maternal qualities to commend her leadership.[123] As Brown notes, Deborah's designation as a mother 'does not signify physical motherhood, but a role and quality of character. The mother's role is to nourish, protect, admonish, teach, and guide; she is compassionate and always mindful of her children'.[124] The Israelite community recognises Deborah's authority: after her death, they lament: 'Behold, a mother has perished from Israel, and a holy one who exercised leadership in the house of Jacob' (*L.A.B.* 33:6). The Israelites also refer to 'Deborah our mother', who commanded them to obey God's commandments (*L.A.B.* 38:2).[125] For *L.A.B.*, the title 'mother' includes leadership qualities and protection of the nation.

Consistent with its attention to female characters, *L.A.B.* 39–40 develops the characterisation of Jephthah's daughter, who is sacrificed after her father makes a foolish vow (Judg 11:29-40).[126] In Judg 11:36-37, Jephthah's daughter expresses her willingness to be sacrificed, but asks that she may first go and lament that she will die a virgin. *L.A.B.* 40 expands on this, portraying this woman, here named Seila, as a willing victim, equal to Isaac during the Aqedah (*L.A.B.* 40:2), and recording the lament that she utters (*L.A.B.* 40:5-7).[127] Seila is regarded positively by

---

120. For 'our mother' in *Genesis Rabbah*, see §3.6.2, 'Uses of the Noun אם as "Matriarch"'.

121. Cf *b. Ber.* 16b. This likely recognises Tamar's status as an ancestress of the Davidic line. Jacobson, 1:409. See also Reiss and Zucker, 'Co-opting the Secondary Matriarchs', 313.

122. On Judg 4–5 in *L.A.B.*, see Brown, *No Longer Be Silent*, 39–71; Jacobson, 2:831–941.

123. See Brown, *No Longer Be Silent*, 66; Halpern-Amaru, 'Women in Pseudo-Philo', 103–4.

124. Brown, *No Longer Be Silent*, 69; cf. 71; van der Horst, 'Portraits of Women in L.A.B.', 38.

125. Neither the Bible nor *L.A.B.* record Deborah saying this (Jacobson, 2:941).

126. See Jacobson, 2:959–77; Brown, *No Longer Be Silent*, 95–117; Halpern-Amaru, 'Women in Pseudo-Philo', 103–5.

127. See Brown, *No Longer Be Silent*, 94–5, 97–9, 101, 103, 109–15; Jacobson, 2:964–5; van der Horst, 'Portraits of Women in L.A.B.', 39–42.

the author of *L.A.B.* Prior to her lamentation in the mountains, the Lord declares: 'Now let her soul be given up in accord with her request, and her death will be precious before me always, and she will go and depart into the bosom of her mothers' (*L.A.B.* 40:4). Jacobson offers several interpretations of the final phrase: it may invoke Lam 2:12, where children are dying and will end up 'on their mothers' bosom'; it may be used in its metaphorical sense, meaning one's homeland (*y. Mo'ed Qaṭ.* 3:1, 81c); or, as in *Pesiqta de Rab Kahana*, it could relate to martyrdom.[128] Perhaps, however, the Lord simply means that Seila's death will allow her to join the great matriarchs of Israel, such as Tamar, Deborah and the patriarchs' wives. Halpern-Amaru agrees, suggesting this to be: 'a phrase that implies the company, if not the status, of the matriarchs'.[129] Though there is no confirmation of this meaning in *L.A.B.*, the text's positive presentation of both Jephthah's daughter and various Jewish ancestresses makes it a realistic possibility.

L.A.B. offers a clear example of the title 'matriarch' being used in early Jewish exegetical literature. Although suggesting some characteristics associated with being a matriarch, *L.A.B.* still provides no clear suggestion of how to identify women known as 'matriarchs', nor any indication of the total number of women included in the group.

3.4.4. *Early Rabbinic Midrash*

In the early rabbinic period, these postbiblical developments combine to form a category of 'the matriarchs' (האימהות). *Mekilta de Rabbi Ishmael*, a tannaitic midrash, is one of the earliest rabbinic texts. Redacted in the third century CE, this halakhic midrash provides commentary on Exod 12:1–35:3.[130] Tractate *Amalek* contains two references to 'the deeds of the mothers' (מעשה אמהות), paralleled each time with 'the deeds of the fathers' (מעשה אבות). These phrases appear in the context of Israel's battle with Amalek in Exod 17:8-16. In Exod 17:9, Moses instructs Joshua to take men to fight Amalek; whilst he 'will stand on the top of the hill with the staff of God in my hand'. The rabbinic exegetes explain the meaning of Moses's words:

---

128. Jacobson, 2:967–8.

129. Halpern-Amaru, 'Women in Pseudo-Philo', 105.

130. See 'Rabbinic Texts'; Ben-Eliyahu, Cohn and Millar, *Handbook*, 63–5; Lauterbach, 'Introduction', 1:xiii–lxiv. Jacob Lauterbach provides the critical text and translation of *Mekilta de Rabbi Ishmael*; quotations will be from Lauterbach.

> *Tomorrow I Will Stand* (Ex 17:9). Tomorrow we shall be prepared to take our
> stand. *Upon the Top of the Hill*, to be taken literally—these are the words of
> R. Joshua. R. Eleazar of Modi'im says: Let us declare tomorrow a fast day
> and be ready, relying upon the deeds of the forefathers (מעשה אבות). For
> 'the top' (*rosh*), refers to the deeds of the fathers (מעשה אבות); 'the hill',
> refers to the deeds of the mothers (מעשה אמהות). (*Amalek* I:94–98).

According to R. Eleazar of Modi'im, Moses prescribes a day of fasting
for the Israelites, suggesting that they should enter a penitent state. The
phrase 'the top of the hill' is interpreted as referring to the meritorious
acts of Israel's ancestors, both male and female. The 'fathers' (אבות) and
'mothers' (אמהות) are used as authoritative categories by the midrash,
and these figures' actions are believed to bring benefits to Israel, such as
victory in battle.

The biblical text describes how, when Moses went up the hill on the
day of the battle, he sat with his arms outstretched. Every time Moses
raised his arms, Israel overpowered Amalek, but each time he lowered
them, Israel began to lose. *Amalek* I.148-152 comments on Exod 17:12,
as Moses struggles to keep his arms lifted:

> *And Aaron and Hur Stayed Up His Hands*. For else he would raise them
> and then have to lower them. 'And his hands were steady until the going
> down of the sun'. This tells that they were having a fast day—these are the
> words of R. Joshua. R. Eleazar of Modi'im says: The sin weighed heavily
> upon the hands of Moses at that hour and he could not bear it. What did he
> do? He turned to the deeds of the forefathers (מעשה אבות). For it is said:
> 'And they took a stone and put under him', which refers to the deeds of the
> fathers (מעשה אבות); 'And he sat thereon', which refers to the deeds of the
> mothers (מעשה אמהות).

Rabbi Joshua first continues the midrash's previous interpretation of Exod
17:9: whilst the Israelites were fasting, Moses's hands remained steady. At
sunset, when the day of fasting ends, R. Eleazar of Modi'im argues that
Moses's strength fails as the full weight of Israel's sin is felt. At this point,
Moses again appeals to the ancestors' good deeds to help secure Israel's
victory. These deeds are the (metaphorical) stones that Aaron and Hur use
to steady Moses's arms.

The battle with Amalek is one of Israel's most notorious battles and
represents defeat of a powerful enemy.[131] Immediately following Israel's
victory, God promises to 'utterly blot out the remembrance of Amalek

---

131. See Gerald L. Mattingly, 'Amalek, Amalekites', *EDB*, 48–9; Samuel
Abramsky, S. David Sperling and Elimelech Epstein Halevy, 'Amalekites', *EncJud*
2:28–31.

from under heaven' (Exod 17:14). *Mekilta* credits 'the fathers' and 'mothers' with this archetypal battle: it is their deeds that secured the victory. This suggests that the rabbis viewed these figures as possessing great authority in Israel. The 'merit of the ancestors' is an important concept in rabbinic literature. As Kaunfer comments, 'The forefathers' faith serves as a reservoir of merit upon which the Jewish people may call to plead their case for mercy in God's judgment of their individual and corporate deeds'.[132] Notably, the midrash names neither 'the fathers' nor 'the mothers'; rather, the rabbinic interpreters assume their audience's understanding of the category even at this early rabbinic stage.[133] *Mekilta de Rabbi Ishmael* demonstrates that the category of 'the matriarchs' (אמהות) was well established by the third century CE, and interestingly, in this tractate, the female group appears to have the same authority as its male counterpart.

Finally, *Sipre Deuteronomy*, another third-century CE midrash, comments on Deut 33:15 as follows:

> 'with the best from the ancient mountains, [and the bounty of hills immemorial]:...' This teaches that the patriarchs and matriarchs are called mountains and hills, as it is said, 'I will go to the mountain of myrrh and to the hill of frankincense' (Song 4:6).[134]

In a similar way to *Mek. R. Ish. Amalek* I:98, *Sipre Deut.* 353:3 links ancestral figures with 'hills' and 'mountains'. Kaunfer notes that the rabbis often interpret the appearance of the word 'hills' in biblical texts as referring to 'the merit of the mothers': 'The choice of "hills" as a metaphor for the Matriarchs would seem to be an apt one, reflecting the contours of the female body'.[135] As in *Mekilta*, *Sipre Deuteronomy*

---

132. Kaunfer, 'Who Knows Four?', 95. See §3.6.3.3, 'The Merit of the Matriarchs (בזכות האימהות)'.

133. They are unlikely simply to be biological mothers and fathers, as so much weight is attached to these individuals' deeds.

134. Jacob Neusner, *Sifre to Deuteronomy: An Analytical Translation*, 2 vols., Brown Judaic Studies (Atlanta: Scholars Press, 1987), 2:435–6. Jacob Neusner offers a translation of *Sipre Deut.* Finkelstein provides the critical Hebrew edition. Louis Finkelstein, *Sifre on Deuteronomy. Published originally by the Gesellschaft zur Foerderung der Wissenschaft des Judentums. And now re-published by The Jewish Theological Seminary of America. Through the Generosity of the Stroock Publication Fund* (New York: The Jewish Theological Seminary of America, 1969).

135. Kaunfer, 'Who Knows Four?', 96. Kaunfer suggests Num 23:9 is the basis for this interpretation, as it appears several times in rabbinic literature. Song 2:8 also appears in connection with 'the merit of the mothers'. He points especially to *Num. Rab.* 20, 19 and *b. Roš Haš* 11a (ibid., nn. 10 and 11 on p. 102).

parallels 'the matriarchs' with the 'patriarchs' and assumes that its readers will understand who is referred to. This implies that the category of 'the matriarchs' was firmly established by the early rabbinic period.

3.4.5. *Summary*

This survey of ancient Jewish literature aids understanding of the category, 'the matriarchs'.[136] *Jubilees* develops the characterisation of women in Genesis and the early chapters of Exodus, but does not refer to these women as a group. Certain common characteristics begin to emerge in this text, particularly female involvement with the Israelite covenant. A fragment of the Qumranite *Damascus Document* employs the title 'the Mothers' (אמות). Even if this title does not refer to biblical women, it shows that by the first century BCE, a group of women had influence within this community. Moving into the first centuries CE, *L.A.B.* provides positive portrayals of women from Genesis to 2 Samuel. Most significantly, this is probably the first Jewish exegetical text to employ the title 'matriarch'. Both Tamar and Deborah are referred to as 'our mother' in *L.A.B.*, recognising their authority as key figures from Israel's history. This usage is paralleled in later rabbinic midrash. Finally, by the third century CE, when the first rabbinic midrashim were compiled, the title 'the matriarchs' (האמהות) was being used increasingly frequently. It referred to a group of authoritative women, who could be paralleled with the male 'patriarchs' (אבות). 'The matriarchs' (האמהות) has finally become a tangible category.

3.5. *Excursus: The Matrilineal Principle*

The matrilineal principle became the primary way of determining a person's Jewish identity.[137] This principle prescribes that in a marriage between a Jew and a non-Jew, any offspring will follow the status of the mother. Thus, if the mother is Jewish and the father gentile, the child will be Jewish; if the mother is a gentile and the father Jewish, the child will be a gentile. The matrilineal principle provides women with an increasingly important role in Jewish identity. It is likely that this principle influenced

---

136. On women in Jewish literature from the Greco-Roman period, including Philo and Josephus, see Levine, ed., *'Women Like This'*; James L. Bailey, 'Josephus' Portrayal of the Matriarchs', in *Josephus, Judaism, and Christianity*, ed. Louis H. Feldman and Gohei Hata (Detroit: Wayne State University Press, 1987), 154–79.

137. Reform and Orthodox Jewish communities today disagree on its importance for determining Jewish identity. See *Judaism* 34, no. 1 (1985).

the portrayal of 'the Mothers' or 'matriarchs' (האימהות) and may even have aided the emergence of that category. Rabbinic texts neither define nor justify the matrilineal principle; it is simply assumed.[138] Two passages

138. The origins of the matrilineal principle are complex and much debated. According to Schiffman, the principle was introduced by Ezra (Ezra 10), based on prohibitions of intermarriage with foreigners (Exod 34:15; Deut 23:4-7): Lawrence H. Schiffman, 'At the Crossroads: Tannaitic Perspectives on the Jewish–Christian Schism', in *Jewish and Christian Self-Definition. Vol. 2, Aspects of Judaism in the Graeco-Roman Period*, ed. E. P. Sanders, with A. I. Baumgarten and Alan Mendelson (London: SCM, 1981), 115–56; Lawrence H. Schiffman, 'Jewish Identity and Jewish Descent', *Judaism* 34 (1985): 78–84. Cohen argues that a comparable Roman law influenced the Jewish principle; he also suggests that rabbinic fascination with mixtures led to consideration of the offspring of mixed marriages. See Shaye J. D. Cohen, 'The Matrilineal Principle in Historical Perspective', *Judaism* 34 (1985): 5–13; Cohen, 'The Origins of the Matrilineal Principle in Jewish Law', *AJS Review* 10 (1985): 19–53. Heger, refuting Schiffman, claims that patrilineality still dominated in the postexilic period (Ezra 2:59; Neh 7:61). Ezra sought to remove foreign influence from Israel; he did not intend to institute a matrilineal principle. Heger suggests that the rabbinic matrilineal principle derives from a legal philosophical principle, claiming that in a mixed marriage, the gentile partner is not subject to Jewish halakhah and any offspring can only be judged according to its mother: Paul Heger, 'Patrilineal or Matrilineal Genealogy in Israel After Ezra', *Journal for the Study of Judaism* 43 (2012): 215–48. The matrilineal principle gained dominance between the Bible and Midrash, the same period that saw the emergence of 'the matriarchs'. It is likely that the matrilineal principle influenced the development of 'the matriarchs'. For what follows, see Shaye J. D. Cohen, *Why Aren't Jewish Women Circumcised? Gender and Covenant in Judaism* (Berkeley: University of California Press, 2005), 13, 141–2; Cohen, *The Beginnings of Jewishness: Boundaries, Varieties, Uncertainties*, Hellenistic Culture and Society XXXI (Berkeley: University of California Press, 1999), 241–307; Cohen, 'Was Timothy Jewish (Acts 16:1-3)? Patristic Exegesis, Rabbinic Law, and Matrilineal Descent', *Journal of Biblical Literature* 105, no. 2 (1986): 251–68; Christine E. Hayes, *Gentile Impurities and Jewish Identities: Intermarriage and Conversion for the Bible to the Talmud* (New York: Oxford University Press, 2002), esp. 151–2; Tal Ilan, *Mine and Yours Are Hers: Retrieving Women's History From Rabbinic Literature* (Leiden: Brill, 1997), 162–4; Mayer I. Gruber, 'Matrilineal Determination of Jewishness: Biblical and Near Eastern Roots', in *Pomegranates and Golden Bells: Studies in Biblical, Jewish, and Near Eastern Ritual, Law, and Literature in Honour of Jacob Milgrom*, ed. David Noel Freedman, Avi Huritz and David P. Wright (Winona Lake: Eisenbrauns, 1995), 437–43; Satlow, *Jewish Marriage*, 133–61, esp. 158–60; Stuart Krauss, 'The Word "Ger" in the Bible and Its Implications', *Jewish Bible Quarterly* 34, no. 4 (2006): 264–70; Susan Sorek, 'Mothers of Israel: Why the Rabbis Adopted a Matrilineal Principle', *Women in Judaism* 3, no. 1 (2002): 1–12; Victor Aptowitzer, 'Spuren des Matriarchats in

in the Mishnah are usually cited by scholars as proof of this principle. First, *m. Qidd.* 3:12 discusses the validity of different marriages and their effects on the status of resulting offspring. This text ends:

> If her betrothal with this man was not valid, and her betrothal with others would also not be valid, the offspring is of her own standing. This is the case when the offspring is by a bondwoman or gentile woman.

Of the four examples of marriages between different people offered in this mishnah, matrilineality ensues only here, where a marriage is contracted between a Jewish man and a gentile- or bondwoman. The union between these individuals cannot be legally valid (have what is called *qiddushin*) when only the male is accounted for under halakhah.[139] As Cohen explains: 'If the mother is legally incapable of contracting a valid marriage, her offspring lacks a legal father and follows its mother'.[140] Importantly, *m. Qidd.* 3:12 states that in a legal marriage between two Jews, where no transgression is enacted, the status of the offspring is still determined patrilineally. *M. Qidd.* 3:12 thus suggests that gentile women marrying Jewish men will produce gentile offspring.

Scholars derive the second part of the matrilineal principle from *m. Yebam.* 7:5, asserting that offspring produced by the marriage of a Jewish woman with a foreign man are Jewish:

jüdischen Schrifftum', *Hebrew Union College Annual* 4 (1927): 207–40; Aptowitzer, 'Spuren des Matriarchats im jüdischen Schrifftum (Schluss)', *Hebrew Union College Annual* 5 (1928): 261–97; Epstein, *Marriage Laws*, 145–219; Satlow, *Tasting the Dish*, 84–118. On women in Ezra–Nehemiah, see Tamara C. Eskenazi, 'Out from the Shadows: Biblical Women in the Postexilic Era', *Journal for the Study of the Old Testament* 54 (1992): 31–42.

139. Cohen notes a similar principle in Roman law: if a marriage is a *justum matrimonium*, 'legal marriage', between two people who have *conubium*, '[t]he capacity to contract a legal marriage', offspring follow the father. Without this, children follow the mother (Cohen, 'Origins of the Matrilineal Principle', 42–6; Cohen, 'Matrilineal Principle in Historical Perspective', 11–12).

140. Cohen, 'Matrilineal Principle in Historical Perspective', 6. He notes that whilst this can explain the examples of a Jewish man marrying a Jewish woman (the marriage is wholly legitimate; the child follows the father) and the case of a Jewish man marrying a gentile woman, it does not account for *m. Qidd.* 3:12's other two examples, following the blemished parent or producing a bastard (Hebrew *mamzer*). Cf. Heger, 'Patrilineal or Matrilineal Genealogy', 222–30.

if the daughter of an Israelite was married to a priest, or a priest's daughter to an Israelite, and she bore a son by him, and the son went and had connexion with a bondwoman, and she bore a son by him, such a child is a bondman...
if the daughter of an Israelite was married to a priest, or a priest's daughter to an Israelite, and she bore a daughter by him and the daughter went and married a slave or a gentile and bore a son by him, such a child is a bastard.

M. Yebam. 7:5 restates the principle found in *m. Qidd.* 3:12: an Israelite man marrying a bondswoman will have children who are bondsmen. The passage then explains that an Israelite woman marrying a slave or a gentile produces a child with the status of a mamzer. This term is often translated as 'bastard' but actually bears different connotations: it refers to 'a Jew of impaired status', who cannot marry a native-born Jew and cannot convert.[141] In *t. Qidd.* 4:16 and the Talmud, however, such offspring are declared full Jews.[142]

Neither *m. Qidd.* 3:12 nor *m. Yebam.* 7:5 defines or explains the matrilineal principle and they must not be regarded in this way by scholars. Both texts speak to particular circumstances, employing the undisputed matrilineal principle as part of a larger argument. Thus, for example, *m. Yebam.* 7:5 explores particular women's right to eat terumah, the priestly portion of sacrifices, not how to determine a child's Jewishness. What *m. Qidd.* 3:12 and *m. Yebam.* 7:5 do show is the widespread acceptance of the matrilineal principle in third-century CE rabbinic Judaism.

In addition, Moshe Reiss and David J. Zucker note that endogamy, an issue connected to the emergence of the matrilineal principle, became increasingly important during and after the Second Temple period, as Jews were concerned to protect their nation and religion from corrupting external influences.[143] The biblical text already indicates that the background and identity of a particular woman can confirm her legitimacy as a 'matriarch' and these characteristics were all the more crucial in post-biblical times.[144] Reiss and Zucker argue that there are two distinguishable

141. Cohen, 'Origins of the Matrilineal Principle', 19 n. 1, 49.

142. See ibid., 33–4.

143. With the loss of the northern kingdom and the later fall of Judah, the Israelites were forced into exile and were more exposed to the influence of surrounding nations. This led to Ezra and Nehemiah's ban on intermarriage. Similar concerns abounded in the Herodian and Hasmonean period, and conversion became a means of allowing outsiders to join the community. It became more unacceptable to marry outside the community. See Reiss and Zucker, 'Co-opting the Secondary Matriarchs', 316–23.

144. See §3.3.2, 'Marriages between Patriarchs and Handmaids'. Cf. Steinberg, 'Alliance or Descent?', 52.

sub-categories of women who may be called 'matriarchs'. First, 'matriarchs' refers to Sarah, Rebekah, Leah, and Rachel, the legitimate wives
of the patriarchs. However, Bilhah, Zilpah, Tamar, and Aseneth are
'Secondary Matriarchs'. This title recognises the significance of foreign
wives who bear key Israelite figures, including heads of Israelite tribes
and the ancestor of the Davidic line, whilst differentiating them from the
primary 'Matriarchs'. In the context of the Hebrew Bible; the patriarchs'
marriages to women outside of Israel were acceptable; postbiblical interpreters corrected the backgrounds of these women in order to affirm their
legitimacy as significant mothers in Israel.[145]

Bilhah and Zilpah provide one example. Genesis gives no background
for these women. *Jubilees*, which encourages endogamy throughout,
explains that Bilhah and Zilpah are sisters, whilst the *Testament of
Naphtali* suggests that Bilhah and Zilpah's father was Rotheus, a member
of Abraham's family and the brother of Rebekah's nurse, Deborah. Finally,
midrashic traditions suggest that they are Laban's daughters by concubines (*Gen. Rab.* 74:13-14). Each of these postbiblical sources attempts
to legitimise Bilhah and Zilpah by explicating their direct relationship
to Israel's ancestral family.[146] A similar phenomenon occurs with Tamar
and Aseneth.[147] Reiss and Zucker's title 'Secondary Matriarchs' is apt. It
recognises the significant role played by these women in Israel's history
and this in turn explains why early Jewish exegetical texts placed them
firmly inside the Jewish community.

3.5.1. *Summary*

Both the introduction of the matrilineal principle and the prohibition
of intermarriages had profound implications for understandings of 'the
matriarchs'. Genesis portrayed these women as legitimate wives, but the
increased importance of mothers in determining their children's Jewish
identity no doubt affected postbiblical portrayals. The matrilineal principle may have directly contributed to the emergence of the category, 'the
matriarchs', as the legitimacy of Israel's mothers was seen to determine
the legitimacy of the very nation itself.[148]

---

145. Reiss and Zucker, 'Co-opting the Secondary Matriarchs', 307–24.

146. Ibid., 309–12. On Bilhah in the *Testament of Naphtali*, see Michael E. Stone,
'The Genealogy of Bilhah', *Dead Sea Discoveries* 3, no. 1 (1996): 20–36.

147. Reiss and Zucker, 'Co-opting the Secondary Matriarchs', 312–15.

148. Patrilineality continued in Judaism, as *m. Qidd.* 3:12 demonstrates. Paternity
and maternity both show the legitimacy of a child.

3.6. 'The Matriarchs' (האימהות) in Genesis Rabbah

The noun אם, in singular or plural form, appears several times in *Genesis Rabbah* with the titular meaning of 'matriarch'.[149] The rabbis assume their audience's knowledge of 'the matriarchs' (האימהות) and their main characteristics. *Genesis Rabbah* offers only one list of women bearing the title and this does not seem to be exhaustive.[150] The content and context of passages containing the term must be carefully considered; and it would be unwise to assume that collating references to individually named 'matriarchs' reveals the group in its entirety. Two main definitions of 'the matriarchs' emerge from the title's use in *Genesis Rabbah*. First, the title refers to the four legitimate wives of the patriarchs (Sarah, Rebekah, Leah and Rachel). This cross-generational use of the term encompasses the mothers of Israel from the earliest generations. Secondly, in certain cases, 'the matriarchs' is a shorthand for 'the mothers of Israel's tribal ancestors' and thus refers to Jacob's four wives (Leah, Rachel, Bilhah and Zilpah). Whichever definition prevails, these women have one thing in common: they bear sons who inherit God's covenant with Israel.

3.6.1. *The Wives of the Patriarchs*

3.6.1.1. *The Title 'the Matriarchs' Paralleled with a Male Equivalent*

Twice in *Genesis Rabbah* (39:11 and 58:4), the title 'matriarchs' (אימהות) is directly paralleled with an equivalent male term. In both cases, it appears to refer to the wives of the patriarchs. *Genesis Rabbah* 39:11 expounds the blessing on Abraham in Gen 12:2. Part of this midrashic interpretation connects occurrences of the words 'greatness' and 'blessing' in Gen 12:2-3 with the number of Israelite patriarchs and matriarchs:

> R. Levi b. R. Aḥyatha and R. Abba said: Thrice is 'greatness' mentioned here, and 'blessings' four times:[151] He thus informed him that there would be three Patriarchs (אבות) and four Matriarchs (אימהות).

---

149. My study has identified eleven midrashim in *Genesis Rabbah* containing אם in a seemingly titular sense.

150. *Gen. Rab.* 58:4. See the discussion below.

151. 'Greatness' only appears twice in Gen 12:2-3. Freedman suggests: 'Some explain that "*I will make thee*" counts as one; others include Gen. XVIII, 18: *Seeing that Abraham shall surely become a great and mighty nation*' (Freedman, n. 6 319). How the rabbis calculate their references to 'greatness' is less important than the subsequent interpretation.

According to these rabbis, both the matriarchs and patriarchs are accounted for at the very beginning of Israel's history, as God makes his covenant with Abraham. No further information is provided about these groups of male and female ancestors, but their importance for Israel is suggested. The covenantal context of this interpretation, as well as the biblical usage of 'fathers' (אבות) as a title, indicates that the 'three patriarchs' must be Abraham, Isaac and Jacob. Correspondingly, the 'four matriarchs' are most likely their wives: Sarah, Rebekah, Leah and Rachel.

Later in *Gen. Rab.* 39:11, R. Berekiah in R. Ḥelbo's name argues that Abraham's 'coinage was current in the world', circulating with pictures of '[a]n old man and an old woman on one side, and a boy and a girl on the other'. Both Neusner and Freedman argue that having his own currency indicates Abraham's greatness and they identify the figures on the coins as Abraham and Sarah, and Isaac and Rebekah.[152] Various other male figures from Israel's history, including King David, are mentioned as having their own coinage; but only in this case are women depicted on the coins alongside men. *Genesis Rabbah* 39:11 parallels 'the mothers' (אימהות) with 'the fathers' (אבות), suggesting the equal importance of both groups within rabbinic thought.

Genesis Rabbah 58:4 provides the midrash's only list of women bearing the title 'the matriarchs'. It interprets Gen 23:3, explaining why the city in which Sarah is buried, Kiriath-Arba (קרית ארבע), is named 'city of four'.[153] The midrash associates various lists of four with the city, including two lists of important individuals who were buried there: 'four righteous (צדיקים) men were buried therein: Adam, Abraham, Isaac, and Jacob.[154] Four matriarchs (אימהות) were buried therein: Eve, Sarah, Rebekah, and Leah'. Although the title 'patriarchs' does not appear, the 'matriarchs' are again paralleled with a group of authoritative men.

This list of 'righteous men' and 'matriarchs' depends on fact or tradition about which key biblical ancestors were buried in Kiriath-Arba. As such, although the categories roughly correspond to the three great patriarchs and their legitimate wives, there is some variation. Sarah, Rebekah and Leah feature, but Rachel cannot because she is buried on the road to Ephrath after dying in childbirth (Gen 48:7).[155] The Bible never mentions the burial place of the first man and woman. This rabbinic tradition maintains a link between the origins of the human race and the emergence of Israel. Eve is named 'the mother (אם) of all living' (Gen 3:20), and because

---

152. Neusner, 2:69, 71; Freedman, n. 2 n. 3 320.
153. The city also has four names. See Sarna, *JPS: Genesis*, 157.
154. Cf. *Tg. Neof.* 23:2.
155. Cf. Pardes, *Countertraditions*, 74.

all people descend from her, this would also qualify her as a 'mother of Israel'. Moreover, this tradition was clearly circulating in the first centuries CE. The Christian priest and theologian Jerome (ca. 347–419 CE) refers to Adam and the patriarchs being buried in Kiriath-Arba.[156] The male and female ancestors buried at Kiriath-Arba are again found in *b. 'Erub.* 53a: 'R. Isaac explained: The city of the four couples: Adam and Eve, Abraham and Sarah, Isaac and Rebekah, Jacob and Leah'.[157]

Genesis Rabbah 58:4 suggests that 'the matriarchs' (האימהות) can refer to slightly different combinations of women depending on the context. Thus, for example, although Rachel is excluded from this list, she is specifically identified as a matriarch elsewhere in *Genesis Rabbah.*[158]

Finally, Neusner suggests that: 'The passage answers an obvious question [about the city's name], with no bearing upon the exegesis of the passage [Gen 23:2]'.[159] Neusner is, however, mistaken: the midrash offers interpretation of the biblical verse by drawing out the historical and national implications of the events it relates. Genesis 23:2 describes how, following Sarah's death, Abraham purchases a burial plot from Ephron the Hittite. Abraham, Isaac, Jacob, Sarah, Rebekah and Leah are subsequently buried here.[160] As Rabow notes, 'it is the resting place for the Matriarchs [and Patriarchs] whose line has continued to the Jews of today'.[161] The first matriarch plays a crucial role in allowing Abraham to

---

156. This is based on Kiriath-Arba as a city relating to four individuals. Josh 14:15 is used to suggest Adam as the fourth man associated with the city. See C. T. R. Hayward, *Saint Jerome's* Hebrew Questions on Genesis, Oxford Early Christian Studies (Oxford: Clarendon, 1995), 56–7, 182–3; Pieter W. van der Horst, 'The Site of Adam's Tomb', in *Studies in Ancient Judaism and Early Christianity*, ed. Martin Hengel, Ancient Judaism and Early Christianity: Arbeiten zur Geschichte des antiken Judentums and des Urchristentums (Leiden: Brill, 2014), 1–6. *Pirqe R. El.* 20 contains a later development of the tradition of Adam's burial and locates the Cave of Machpelah at the Temple site, instead of Kiriath-Arba. There is discussion of this text in eds. Emmanouela Grypeou and Helen Spurling, *The Book of Genesis in Late Antiquity: Encounters Between Jewish and Christian Exegesis*, Jewish and Christian Perspectives 24 (Leiden: Brill, 2013), 50–4. Darr briefly discusses Jewish tradition placing Adam and Eve in the Cave of Machpelah (Darr, *Far More Precious*, 112).

157. Cf. *b. Soṭah* 13a.

158. E.g. *Gen. Rab.* 72:6. See §3.6.2, 'Uses of the Noun אם as "Matriarch"'.

159. Neusner, 2:297.

160. See Gen 49:29-32. See Schneider, *Sarah*, 113, 115, 117, 122; Wenham, *Genesis 16–50*, 130; Claus Westermann, *Genesis 12–36: A Commentary*, trans. John J. Scullion SJ from the German 1981 published by Neukirchener Verlag (Minneapolis: Augsburg, 1986), 376; Rabow, *Lost Matriarch*, 2, 20.

161. Rabow, *Lost Matriarch*, 184.

secure a portion of the promised land, a place that future generations will forever remember as the burial place of their ancestors.[162] This testifies to Sarah's significance within Israel. In this regard, she is 'unique among biblical women, in that both her age at her death and her burial place are noted'.[163] *Genesis Rabbah* 58:4 builds upon this notion, recognising the enduring, authoritative status of both male and female ancestors within the nation's history.

3.6.1.2. *Summary*

In *Gen. Rab.* 39:11 and 58:4, the category of the 'matriarchs' (אימהות) is paralleled by the male terms 'patriarchs' (אבות) and 'righteous men' (צדיקים). The referents of the traditions are largely the wives of the patriarchs, but the women included may change depending on context. Neither midrash offers concrete evidence for defining or identifying the figures belonging to either the male or female groups, but they are clearly respected greatly by the rabbis, the women as much as the men.

3.6.2. *Uses of the Noun* אם *as 'Matriarch'*

Genesis Rabbah also uses the title 'matriarch' (אם) of individual biblical women as it retells their stories. Sarah and Rebekah are both referred to as 'our mother' (אימנו), which appears to function as the singular form of the title 'the matriarchs' (האימהות). After Isaac's birth, Sarah exclaims: 'God has brought laughter for me; everyone who hears will laugh with me' (Gen 21:6). The rabbinic interpreters conclude that: 'when the matriarch (lit. "our mother", אימנו) Sarah was remembered [gave birth], many other barren women were remembered with her' and those suffering from other infirmities and disabilities were also cured (*Gen. Rab.* 53:8).[164] The rabbis claim Sarah as 'our mother' because 'the matriarchs' are regarded as the mothers of Israel, from whom all Jews descend.[165] The use of the singular noun אם plus suffix in relation to Sarah helps to establish a more nuanced understanding of what the term 'matriarch' meant to the rabbis. The title recognises the enduring significance of Sarah's motherhood and celebrates the widespread consequences of events occurring in her lifetime.[166]

---

162. Exum, *Fragmented Women*, 106; Teubal, *Sarah the Priestess*, 94–5; Sarna, *JPS: Genesis*, 156.

163. David J. Zucker, 'Sarah: The View of the Classical Rabbis', in Hunt, ed., *'Perspectives on Our Father Abraham'*, 248.

164. See §5.3.2, 'The Reversal of Barrenness and Its Consequences'.

165. Neusner translates אימנו as 'our mother' (2:250); Freedman as 'the matriarch' (467).

166. Cf. Baskin, *Midrashic Women*, 160.

In *Gen. Rab.* 63:6, Rebekah's struggle with her painful pregnancy (Gen 25:22) is interpreted by the rabbis. The midrash depicts 'our mother (אימנו) Rebekah' travelling to other women's houses and asking about their experiences. In the next part of the midrash, R. Huna and R. Nehemiah connect Rebekah's physical experiences of pregnancy and childbearing with her worthiness to become the mother of Israel's tribal ancestors through her son, Jacob. Rebekah is deserving of the title 'our mother' because her maternity will endure.[167] In *Gen. Rab.* 53:8 and 63:6, this matriarchal title notes Sarah and Rebekah's significance not only as the physical mothers of covenant sons, but also as the national mothers of Israel.

Leah and Rachel are referred to as 'matriarchs' in *Gen. Rab.* 68:5. This midrash calculates the age at which Jacob married by reference to several events in his life. One time span given is: 'a further seven years were spent by him in working for the matriarchs (באימהות)'. Anyone familiar with the biblical text will recognise that this must refer to Leah and Rachel, the two wives whom Jacob married only after several years working for Laban. Although this midrash does not name 'the matriarchs', the rabbis assume that their audience will know which women are being discussed.[168] The use of 'matriarchs' in *Gen. Rab.* 68:5 to refer to Jacob's two primary wives provides further support for the notion that when the noun אם is used as a title, it refers to the legitimate wives of the Genesis patriarchs.

Finally, *Gen. Rab.* 67:9 and 72:6 state: 'The matriarchs were prophetesses, and Rebekah/Rachel was one of the matriarchs'. Two of the wives of the patriarchs, Rebekah and Rachel, are individually declared to be matriarchs because they have prophetic abilities.[169] The use of this identical phrase suggests that the title 'matriarchs' is a cross-generational term, uniting women from different generations of Israel's history through characteristics that they share.

3.6.2.1. *Summary*

The passages discussed in this section indicate that individual wives may be referred to as 'matriarch' in rabbinic midrash. No justification is given for these women bearing that title, suggesting that the category was familiar to the rabbis and their audience. It is reasonable to assume that the wives of the patriarchs may be referred to collectively as 'the

167. See §6.1.1, 'The Physical Act of Childbearing'.
168. The title cannot refer to Bilhah and Zilpah: Leah and Rachel gave them to Jacob.
169. See §3.6.3.1, 'The Matriarchs (האימהות) Were Prophetesses'.

matriarchs' (האימהות), especially as *Genesis Rabbah* does not refer to any other biblical women using the singular form of the title אם, 'matriarch'.[170]

3.6.3. *Characteristics of the Matriarchs (האימהות)*

3.6.3.1. *'The Matriarchs (האימהות) Were Prophetesses'*
Genesis Rabbah presents several characteristics that define 'the matriarchs' as a group. One of these is prophecy. Two separate midrashim claim that 'The matriarchs were prophetesses' (*Gen. Rab.* 67:9; 72:6), and they provide Rebekah and Rachel as examples.[171] *Genesis Rabbah* 67:9 comments on Gen 27:42, where Rebekah discovers that Esau plans to kill Jacob as revenge for stealing his birthright:

> AND THE WORDS OF ESAU HER ELDER SON WERE TOLD TO REBEKAH (XXVII, 42). Who told her? R. Haggai said in R. Isaac's name: The matriarchs (אימהות) were prophets, and Rebekah was one of the matriarchs (האמהות).

The midrash attempts to fill a gap in the biblical text by explaining the source of Rebekah's information. According to R. Haggai in the name of R. Isaac, as a matriarch Rebekah had prophetic abilities and could therefore discern Esau's murderous intentions. *Genesis Rabbah* 67:9 confirms Rebekah's authority and connects her to the group, 'the matriarchs', through these women's shared prophetic abilities.

Here, Rebekah ensures Jacob's protection from his brother and, by implication, protects the covenant and the Israelite nation. The noun אם means 'mother', and the term 'matriarch', also אם, is an extension of biological motherhood. The matriarchal figures bear children and protect their sons throughout their lifetimes, ensuring that the correct covenantal line is secured.[172] The biblical Rebekah provides a particular model for this: she, not Isaac, is 'the intermediary, who has to actively transmit the promise and blessing to the next generation'.[173] The rabbis identify 'the matriarchs' as their ancestresses and portray them with great respect

---

170. There are instances where אימהות refers to Jacob's wives. This is a collective identity, rather than recognition of an individual woman's matriarchal status. See §3.6.4.1, 'The Matriarchs as "Mothers of the Tribal Ancestors", in Reference to their Children'. Cf., however, *L.A.B.*'s 'our mother Tamar'.

171. See §3.6.2, 'Uses of the Noun אם as "Matriarch"'.

172. See also §6.4, 'Maternal Protection of the Covenant Son'.

173. Teugels, *'The Wooing of Rebekah' (Gen. 24)*, 125. Cf. Teugels, *'The Wooing of Rebekah' (Gen. 24)*, 119–29; Schneider, *Mothers of Promise*, 49–53. 57.

because without them, Israel would not have emerged. Moreover, as Rebekah's matriarchal status may be inferred from events occurring in her own life, this suggests that the individual characterisation of each woman contributes directly to an understanding of 'the matriarchs' as a group.

Genesis Rabbah 72:6 establishes a causal connection between Gen 30:21: 'Afterwards she (Leah) bore a daughter'; and Gen 30:22: 'Then God remembered Rachel...and opened her womb'. Basing itself on *m. Ber.* 9:3, the midrash debates the latest point at which God can change the sex of an unborn child. Genesis 30:22, where Dinah is born, is then discussed:

> R. Abba replied [He said to them]: Actually she was created a male, but she was turned into a female through Rachel's prayers when she said, *The Lord add to me another son* (Gen. XXX, 24). Said R. Ḥanina b. Pazzi: The matriarchs (אמהות) were prophetesses, and Rachel was one of the matriarchs (האימהות). It is not written, '*The Lord add to me* other sons', but '*another son*': she said: 'He is yet destined to beget one more; may it be from me!' R. Ḥanina said: All the matriarchs (אימהות) assembled and prayed: 'We have sufficient (*dayyenu*) males; let her [Rachel] be remembered'.

Leah's final child was supposed to be a boy but various prayers led instead to the birth of a daughter, Dinah. When Rachel bore Joseph (יוסף), she asked: 'May the Lord add (יסף) to me another son' (Gen 29:24). If Dinah were born male, Leah would have provided Jacob with his twelfth son. Rabbi Ḥanina b. Pazzi argues that, as a matriarch, and thus a prophetess, Rachel discerned that Jacob would only bear twelve sons and she prays that she will mother Jacob's final son. The power of female prayer is further suggested as 'the matriarchs' collectively prayed for Rachel to bear the final covenant son.[174]

Like *Gen. Rab.* 67:9, *Gen. Rab.* 72:6 shows how an episode from Rachel's life reveals her status as a matriarch. The midrash emphasises the link between the final patriarchal generation and the origins of Israel. *Genesis Rabbah* develops Rachel's characterisation, building on her biblical statement in Gen 29:24 and connecting her words to an awareness of Israel's structure as a nation of twelve tribes descending from Jacob's twelve sons.

---

174. See §3.6.4.1, 'The Matriarchs as "Mothers of the Tribal Ancestors", in Reference to their Children'; §8.1.1, 'Prayer and Praise'. See also Rabow, *Lost Matriarch*, 111–17.

Midrashic sources portray only a few women as prophetesses.[175] Seven female prophetesses are identified in *b. Meg.* 14b: Sarah, Miriam, Deborah, Hannah, Abigail, Huldah and Esther. Bronner notes that rabbinic interpreters had an ambivalent attitude towards women in this role.[176] Deborah is depicted as arrogant in spite of her positive portrayal in the Bible.[177] Sarah and Esther are portrayed positively as prophetesses in midrash, as is Miriam, who predicts Moses' greatness, ensures that Israel is not destroyed at the hands of the Egyptians, and regains her beauty following a life-threatening illness.[178] The rabbis respected certain biblical females for their prophetic abilities and added 'the matriarchs' to this list.

3.6.3.2. *The Matriarchs (האימהות) as 'Women in the Tent'*

Turning now to *Gen. Rab.* 48:15, a rather different picture of 'the matriarchs' emerges. In Gen 18, three angelic visitors come to announce Isaac's birth to Abraham. When asked about Sarah, Abraham says that she is 'in the tent' (באהל) (Gen 18:9). The rabbinic interpreters connect this with Judg 5:24: 'Most blessed of women be Jael, the wife of Heber the Kenite, of tent-dwelling women most blessed (lit. "above all women in the tent [באהל] she shall be blessed")', and they try to explain what this latter verse means:

> R. Eleazar said: It means, above the women of the generation of the wilderness. They gave birth to children, yet but for her [Jael] they [the children] would have been destroyed. R. Samuel b. Naḥman said: Above the Matriarchs (האמהות). They gave birth to children, yet but for her they would have been destroyed.

---

175. As Tal Ilan notes, there were no prophets (or classical prophecy) by Second Temple times. Torah study, from which women were excluded, replaced prophecy (Ilan, *Mine and Yours Are Hers*, 128). For women in the Israelite cultus, see Phyllis Bird, 'The Place of Women in the Israelite Cultus', in *Ancient Israelite Religion: Essays in Honour of Frank Moore Cross*, ed. Paul D Hanson, Patrick D. Miller, and S. Dean McBride (Philadelphia: Fortress, 1987), 397–419; and on prophetesses in the Talmudic tradition, see Bronner, *From Eve to Esther*, 163–84. Goitein and Carasik discuss poetry and prophecy as women's genres: S. D. Goitein and Michael Carasik, 'Women as Creators of Biblical Genres', *Prooftexts* 8, no. 1 (1998): 1–33. Cf. Brenner-Idan, *The Israelite Woman*, 47–57.

176. Bronner, *From Eve to Esther*, 163–84.

177. Ibid., 170–4.

178. Ibid., 164–70, 177–80. Steinmetz offers a study of Miriam in midrash: Devora Steinmetz, 'A Portrait of Miriam in Rabbinic Midrash', *Prooftexts* 8, no. 1 (1988): 35–65.

Rabbi Eliezer identifies the 'women in the tent' as the women of the exodus, who dwelt in tents in the wilderness. Rabbi Samuel b. Naḥman claims, however, that they are 'the matriarchs' (האמהות), an interpretation which links back to Sarah in Gen 18:9. In both cases, Jael is said to be greater than these women who bore children: she prevented the destruction of those offspring at the hands of Sisera (Judg 4–5).[179]

The final part of this midrash offers an alternative definition of 'the matriarchs' as 'women in the tent' and suggests that Sarah belongs to this group. The rabbis rely on their audience's knowledge of the biblical text to realise that the wives of the patriarchs are being referred to here.[180] Sarah, Rebekah, Leah and Rachel are all said to dwell in tents (Gen 18:6, 9-10; 24:67; 31:33-34), and in the case of Rebekah, her entry into Sarah's tent indicates her transition into the matriarchal role.[181] These four women are the central maternal figures preceding the exodus generation; and in biblical chronology, these two sets of women lead to the period of Judges. It is their offspring, therefore, put in danger by Sisera. *Genesis Rabbah* 48:15 suggests a limit to the matriarchal role. In *Gen. Rab.* 48:15, the matriarchs represent physical motherhood. National motherhood, elsewhere associated with 'the matriarchs', is transferred to Jael, who kills Sisera and ensures Israel's survival.[182]

Whilst the role of 'the matriarchs' is downplayed in this midrash, another woman, Jael, is credited with Israel's protection. Women play a central role in Judg 4–5.[183] The Canaanites and their commander, Sisera, are oppressing Israel. Deborah the prophetess tells Barak to fight the Canaanites and goes into battle with him. Deborah is referred to as 'a mother in Israel' (אם בישראל) in Judg 5:7, the closest that the biblical text comes to the title 'matriarch'. The Kenites are allied with Israel and one

179. On Jael, see Meir Bar-Ilan, *Some Jewish Women in Antiquity*, Brown Judaic Studies 317 (Atlanta: Scholars Press, 1998), 5–6, 90–1; Sasson, *Judges 1–12*, 264–71, 306–8.

180. This assumption is supported by *b. Naz.* 23b, which specifically identifies 'the women in the tent' as these four women.

181. See §3.3.1, 'The Matriarchs in the Hebrew Bible'; §7.4, 'Matriarchal Succession'; §8.1.2, 'Piety'; Sasson, *Judg 1–12*, 265, 306. Cf. Claus Westermann, *Isaiah 40–66*, trans. David M. G. Stalker from the German Das Buch Jesaia 40–66, das Alte Testament Deutsch 19, first edition 1966 published by Göttingen: Vandenhoeck & Ruprecht, Old Testament Library (London: SCM, 1969), 272–3.

182. Sasson notes that the order of tribes given in Judg 5:14-18 is grouped by mother (Sasson, *Judges 1–12*, 320–2). Cf. §6.2, 'Identity'.

183. Bar-Ilan, *Some Jewish Women*, 80. On Judg 4–5, see Sasson, *Judg 1–12*, 250–323.

of their women, Jael, kills Sisera with a tent pole when he seeks refuge with her. These events are related in Judg 4 and then, in Deborah's song (Judg 5), Jael is praised for her actions. Judges 4–5 thus depicts female characters acting assertively to positively influence Israel's history. In *Gen. Rab.* 48:15, Jael is suggested to be more important than even 'the matriarchs'.[184] Whilst they protected individual Israelite ancestors prior to the inception of the nation, Jael protects the emergent nation, as Israel struggles to claim its place among its often hostile neighbours. Within *Genesis Rabbah*, the rabbis commend the actions of both 'the matriarchs' and Jael. In this particular instance, Jael is elevated above the ancestresses because of the time in which she lived.

3.6.3.3. *'The Merit of the Matriarchs' (*בזכות האימהות*)*
As a group, 'the matriarchs' had power and influence. *Genesis Rabbah* 73:3 discusses Gen 30:22, where 'God remembered Rachel, and God heeded her and opened her womb', finally allowing her to bear a child:

> *He hath redeemed my soul in peace*, etc. (Ps. LV, 19):[185] this alludes to Jacob; *So that none came nigh to me (ib.)*—that the counsel of the wicked man [Laban] may not come nigh to me, that he may not say, 'The one who bore children he can take away, but the one who did not bear children he must not take away'. *For the many* [prayers] *were with me (ib.)*. For R. Judan said in R. Aibu's name: Through many prayers was Rachel remembered. First, for her own sake (or, 'by her own merit', בזכותה), as it says, AND GOD REMEMBERED (ETH) RACHEL. ETH RACHEL, implies for the sake of her sister (בזכות אחותה). AND GOD HEARKENED TO HER—for Jacob's sake; AND OPENED HER WOMB—for the sake of the matriarchs (בזכות האימהות).

Laban threatens to allow Jacob to leave Haran with Leah, who had borne him several children, but without the barren Rachel. Rabbi Judan in R. Aibu's name argues, using Ps 55:19, that Laban's threat was removed because many people prayed for Rachel and she gave birth. Each phrase of Gen 30:22 corresponds to the actions of a particular person or group who prayed for an end to Rachel's barrenness.

---

184. Sasson notes that: 'Jael should be blessed *minnāšîm*, "among women", so a most powerful accolade; but the phrase's construction might allow us to treat *minnāšîm* as a superlative, making Jael more worthy than the matriarchs, who likewise lived in tents' (Sasson, *Judges 1–12*, 306).

185. See Mitchell Dahood, *Psalms II: 51–100*, Anchor Bible 17 (New York: Doubleday, 1970), 35–6; Marvin E. Tate, *Psalms 51–100*, Word Biblical Commentary 20 (Dallas: Word, 1990), 53–4, 58–60.

The merit of Israel's ancestors is a widespread and influential notion in rabbinic literature. The biblical Hebrew verb זכה means 'to be clear, clean, pure, always in a moral sense'.[186] In rabbinic terminology, this becomes a noun, זכות, which has a range of connotations, including legal 'acquittal'; 'blessing' for good acts; 'benefit'; and 'the protecting influence of good conduct, merit'.[187] The rabbis believed that the patriarchs were more righteous than other people and their good deeds set them in God's good favour. The effects of this are felt through the centuries, as Israel is protected by and rewarded for the merit of these individuals.[188] *Genesis Rabbah* 73:3 associates such merit not only with the patriarch Jacob, but also with Rachel, Leah and 'the matriarchs'. Schechter points to the existence of 'merit of the mothers', corresponding to the 'merit of the fathers';[189] whilst Marmorstein discusses not only the 'merit of the mothers', but also 'the merit of pious women', which is credited with enabling the exodus from Egypt in certain talmudic sources.[190]

The rabbis accorded the Genesis matriarchs great respect, believing that their merit could influence God's action towards his people. In this midrash, the 'merit of the matriarchs' is associated with the phrase 'and (God) opened her womb' (Gen 30:22). This reinforces the link between 'the matriarchs' (האימהות) and motherhood and helps us to identify those women whom the rabbis regarded as matriarchs. 'The matriarchs' are not named, but are probably the wives of the patriarchs, especially as Leah and Rachel's merit is specifically mentioned by the midrash. This would then create a parallel between the common phrase the 'merit of the fathers' (זכות אבות), which usually connotes the merit of Abraham, Isaac and Jacob, and the 'merit of the mothers' (זכות אימהות), which appears here. For the rabbis, the patriarchs and their wives were authoritative figures in Israel's history and their actions had long-lasting consequences.

---

186. BDB, 269. See e.g. Job 15:14; 25:4, where the term is paralleled with צדק, meaning 'righteous'.

187. Jastrow, 398.

188. See Urbach, *The Sages*, 496–508; Solomon Schechter, *Aspects of Rabbinic Theology: Major Concepts of the Talmud*, International Journal for Philosophy and Theology (New York: Schocken, 1965), 170–98; A. Marmorstein, *The Doctrine of Merits in Old Rabbinical Literature* (London: Jews' College Publications, 1920); Joshua H. Schmidman, 'Zekhut Avot', *EncJud* 21:497–8; Ramon, 'Torah of Hesed', esp. 162–3.

189. Schechter, *Aspects*, 172.

190. E.g. *b. Sotah* 11b. See Marmorstein, *Doctrine of Merits*, 35, 41–4, 62, 172, etc.

3.6.3.4. *'Why Were the Matriarchs Made Barren?'* (ולמה נתעקרו אמהות)
Genesis Rabbah 45:4 emphasises barrenness as a central characteristic
of 'the matriarchs'.[191] This midrash interprets Gen 16:4, where Hagar
conceives a child and scorns her mistress. This midrash is formed of three
interconnected parts. First, the relationship between sexual intercourse
and conception is considered. This is followed by a discussion around
the question: 'Why were the matriarchs barren?' Finally, the midrash
expands on the pregnant Hagar's disregard for Sarah. Overall, the midrash
suggests that Hagar's quick conception reflects the lesser quality of her
pregnancy; whilst Sarah and the other matriarchs' barrenness highlights
the worthiness of these women and their offspring.

Genesis Rabbah 45:4 opens by quoting part of Gen 16:4: 'And Abraham
went in to Hagar and she conceived'. The following debate ensues:

> R. Levi b. Ḥaytha said: She became pregnant through the first intimacy. R.
> Eleazar said: A woman never conceives by the first intimacy. An objection
> is raised: surely it is written, *Thus were both the daughters of Lot with
> child by their father* (Gen. XIX, 36)? Said R. Tanḥuma: By an effort of will
> power they brought forth their virginity, and thus conceived at the first act
> of intercourse.

Although R. Eleazar argues that a woman cannot conceive the first time
she has sex, the case of Lot's daughters provides proof that this is untrue:
they slept with their father once and became pregnant (Lev 19). Hagar too
became pregnant immediately.[192]

A comparison is then made between the quality of wheat, which takes
a long time to grow, and thorns, which are often prolific despite a lack of
cultivation:

> R Ḥanina b. Pazzi observed: Thorns are neither weeded nor sown, yet of
> their own accord they grow and spring up, whereas how much pain and toil
> is required before wheat can be made to grow!

This becomes an analogy for the differing qualities of pregnancies:
those that happen quickly, as mentioned above, are worth less than those
resulting from a prolonged period of struggle. In Gen 16, Hagar conceives

---

191. See Chapter 5, 'Barrenness'.
192. Cf. Satlow, *Tasting the Dish*, 238. For Jewish views on sexuality, see Biale,
Eros; Satlow, *Tasting the Dish*; Daniel Boyarin, *Carnal Israel: Reading Sex in
Talmudic Culture* (Berkeley: University of California Press, 1993); Biale, *Women and
Jewish Law*, 121–46.

easily, whilst Sarai, who desperately longs for a child, remains childless.[193] Rabbi Ḥanina b. Pazzi suggests that Sarah's pregnancy will be of high value when she finally conceives.[194] Barrenness is therefore regarded as indicative of Sarah's legitimacy.

Out of this discussion arises the question: 'And why were the matriarchs made barren?' (ולמה נתעקרו אמהות).[195] Paradoxically, this question assumes that 'the matriarchs', women who are defined by their maternity (as 'mothers', אמהות), were all also barren (root עקר) and hence technically unable to have children. The rabbis must therefore have a particular group of women in mind, who struggled with barrenness before becoming mothers. Although 'the matriarchs' are not listed, it is fair to assume that the rabbis have Sarah, Rebekah, Leah and Rachel in mind. These women are all known to have been barren; even Leah is made barren in rabbinic interpretation.[196] The title 'the matriarchs' appears to refer again to the wives of the patriarchs, and barrenness is a necessary precursor to their motherhood.

The midrash then offers various explanations of the matriarchs' barrenness, presented by different rabbis. *Genesis Rabbah* 45:4 exemplifies the multivocality which characterises so much of rabbinic thought. The midrash explores a number of possible explanations of the matriarchs' prolonged barrenness, but ultimately offers no definitive answer:

> Why were the matriarchs barren? R. Levi said in R. Shila's name and R. Ḥelbo in R. Joḥanan's name: Because the Holy One Blessed be He, yearns for their prayers and supplications. Thus it is written, *O my dove, thou art as the clefts of the rock* (S.S. II, 14): Why did I make thee barren? In order that, *Let me see thy countenance, let Me hear thy voice (ib.)*. R. 'Azariah said in R. Ḥanina's name: So that they might lean on (מתפרקדות) their husbands in [spite of] their beauty. R. Huna and R. Jeremiah in the name of R. Ḥiyya b. Abba said: So that their husbands might derive pleasure from them, for when a woman is with child she is disfigured and lacks grace (מיתאזבת).[197] Thus the whole ninety years that Sarah did not bear she was like a bride in her canopy.

193. Cf. Baskin, *Midrashic Women*, 150; Trible, *Texts of Terror*, 6.

194. Cf. *Gen. Rab.* 45:1, suggesting that Sarah's pregnancy is highly valuable. See §7.1, 'Sarah as the "Capable Wife" (אשת חיל)'.

195. For discussion of this passage and what follows here, see Callaway, *Sing, O Barren One*, 126–7; Baskin, *Midrashic Women*, 131–3.

196. See *Gen. Rab.* 72:1. See also Chapter 5, 'Barrenness'; §8.1.1, 'Prayer and Praise'.

197. Jastrow derives from the Hithpael of עזב (Jastrow, 1061).

The midrash first suggests that God viewed the matriarchs positively because they were pious. This positive relationship between God and the matriarchs is confirmed by quotations from Song 2:14. The Song of Songs has been understood by Jewish interpreters throughout the centuries to represent God's relationship with Israel.[198] The matriarchs exemplify that relationship, becoming 'models of the faithful and pious Jew', whose behaviour should be emulated.[199]

In the Theodor-Albeck text, the second explanation contains the unusual verb form מתפרקדות.[200] Following the Vilna edition, Jastrow reads מתרפקות, the Hithpael of רפק, '*to join one's self*', translating as: 'In order that they might endear themselves to their husbands in their beauty'.[201] Freedman's translation, cited above, implies that, 'The matriarchs, possessing both beauty and wealth, would have felt quite independent of their husbands had they also been blessed with children in their early years'.[202] Neusner adds: 'It was so that they should depend upon their husbands despite their beauty [since they would want to have sexual relations to produce children]'.[203] Barrenness is such a debilitating condition that it would ensure the matriarchs' dependency on their husbands in spite of their other assets.

Next, R. Huna and R. Jeremiah in the name of R. Ḥiyya b. Abba suggest that 'the matriarchs' remained barren to prolong their freedom prior to the burden of raising children. Finally, the midrash suggests that 'the matriarchs' were more beautiful, and thus more pleasing to their husbands, before they bore children. Baskin suggests that this was meant to be encouraging for women, because, as *b. Yebam.* 63*b* explains: 'A beautiful wife is a joy to her husband; the number of his days shall be [as if] double'.[204]

198. Rachel Adler, *Engendering Judaism: An Inclusive Theology and Ethics* (Philadelphia: The Jewish Publication Society, 1998), 135–6, 140; Biale, *Eros*, 31–2; Keith N. Schoville and S. David Sperling, 'Song of Songs', *EncJud*, 19:16–17.

199. Callaway, *Sing, O Barren One*, 138. Cf. Baskin, *Midrashic Women*, 141.

200. Cf. Jastrow posits an Aramaic root פרקד with the meaning '*to lie on the back; to be slanting*' (Jastrow, 1240).

201. Jastrow, 1491. For more information on the Vilna edition of the text, see Ben-Eliyahu, Cohn and Millar, *Handbook*, 81–2.

202. Freedman, 382, n. 2 382. Cf. Jastrow, 1240.

203. Neusner, 2:148.

204. Baskin, *Midrashic Women*, 133.

In *Gen. Rab.* 45:4, the rabbis attempted to explain why barrenness was a feature characterising the group of women known as 'matriarchs' (אמהות).[205] The direct nature of the question, 'Why were the matriarchs barren?', and of the ensuing debate, highlight the importance of barrenness as a necessary precursor to the matriarchs' motherhood. This midrash is at points demeaning towards women, focusing on their physical attributes and clearly subordinating them to men.[206]

Sarah is said to resemble 'a bride in the bridal canopy' all the time she remains barren.[207] This reference links the abstracted debate about matriarchal barrenness back to the biblical base text.[208] After becoming pregnant, Hagar 'looked with contempt on her mistress' (Gen 16:4). Instead of directly quoting this phrase, the midrash expands on its meaning, portraying Sarai and Hagar in conversation with other women:

> Ladies used to come to inquire how she was, and she would say to them, 'Go and ask about the welfare of this poor woman [Hagar]'. Hagar would tell them: 'My mistress Sarai is not inwardly what she is outwardly: she appears to be a righteous woman, but she is not. For had she been a righteous woman, see how many years have passed without her conceiving, whereas I conceived in one night!' Said Sarah: 'Shall I pay heed to this woman and argue with her! No; I will argue the matter with her master!'

Sarai demonstrates concern for Hagar, sending the noblewomen to ask after Hagar's health instead of her own. Hagar uses this opportunity to defame Sarai, invoking the popularised notion that pregnancy is linked with righteousness.[209] Hagar's comments are recognisably naive. The preceding debates in *Gen. Rab.* 45:4 now shape the way in which Gen 16 is to be understood. Hagar's immediate conception does not convey

205. See ibid., 131–3; Callaway, *Sing, O Barren One*, 126–7 for expositions of this passage.

206. See Chapter 8, 'The Rabbis and the Matriarchs as Women'.

207. Callaway notes that the parallel passage of *Cant. Rab.* 82 instead places God's desire to hear the matriarchs' prayers at its climax. She suggests that this highlights how the same tradition, 'Why were the matriarchs barren?', could be adapted for use in different contexts (Callaway, *Sing, O Barren One*, 126–7). Discussing a different tradition, Kugel comments: 'The very insularity of midrash's verse-centredness meant that one interpretive story could be combined with another and/or incorporated into many different collections' (Kugel, 'Introductions', 99).

208. The 'base text/verse' describes the main verse interpreted by the midrash. The 'intersecting verse' interprets the 'base text'.

209. See §5.1, 'The Anguish of Barrenness'.

righteousness; Sarai's struggle for a child is necessary for her role as a mother of Israel. Sarah's legitimacy is clear and she becomes a prototype for the other Genesis matriarchs. Additionally, at the very end of this midrash, Sarai suggests her own awareness of Hagar's false claims and refuses to argue with her maidservant.

Genesis Rabbah 45:4 advances its argument in three stages, each of which builds upon the previous. First, the midrash establishes that long-sought-after pregnancies are more valuable than immediate conception. This leads into a debate querying, 'why were the matriarchs barren?' Returning finally to the narrative context of Gen 16, Hagar's judgment of Sarai's barrenness is clearly misguided, as it is this quality that confirms her matriarchal status.

3.6.3.5. *Summary*

Genesis Rabbah offers four main characteristics that the wives of the patriarchs possess as matriarchs: prophetic abilities, maternal roles as 'women in the tent', 'the merit of the matriarchs' and, finally, barrenness. This last point is perhaps the most important for defining the wives of the patriarchs as 'matriarchs'. Baskin argues that the rabbis offer only 'trivial responses to childlessness', which 'constitute a powerful declaration of the futility of all human efforts in explaining the mysteries of suffering'.[210] Whilst this may be true, the claims made in *Gen. Rab.* 45:4 are crucial. 'The matriarchs' are a particular group of women, all of whom were barren before they became mothers (אמהות). This forms the basis of the 'matriarchal cycle' in *Genesis Rabbah*, which traces the transformation of each matriarch from a barren woman to the mother of covenant sons.[211] All of the passages discussed in this part of the chapter contribute to an understanding of exactly what is meant in rabbinic parlance by 'the matriarchs' (האימהות).

3.6.4. *The Mothers of the Tribal Ancestors*

3.6.4.1. *The Matriarchs as 'Mothers of the Tribal Ancestors', in Reference to Their Children*

An alternative, and less common, definition of 'the matriarchs' is evident in parts of *Genesis Rabbah*. In these cases, the title refers to Jacob's four wives, the mothers of Israel's twelve tribal ancestors: Leah, Rachel, Bilhah and Zilpah.[212] *Genesis Rabbah* 70:7 discusses Jacob's promise: 'of

---

210. Baskin, *Midrashic Women*, 133.
211. See 'Part II: The Matriarchal Cycle in *Genesis Rabbah*'.
212. Cf. Ramon, 'Torah of Hesed', 162.

all that you give me I will surely give one tenth to you' (Gen 28:22). A Cuthean questions Jacob's sincerity in this verse, as he only set aside the tribe of Levi as holy, which equates to less than a tenth of the twelve tribes of Israel. Rabbi Meir explains:

> 'Were there then only twelve tribes?' he replied; 'surely there were fourteen, for its (*sic*) says, *Ephraim and Manasseh, even as Reuben and Simeon, shall be mine*' (Gen. XLVIII, 5). 'Then the difficulty is all the greater', he exclaimed; 'if you add water you must add flour'. 'Will you not admit that there were four matriarchs?' said he to him. 'Yes', he replied. 'Then deduct the four firstborn of the four matriarchs from these [fourteen], since the firstborn is holy, and what is holy does not exempt what is holy'.[213] 'Happy the people in whose midst you dwell!' he exclaimed.

Based on Gen 48:5, where Jacob adopts Ephraim and Manasseh, making them of equal status to his sons, R. Meir argues that there are fourteen tribes.[214] The Cuthean believes that increasing the number of tribes makes Jacob's infraction more acute, but R. Meir explains that if the holy firstborn sons of the four matriarchs are removed, because they do not need to be tithed, this leaves ten tribes.[215] Jacob's tithe was thus appropriate.

The term 'matriarchs' (אימהות) clearly refers here to the mothers of the tribal ancestors. Although R. Meir may simply be asking the Cuthean to recognise that four (physical) 'mothers' (אימהות)[216] bore Jacob's sons, the question, 'Will you not admit that there were four matriarchs?' suggests a recognised category of women. By using this title in *Gen. Rab.* 70:7, the rabbis acknowledge the unique status that Rachel, Leah, Bilhah and Zilpah hold within Israel's history. Ephraim and Manasseh's appearance

---

213. 'I.e. no tenth is needed to exempt what is holy' (Freedman, 640). On redemption of the firstborn son, see Biale, *Women and Jewish Law*, 10–11.

214. As with Isaac and Ishmael, and Jacob and Esau, the younger son (Ephraim) is given the firstborn's blessing, not his elder brother (Manasseh). On Ephraim and Manasseh's adoption, see Robert D. Miller II, 'Ephraim', *EDB*, 416; Lynn Tatum, 'Manasseh', *EDB*, 851–2; Gruber, 'Matrilineal Determination', 442; Dan W. Forsyth, 'Sibling Rivalry, Aesthetic Sensibility, and Social Structure in Genesis', *Ethos* 19, no. 4 (1991): 499–500; Laurie J. Braaten, 'Adoption', *EDB*, 21–2; Sarna, *JPS: Genesis*, 324–9; Westermann, *Genesis 37–50*, 185–92; Wenham, *Genesis 16–50*, 462–6.

215. On tithing of the firstborn, see C. T. R. Hayward, *Interpretations of the Name Israel in Ancient Judaism and Some Early Christian Writings: From Victorious Athlete to Heavenly Champion* (New York: Oxford University Press, 2005), 130–2; Michael D. Hildenbrand, 'Firstborn', *EDB*, 462; Hemchand Gossai, 'Tithe', *EDB*, 1315.

216. I.e. translating the term as purely biological.

among Jacob's sons makes no mention of their mother. There are two reasons for this. As a foreigner, Joseph's Egyptian wife, Aseneth, lacks the heritage necessary for an Israelite matriarch.[217] Moreover, Ephraim and Manasseh were only adopted by Jacob later in their lives. Joseph's credentials are sufficient to allow his sons' inclusion in Israel's tribes; Aseneth plays no role in this agreement.[218] *Genesis Rabbah* 70:7 thus limits the term 'matriarchs' (אימהות) to Jacob's four wives.

Genesis Rabbah 71:4 provides further proof that Jacob's wives could be referred to as 'matriarchs'. Leah's naming of three of her sons (Gen 29:33-35) is dealt with in this pericope. Whilst the midrash indicates that Simeon and Levi's names reveal roles that their descendants will play in Israel's later history, Judah's name is connected with his mother's personal experience. In the Bible, she claims: 'This time I will praise the LORD' (Gen 29:35). R. Berekiah in the name of R. Levi addresses this through analogy:

> This may be illustrated by a priest who went down into a threshing-floor: one man gave him a *kor* of tithe, yet he showed no gratitude to him, while another gave him a handful of non-sacred corn and he showed himself grateful. Said the former to him, 'Sir priest, I gave you a *kor* yet you evinced no gratitude, while this man gave you merely a handful, and you showed yourself grateful to him'. 'You gave me of my own portion', he replied, 'whereas this man gave me of his own'. Similarly, since the matriarchs thought that each was to produce three, when Leah bore a fourth son she exclaimed, *THIS* TIME WILL I PRAISE THE LORD.

Rabbi Berekiah argues that just as a priest is grateful when he receives more than is his due, so too does Leah praise God when she bears an unexpected fourth son. The title 'matriarchs' (אמהות) must refer to

---

217. As Baskin notes: 'the themes of overriding importance for the biblical editors were the covenantal relationship and the unimpeachable genealogy of Israel's fathers and mothers' (Baskin, *Midrashic Women*, 150). Baskin discusses the Egyptian Hagar's foreignness (ibid., 150–3). Perhaps Aseneth reminded the rabbis of Hagar, another Egyptian woman and potential usurper of Sarah's matriarchal status. Interestingly, Bilhah and Zilpah's heritage is not clear from the biblical text. See Chapter 7, 'Legitimacy and Succession'. See also Brenner-Idan, *The Israelite Woman*, 115–22; Baskin, *Midrashic Women*, 163.

218. Westermann notes that: 'This can be called "adoption" in a rather broad sense…; in fact, it is meant as legitimation, because the sons remain with their parents; and it is a subsequent legitimation which refers only to their future as fathers of tribes' (Westermann, *Genesis 37–50*, 185).

Jacob's wives: four 'matriarchs' expecting to bear three sons each yields the expected twelve tribes of Israel. It also suggests that these 'matriarchs' had prophetic abilities, as they foresaw how many sons they would collectively bear.[219] Jacob's wives are recognised and respected for their national, maternal roles. Bilhah and Zilpah are again included, whilst Sarah and Rebekah are excluded from this particular use of the title.

Genesis Rabbah 72:6 notes that Leah bore a daughter after 'the matriarchs' prayed that Rachel would bear another of Jacob's sons.[220] Rabbi Ḥanina adds: 'All the matriarchs (אימהות) assembled and prayed: "We have sufficient (*dayyenu*) males; let her [Rachel] be remembered"'. The rabbis explain Dinah's name (דינה) through a play on the word 'enough' (דיינו), envisaging this as the matriarchs' recognition that they each have more sons than Rachel. Although the verb דין can mean 'to judge' (negatively) or 'to punish', the midrash may also follow here the more positive meaning of 'to vindicate' or 'plead the cause of' someone.[221] 'The matriarchs' must be Jacob's wives, who between them bore his twelve sons.

Leah, it seems, joins in with these prayers. In the biblical text, Leah hopes that Jacob will love her if she bears more sons and it is surprising that she concedes here that her sister and rival co-wife should bear Jacob's final son.[222] The sisters have a more amicable relationship in midrash compared to the Bible, perhaps explained by their shared understanding of their roles as 'matriarchs'.[223]

A parallel tradition regarding the alteration of Dinah's sex between conception and birth is found in *b. Ber.* 60a. Like *Gen. Rab.* 72:6, this talmudic portion comments on *m. Ber.* 9:3. According to Rab (*b. Ber.* 60a), Leah realises that if she bears another son, Rachel will have borne fewer

---

219. See §3.6.3.1, 'The Matriarchs (האימהות) Were Prophetesses'.

220. It is unusual for female births to be recorded in the Bible (Schneider, *Mothers of Promise*, 67). This midrash explains why notice of the birth of Leah's daughter is important.

221. Based on the use of the root דין in this passage compared with Dinah's name דינה. Baskin interprets this verb negatively (Baskin, *Midrashic Women*, 148). See Jastrow, 300–301; BDB, 192.

222. Schneider argues that this hope diminishes as Leah's narrative continues and she instead finds fulfilment in childbearing and her children (Schneider, *Mothers of Promise*, 67–72). See also Rabow, *Lost Matriarch*, 76–9.

223. See Baskin, *Midrashic Women*, 145–6, 148; Rabow, *Lost Matriarch*, 16, 116–18, 189. Rabow suggests that after the family leave Laban, Rachel puts her own interests first, whilst Leah is silent (Rabow, *Lost Matriarch*, 135).

tribal ancestors than the handmaids. The passage does not suggest that Rachel and 'the matriarchs" prayers alter the situation; but Leah is still said to pray that Rachel would bear another son for Jacob.[224]

3.6.4.2. *Summary*

In certain specific contexts, where the twelve tribal ancestors of Israel are being discussed, the title 'the matriarchs' (האימהות) may refer to Jacob's four wives. Thus, although they are largely excluded, Bilhah and Zilpah are occasionally included within the matriarchal group. This title recognises the important role that Rachel, Leah, Bilhah and Zilpah played in bearing covenant sons immediately prior to Israel's emergence as a nation.[225]

3.7. *Conclusions*

Modern scholarship has failed to define adequately the term 'matriarch', although it often appears in the literature as a way of referring to key women from Genesis. This lack of clarity necessitated a return to biblical and early exegetical texts in order to explore the origins of the title 'matriarchs'. The emergence of the category followed both sustained development of biblical women's characterisation in early Jewish exegetical material and the increased prominence of the matrilineal principle, which claimed that a mother determines her offspring's Jewish identity. In pre-rabbinic literature, 'the matriarchs' refers to influential female figures early in Israel's history. It is not always clear which individuals are included in the category, although it often refers to the wives of the patriarchs.

Turning then to *Genesis Rabbah*, this text presents two accepted definitions of 'the matriarchs' (האימהות): one referring to the legitimate wives of Israel's three great patriarchs; and the other to the mothers of Jacob's children. In the case of the former, the rabbis present various characteristics that the wives of the patriarchs share. Most significant is barrenness prior to motherhood, a concept that will be explored in much greater detail in Part II. The second use of the term, referring to the mothers of Jacob's children, appears in very specific contexts where the role of Jacob's sons as tribal ancestors of Israel is a focus.

---

224. Bronner, *From Eve to Esther*, 100–101.

225. If the term אימהות were simply translated 'mothers' in these instances, the significance of these women for Israel's national history would be obscured.

In line with these findings, for the remainder of this study, the title 'the matriarchs' will generally be understood as meaning the legitimate wives of the patriarchs. Where *Genesis Rabbah* does include Bilhah, Zilpah, or other biblical females within the category, these women will be identified and discussed.

Part II

'THE MATRIARCHAL CYCLE':
THE PORTRAYAL OF THE MATRIARCHS IN *GENESIS RABBAH*

Chapter 4

PREFACE TO PART II:
'THE MATRIARCHAL CYCLE'

4.1. *The Biblical Barren Matriarch Tradition*

To understand the portrayal of 'the matriarchs' in *Genesis Rabbah*, one
must first explore the biblical development of the barren matriarch tradition.[1] For the rabbis, Scripture was a unity and later developments of the
barrenness tradition could be used to shed light on earlier occurrences
of the theme.[2] The motif of barrenness recurs throughout the Hebrew
Bible, most commonly expressed by the narrative of a barren woman who
eventually bears children. The motif first appears in the patriarchal narratives in Genesis, where three of the patriarchs' wives, Sarah, Rebekah and
Rachel, are said to be 'barren' (עקרה).[3] In each case, this barrenness is
only reversed when God intervenes to ensure that the woman gives birth.[4]
Thus, 'the connection between infertility and birthing the distinguished
heir is strongly implied', as three of the four primary matriarchs portrayed
in Genesis bear this characteristic.[5]

---

1. 'The matriarchal cycle' (barrenness, motherhood, matriarchal succession)
applies in its entirety only to the four wives of the patriarchs. At times, however,
Bilhah and Zilpah will be discussed in these chapters, as *Genesis Rabbah* sometimes
includes them within the matriarchal category. See Chapter 3, '"The Matriarchs"
(האימהות)'.

2. See §2.2, 'The Theory of Midrash: The Rabbinic Worldview'.

3. Gen 11:30 (Sarah); 25:21 (Rebekah); 29:31 (Rachel). On עקר, see BDB, 785;
Jastrow, 1108. Teugels describes the barren woman who bears as a type-scene because
it recurs throughout the Bible (Teugels, *'The Wooing of Rebekah' [Gen. 24]*, 51).

4. Gen 21:1 (Sarah); 25:21 (Rebekah); and 30:22 (Rachel).

5. Halpern-Amaru, *Women in the Book of Jubilees*, 100. On the Genesis barren
matriarch narratives, see Callaway, *Sing, O Barren One*, 13–33. Cf. Brenner-Idan,
The Israelite Woman, 92–105.

The next appearance of the motif is in Judg 13.[6] This entire chapter is devoted to the announcement of Samson's birth. The wife of Manoah is visited by a divine emissary who informs her that although she is barren (עקרה), she will soon bear a son (Judg 13:3). This 'angel of God' appears several times, specifying that the woman, 'be careful not to drink wine or strong drink, or to eat anything unclean' because her child will be a Nazirite (Judg 13:4-5; cf. 13:14). Manoah ultimately recognises this figure's divinity and his wife bears Samson (Judg 13:22, 24).

This narrative is a clear development of the biblical barrenness tradition.[7] In Genesis, the covenant was the driving force of the narrative. Barrenness was an obstacle that had to be overcome in order to fulfil God's promises to the patriarchs by providing the next covenant son. In Judg 13, the birth of a significant male figure again elicits the reversal of barrenness; but in this narrative, the woman is the primary recipient of the divine promises. It is to her alone that the angel appears for the first and second times, and the restrictions concerning what she may eat and drink, as well as the future role of her son, are told to her before her husband. Exum comments: 'Narrative arrangement in Judges 13 teaches us, as well as Manoah, a lesson: in the events surrounding the birth of this wonder-child, the father is not more important than the mother'.[8] The mother plays a more central role in this barrenness narrative than the matriarchs did in Genesis.

1 Samuel 1–2 further advances the barrenness motif from Genesis and Judges.[9] Hannah, the wife of Elkanah, 'had no children' (ולחנה אין ילדים) (1 Sam 1:2) 'because the LORD had closed her womb' (1 Sam 1:6). Her

---

6. On Judg 13 and what follows here, see Callaway, *Sing, O Barren One*, 36–8; Exum, *Fragmented Women*, 62–9; Esther Fuchs, 'The Literary Characterisation of Mothers and Sexual Politics in the Hebrew Bible', *Semeia* 46 (1989): 155–7; J. Cheryl Exum, 'Promise and Fulfilment: Narrative Art in Judges 13', *Journal of Biblical Literature* 99 (1980): 43–59; Robert C. Boling, *Judges: Introduction, Translation, and Commentary*, Anchor Bible 6A (New York: Doubleday, 1975), 217-24.

7. According to Esther Menn, 'The reappearance of the motifs of the barren wife and of divine intervention leading to childbirth…stresses the continuity between the patriarchal period and later periods of Israelite history and underscores God's active involvement with a chosen lineage of Abraham's descendants' (Menn, *Judah and Tamar*, 89).

8. Exum, 'Promise and Fulfilment', 58.

9. On 1 Sam 1–2, especially Hannah's role, see Callaway, *Sing, O Barren One*, 35–57; Bar-Ilan, *Some Jewish Women*, 81–3; Joan E. Cook, *Hannah's Desire, God's Design: Early Interpretations of the Story of Hannah*, JSOT Supplement Series 282 (Sheffield: Sheffield Academic, 1999); Ralph W. Klein, *1 Samuel*, Word Biblical

rival co-wife torments Hannah because of her childlessness, causing her great distress (1 Sam 1:6).[10] On one of the family's regular visits to the sanctuary, Hannah prays that God will provide her with a son, in return promising to dedicate that son to the Lord (1 Sam 1:10-11). The role of the mother has undergone another noticeable development. As Callaway notes: 'While Hannah, like the other mothers, is barren, her desire for a child is expressed more fully and deeply than in the other narratives'.[11] Hannah's determination to produce a child is expressed through her direct address to God. In short, '[s]he does what none of the matriarchs did; she simply asks Yahweh for a child'.[12]

Hannah's narrative stands in clear continuity with the preceding biblical accounts concerning barren women: Samuel will play an important role in the history of Israel; Hannah faces rivalry with a fertile co-wife, as do Sarah and Rachel; and her barrenness is reversed by God's interven-tion.[13] Yet Hannah is more vocal than those women who precede her. Her dialogue is more extensive and we are provided with greater detail about her thoughts, feelings and motivations. She even successfully defends

---

Commentary 10 (Nashville: Thomas Nelson, 2008), 4–20; Fuchs, 'Literary Charac-terisation', 157–9, 162, 164; Fewell and Gunn, *Gender, Power, & Promise*, 70; Cynthia Ozick, 'Hannah and Elkanah: Torah as the Matrix for Feminism', in *Out of the Garden: Women Writers on the Bible*, ed. Christina Büchmann and Celina Spiegel (London: HarperCollins, 1994), 88–93; Marcia Falk, 'Reflections on Hannah's Prayer', in Büchmann and Spiegel, eds., *Out of the Garden*, 94–102; Randall C. Bailey, 'The Redemption of YHWH: A Literary Critical Function of the Songs of Hannah and David', *Biblical Interpretation* 3, no. 2 (1995): 213–31; Walter Brueg-gemann, '1 Samuel 1: A Sense of a Beginning', *Zeitschrift für die Alttestamentliche Wissenschaft* 102, no. 1 (1990): 33–48. *L.A.B.* notably expands Hannah's role. See Joan E. Cook, 'Pseudo-Philo's Song of Hannah: Testament of a Mother in Israel', *Journal for the Study of the Pseudepigrapha* 9 (1991): 103–14.

10. In the LXX, Hannah's distress arises from her childless situation, not out of any action by Peninnah. See Callaway, *Sing, O Barren One*, 45–6; Stanley D. Walters, 'Hannah and Anna: The Greek and Hebrew Texts of 1 Samuel 1', *Journal of Biblical Literature* 107, no. 3 (1988): 385–412.

11. Callaway, *Sing, O Barren One*, 41.

12. Ibid., 42. On differences between 1 Sam 1, and Gen 16 and 30, see ibid., 41–2.

13. Joan E. Cook splits the barrenness traditions into three categories: the 'compe-tition' model, where a rival wife threatens the childless, favoured wife by bearing a son first (Sarah, Rachel, Hannah); the 'promise' model, where a son is promised (Sarah, wife of Manoah, Hannah, Shunammite woman); and the 'request' model, where the woman asks for a child (Rebekah, Rachel, Hannah). See Cook, *Hannah's Desire, God's Design*, esp. 14–20.

herself against Eli's accusations of drunkenness, leading the High Priest to bless her (1 Sam 1:13-18). Furthermore, although the narrative does not explicitly describe Hannah as 'barren' (עקרה), the term features in Hannah's psalm of thanksgiving in 1 Sam 2:1-10, where she praises God's ability to exalt the low and bring down the mighty. In this psalm, she proclaims: 'The barren (עקרה) has borne seven, but she who has many children is forlorn' (1 Sam 2:5).[14] The use of the term עקרה, '[t]he key catchword in the psalm', ensures that 1 Sam 1–2 is read in conjunction with Genesis and Judg 13.[15]

There is one other short biblical narrative that deals with a child-less woman eventually bearing a son. In 2 Kgs 4:8-37 the story of the Shunammite woman is related.[16] This woman shows hospitality towards Elisha, whom she recognises as a man of God. In return, Elisha asks what he can do for her; Elisha's servant recounts: 'she has no son, and her husband is old' (בן אין־לה ואישה זקן, 2 Kgs 4:14). Elisha promises that she will bear a child 'at this season ("this appointed time", למועד הזה), in due time ("at the time of reviving", כעת חיה)' (4:16).[17] Although the term עקר, 'barren', appears nowhere here, this woman shares many characteristics with the other barren matriarchs.[18] The language resonates with those narratives, particularly with certain circumstances surrounding Sarah's conception.[19] Interestingly, Fuchs notes that: 'This annunciation type-scene is the first to present the female protagonist as character before focusing on her as a maternal role model'; thus, the woman's hospitality to Elisha, rather than her barrenness, is the focus of the narrative.[20] 2 Kings 4:8-37 develops the barren matriarch tradition, clearly drawing on earlier tradition.

Each of these narratives concerns a barren woman, who finally conceives a child following divine intervention. The sons born to these women become great figures in the history of Israel. A number of scholars have

---

14. Cf. Pardes, *Countertraditions*, 111. On 1 Sam 2:5, see Theodore J. Lewis, 'The Songs of Hannah and Deborah: ḤDL-II ("Growing Plump")', *Journal of Biblical Literature* 104, no. 1 (1985): 105–8.

15. Callaway, *Sing, O Barren One*, 54.

16. See Fuchs, 'Literary Characterisation', 158–60.

17. Translation of כעת חיה is taken from BDB, 312.

18. Rachel Havrelock, 'The Myth of Birthing the Hero: Heroic Barrenness in the Hebrew Bible', *Biblical Interpretation* 16 (2008): 161–2.

19. Cf. Sarah 'had no child' (אין לה ולד, 11:30); she will conceive כעת חיה (Gen 18:10, 14); and Abraham is זקן, 'old' (18:12).

20. Fuchs, 'Literary Characterisation', 158.

offered studies of these traditions. Esther Fuchs notes the increasingly prominent role played by the mother in biblical annunciation scenes.[21] In Genesis, Sarah is a rather passive figure, subordinate to Abraham and the Deity. She plays no direct role in the birth announcement, as the promises are revealed to Abraham and fulfilled for his sake (Gen 17–18). However, by 1 Samuel, the husband (Elkanah) plays a much smaller role, being needed only for the conception of the child, whilst 'Hannah emerges as the incontestable heroine of the scene', acting independently as she petitions God for a son.[22] For Fuchs: 'The growing emphasis on the figure of the potential mother may be misinterpreted as a growing recognition of the importance of woman's reproductive powers'.[23] In fact, these narratives are merely vehicles for promoting the patriarchal ideology of the biblical writers, who recognise the necessity of motherhood for the continuation of the male line.[24]

Fuchs does not adequately explain why the father's role in these narratives drastically decreases, whilst that of the wife increases. According to Fuchs's analysis of the dominance of patriarchy in shaping biblical narratives, one would expect the male to continue to play a central role. Whilst the patriarchal context of the biblical narratives must be accounted for, Fuchs allows this to dominate her interpretation of the barrenness narratives.

The most comprehensive study of these barrenness narratives is Callaway's *Sing, O Barren One: A Study in Comparative Midrash*.[25] Callaway considers the development of the barren matriarch tradition from Genesis through to the rabbis, presenting a more neutral analysis of the evidence than Fuchs. Although devoting little attention to Judg 13, her analysis of the Genesis and 1 Samuel narratives is insightful.[26] She concludes that whilst the Genesis accounts of the barren woman giving birth are designed to emphasise God's power and control over life, in 1 Sam 1–2 Hannah becomes a representative figure. Callaway argues in particular that the psalm in 1 Sam 2:1-10 provides important information

---

21. Ibid., 151–66. This article was reprinted in 1999: Esther Fuchs, 'The Literary Characterisation of Mothers and Sexual Politics in the Hebrew Bible', in *Women in the Hebrew Bible: A Reader*, ed. Alice Bach (New York: Routledge, 1999), 127–39. Cf. Exum, 'Promise and Fulfilment', 58.

22. Fuchs, 'Literary Characterisation', 158.

23. Ibid., 161.

24. Ibid., 159–60, etc. Fuchs draws on Adrienne Rich's 'institution of motherhood'.

25. Callaway, *Sing, O Barren One*.

26. Ibid., 13–57.

about the way in which this narrative should be interpreted. She argues that it transforms the experience of one woman into a message of hope for others that God will also intervene to reverse their misfortunes, even those of the nation Israel.[27] In this way, the narrative of the barren woman takes on a new significance, bearing relevance for the contemporary age. This is a change that 'was to alter the shape of the barren matriarch tradition permanently'.[28]

The biblical barrenness motif reaches its culmination in Isa 54:1. As Callaway argues: 'For the first time, there is no birth narrative into which the story of the barren woman is set; there is rather an oracle of salvation addressed to the woman herself'.[29] In this verse, Zion is called a barren woman (עקרה), a designation which explicitly nationalises the representative role accorded to the barren woman in 1 Sam 1–2. The image of the barren woman who eventually gives birth offers hope to the exiled nation that it will one day be restored. The image of the barren woman producing more children than her married counterpart recalls Hannah's comparison of the fruitful woman's demise with the barren woman's exultation, as well as the rivalry between co-wives displayed by Sarah and Hagar (Gen 16; 21), Rachel and Leah (Gen 29–33) and Hannah and Peninnah (1 Sam 1).[30] The oracle provided in Isa 54 stands in clear continuity with the preceding barrenness narratives, but further develops the biblical tradition. As Callaway remarks, the mother, rather than her son, has now become the focus of the motif and the prophet has 'radically transformed the tradition from a story about the birth of a child to the story of the birth of a people'.[31]

Traditions depicting Jerusalem/Zion as a barren woman and as the mother of the nation continue into the Second Temple period. This suggests the continued popularity of the imagery.[32] The rabbinic interpreters of the first centuries CE thus had a rich interpretive tradition upon which to draw as they developed their interpretations of the matriarchs.

---

27. Ibid., 54.

28. Ibid., 56.

29. Ibid., 63. I draw on Callaway's comprehensive analysis of Isa 54:1-3 (ibid., 59–72). See also John D. W. Watts, *Isaiah 34–66*, Word Biblical Commentary 25 (Nashville: Thomas Nelson, 2005), 794–801; Westermann, *Isaiah 40–66*, 269–76.

30. Callaway, *Sing, O Barren One*, 67–8.

31. Ibid., 63.

32. So ibid., 73–90. Callaway discusses Isa 56–66 before moving into the Second Temple period, looking at *Baruch* and *4 Ezra*.

4.2. *'The Matriarchal Cycle'*

The rabbinic interpreters adopted, developed and emphasised the various parts of the biblical barrenness tradition, using it to inform their portrayal of the earliest Israelite matriarchs in Genesis. As the rabbis reflect on these women's significance in *Genesis Rabbah*, a 'matriarchal cycle' emerges.[33] I use this term to describe the transformation of each individual matriarch from a barren woman to a mother through a series of repeated stages. The cycle is traceable in the lifetime of each matriarch, beginning afresh in every generation as the next woman assumes her matriarchal role. Sarah, Rebekah, Leah and Rachel each complete this 'matriarchal cycle', although different aspects are emphasised in each case. The cycle thus becomes a unifying factor, connecting the matriarchs to one another and also to the wider history of Israel. For the rabbis, it proves that each of the wives of the patriarchs was worthy of becoming a matriarch, a woman who is respected for her roles in both the historical and present life of Israel.

Ultimate proof of the cycle's importance lies in the portrayal of Leah in *Genesis Rabbah*.[34] In Genesis, Leah is never described as barren and she is in fact given little attention beyond descriptions of her rivalry with Rachel and her strained marital relationship with Jacob, who prefers her sister (Gen 29–33). Yet, in *Genesis Rabbah*, Leah too participates in the 'matriarchal cycle', undergoing the same transformation from barren woman to beloved mother as the other matriarchs.[35] That the rabbis increased her role, bringing her experiences into line with those of the other matriarchs, highlights the centrality of the 'matriarchal cycle' for *Genesis Rabbah*'s characterisation of these women.

The biblical text provides the basis for the rabbinic 'matriarchal cycle'. The biblical barrenness tradition increasingly focused on the role of the mother. Barrenness is as much a part of the matriarchs' motherhood as childbirth and the raising of children because it sets these women aside as worthy of becoming the mothers of the Israelite nation. Each woman is barren; God intervenes to reverse the condition. In the Bible and in ancient Israelite society, women were valued for their roles as mothers;

---

33. Teugels coins this term. See Teugels, 'A Matriarchal Cycle?', 61–72, and *'The Wooing of Rebekah' (Gen. 24)*. My own usage is slightly different, as explained below.

34. See Rabow, *Lost Matriarch*.

35. See e.g. *Gen. Rab.* 71:1. 2. See also §5.2.2, 'God's Support of the Disadvantaged, Especially Barren Women'; §7.4, 'Matriarchal Succession'.

yet the biblical text rarely explores this maternal role, often providing only 'the indistinct shapes of a host of unnamed mothers, who, silent and unacknowledged, bear all the endless genealogies of males'.[36] Even in the barrenness traditions, the mother is soon forgotten following the birth of her children.[37] For the rabbis, both barrenness and motherhood were central to their understanding of the matriarchs. They developed the Bible's notion that barrenness represents matriarchal legitimacy. They also accentuated respect for the maternal role by portraying the Genesis matriarchs as mothers who actively protect their sons, enabling the covenant to continue and Israel to emerge. Thus, whilst Fuchs suggests that 'Woman's parenthood in the biblical narrative is largely restricted to reproductive and protective functions', it is these very roles that the rabbis expand to highlight the significance of the matriarchs.[38]

The 'matriarchal cycle' has several stages. First, a legitimate wife for the patriarch is found. This is proved through the use of genealogies and, often, through God's choice of a particular woman. This woman is barren, which threatens the continuation of the patriarchal line. Yet, following divine intervention, she gives birth to a son. She then protects that son and promotes his interests above other potential covenant heirs. Finally, following the mother's actions, the son's inheritance is secured and there is a movement to the next generation. This final stage is also predicated in the biblical text: in Gen 24:67, Rebekah is suggested to take on Sarah's role as a matriarch.[39] Furthermore, in Gen 27:46, Rebekah declares the Hittite women unfit to become Jacob's wife, thus showing the second matriarch to play an active role in determining who will become the next matriarch.[40] In basic terms, the 'matriarchal cycle' is a three-tier process of matriarchal barrenness, matriarchal motherhood and matriarchal succession.

Scholars have identified similar patterns within the Bible. Rachel Havrelock suggests that 'the movement from barrenness to fertility is a mode of female initiation into a relationship with the divine'.[41] She identifies seven stages in this process and then explores how these stages

36. Phyllis A. Bird, *Missing Persons and Mistaken Identities: Women and Gender in Ancient Israel*, Overtures to Biblical Theology (Minneapolis: Fortress, 1997), 13.

37. Fuchs, 'Literary Characterisation', 164.

38. Ibid., 163. On the positive portrayal of the matriarchs in Genesis, see Davidson's introductory article (Davidson, 'Genesis Matriarchs', 169–78).

39. See §3.3.1, 'The Matriarchs in the Hebrew Bible'; §7.4, 'Matriarchal Succession'; §8.1.2, 'Piety'.

40. See Chapter 7, 'Legitimacy and Succession'.

41. Havrelock, 'Heroic Barrenness', 154.

are manifested in each of the biblical barrenness narratives.[42] Havrelock argues that in order for the male line to continue, the mothers themselves must establish a covenant with God, paralleling the patriarchal heroes who form relationships with the divinity.[43] Havrelock essentially identifies a barrenness cycle within the biblical text, as characters develop from passive and infertile wives to mothers. The rabbinic interpreters developed this biblical cycle in their midrashic exegesis of the Genesis narratives, particularly expanding on the maternal actions of these women and emphasising the importance of passing the matriarchal title on to the correct woman in the following generation.

Lieve Teugels also offers an interesting forerunner to the rabbinic notion of the 'matriarchal cycle'. She uses this same term when discussing the biblical narratives concerning Isaac and Rebekah as part of her wider study of Gen 24 in the Bible and Midrash.[44] Teugels notes that scholars have struggled to identify an 'Isaac Cycle', a substantial set of biblical episodes featuring the second patriarch, particularly to match the extensive material about Abraham and Jacob. This relates both to a lack of narrative material concerning Isaac in Genesis and to his passive role in episodes such as the Aqedah (Gen 22) and his betrothal to Rebekah (Gen 24). For Teugels, scholars have not acknowledged the active role played by the matriarch Rebekah in this second covenantal generation. Because Rebekah ensures that the covenant passes on to the correct son, Jacob, Teugels concludes that 'this is more of a matriarchal than a patriarchal cycle'; and she ultimately suggests that the 'patriarchal stories' might be renamed as 'stories of the ancestors'.[45] Teugels recognises the central role played by Rebekah in Israel's early history and she identifies a set of biblical narratives that support this.

My own use of the term 'matriarchal cycle' in this study extends Teugels's use of the phrase, recognising that each matriarch plays a central, active role in ensuring the continuation of the covenant and the

---

42. Ibid., 154–78. Havrelock identifies the seven stages as: barrenness; statement of protest; direct action; encounter with God; conception; birth; naming (p. 159).

43. Ibid., esp. 155–7, 168–9, 178. Cf. Ramon: 'Throughout Jewish history, insufficient attention has been devoted to the covenant that God made with the matriarchs' (Ramon, 'Torah of Hesed', 170).

44. Teugels, *'The Wooing of Rebekah' (Gen. 24)*, 119–29, 132; Teugels, 'A Matriarchal Cycle?', 61–72.

45. Teugels, *'The Wooing of Rebekah' (Gen. 24)*, 124, 129. Terminology from Turner. See Mary Donovan Turner, 'Rebekah: Ancestor of Faith', *Lexington Theological Quarterly* 20 (1985): 42–a50.

emergence of Israel. A 'matriarchal cycle' can therefore be identified in each generation: from Sarah to Rebekah to Leah and Rachel, with the same stages being repeated, as Havrelock's study demonstrates for the biblical barrenness narratives. This 'matriarchal cycle' is evident in the biblical text but is emphasised in *Genesis Rabbah*.

4.3. *'The Matriarchal Cycle' in* Genesis Rabbah

I will now examine the portrayal of the matriarchs as individual characters in *Genesis Rabbah*. A large part of the matriarchs' characterisation centres around motherhood, portrayed through the 'matriarchal cycle', and this will be the focus of my analysis. Israel's national identity has its basis in physical and familial identity, through genealogies and correct descent. As such, childbearing and motherhood become metaphors for the emergence of the nation, as the matriarchs produce Israel's patriarchs and tribal ancestors. This helps to explain why the rabbis held the matriarchs in such high regard and why they developed their roles in the midrash. By emphasising the recurrence of the matriarchal cycle, the rabbis confirmed the legitimacy of each mother and ensured continuity across the generations, establishing connections between those women who bear the title 'matriarch'.

The following chapters will deal with the three parts of the 'matriarchal cycle' as they are portrayed in *Genesis Rabbah*: barrenness; motherhood; legitimacy and succession. It will become clear that each of the matriarchs partakes in the matriarchal cycle from barrenness to motherhood and that this indicates their superior status as the ancestresses of Israel.

Chapter 5

Barrenness

In Genesis, three of the patriarchs' wives, Sarah, Rebekah and Rachel, are described as 'barren' (עקרה) (Gen 11:30; 25:21; 29:31) and the rabbis did not ignore this shared trait. In fact, barrenness became a central part of rabbinic characterisation of the matriarchs; the rabbis even declared Leah to be barren to ensure recognition of her matriarchal status.[1] Barrenness forms the first part of the 'matriarchal cycle' experienced by each matriarch during her lifetime. It is a necessary precursor to matriarchal motherhood, proving that these women are worthy of becoming the mothers of Israel. Barrenness was a physical condition that drastically impacted upon a woman's position in her family and society. *Genesis Rabbah* recognises the plight of the barren woman and challenges presuppositions concerning a connection between righteousness and fertility. God is in control of childbirth and this is emphasised throughout *Genesis Rabbah*. It is thus his prerogative to reverse the matriarchs' barrenness and his intervention ensures that the matriarchs conceive. Finally, barrenness allows these women to become representatives of the disadvantaged and of Israel. It provides hope to others that their own misfortunes can be reversed and reflects God's commitment to his covenant people. Matriarchal barrenness prepares these women for their maternal roles. This ultimately enables the nation Israel to emerge through their sons.

5.1. *The Anguish of Barrenness*

There is no doubt that barrenness was considered a 'grave misfortune' in the ancient world and notably, 'tension abounds' in the Genesis patriarchal narratives as the ancestral family grapples with the barrenness of

---

1. See *Gen. Rab.* 72:1.

its women.[2] Such attitudes continued into later periods. Judith Baskin discusses rabbinic laws about procreation, noting the male duty to produce children and the societal pressure on a woman to bear. Baskin explains that such views created numerous problems for a couple without offspring, ranging from an eventual obligation to divorce and remarry because of barrenness to the lack of security for, and taunting endured by, a woman without children.[3] The mishnaic ruling that after ten years a barren couple must divorce and remarry is quoted in *Genesis Rabbah*, drawing support from Gen 16:3, where Sarah gives Hagar to Abraham after ten years in Canaan (*m. Yebam.* 6:6; *Gen. Rab.* 45:3).[4] This provides an example of Israel's Scriptures foreshadowing later circumstances and links the theme of matriarchal barrenness into the wider development of the Jewish religion. Even if it was often contravened in practice, the very existence of such a law highlights the expectations of the society in which the rabbis were living.[5]

Furthermore, feelings of anguish and the adversity faced by those without children are well documented in the midrashic literature. *Genesis Rabbah* 45:2 explains: 'It is taught (on tannaitic authority) that anyone who does not have a child, it is as if he were dead, as if he were demolished'. The following are cited as proof: Rachel's cry in Gen 30:1, 'Give

---

2. Baskin, *Midrashic Women*, 130; Halpern-Amaru, *Women in the Book of Jubilees*, 33. On Hebrew terms conveying barrenness, see Jeansonne, *Women of Genesis*, 75; Sarna, *JPS: Genesis*, 87 ('*'akarah* simply means "childless" but not necessarily infertile'). On childlessness in antiquity, see Byron, 'Childlessness and Ambiguity', 17–46; Callaway, *Sing, O Barren One*, 13–18.

3. Baskin, *Midrashic Women*, 119–31. Cf. Bronner, *From Eve to Esther*, 88, 98, 153; Callaway, *Sing, O Barren One*, 13; Jeansonne, *Women of Genesis*, 75; Trible, 'Ominous Beginnings', 34; Gordon J. Wenham, *Genesis 1–15*, Word Biblical Commentary 1 (Nashville: Nelson; Nelson Reference and Electronic, 1987), 273; Byron, 'Childlessness and Ambiguity', 21–7; Biale, *Women and Jewish Law*, 198–203; Wegner, *Chattel or Person?*, 41–2.

4. Epstein notes that *m. Yebam.* 61b and *m. Soṭah.* 24a suggest taking an additional wife if the first is barren (Epstein, *Marriage Laws*, 18). Also Leonard Swidler, *Women in Judaism: The Status of Women in Formative Judaism* (Metuchen: Scarecrow, 1976), 155–6. Byron discusses this practice as well as comparable practices of other ancient Near Eastern societies (Byron, 'Childlessness and Ambiguity', 35–9, 21–4). On the rabbis and barrenness, see Judith R. Baskin, 'Rabbinic Reflections on the Barren Wife', *The Harvard Theological Review* 82 (1989): 101–14; 'Barrenness'.

5. Baskin, *Midrashic Women*, 128–30; Bronner, *From Eve to Esther*, 88–9; Hauptman, *Rereading*, 130–46; Satlow, *Jewish Marriage*, 19; Satlow, *Tasting the Dish*, 231.

me children, or I shall die!'; and Sarah's hope that 'it may be that I shall obtain children by her (lit. "be built up from her")' (Gen 16:2). The tannaitic authority with which this claim is imbued,[6] and the matriarchal examples provided as proof, lend credence to this claim's presentation as recognised fact.

In the Torah, Exod 23 and Deut 7 associate an end to barrenness with the blessings that follow from adhering to God's commands.[7] Barrenness then automatically represents retribution suffered by those turning from God, whether Israel or the nations surrounding her. Callaway argues that this theology was wrongly believed to be true also for individuals, an interpretation that led to the unfair vilification of the childless.[8] In particular, it seems that the connection between childbearing and personal piety was assumed by many in an ancient context. In *Genesis Rabbah*, Hagar tells other women that whereas she conceived quickly, Sarah has been barren for years and so cannot be as righteous as she seems (*Gen. Rab.* 45:4). Similarly, the rabbis interpret Rachel's jealousy in Gen 30:1 as conveying her assumption that Leah must be righteous because she has children (*Gen. Rab.* 71:6). Rachel's view suggests that the relationship between fertility and righteousness was embedded in the social consciousness, a point further suggested by Hagar's attempts to defame Sarah's character on the basis of her continued barrenness.[9]

An even more explicit presentation of this viewpoint emerges in *Gen. Rab.* 71:7. When Rachel's maid Bilhah conceives, the midrash further explains Rachel's comment: '"God has judged me"' (Gen 30:6). Rachel asserts that: 'He hath judged me and condemned me; He hath judged me and pronounced in my favour', the first statement referring to her barrenness (Gen 29:31) and the second to Dan's birth (Gen 30:6). The legal language used here links barrenness to punishment for wrongdoing. Baskin states: 'it seems likely…that in the popular imagination childlessness for women was often seen as a divine punishment. On the whole, however, rabbinic literature shows compassion for the childless and hesitates to explain the divine dispensation in a facile manner.'[10]

---

6. See Strack and Stemberger, *Introduction*, 60, 65–83, 109; Daniel Sperber, 'Tanna, Tannaim', *EncJud*, 19:505–7.

7. Exod 23:26 and Deut 7:14 both use the term עקר. See Byron, 'Childlessness and Ambiguity', 21.

8. Following J. A. Sanders. Callaway, *Sing, O Barren One*, 91–2.

9. See *Gen. Rab.* 45:4. See also §3.6.3.4, '"Why Were the Matriarchs Made Barren?" (ולמה נתעקרו אמהות).

10. Baskin, *Midrashic Women*, 132.

5.1.1. *Summary*

Barrenness was an unfortunate and harrowing state in the ancient world. Women were expected to bear children and faced vilification and insecurity if unable to have children. Whilst the midrash acknowledges these problems, the rabbis present an alternate strand of interpretation, challenging society's assumptions about this condition and suggesting a more considerate approach to barren women.

5.2. *God's Role in Childbirth and the Reversal of Barrenness*

5.2.1. *God's Control over Childbirth*

In the Pentateuch, the Lord is explicitly connected with the prevention of barrenness, as Israel is promised prosperity and fertility if she follows God's commands.[11] Fecundity will characterise the faithful Israel, differentiating her from the nations that she will dispossess when entering the promised land. In Genesis, a personal counterpart to these national blessings is found. Here too, God is presented as the instigator of life and at the appropriate moment, he is able to reverse the matriarchs' barrenness. As Callaway summarises: 'in the biblical stories the initiative is always Yahweh's and the barrenness of the women seems to be all part of his plan'.[12]

Genesis Rabbah develops the themes of God's central role in childbirth and the reversal of barrenness, using them to prove God's power and the legitimacy of those whom he chooses to become the mothers of Israel. The significance of these choices cannot be overstated. Not only are these women the historical mothers of Israel who bore the founding figures of the Israelite nation; they are also the present mothers of Israel, whom the rabbis see as continuing to contribute to and embody Israel's identity.

Genesis Rabbah 73:4 is central to the rabbinic presentation of God as life-giver. This pericope comments on Gen 30:22, where God 'opened (ויפתח) her (Rachel's) womb (רחמה)'. R. Menahema in the name of R. Bibi explains that: 'Three keys (מפתחות) are in the hands of the Holy One, blessed be He: the keys of burial [i.e. resurrection], rain, and the womb (רחם)... Some add, the key of sustenance too.' The entire pericope centres around the verb פתח, 'to open', which appears in the Genesis verse

---

11. E.g. Exod 23:26; Deut 7:14.
12. Callaway, *Sing, O Barren One*, 138.

cited. Genesis 30:22 is used in support of God's control over the womb, meaning childbirth. Another three biblical verses containing the verb פתח, 'to open', with God as its subject are quoted in support of the other keys.[13] As such, this midrash shows this verb describing divine action which promotes and sustains life. Furthermore, the word 'key' (מפתיח) is a rabbinic word play on this root, indicating that God is able to open up the possibility of new or renewed life.

This interpretation appears elsewhere in rabbinic literature. In *b. Ta'an.* 2a, R. Joḥanan presents three keys under slightly different names: the keys of rain, of childbirth and of the resurrection of the dead. He rejects the addition of sustenance, arguing that this is accounted for in the mention of rain. *Targum Neofiti* also offers the four keys as an aggadic addition to its translation of Gen 30:22.[14] This suggests widespread acceptance of this interpretation in ancient Judaism.

In *Genesis Rabbah*, this pericope draws attention to Rachel's pregnancy as an act of divine intervention to enable life. By including the reversal of Rachel's barrenness in this exploration of God's life-giving power, the rabbis suggest the wider significance of the matriarchal narratives. The representative role of the matriarchs is central to their portrayal in *Genesis Rabbah* and God's intervention in the lives of these women has consequences for his treatment of Israel throughout its history.[15]

God's control over childbirth is demonstrated throughout *Genesis Rabbah*. *Genesis Rabbah* 72:6 quotes R. Judah b. Pazzi's statement that God can change the sex of a baby right up until the moment of birth. This is based on Jer 18:6, depicting God as a potter, able to mould Israel like clay. Furthermore, in *Gen. Rab.* 53:6, R. Judah explains: 'Although R. Huna said that there is an angel appointed over desire, Sarah had no need for such, but He in His glory [made her conceive]; hence, AND THE LORD REMEMBERED SARAH (Gen 21:1)'. God is seen to play an active role in the process of childbearing and this is particularly important for the narratives in Genesis, where the birth of sons is necessary for the emergence of Israel.

Genesis Rabbah records human responses to divine power over life. Genesis 16:2 reads: 'Sarai said to Abram, "You see that the LORD has

---

13. Ezek 37:12; Deut 28:12; Ps 145:16.

14. See Martin McNamara, *Targum Neofiti 1: Genesis Translated, with Appartus and Notes By Martin Mcnamara*, The Aramaic Bible, The Targums 1A (Edinburgh: T. & T. Clark, 1992), 148–9.

15. Callaway, *Sing, O Barren One*, 123.

prevented me from bearing children"'.[16] *Genesis Rabbah* 45:2 expands, as 'Sarah is said to reject the amulets and spells of popular religion, because she knows it is God who can open the womb whenever God wills it'.[17] This contributes to the rabbinic portrayal of Sarah's character, which emphasises her legitimacy to become a matriarch and also provides a 'model' for how Israel should respond to Yahweh.[18] In contrast to this, Jacob's anger at Rachel in Gen 30:2 is met with divine reproach in the midrash, as God recognises the anguish of her situation. Jacob's biblical claim, 'Am I in the place of God, who has withheld from you the fruit of the womb?', is explained as meaning: 'From thee He withheld it, but not from me (lit. "but from me he did not withhold it")'[19] (*Gen. Rab.* 71:7). This terse comparison draws implications from the use of ממך, 'from you' (second person singular), in the biblical text. Jacob shows a lack of sympathy for Rachel's barrenness, noting that this only affects her: he already has children through Leah (Gen 29:32-35).[20]

Whilst Jacob and Sarah both acknowledge God's primary role in conception, Jacob uses this to distance himself from the problem of barrenness, blaming Rachel alone for her misfortune. Sarah, however, does not use God's control over childbirth as an excuse to turn to magical practices or to give up hope of becoming a mother. Instead, she demonstrates her determination by giving Hagar to Abraham with the hope that 'it may be that I shall obtain children by her' (Gen 16:2).[21] Furthermore,

16. Wenham comments: 'Though the term "prevent" (עצר) is used of infertility only here and in 20:18, the idea that it is God who gives or denies conception is commonplace in the Old Testament (25:21; 30:2; Lev 20:20, 21; Deut 28:11; Ps 113:9)' (Wenham, *Genesis 16–50*, 6).

17. Baskin, *Midrashic Women*, 133. Baskin and Freedman (n. 4 380) note translational difficulties and thus uncertain meaning. Freedman translates: 'Said she: I know the source of my affliction: it is not as people say… "she needs a talisman, she needs a charm", but BEHOLD NOW, *THE LORD* HATH RESTRAINED ME FROM BEARING' (Freedman, 380). On magic and medicine to overcome barrenness, see Byron, 'Childlessness and Ambiguity', 29–31.

18. For biblical figures as 'models', see Exum, *Fragmented Women*, 135; Fuchs, 'Literary Characterisation', 165; Callaway, *Sing, O Barren One*, 138–9; Baskin, *Midrashic Women*, 141, 160.

19. Freedman's translation does not replicate the Hebrew parallel phrases. These contrast Jacob's view of his own and Rachel's relationships with God.

20. So also Fuchs, 'Literary Characterisation', 155. On this event, see Rabow, *Lost Matriarch*, 80–7.

21. Callaway, *Sing, O Barren One*, 21; Wenham, *Genesis 16–50*, 7; Sarna, *JPS: Genesis*, 119; Trible, *Texts of Terror*, 15. For Fuchs, 'What seems to be a sentimental

Gen. Rab. 53:3 states that Sarah continued to praise the Lord and to trust in him despite her continued barrenness, a commitment later rewarded when she is remembered by God:

> Sarah exclaimed, 'What! am I to lose faith in my Creator! Heaven forfend! I will not lose faith in my Creator, *For I will rejoice in the Lord, I will exalt in the God of my salvation*' (Hab. III, 18). Said the Holy One, blessed be He, to her: 'Since thou didst not lose thy faith, I too will not give thee cause to lose faith'. But rather, AND THE LORD REMEMBERED SARAH, etc.

These rabbinic passages present Sarah as a matriarchal figure, for whom motherhood is a priority. Barrenness was understood by the biblical writers, but even more explicitly by the rabbis, to be a necessary precursor to motherhood for the women in Genesis.[22] Biale notes that through this, 'the biblical authors reinforced the theology of divine election: just as God chooses the younger son and allows violations of legal norms to establish the Israelite nation, so there is divine intervention in procreation to provide the nation's heroes'.[23] Fuchs interprets this more negatively, arguing that the biblical annunciation scene confirms 'that woman has no control at all over her reproductive potential'; she is wholly subject to God's power and will.[24] To the rabbis, Sarah is the model of true faith, who puts her trust in God. Sarah shows an inherent acceptance of her matriarchal role through her actions. In contrast, Jacob misunderstands the nature of matriarchal barrenness and God's part in ensuring that the right woman bears the right son at the right time.[25]

5.2.2. *God's Support of the Disadvantaged, Especially Barren Women*

Midrash makes clear that God is sympathetic to the plight of the weak and disadvantaged, including barren women, and that he works to improve their situation. This is demonstrated in several pericopae, often by interpreting Psalm verses with reference to the matriarchs' barrenness and its reversal. *Genesis Rabbah* 53:5 identifies Sarah as the barren woman who bears children in Ps 113:9. *Pesiqta de Rab Kahana*, a later midrash, makes

---

narrative about the happy transition from emptiness to fullness and from failure to victory is a carefully constructed story intended among other things to promote the institution of motherhood' (Fuchs, 'Literary Characterisation', 160–1).

22. See Teubal, *Sarah the Priestess*, 106.
23. Biale, *Eros*, 25.
24. Fuchs, 'Literary Characterisation', 161.
25. Cf. Hauptman, *Rereading*, 130.

the same connection between Sarah and Ps 113:9, then extends the application to seven barren women, namely Sarah, Rebekah, Leah, Rachel, Samson's mother (Judg 13), Hannah (1 Sam 1–2) and Zion.[26] Psalm 113 praises the Lord for his majesty and power and notes his ability to reverse the helpless situation of the poor. The barren woman (עקרה) becomes an example of a disadvantaged individual whose situation is dramatically changed by God.[27]

Genesis Rabbah 71:1 and 71:2 build on this theme. Both passages cite further Psalm verses (Pss 69:34; 145:14), said to relate to the Lord making Leah conceive immediately to give her security in the home.[28] In their entireties, both of these Psalms present the psalmists' praise of the Lord alongside proclamations of hope and confidence that he will support the weak and intervene at times of despair. Neither of these Psalms makes reference to barrenness, but there is precedence for this connection in Ps 113:9, where the 'poor' (דל) and 'needy' (אביון) are brought into relation with the barren woman (עקרה).[29] Biblical statements regarding the disadvantaged were applicable to the barren woman's plight and the reversal of barrenness could be equated with the empowerment of the weak. Most importantly, God is central to both processes and has ultimate control over individuals' fate.

5.2.3. *God Ensures the Reversal of Barrenness by His Power*

God's direct responsibility for childbirth combined with the matriarchs' barrenness means that the Lord must directly intervene in the matriarchs' lives to ensure that they bear children. One indication of this intervention appears in *Gen. Rab.* 44:10:

---

26. *Pesiq. Rab Kah.* 20:1. Callaway translates and interprets an extended form of this pericope (Callaway, *Sing, O Barren One*, 120–2). See also Callaway, *Sing, O Barren One*, 117–23; Zucker, 'Sarah', 227; Baskin, *Midrashic Women*, 134–6. See also Jacob Neusner, *Pesiqta Derab Kahana: An Analytical Translation*, 2 vols., Brown Judaic Studies (Atlanta: Scholars Press, 1987), 2:63–5. See also 'Preface to Part II: The Matriarchal Cycle'.

27. See Callaway, *Sing, O Barren One*, esp. 120–2, 137; Byron, 'Childlessness and Ambiguity', 21.

28. Callaway, *Sing, O Barren One*, 131–2, interprets and connects these passages. See §5.2.2, 'God's Support of the Disadvantaged, Especially Barren Women'.

29. Callaway, *Sing, O Barren One*, 122. Callaway also compares Hannah's psalm (1 Sam 2) to the lament Psalms (pp. 46–57).

AND ABRAHAM SAID: BEHOLD, TO ME THOU HAST GIVEN NO
SEED (XV, 3). R. Samuel b. Isaac commented: [Abraham said:] My
planetary fate oppresses me, and declares, 'Abram cannot beget a child'.
Said the Holy One, blessed be He, to him: 'Let it be even as thy words:
Abram and Sarai cannot beget but Abraham and Sarah can beget'.

This passage links Gen 15:3 to the change of Abraham and Sarah's names
in Gen 18. Although barrenness may seem like a hopeless and irreversible
condition, God has the power to change a person's destiny.[30] As with
Sarah's rejection of magical practices in *Gen. Rab.* 45:2, this pericope
creates an opposition between God and popular understandings of the
forces controlling human life and reproduction. God is life-giver and he
cannot be displaced by any other power.

Sarah is the first matriarch and thus the first woman to bear a son within
the covenant. God promises that she will conceive and that promise is
fulfilled (Gen 17:15-21; 18:10, 14; 21). *Genesis Rabbah* emphasises
God's commitment to these promises.[31] Interpreting Gen 17:2, *Gen. Rab.*
47:2 comments:

AND I WILL BLESS HER (Gen 17:16), that she should give thee a son;
YEA, I WILL BLESS HER in respect of milk. Said R. Nehemiah to him:
Had she then already been informed about her milk? This teaches, however,
that God restored to her her youth (נערות).[32] R. Abbahu explained it thus in
the name of R. Jose b. R. Ḥanina: I will inspire all peoples with awe of her,
so that they should not call her, 'barren woman'. R. Judan said in the name
of Resh Lakish: She lacked an ovary, but the Lord fashioned an ovary for
her.

---

30. Freedman also expresses this (n. 2 367). A number of ancient traditions link
Abraham with astrology. See Devorah Dimant, 'Abraham the Astrologer at Qumran?
Observations on Pseudo-Jubilees (4Q225 2 I 3-8)', in *Textual Criticism and Dead
Sea Scroll: Studies in Honour of Julio Trebolle Barrera*, ed. Andrés Piquer Otero, and
Pablo A. Torijano Morales, Supplements to the Journal for the Study of Judaism 157
(Leiden: Brill, 2012), 71–82; James L. Kugel, *Traditions of the Bible: A Guide to the
Bible As It Was at the Start of the Common Era* (Cambridge, MA: Harvard University
Press, 1998), 259–64, 249–51. In *Gen. Rab.* 44:12, God tells Abraham '"You are a
prophet, not an astrologer..."'

31. Cf. Sarna, *JPS: Genesis*, 93; Westermann, *Genesis 12–36*, 267.

32. נערות, 'youth, vitality', is the feminine noun used for '*maidenhood, the age* or
the legal status of a נערה' (Jastrow, 922).

This pericope is repeated, almost verbatim, in *Gen. Rab.* 53:5, when these promises to Sarah are finally fulfilled (Gen 21:1).[33] No obstacle is so great that it cannot be overcome by God and he intervenes to make his choice for a matriarch viable.[34] Literary repetition emphasises the correspondence between God's words and actions, affirming his complete control over all.[35] This also affects understandings of God's interaction with humans on both an individual and national scale. Sarah's story is therefore significant for the rabbis and all Jews.[36]

Genesis 21:1 records the reversal of Sarah's barrenness, as 'the LORD visited ("remembered", פקד) Sarah', and she conceived. Elsewhere in the barren matriarch tradition, the verb זכר, 'to remember', is employed to the same effect. With God as its subject, these verbs indicate action on behalf of the individual concerned.[37] Overall, the reversal of Sarah's barrenness represents the beginnings of Israel and God's firm commitment to the covenant and its promises.[38] Sarah has become the first mother of Israel and this is enabled by God's intervention. *Genesis Rabbah* devotes several pericopae to interpretations of Gen 21:1 (*Gen. Rab.* 53:1-5). These midrashim apply different biblical verses to Sarah's situation, demonstrating her universal significance. For example, *Gen. Rab.* 53:1 employs Ezek 17:24 and *Gen. Rab.* 53:5 uses 1 Kgs 8:24, to confirm that God did exactly what he promised for Abraham and Sarah.[39] This exegetical technique also demonstrates the unity of Scripture as later biblical verses are used to comment on events occurring in the patriarchal narratives.[40]

---

33. The differences between the two parallel passages are negligible and do not affect interpretation.

34. Cf. *b. Yebam.* 64a-b.

35. Cf. Callaway, *Sing, O Barren One*, 23; Rachel Adelman, 'Laughter and Re-Membering', *Nashim: A Journal of Jewish Women's Studies & Gender Issues* 8 (2004): 231.

36. Callaway, *Sing, O Barren One*, 32–3.

37. זכר, 'to remember', is used regarding the reversal of Rachel and Hannah's barrenness (Gen 30:22; 1 Sam 1:19). פקד is also used regarding Hannah in 1 Sam 2:21. Cf. *Gen. Rab.* 38:14; 73:1-4. See also §5.4.1, 'Use of the Biblical Barren Matriarch Tradition and its Development'. See Adelman, 'Laughter and Re-Membering', 230.

38. Callaway, *Sing, O Barren One*, 132–3.

39. For these passages, see §5.4.3, 'Scriptural Texts Applied to the Matriarchal Narratives'.

40. See Callaway, *Sing, O Barren One*, 123. See also §2.2, 'The Theory of Midrash: The Rabbinic Worldview'. See further §5.4, 'The Matriarchs as Representatives: Of the National Identity'; §8.1.1, 'Prayer and Praise'.

The importance of themes explored in Sarah's narrative, including the woman's legitimacy and God's control over childbirth, is confirmed as each matriarch overcomes barrenness and mothers the next generation of Israel.[41] The biblical text declares Rebekah's barrenness only once (Gen 25:21) and she conceives in the same verse.[42] Isaac prays for Rebekah and the Lord responds to his supplication. The rabbis expand on this verse in *Gen. Rab.* 63:5, picturing both Isaac and Rebekah praying that they may have children with each other:

LENOKAH (FOR) HIS WIFE: This teaches that Isaac prostrated himself in one spot and she in another [opposite him], and he prayed to God: 'Sovereign of the Universe! May all the children which Thou wilt grant me be from this righteous woman.' She too prayed likewise.

There is a recognition by the second patriarch and matriarch that God is in control of childbirth and they, like Sarah, are not distracted by false solutions to barrenness.[43] The Lord responds positively to this recognition of his power and 'was entreated by' Isaac (Gen 25:21).[44] The same verb is used in Gen 25:21 to describe both Isaac's prayer (עתר, Qal) and God's response to that prayer (עתר, Niphal). This suggests reciprocity between the two characters as Isaac appeals to God's authority and God rewards his action, providing Isaac with a child. In the midrash, R. Levi illustrates this with the following image: 'This may be compared to the son of a king who was digging through to his father to receive a *litra* (pound) of gold from him, and thus one [the king] dug from within while the other [his son] dug from without'. God and Isaac are shown working towards a common cause, with God graciously quickening the process.[45]

Prayer is present in the biblical text, but the rabbinic midrash develops the implications of biblical language and includes Rebekah praying alongside Isaac. This contrasts with the biblical text, where, as Fewell and Gunn comment, 'unlike Sarah before her and Rachel after her, Rebekah

---

41. Schneider notes that God is said to have 'opened her [Leah's] womb, ויפתח את־רחמה' (Gen 29:31), the same phrase used when Rachel's barrenness is reversed in Gen 30:22. This may suggest that Leah was also barren prior to divine intervention (Schneider, *Mothers of Promise*, 72–3). See also Schneider, *Mothers of Promise*, 96; Rabow, *Lost Matriarch*, 73–5.

42. See Wenham, *Genesis 16–50*, 172; Turner, 'Rebekah', 44.

43. Cf. Byron, 'Childlessness and Ambiguity', 29.

44. My translation.

45. Freedman (n. 2 559) and Neusner (2:352) make similar points. Cf. Callaway, *Sing, O Barren One*, 138–9.

does not seem too bothered by her barrenness. She indulges in no schemes to have children...; she gives no evidence of desperation or frustration'.[46] The midrash develops Rebekah's role and supports Callaway's claim that, 'in the rabbinic midrashim the barrenness of the woman is a problem which Yahweh and the characters involved deal with together'.[47] The matriarchs and patriarchs play an increased role in *Genesis Rabbah*. Notably, their total deference to God's authority confirms their worthiness to become ancestors of the nation.[48]

R. Johanan links the verb עתר in Gen 25:21, 'Isaac prayed (יעתר) to the LORD', with עושר, 'plenty', to indicate the multitude of Isaac's prayers. Resh Laqish argues instead that: 'He reversed (הפך) her destiny (lit. "decree", גזירה), and for that reason a pitchfork is called *'athra* (עתרה), because it turns (הפך) the grain'.[49] This reversal of destinies is reminiscent of *Gen. Rab.* 44:10, where the change in Abram and Sarai's names allows an alternate fate for these figures. God's central role is clear as the couple's prayer elicits a divine response.

Genesis Rabbah 63:5 contains an even more explicit connection to rabbinic interpretations of Sarah's barrenness. Using the same language as *Gen. Rab.* 47:2 and 53:5, R. Judan explains that the Lord created an ovary for Rebekah: 'R. Judan said in the name of Resh Laḳish: She lacked an ovary, whereupon the Lord fashioned an ovary for her'. This draws a parallel between Sarah, the first matriarch, and Rebekah, her successor. The same kind of divine intervention was necessary to ensure that both women could bear children. The construction of a female sexual organ, without which these women were physically unable to conceive, highlights the extent to which the matriarchs' lives are determined by God's action and his plan for his people.

5.2.4. *Summary*

God is in complete control of life and childbirth and it is he who must intervene in the barren matriarchs' lives to ensure that they bear children. *Genesis Rabbah* continues these biblical themes and uses them to demonstrate the legitimacy of the matriarchs, who act as models of faith, representatives of Israel, and prove themselves worthy of bearing Israel's covenant sons. God pays particular attention to the disadvantaged and his reversal of the matriarchs' barrenness emphasises this (*Gen. Rab.* 53:5,

---

46. Fewell and Gunn, *Gender, Power, & Promise*, 73.
47. Callaway, *Sing, O Barren One*, 138.
48. See ibid., 129, 134.
49. See Freedman, n. 2 558.

71:1 and 71:2). Ultimately, the midrash demonstrates that barrenness is part of God's plans for Israel.

5.3. *The Matriarchs as Representatives: Of the Disadvantaged*

5.3.1. *Matriarchs as Representatives of the Disadvantaged*

As figures overcoming adversity, the matriarchs had relevance for the contemporary rabbinic audience. These women took on a representative role, first coming to represent all barren women and then, by extension, all who are disadvantaged. This is demonstrated in *Gen. Rab.* 71:6. The rabbinic discussion centres around Rachel's outcry in Gen 30:1 that Jacob should: 'Give me children, or I shall die!'[50] Rabbi Samuel argues that: 'Four are regarded as dead (מת): the leper, the blind,[51] he who is childless, and he who has become impoverished'. Biblical verses containing the root מות, 'to die', can be identified in relation to each of these groups.[52] For example, Aaron appeals to Moses that Miriam be healed of her leprosy with the statement: 'Let her not be like the dead (מת)' (Num 12:12).[53]

As this midrash shows, there were a number of disadvantaged groups in rabbinic society, the barren being only one.[54] The experiences of Rachel and her fellow matriarchs could be linked with these people and would eventually give them hope that just as barrenness could be overcome, their own misfortunes did not have to be permanent.[55] The rabbis thus ensure the continued relevance of Israel's earliest ancestresses. This pericope is *Genesis Rabbah*'s clearest expression of the correspondence between the childless and others who are disadvantaged in society.

5.3.2. *The Reversal of Barrenness and Its Consequences*

The reversal of barrenness is a key moment in each matriarch's life as God intervenes to ensure that she bears children. As representatives of the disadvantaged in the midrash, the reversal of the matriarchs' barrenness has profound implications for those who are suffering. *Genesis Rabbah*

---

50. Ilana Pardes, 'Rachel's Dream of Grandeur', in Büchmann and Spiegel, eds., *Out of the Garden*, 30. Schneider notes that Rachel's anger is misdirected here: it is God, not Jacob, who enables fertility (Schneider, *Mothers of Promise*, 83).

51. Theodor-Albeck's text reads 'blind' then 'leper'.

52. Gen 30:1; Exod 4:19 Num 12:12; Lam 3:6.

53. My translation.

54. Cf. Wegner, *Chattel or Person?*, 12, 149–50; Baskin, *Midrashic Women*, 76–7.

55. Baskin, *Midrashic Women*, 135–6.

53:5 equates Sarah with the barren woman who bears children in Ps 113, which praises God for his ability to reverse the situation of the vulnerable.[56] Sarah's role as a representative of the disadvantaged is further explored in *Gen. Rab.* 53:8. Sarah claims following Isaac's birth that, 'God has brought laughter for me; everyone who hears will laugh with me' (Gen 21:6). Sarah suggests that her personal transformation from barren woman to mother elicits a joyful response from others; the rabbinic interpreters question how this can be so:[57]

> R. Berekiah, R. Judah b. R. Isaac said: If Reuben has cause to rejoice, what does it matter to Simeon? Similarly, if Sarah was remembered (root פקד), what did it matter to others? But when the matriarch Sarah was remembered [gave birth] (root פקד), many other barren women were remembered with her (root פקד); many deaf gained their hearing; many blind had their eyes opened, many insane became sane.

This midrash explains the full implications of the verb פקד, 'to remember', which describes the action taken by God to reverse Sarah's barrenness in Gen 21:1. When Sarah's barrenness was reversed, the misfortunes of others were also reversed. Sarah acts as a representative figure, offering hope that those suffering misfortune may see their situations change.

The rabbinic interpreters do not simply assert Sarah's representative role; they also try to explain it. This is achieved in *Gen. Rab.* 53:8 through the rabbinic principle of *gezerah shawah*.[58] It reads:

> For 'making' [HATH MADE (Gen 21:6)] is mentioned here, and also elsewhere, viz. *And he made a release to the provinces* (Est. II, 18). As the making mentioned there means that a gift was granted to the world, so the making mentioned here means that a gift was granted to the world.[59] R. Levi said: She increased the light of the luminaries: 'making' is mentioned here, viz. GOD HATH MADE FOR ME, while elsewhere it says, *And God made the two lights* (Gen. I, 16).

---

56. See §5.2, 'God's Role in Childbirth and the Reversal of Barrenness'.

57. Jeansonne suggests that in Gen, '[a]lthough the phrasing is ambiguous, it is clear that Sarah's esteem among other women (as well as among men) is related to giving birth to her son' (Jeansonne, *Women of Genesis*, 75). Cf. Wenham, *Genesis 16–50*, 81; Westermann, *Genesis 12–36*, 334.

58. See §2.3, 'Common Midrashic Exegetical Techniques'.

59. According to this midrash, both Esther and Sarah generated positive consequences for the world around them. Both women play a significant role in Israelite history, recognised by the rabbis. See Bronner, *From Eve to Esther*, esp. 178–81.

The midrash builds on Est 2:18's use of the verb עשׂה, 'to make', to describe an action that affects 'provinces' (מדינות), thus large areas of land. Rabbinic exegetes assert that because the same verb is used in Gen 21:6, the reversal of Sarah's barrenness was also an action with far-reaching consequences.[60] Rabbi Levi explains this differently, connecting the verb עשׂה, 'to make', in Gen 21:6 with its use in Gen 1:16. Using *gezerah shawah*, he deduces that Sarah 'increased the luminaries'. This adds a cosmic dimension to Sarah's characterisation and highlights the unparalleled significance of her role.[61] There is no doubt that the rabbis respected Sarah and recognised her continued influence. That she and the other matriarchs could represent the experiences of the poor and vulnerable only increased their relevance.

Although the categories of the disadvantaged differ slightly, this midrash parallels *Gen. Rab.* 71:6. Both Rachel and Sarah become representative figures through their experiences of barrenness. Whilst *Gen. Rab.* 71:6 establishes a connection between a barren matriarch and the disadvantaged, *Gen. Rab.* 53:8 shows the full implications of the connection: as matriarchal barrenness is not permanent, the disadvantaged are offered hope. Furthermore, Sarah is referred to as 'our mother' (אימנו) in *Gen. Rab.* 53:8.[62] The rabbis associate themselves with Sarah, claiming her as a figure of continued importance and authority. Given this status, it is not surprising that Sarah's life affects the world in this extraordinary way.

Finally, it is important to mention again *Gen. Rab.* 71:1 and 71:2.[63] These passages connect the experiences of a barren matriarch, Leah, with the anguish of the poor. Both take the literary and rhetorical form of a proem, where: 'A verse from the prophets or the writings usually provided a general statement by which the story from the Torah was interpreted, indicating again the liturgical origins of the midrash'.[64] The experiences of this Genesis matriarch are shown to have a universal quality, bearing

60. This point is made anonymously, which may suggest general acceptance of this view.

61. Discussing an almost identical midrash in *Pesiq. Rab Kah.* 42, Callaway notes that the curing of disabilities and the increased luminary-light are eschatological signs (Callaway, *Sing, O Barren One*, 135–6). See also Darr, *Far More Precious*, 123; Zucker, 'Sarah', 238. In the Hebrew Bible and the New Testament, various passages discuss God's ability to cure disabilities, particularly blindness and deafness, often in an eschatological context. See Exod 4:11; Isa 29:18; 35:5; Matt 11:5; Luke 7:22.

62. See §3.6.2, 'Uses of the Noun אם as "Matriarch"'.

63. For what follows, see Callaway, *Sing, O Barren One*, 130–2.

64. Ibid., 130. See also Jacobs, *Midrashic Process*. See also §2.3, 'Common Midrashic Exegetical Techniques'.

relevance throughout time. Psalm verses (69:34 and 145:14) are used to express the change in a woman's status when she has children, as her position in the household is secured.[65] The midrashim conclude with exactly the same phrase: 'when the Holy One Blessed Be He remembers them with children, they are raised up (נזקפות)'.[66] Leah is then provided as an example of this. Callaway argues that: 'The use of נזקפות "raised up" in both midrashim about Leah, though it occurs in Ps 145:14 and not in the Psalm cited in the other midrash about Leah [Ps 69:34; *Gen. Rab.* 71:1], indicates an accepted tradition that Leah was נזקפה'.[67] The biblical text reports that: 'the Lord saw that Leah was hated and he opened her womb' (Gen 29:31). The midrash explains that this secured her position within the household as the mother of Jacob's children.[68]

Genesis Rabbah 71:1 further develops the representative role of Leah. The beginning of the midrash discusses the language used in Ps 69:34 (ET 69:33), 'For the LORD hears the needy, and does not despise his own that are in bonds':

> R. Benjamin b. Levi said: The beginning of this verse does not match its end, nor the end the beginning. The verse should surely have read either, 'For the Lord hearkeneth unto the needy and despiseth not *the* prisoners', or 'For the Lord hearkeneth unto *His* needy and despiseth not His prisoners'. But, '*For the Lord hearkeneth unto the needy*' refers to Israel, for R. Johanan said: Wherever 'poor', 'afflicted', or 'needy' occurs, Scripture refers to Israel. '*And despiseth not his prisoners*' alludes to childless women who are as prisoners in their houses, but as soon as the Holy One, blessed be He, visits [i.e. blesses] them with children, they become erect [with pride].[69] The proof is that Leah was hated in her house, yet when God visited her she became erect; hence it is written, AND THE LORD SAW THAT LEAH WAS HATED, AND HE OPENED HER WOMB.

65. See e.g. Baskin, *Midrashic Women*, 130–1; *Gen. Rab.* 71:5.

66. My own translation. *Gen. Rab.* 71:2 reads: '*The Lord upholdeth all who fall* (Ps. CXLV, 14)—viz. childless women who fall [i.e. are disgraced] in their own homes; *And raiseth up all those who are bowed down (ib.)*: as soon as God visits them with children, they are raised up. The proof is that Leah was hated in her house, yet when the Holy One, blessed be He, visited her, she was raised up. Thus it is written, AND THE LORD SAW THAT LEAH WAS HATED, etc.' *Gen. Rab.* 71:1 is quoted below.

67. Callaway, *Sing, O Barren One*, 132.

68. *Gen. Rab.* 71:2 explores this further. See §6.3.1, 'Husbands' Respect for Their Wives as Mothers'.

69. The barren are understood as the Lord's prisoners because he alone is in control of childbirth (Freedman, n. 1 652). See §5.2.1, 'God's Control Over Childbirth'.

Rabbi Benjamin b. Levi proposes an alteration to ensure true parallelism between the two parts of the verse. However, a statement is then made which interprets the verse as it stands. God can reverse barrenness and Leah acts as a representative of barren women.

The group mentioned in the other part of the verse, 'the needy', is said to refer to Israel. This statement is parallel to that regarding the barren woman and so Leah can be understood to represent both categories. As Callaway argues: 'In a homiletical setting, this point is made more eloquently by analogy than by explicit statement'.[70] A link is made between the barren, the vulnerable and Israel. Leah is a mother of Israel who suffered much anguish and yet God ensured that her situation would be reversed. She thus provides hope for the weak and for Israel. *Genesis Rabbah* 71:1 charts the development in the representative role of the biblical matriarchs: the experiences of these individual women allow them to be viewed first as representatives of barren women and of the disadvantaged, and then as representatives of Israel.[71]

5.3.3. *Summary*

The matriarchs act as representatives of the disadvantaged. When these women's barrenness is finally reversed, this offers hope to others struggling within their own lives that they may also see their fortunes improve. Leah is a particularly important example, as in *Gen. Rab.* 71:1, she becomes a representative not only of the disadvantaged, but also of Israel.

5.4. *The Matriarchs as Representatives: Of the National Identity*

5.4.1. *Use of the Biblical Barren Matriarch Tradition and Its Development*

The biblical barren matriarch tradition, culminating in the presentation of Zion as a barren woman in Isa 54, allowed Sarah, Rebekah, Leah and Rachel to become representatives of Israelite and Jewish identity in *Genesis Rabbah*. Rabbinic exegesis of the Genesis narratives freely incorporated all layers of the tradition as the matriarchs' significance was considered. When viewed in light of the biblical barrenness tradition and as a necessary part of 'the matriarchal cycle' from infertility to motherhood, barrenness becomes a symbol of hope. In Isaiah, the image offered encouragement that the exiled nation would one day be restored

---

70. Callaway, *Sing, O Barren One*, 131.
71. Cf. Baskin, *Midrashic Women*, 136–8.

by God; and for the rabbis, matriarchal barrenness and its reversal continued to influence Jewish identity into their own times.[72]

Genesis Rabbah 38:14 clearly demonstrates the rabbinic use of the biblical barren matriarch tradition. This midrash provides commentary on Gen 11:29-30, where Sarah is introduced into the biblical narrative. Here, barrenness defines her. It is the only information provided about Sarai, other than her status as Abram's wife; and as Halpern-Amaru notes, 'Such a presentation is appropriate in Genesis where infertility is the primary motif in the writer's portrayal of the first matriarch'.[73] *Genesis Rabbah* 38:14 first discusses Gen 11:29, where Abram and his brother, Nahor, marry.[74] Based on an assumed age gap of one year between each of Terah's sons, the rabbis calculate that 'Haran fathered children at the age of six, but Abram did not father children'.[75] The rabbis express surprise at Abram's continued childlessness and this statement is then juxtaposed with Gen 11:30: 'Now Sarai was barren; she had no child'. This offers an apparent explanation for Abram's childlessness and at first glance seems to lay blame on Sarai.[76]

72. For the barren matriarch motif from biblical to rabbinic times, see Callaway, *Sing, O Barren One*. For the biblical tradition, see §4.1, 'The Biblical Barren Matriarch Tradition'. See also Darr, *Far More Precious*, 114–16.

73. Halpern-Amaru, *Women in the Book of Jubilees*, 34. Cf. Jeansonne, *Women of Genesis*, 11.

74. Gen 11:29 declares that Haran was 'the father of Milcah and Iscah'. The biblical text identifies Milcah as Nahor's wife, so the rabbis assume that Haran's other daughter, Iscah, must be Sarah, Abraham's wife (so Freedman, n. 1 312). In *Jubilees*, the matriarchs descend from Terah. Their genealogies legitimise their matriarchal roles (Halpern-Amaru, *Women in the Book of Jubilees*, 130 et passim). A similar legitimisation of Sarah may be at work here.

75. Gen 11:26 names Terah's three sons one after another; the rabbis assume that they must have been born in three successive years: 'Abram was a year older than Nahor and Nahor was a year older than Haran; [hence Abram was] two years older [than Haran]; [now deduct] the year of pregnancy with Milcah and the year of pregnancy with Iscah, and you find that Haran begot children at six years of age, yet you say that Abram could not beget a child!' (*Gen. Rab.* 38:14). As Freedman explains: 'According to the Rabbis, Iscah was Sarah. Now Abram was ten years older than Sarah (v. [Gen] XVII, 17); since he was two years older than Haran, Sarah's father, Sarah was born when Haran was only eight years old. Again, she was his second daughter, and since the period of pregnancy and child-bearing is roughly a year for each child, Haran must have been six years old when he begot a child, i.e. when his wife conceived by him. The point of the difficulty, "and yet you say that Abram, could not beget child", is not clear' (Freedman, n. 1 312).

76. Cf. Darr, *Far More Precious*, 94; Schneider, *Sarah*, 17, 30, 121; Trible, 'Ominous Beginnings', 34–6; Wenham, *Genesis 1–15*, 271; Westermann, *Genesis*

Yet *Gen. Rab.* 38:14 continues, connecting Sarah's experiences to the wider biblical barrenness tradition and proving that barrenness is not a sign of her moral or physical shortcomings. Genesis 11:30 twice states that Sarah is childless: 'Now Sarai was barren (עקרה); she had no (אין לה) child'.[77] For the rabbis, the second proclamation must serve a purpose because repetition in biblical texts is never accidental:[78]

> R. Levi said: Wherever 'she had not' (אין לה) is found, it means that eventually she did have (הוה לה). Thus: AND SARAI WAS BARREN; SHE HAD NO CHILD; eventually she did have, as it is written, *And the Lord remembered Sarah* (Gen. XXI, 1). *And Peninah had children, but Hannah had no children* (1 Sam. I, 2): eventually she did have, as it is written, *And she bore three sons*, etc. (*ib.* II, 21). Again, *She is Zion, there is none that careth for her* (lit. 'seeking her', דרש אין לה) (Jer. XXX, 17). Yet eventually she will have [one to care for her, as it is written], *And a redeemer will come to Zion, and unto them that turn from transgression*, etc. (Isa. LIX, 20).

This midrash suggests that barrenness was a necessary precursor to Sarah's motherhood, a point reinforced by comparison to Hannah's narrative in 1 Sam 1–2. In both narratives, the Hebrew phrase אין לה, 'she did not have', is used to express the woman's barrenness (Gen 11:30; 1 Sam 1:2).[79] Later, both Hannah and Sarah are said to be remembered (זכר/פקד) by the Lord (Gen 21:1; 1 Sam 1:19);[80] and following divine intervention, they each 'conceived and bore' (ותהר ותלד) a son (Gen 21:2; 1 Sam 1:20). The strong linguistic connection between these two narratives allows parallels to be drawn between them.[81]

Compared to Genesis, 1 Sam 1–2 represents a more developed stage in the barren matriarch tradition.[82] Callaway suggests that the two major developments are Hannah's victimisation at the hands of her rival co-wife, Peninnah, and the presentation of Hannah as a pious woman,

---

12–36, 138, 141; Callaway, *Sing, O Barren One*, 20–1. Porton suggests that *Genesis Rabbah* does not always lay the blame for childlessness on the woman. See Gary G. Porton, 'How the Rabbis Imagined Sarah: A Preliminary Study of the Feminine in *Genesis Rabbah*', in *A Legacy of Learning: Essays in Honour of Jacob Neusner*, ed. Bruce Chilton, Alan J. Avery-Peck, William Scott Green and Gary G. Porton, The Brill Reference Library of Judaism 43 (Leiden: Brill, 2014), 204–5.

77. See Callaway, *Sing, O Barren One*, 21.

78. See Alexander, 'Midrash', 458.

79. The latter has לחנה אין, thus specifying the name, '*Hannah* did not have', rather than simply using a feminine singular suffix, '*she* did not have'.

80. The verb פקד, 'to remember', is also used of Hannah in 1 Sam 2:21.

81. See Callaway, *Sing, O Barren One*, 122.

82. Ibid., 35–57.

to whom God gives a son.[83] No explanation is offered for Hannah's barrenness and Callaway argues that 1 Sam 1–2 draws on the language of the lament psalms, portraying Hannah as a faithful individual who suffers without due cause.[84] As a result, 'Hannah functions as a symbol of a group', as her life 'gives graphic and poignant content to the Psalms of lament and gives concrete meaning to the affirmation that Yahweh raises the lowly and rewards his righteous ones'.[85] There is no doubt that the portrayal of Hannah in 1 Sam 1–2 influenced rabbinic interpretations of the Genesis matriarchs.[86] *Genesis Rabbah* 38:14 brings Sarah and Hannah's narratives together on account of their shared language; for the rabbis, this also implied further thematic parallels between the two stories. The notion of undeserved suffering removes any suggestion of blame on Sarai for her barrenness and, like Hannah, Sarai also assumes a representative role.

Callaway suggests that: 'Hannah is more truly the mother of Israel than Sarah, for in the figure of the poor one of low estate who was visited and remembered by Yahweh Israel could see herself'.[87] *Genesis Rabbah* 38:14 uses this development in the barrenness tradition as a link to the national identity. The final stage of the biblical barren matriarch tradition was to view Zion as a barren woman who will eventually produce many children (Isa 54:1). This functioned as a symbol of hope that the exiled nation would one day be restored.[88] *Genesis Rabbah* 38:14 alludes to this stage of the barrenness tradition. The midrashist contrasts Jer 30:17 with Isa 59:20. Neither of these prophetic verses refers to the barren woman; rather, the connection to Sarah and Hannah is established through the use of the

83. Ibid., 42. On Hannah and Peninnah, see Klein, *1 Samuel*, 7. On Hannah's piety, see Fuchs, 'Literary Characterisation', 157. For 1 Sam 1–2, see Klein, *1 Samuel*, 1–20; Keith Bodner, *1 Samuel: A Narrative Commentary*, Hebrew Bible Monographs 19 (Sheffield: Sheffield Phoenix, 2009), 11–36.

84. Callaway, *Sing, O Barren One*, 46–51, 54, 56–7, 137. Callaway notes similar language and themes in 1 Sam 1–2 and in the lament psalms and the cries of the *anawim*. For example, the call to God not to forget those who suffer; the use of the roots כעס, 'to be vexed', and צרר, 'to suffer distress'; weeping and praying.

85. Callaway, *Sing, O Barren One*, 57.

86. Cf. e.g. Hagar's increased cruelty towards Sarah after Hagar has conceived (*Gen. Rab.* 45:4) and images of the matriarchs praying (e.g. *Gen. Rab.* 41:2; see further §8.1.1, 'Prayer and Praise'). So also Callaway, *Sing, O Barren One*, 56–7.

87. Ibid., 57.

88. See §4.1, 'The Biblical Barren Matriarch Tradition'. See also Darr, *Far More Precious*, 114–16.

third person feminine pronoun (היא) and the phrase אין לה, 'she did not have', in relation to Zion in Jer 30:17. The rabbis assume their audience's knowledge of the biblical barren matriarch tradition and its development.

Isaiah's depiction of Zion as a barren woman (Isa 54:1-3) uses themes present in earlier strands of the barren matriarch tradition, raising them to a national scale.[89] There is a comparison between two women, one without children and one with many, a situation recalling that of rival co-wives in Genesis and 1 Samuel. Furthermore, just like Sarah (Gen 11:30), Rebekah (25:21) and Rachel (29:31), Zion is 'barren' (עקרה); and like Rachel (30:1) and Sarah (16:1), 'she did not bear' (לא ילדה). The two phrases even appear together in Isa 54:1, just as they do in Judg 13:2-3.[90] The barren woman who is eventually blessed with children became a model for Israel in exile, offering hope that one day she too would be restored by God.[91] Thus, the development of the earlier narrative tradition into a prophetic oracle concerning Zion provided a national dimension to the experiences of barren women earlier in the Hebrew Bible. *Genesis Rabbah* 38:14 brings together the different stages of the barren matriarch tradition, highlighting the significance of matriarchal barrenness and its reversal for Israel's history and her future. Although not directly quoting Isa 54, this midrash draws on the tradition of Zion as the barren woman and thus suggests that Sarah and the other barren matriarchs may be viewed as representatives of the nation.

5.4.2. *Matriarchs as Representatives of the National Identity*

For the rabbis, the matriarchs' experiences reflected their authoritative roles as the mothers of Israel and foreshadowed events taking place later in Israel's history.[92] *Genesis Rabbah* contains midrashim that deal explicitly with the matriarchs' roles as representatives of Israel. *Genesis Rabbah* 71:2 interprets Gen 29:31, including the statement: 'Rachel was barren (עקרה)'. In the midrash, עָקָר, 'barren', is revocalised as עִקָּר, meaning 'principal' or 'chief':[93]

---

89. For all that follows, see Callaway, *Sing, O Barren One*, 59–72. Callaway also discusses the use of the barren matriarch in *4 Ezra* (pp. 83–9).

90. Ibid., 67.

91. Darr, *Far More Precious*, 114–16.

92. Rabow, *Lost Matriarch*, 4.

93. This is expressed several times in *Gen. Rab.* 71:2 with slightly differing phrases: רחל היתה עקרו שלבית [עיקר הבית]; עקר; רחל היתה עקר הבית.

R. Isaac said: Rachel was the chief of the house, as it says, BUT RACHEL
WAS 'AKARAH, which means, she was the chief (*'ikar*) of the house. R.
Abba b. Kahana said: The majority of those who dined [at Jacob's table]
were Leah's children, therefore Rachel was declared the principal, BUT
RACHEL WAS 'AKARAH, meaning that Rachel was the chief of the
house. R. Samuel b. Naḥman said: Because the incidents are related about
Rachel, Israel was called by her name, as it says, *Rachel weeping for her
children* (Jer. XXXI, 15); and not only by her name, but by her son's name:
*It may be that the Lord, the God of hosts, will be gracious unto the remnant
of Joseph* (Amos V, 15); and not only by her son's name, but also by the
name of her grandson, as it says, *Is Ephraim a darling son unto Me* (Jer.
XXXI, 20)?

Through wordplay, Rachel's hardship is reinterpreted and understood to
reflect her significance as a matriarch in Israel. According to this view,
barrenness is a sign of Rachel's authority, not her condemnation. As
Halpern-Amaru states: 'Rachel, the beloved wife, is barren—clearly,
given the stories of Sarah and Rebekah, a forecast that she, like her predecessors, will give birth to the covenantal heir'.[94] The biblical text assumes
barrenness to be a particular characteristic of the matriarchs and the rabbis
accentuate this point using their own exegetical methods.

Rachel's position as 'chief of the household' ensured that both she and
Leah remain of equal status in Jacob's house, even though Leah bore
more children.[95] However, this statement should equally be understood
to reflect Rachel's wider significance as a matriarchal figure in Israel.
Events in the lives of the Genesis matriarchs are understood by the rabbis
to automatically have a wider significance. Rachel's enduring influence
is further suggested as R. Samuel b. Nahman explains that: 'Because the
matters speak about Rachel, therefore Israel are called by her name'. This
raises Rachel's significance to the national level, linking her directly to
Israel's identity. Jeremiah 31:15, 'Rachel is weeping for her children', is
cited in support of the rabbi's claim, before biblical verses from Amos and
Jeremiah demonstrate that the names of Rachel's descendants, Joseph and
Ephraim, become designations for Israel. Given the importance of names
in the ancient world as a reflection of character and status,[96] referring to

94. Halpern-Amaru, *Women in the Book of Jubilees*, 101. Cf. Teubal, *Sarah the
Priestess*, 102; Sarna, *JPS: Genesis*, 87.

95. So Freedman, n. 6 653. Cf. Jeansonne, *Women of Genesis*, 75. Byron notes
that: 'Without a child, particularly a son, her position in the marriage as primary wife
was not necessarily fixed' (Byron, 'Childlessness and Ambiguity', 27).

96. See Ronald A. Simkins, 'Names and Naming', *EDB*, 944–6; Rabow, *Lost
Matriarch*, 7–8; Havrelock, 'Heroic Barrenness', 175–8.

Israel through Rachel or one of her immediate descendants highlights this matriarch's importance for Jewish identity. In Jer 31:15, Rachel is portrayed as the archetypal mother of Israel, who mourns as 'her children' are exiled.[97]

Thus, according to the rabbis, there is an inherent link between Rachel's barrenness and her status as a mother of Israel. Mary Callaway offers a study of traditions concerning the barren matriarch from Genesis to rabbinic times; yet she does not deal at all with this pericope, where the term עָקָר, 'barren', is present in the biblical text and specifically addressed by the rabbis.[98] Although she notes the influence of Jer 31:15 on postbiblical texts such as *Baruch* and *4 Ezra*, Callaway overlooks this direct link between Jer 31:15 and barrenness in the rabbinic literature.[99] In *Gen. Rab.* 71:2, the rabbinic interpreters emphasise the matriarchs' continued influence over national and religious identity. The development of the barren matriarch tradition allowed these women to transcend their own historical contexts and represent the nation that descended from them. Matriarchal barrenness prefigures these women's roles as ancestresses of Israel. In this way, the historical mothers of Israel are portrayed as the present mothers of Israel.

5.4.3. *Scriptural Texts Applied to the Matriarchal Narratives*

The technique of relating a seemingly unconnected biblical verse to the specific verse being expounded in a given midrash is common in rabbinic exegesis.[100] In *Genesis Rabbah*, this technique highlights the matriarchs' continued relevance. Many examples have already been discussed: for example, *gezerah shawah* creating a connection between the use of עָשָׂה, 'to make', in Est 2:18 and Gen 21:6, clarifying how Sarah's pregnancy could benefit others (*Gen. Rab.* 53:8); and the application of Ps 69:34 to Leah in *Gen. Rab.* 71:1.[101] The matriarchs' lives and experiences resonate throughout Scripture.

Genesis Rabbah 53:5 begins by quoting 1 Kgs 8:24, where Solomon praises God for having fulfilled his promises to David. The midrashist applies each part of this verse to Abraham and Sarah's narrative:

---

97. Freedman, 654 n. 1.
98. Callaway, *Sing, O Barren One*.
99. Ibid., 81–2, 86–7, 112.
100. See §2.2, 'The Theory of Midrash: The Rabbinic Worldview'.
101. See §5.2, 'God's Role in Childbirth and the Reversal of Barrenness'; §5.3.2, 'The Reversal of Barrenness and Its Consequences'. See also Callaway, *Sing, O Barren One*, 120–3; Baskin, *Midrashic Women*, 137–8.

> *Who hast kept with Thy servant David my father*, etc. (1 Kings VIII, 24).
> *'Who hast kept with Thy servant'* alludes to Abraham. *That which Thou
> didst promise him,* viz. *At the set time I will return unto thee,* etc. (Gen.
> XVIII, 14). *Yea, Thou speakest with thy mouth, and hast fulfilled it with Thy
> hand, as it is this day* (1 Kings *loc. cit.*), viz. AND THE LORD REMEM-
> BERED SARAH.

The moment of Sarah's conception (Gen 21:1) provides an opportunity to
reflect on the fulfilment of God's promises, just as the dedication of the
Temple evoked Solomon's praise of the Lord.[102] The midrash connects the
Genesis narrative to the monarchic period when Israel was thriving as a
nation, and in particular to David, a figure central to Israel's history and
identity. The national import of the Genesis narratives is thus confirmed
as the theological principles of covenant and God's steadfast commitment
to his promises are shown to be active throughout history, even in the
earliest period.

Similarly, in *Gen. Rab.* 53:1, Ezek 17:24 is applied to the events narrated
in Gen 20.[103] Again, the verse is taken phrase by phrase, as the rabbinic
exegetes demonstrate the exact correspondence between the prophetic
oracle and Abraham and Sarah's encounter with Abimelech. It reads:

> *'And all the trees of the field shall know'* refers to the people, as you read,
> *For the tree of the field is man* (Deut. XX, 19). *'That I the Lord have brought
> down the high tree'* alludes to Abimelech; *'Have exalted the low tree'*—to
> Abraham; *'Have dried up the green tree'*—to Abimelech's wives, as it
> is written, *For the Lord had fast closed up all the wombs of the house of
> Abimelech* (Gen. XX, 18). *'And have made the dry tree to flourish'* alludes
> to Sarah. *'I the Lord have spoken':* Where did He speak it? *'At the set time I
> will return unto thee',* etc. *'And I have done it':* thus it is written, AND THE
> LORD DID UNTO SARAH AS HE HAD SPOKEN.

Ezekiel 17:24 provides an analogy, describing Israel and the nations as
trees. God will intervene to raise up Israel, who were once a 'low' and
'dry' tree, whereas the nations, once 'high' and 'moist', will decline. This
oracle gives hope to Israel that she will be redeemed by God and that
God's power will be recognised by all.[104] The midrash applies the oracle
to a concrete historical situation, using as its starting point the biblical
base text of Gen 21:1.

---

102. Cf. Callaway, *Sing, O Barren One*, 130.
103. See §5.2.3, 'God Ensures the Reversal of Barrenness by His Power'.
104. On Ezek 17:24, see e.g. Leslie C. Allen, *Ezekiel 1–19*, Word Biblical
Commentary 28 (Dallas: Word, 1994), 255, 261–2.

Ezekiel 17:24 claims that God fulfils his word. In the midrash, this twofold statement is demonstrated by Gen 18:14, giving the promise of a son for Sarah; and Gen 21:1, where that promise is fulfilled. These same verses appeared in *Gen. Rab.* 53:5 and here again they highlight God's commitment to his covenant promises. This sets the context for the remainder of the midrash as the prophetic oracle is shown to refer directly to characters appearing in Gen 20, despite its own origins centuries later. In Gen 20, Abimelech, king of Gerar takes Sarah into his household, believing that she is Abraham's sister. Following a warning from God that she is in fact a married woman, Sarah is returned to Abraham. In this midrash, the rabbis read the consecutive biblical verses (Gen 20:17-18; 21:1) together, regarding them as the fulfilment of the Ezekiel oracle.[105] The imagery of fecundity plays a significant role here. The barrenness of Abimelech's wives is punishment for Sarah's presence in the royal household. This prevents God's covenant promises to Abraham from being fulfilled because the matriarch and patriarch are separated; so when Sarah is restored, this punishment is reversed. By contrast, Gen 21:1 records the reversal of Sarah's undeserved barrenness, thus confirming God's choice of the matriarch as a mother of Israel. In this way, the 'low' and 'dry' trees, Abraham and Sarah, are made great by God.

Genesis Rabbah 53:1 portrays Sarah and Abraham as representatives of Israel, emphasising God's commitment to his covenantal promises. The connection to the prophetic oracle in Ezek 17:24 indicates the enduring relevance of Abraham and Sarah's lives. The birth of Isaac represents the past fulfilment of God's promises and, as such, also offers hope for the nation's future restoration. There is a continuity in God's treatment of his chosen people, Israel, throughout history. *Genesis Rabbah* focuses much attention on the verse, 'The LORD dealt with Sarah as he had said, and the LORD did for Sarah as he had promised' (Gen 21:1), because this is the very point at which God intervenes to reverse Sarah's barrenness and fulfil his covenant promise to the first of Israel's ancestors. As a result of this, Israel, and the Jewish religion that ultimately descends from it, can begin to emerge. Whilst Fuchs argues that God acts only to fulfil promises made to Abraham, and recognises only the male's merits, the rabbis prove that the matriarch is just as significant to Israel's covenantal history.[106] These women are legitimate figures who demonstrate true faith in God and to whom God promises (and delivers) covenant sons.

---

105. So also Sarna, *JPS: Genesis*, 145. Cf. Callaway, *Sing, O Barren One*, 124–5.
106. Fuchs, 'Literary Characterisation', 152–4.

5.4.4. *Summary*

The barren matriarchs become representatives of the nation, Israel. This is based on biblical traditions, such as Isa 54, which portrays Zion as a barren mother bearing children, and Jer 31:15-17, where Rachel weeps for her children, the Israelite exiles. *Genesis Rabbah* 38:14 expertly weaves together several layers of the biblical barrenness tradition, the narratives of Sarah and Hannah and the prophetic image of Zion, to emphasise the significance of barrenness within Israel's history. *Genesis Rabbah* 71:2 supports this, depicting the barren Rachel as the ultimate advocate of Israel. Furthermore, later biblical texts are understood to comment upon the matriarchs' situations. Once again, the experiences of the matriarchs are shown to have relevance beyond their own lifetimes, foreshadowing the restoration of Israel and God's continued attention to his people.

5.5. *Conclusions*

In *Genesis Rabbah*, the rabbinic interpreters build on details given in the biblical text of Genesis and present barrenness as a major part of their characterisation of the matriarchs. Barrenness forms a key component in the rabbinic 'matriarchal cycle', as each matriarch must overcome this adversity in order to become the next mother of Israel. In fact, even Leah was declared barren in order to confirm her matriarchal status. Thus, although barrenness was commonly regarded as a punishment in biblical and rabbinic times, the reversal of this misfortune confirms that Sarah, Rebekah, Leah and Rachel are worthy of becoming the mothers of Israel. God has ultimate control over childbirth, and as such, he intervenes to ensure that each of the women is able to bear. The experiences of these women allowed them to become representatives of the disadvantaged, offering hope to the weak that their misfortunes could be overcome; but, most importantly, they became representatives of the nation, embodying Israel's experiences and identity. When their barrenness is reversed through God's intervention, these women bear sons. It is to their matriarchal motherhood that my attention will now turn.

Chapter 6

MOTHERHOOD

Schneider notes that 'The main role and function of women in Genesis concerns women's capacity to bear children'.[1] Whilst barrenness may be central to understanding rabbinic portrayals of the matriarchs, it is only one half of these women's story. Following the anguish of barrenness and the difficulties of conception, the matriarchs finally become mothers. For the rabbis, motherhood defined these women from Genesis. Motherhood is the next stage of the rabbinic 'matriarchal cycle' as Sarah, Rebekah, Leah and Rachel give birth to sons.

Genesis Rabbah explores the physical phenomenon of childbirth, recording details about the matriarchs' pregnancies and labour. Bearing children, and particularly sons, secured a woman's position in society and entailed respect for her within the family.[2] Following childbirth, the matriarchs protect their offspring, ensuring that the correct son inherits the covenant. Here, the matriarchs' development from passive, infertile wives

---

1. Only a handful of Genesis women do not bear; see Schneider, *Mothers of Promise*, 217.

2. Bronner (*From Eve to Esther*, 186) speaks of 'the valorised roles of matrimony and motherhood'. See also Bronner, *From Eve to Esther*, 2–3, 29, 33, 99, 142, 163; Claudia V. Camp, *Wisdom and the Feminine in the Book of Proverbs*, Bible and Literature Series 11 (Sheffield: Almond, 1985), 79, 81; Naomi Graetz, 'Dinah the Daughter', in *A Feminist Companion to Genesis*, ed. Athalya Brenner, The Feminist Companion to the Bible 2 (Sheffield: Sheffield Academic, 1993), 306; Fewell and Gunn, *Gender, Power, & Promise*, 168; Judith Romney Wegner, 'The Image and Status of Women in Classical Rabbinic Judaism', in *Jewish Women in Historical Perspective*, ed. Judith R Baskin (Detroit: Wayne State University Press, 1998), 91; Byron, 'Childlessness and Ambiguity', 18, 26; Baskin, *Midrashic Women*, 161. On the wife's status, see Wegner, *Chattel or Person?*, 40–96. On good and bad wives, see Baskin, *Midrashic Women*, 100–118.

to active mothers is clear as they enact the divine will, promoting the son that God intends to inherit the covenant. Finally, the twofold significance of matriarchal motherhood is emphasised in *Genesis Rabbah*. These women do not just bear and protect the covenant sons; they also continue to be viewed throughout history as 'the mothers of Israel', representing and embodying the nation.

6.1. *Pregnancy and Childbirth*

6.1.1. *The Physical Act of Childbearing*

Matriarchal motherhood begins as a physical phenomenon, whereby a woman conceives and carries a child in her womb, before giving birth to, nursing and nurturing that child through to adulthood.[3] In Genesis, the wives of the patriarchs bear children to their husbands; this physical descent becomes the basis for national identity, as Israel emerges from Jacob's sons. The matriarchs' role as mothers was central to the rabbis' self-understanding as Jews and in *Genesis Rabbah*, they preserved and expanded on biblical details concerning pregnancy and childbirth. Whilst Baskin notes that 'To study women in rabbinic literature is actually to study men…[it] reveals far more about men's assumptions and anxieties than actual female concerns', the rabbis did acknowledge the struggles associated with childbirth.[4]

In Gen 3:16, God curses woman following her expulsion from the garden: 'I shall greatly increase your pangs in childbearing;[5] in pain you shall bring forth children'. The biblical text remains silent on the effects of this curse until the matriarchal narratives, when Rebekah becomes pregnant with Jacob and Esau.[6] The biblical text records her difficult pregnancy as, 'the children crushed one another inside her and she said, "If it is to be this way, why do I live?"' (Gen 25:22).[7] The twins inside Rebekah's womb cause her pain, and in *Gen. Rab.* 63:6 the rabbis examine the implications of their struggle.

The midrash begins by linking Jacob and Esau's struggles in the womb to their opposing personalities. Most notably:

---

3. Cf. Schneider's description of Sarah's actions in Gen, which largely revolve around her childbearing (Schneider, *Mothers of Promise*, 40).

4. Baskin, *Midrashic Women*, 11. Cf. Baskin, *Midrashic Women*, 16–17, 161–4.

5. See GKC §154a, n. 1(b) 484.

6. Fewell and Gunn, *Gender, Power, & Promise*, 74.

7. See Wenham, *Genesis 16–50*, 175. See BDB, 261, 4 for the use of זה.

When she (Rebekah) stood near synagogues or schools, Jacob struggled to come out; hence it is written, *Before I formed thee in the belly I knew thee* (Jer. I, 5). While when she passed idolatrous temples, Esau eagerly struggled to come out; hence it is written, *'The wicked are estranged from the womb'* (Ps. LVIII, 4).[8]

Jacob and Esau will later found conflicting nations, Israel and Edom, and their opposition is shown to have its roots before birth. Frequent womb references in the midrash confirm that Rebekah's body provides the setting for these initial struggles.[9] Woman's role 'as a vessel for the reception and nurturing of…new life' thus receives a dual interpretation here.[10] Not only does Rebekah's role as mother entail physical maternity, as her sons grow and develop inside her, but their individual personalities are fostered inside her, which ultimately has implications on a national scale.

Having considered the relationship between Rebekah's foetal sons, the midrash interprets the second half of its biblical base verse. Here Rebekah's own experience of pregnancy is recorded as she complains about its painfulness: 'If it is to be this way, why do I live?' (Gen 25:22). *Genesis Rabbah* 63:6 expands as follows:

R. Haggai said in R. Isaac's name: This teaches that our mother Rebekah went about to women's houses and asked them: 'Did you suffer so much in your time? If the pain of children is so great, would that I had not become pregnant!' R. Huba said: [She exclaimed]: 'If I am (lit. "destined", אני עתידה) to produce the twelve tribes only with such suffering, would that I had not conceived!' It was taught in R. Nehemiah's name: Rebekah merited that the twelve tribes should spring directly from her.

The midrash preserves Rebekah's voice and actions as she questions other women about their experiences of pregnancy. The rabbis develop Rebekah's own perspective and do not simply gloss over it. Furthermore, Rebekah is referred to as 'our mother', a term indicating rabbinic recognition of her status as an ancestress of Israel.[11] Referring to Rebekah in this way acknowledges and legitimises her experiences of pregnancy.

---

8. In Theodor-Albeck, the information about Esau is presented before that concerning Jacob.

9. מעי אמו ('the womb of his mother', twice); רחם ('womb', in a citation of Ps 58:4, twice); קרבה (lit: 'her inward part', twice, one of which is in a quotation of Gen 25:22); בטן ('womb', in a citation of Jer 1:5).

10. Baskin, *Midrashic Women*, 1.

11. See §3.6.2, 'Uses of the Noun אם as "Matriarch"'.

Such attention to the female perspective is unexpected in this male-oriented midrash.

Rebekah next exclaims that she does not want to bear the twelve tribes of Israel if it will be this painful. Physical motherhood forms the basis of the matriarchs' national motherhood and here, the woman herself shows an awareness of her role. The tannaitic tradition closing this section provides further support for Rebekah's legitimacy as a mother of Israel.

Genesis Rabbah 63:6 acknowledges the physical experience of childbirth, recording the reality of painful pregnancy and preserving Rebekah's search for comfort from other women.[12] Yet matriarchal motherhood is not simply a physical phenomenon; it points to the role that the Genesis women play in Israelite history. Baskin notes that any female perspective contained within rabbinic literature is shaped and influenced by the male author or compiler's own prejudices.[13] Women's experiences may ultimately serve an agenda, highlighting national or covenantal themes, but the female perspective is not devalued as the rabbinic interpreters show in *Gen. Rab.* 63:6 by allowing Rebekah's voice to be heard.

6.1.2. *Death during Childbirth*

Childbirth can be fatal and Genesis provides the first biblical instance of a woman dying whilst bearing her child. In an ironic twist, 'the woman who exclaimed, "Give me children or I am as dead" (Gen 30:1), dies in childbirth' as Rachel bears Benjamin and perishes (Gen 35:16-19).[14] Genesis 35:17 records how, 'When she was in her hard labour, the midwife said to her, "Do not be afraid; for now you will have another son"'.[15] These words of comfort are discussed in *Gen. Rab.* 82:8. This midrash presents the questioning of two disciples of R. Joshua by a Roman officer during a time of persecution. The disciples are asked to interpret certain biblical verses. Each time, the officer argues that their teacher, R. Joshua, interpreted the verses differently. The final section turns to Gen 35:17, the base verse for the midrash. The apostate Roman officer asks the disciples to interpret the midwife's words. They reply that '"A woman in confinement

---

12. Cf. Fewell and Gunn, *Gender, Power, & Promise*, 69.

13. Baskin, *Midrashic Women*, 3. Cf. Satlow, *Tasting the Dish*, 332–3.

14. Exum, *Fragmented Women*, 142. See also Schneider, *Mothers of Promise*, 83; Helena Zlotnick, *Dinah's Daughters: Gender and Judaism From the Hebrew Bible to Late Antiquity* (Philadelphia: University of Pennsylvania Press, 2002), 4–5, 163. Sarna suggests that: 'Rachel is comforted in her death agony by the knowledge that God answered the prayer she had uttered after the birth of Joseph...' (Sarna, *JPS: Genesis*, 243).

15. See Westermann, *Genesis 12–36*, 554–5.

is thus soothed", they replied, "and she is told when she is giving birth, 'Fear not, for you have given birth to a male child'"'. This provides a literal interpretation of the biblical text. The midwife reassures the new mother that her labour pain is worthwhile because she is bearing a son. The gender of the child is emphasised by the twofold description: 'male son'.[16] This explanation reflects the social benefits of having a son, namely the security it brought a woman.

In response, the Roman officer argues that R. Joshua interpreted the verse as revealing that a twin sister was born at the same time as each of the covenant sons. This point is partly supported by Abba Ḥalpa, the son of Koriah, who argues that: 'An additional twin sister (תאומה יתירה) was born with Benjamin'.[17] This interpretation probably arises from the use of גם, 'also', in Gen 35:17, a particle signifying addition in rabbinic hermeneutics.[18] When גם appears in a biblical verse, it is said to conceal extra information, such as additional subjects or objects in the sentence. In this case, the midwife confirms that the woman is bearing a son; but גם reveals that she bore a daughter at the same time.[19] Midrash often includes alternate interpretations of biblical texts, with no indication that one of them is correct. The birth of a healthy son is confirmed by this interpretation of Gen 35:17, but it reads specific language in the biblical verse as providing additional details about the events recorded.

Genesis Rabbah 82:8 offers a simple interpretation of Gen 35:17, but even here, patriarchal assumptions about women lie at its basis. As Exum explains: 'it is in the interest of patriarchal ideology not only that women bear children but also that they desire to do so. Thus these narratives represent the matriarchs as desiring children, especially sons... at all costs'.[20] The midwife's words in Gen 35:17, and their midrashic interpretation in *Gen. Rab.* 82:8, assume that news of a son is the only

---

16. Cf. *Tg. Neof.*; *Ps.-J.* to Exod 1:16 and 1:22, where the same phrase 'male child' is used. See Martin McNamara, Robert Hayward and Michael Maher, *Targum Neofiti 1: Exodus. Translated, With Introduction and Apparatus by Martin McNamara, and Notes by Robert Hayward; Targum Pseudo-Jonathan: Exodus. Translated, with Notes by Michael Maher*, The Aramaic Bible: The Targums 2 (Edinburgh: T. & T. Clark, 1994), 162 n. 33.

17. Though this would suggest two twin sisters were born with Benjamin (Freedman, n. 1 759). See also Rabow, *Lost Matriarch*, 112.

18. Freedman, n. 1 759; Strack and Stemberger, *Introduction*, 23.

19. This hermeneutical technique is one of R. Eliezer's 32 *Middot*. See §2.3, 'Common Midrashic Exegetical Techniques'. See also Strack and Stemberger, *Introduction*, 23.

20. Exum, *Fragmented Women*, 121. Cf. Ramon, 'Torah of Hesed', 165–8.

encouragement a woman needs as she gives birth, even when she is dying as a result. Women's voices and experiences are found in Genesis and in *Genesis Rabbah*; however, the patriarchal background of these texts influences interpretation of these experiences.

In *Gen. Rab.* 82:7, Rachel, the wife of Phinehas (1 Sam 4:19-22), and Michal, David's wife (2 Sam 6:23), are named as women who died during childbirth. The pregnant wife of Phinehas, daughter-in-law to Eli the priest, dies when news reaches her that the Philistines have captured the Ark of the Covenant and her father-in-law and husband are dead. This triggers an extremely painful labour. Like Rachel, she dies immediately afterwards, despite the attempts of those around her to comfort her with the announcement that she has borne a son. The connection with Michal is based on 2 Sam 6:23, which states that 'Michal the daughter of Saul had no child to (עד) the day of her death'. Whilst the biblical text implies that Michal died childless, the midrash reads the preposition עד, 'until', as indicating that she bore a child on the day she died, hence childbirth killed her.[21] This is justified by reference to 2 Sam 3:5, where David is said to have fathered his sixth son, Ithream, by his wife Eglah.[22] As an otherwise unknown figure, the rabbis identify Eglah with David's wife, Michal; just as Iscah was identified with Sarah in *Gen. Rab.* 38:14 (Gen 11:29). As proof, R. Judah explains that Michal became known as Eglah '[b]ecause she lowed [cried out] like a calf (*'eglah*) (lit. "heifer", עגלה) and died'. *Genesis Rabbah* 82:7 acknowledges that women die in childbirth, demonstrating this through examples taken from the Hebrew Bible. Through a careful reading of 2 Sam 6:23, Michal is included among these women and is identified with an otherwise unidentifiable wife of David, who bore him a child. The physical aspect of motherhood is considered in the midrash and the harsh realities of childbirth are recorded. As Fewell and Gunn conclude, 'Here lies the poignant trap of patriarchal motherhood: women face social death without children and physical death to bear children'.[23]

6.1.3. *Summary*

The midrashists consider the physical phenomena of pregnancy and childbirth as they interpret those biblical narratives where the birth of children is central to the emergence of Israel. The biblical text itself records some detail about childbearing and the rabbis do not quell the female

---

21. Cf. Freedman, 757.
22. Eglah's other mention is in the corresponding genealogy in 1 Chr 3:3.
23. Fewell and Gunn, *Gender, Power, & Promise*, 79.

perspective in their midrashic interpretations. Thus, the pain and potential trauma associated with childbirth, including death, appear in *Genesis Rabbah*. As Baskin and Exum note, the preservation of such material may often serve a patriarchal purpose. Yet, at times, the rabbis allowed women their own voice in the midrash and they acknowledged the difficulties that childbirth presented. Motherhood begins as a physical phenomenon in Genesis, as the matriarchs bear children to their patriarchal husbands; and the rabbis did not ignore this experience.

6.2. *Identity*

6.2.1. *Sons Are Identified through Their Mothers: By Name*

Both Genesis and *Genesis Rabbah* exhibit a 'narrative insistence on descent from the proper mother'.[24] Israel's covenant with God is constantly in view and '[a]s this promise will be passed from generation to generation, the crucial question becomes, How is a pure line of descent to be maintained?'[25] The mother plays an important role here, distinguishing the covenant son from his patriarchal father's other offspring.[26] Identity becomes an important theme in *Genesis Rabbah*, as the rabbis emphasise the legitimacy of mothers and their sons. These individuals become the founding figures of Israel; thus physical identity forms the basis for national identity.

Although children are often identified through their fathers in the Hebrew Bible,[27] there are instances of identification through the mother. For example, in Gen 21:9, Ishmael is designated 'the son of Hagar' (בן־הגר) and in Gen 24:15, Rebekah's father Bethuel is called 'son of Milcah, the wife of Nahor' (בן־מלכה אשת נחור). *Genesis Rabbah* contains similar phrases, such as Joseph's identification as 'the son of Rachel' (בנה שלרחל) twice in *Gen. Rab.* 84:18. Furthermore, it is often the female prerogative to name a child after birth. This is most clearly seen in Gen 29–30, where eleven of Jacob's sons and his only daughter, Dinah, are all named by Rachel and Leah.[28] Fuchs notes: 'The act of naming signifies a recognition of identity, an endowment of new essence and being, and it suggests

---

24. Exum, *Fragmented Women*, 112. See §3.5, 'Excursus: The Matrilineal Principle'.

25. Exum, *Fragmented Women*, 107.

26. See ibid., 107–17, 145–7.

27. E.g. 'Joshua, son of Nun' (Exod 33:11).

28. In Gen 35:18, Rachel names her final son Ben-Oni, 'son of my sorrow', but Jacob changes this to Benjamin. See Pardes, *Countertraditions*, 35.

the namer's authority'.[29] Mothers play a central role in determining the identity of their sons. The Bible and midrash testify that sons can be named by, and subsequently identified through, their mothers as well as their fathers.

Genesis Rabbah 53:7 explores the meaning of Isaac's name (Gen 21:3). Each letter of יצחק is shown to represent a number, and meaning is attributed to those values through *gematria*.[30] The *yôd* (י) has a numeric value of ten and the *ḥêt* (ח) is eight. These are linked with the Ten Commandments and the eighth day for circumcision. The other two letters, *ṣādē* (צ) and *qôp* (ק), have numerical values of ninety and one hundred, reflecting Abraham and Sarah's respective ages when Isaac was born. According to this midrashic interpretation, Isaac's name contains reference to two key markers of Israel's identity, alongside reference to both of his parents. These things are integral to Isaac's identity and highlight God's miraculous intervention to ensure the fulfilment of his covenant promises. Explicit reference is made to the mother, as well as the father, suggesting the equal importance of both parents in determining identity.

In *Gen. Rab.* 71:7, God chastises Jacob for showing anger towards his barren wife, Rachel (Gen 30:2): 'Said the Holy One, blessed be He, to him: "Is that a way to answer a woman in distress? By thy life, thy children will one day stand [in supplication] before her son [Joseph]."' The Lord sets Joseph apart from Jacob's other offspring by identifying him solely as Rachel's son.[31] Jacob has twelve sons and one daughter and so their different mothers become a useful way of distinguishing between them. As punishment for Jacob's harsh treatment of Rachel, the Lord elevates this woman's son above Jacob's other offspring. This foreshadows the events of Gen 42–50, where Joseph's authoritative position in Egypt puts

---

29. Fuchs, 'Literary Characterisation', 153. See also Simkins, 'Names and Naming', *EDB*, 944–6.

30. See §2.3, 'Common Midrashic Exegetical Techniques'.

31. Rachel only bears two children: Joseph and Benjamin. Freedman's 'cur. edd.', which cite Joseph's words from Gen 50:19, 'Am I in the place of God?', confirms that Joseph is referred to here. These are the exact words that Jacob says to Rachel when she complains about her barrenness (Gen 30:2). Joseph uses the words kindly, promising to care for his brothers following their father's death. In contrast with Joseph, Jacob uses these same words to relinquish any responsibility for Rachel's barrenness. This additional line in the cur. edd. uses a verbal connection between the two biblical passages. It brings the midrash to its logical conclusion, as Gen 50:19 shows Jacob's sons at the mercy of Joseph in Egypt (Freedman, 658).

his impoverished brothers at his mercy.[32] Hence, identity through the mother can determine the status of sons, a significant factor when issues of covenantal inheritance are at stake.

Maternal identification can have practical implications, determining a son's rank within the family.[33] A particularly acute example concerns the contrasting phrases 'the son of the bondmaid' and 'the son of the mistress'. Here, the legitimacy of the mother is used to contest the legitimacy of her children. *Genesis Rabbah* 84:7 discusses Gen 37:2, where 'Joseph brought a bad report of them (his brothers by Bilhah and Zilpah) to their father':

> R. Meir said: [He told Jacob]: Thy children are to be suspected of [eating] limbs torn from the living animals. R. Judah said: They insult the sons of the bondmaids (בני השפחות) [Bilhah and Zilpah] and call them slaves. R. Simeon said: They cast their eyes on the daughters of the country.

Three rabbis offer different explanations of Joseph's 'bad report'. Rabbi Judah's interpretation suggests the inferior nature of Joseph's brothers based on their maternal background. Bilhah and Zilpah are maidservants to Leah and Rachel; their sons are suggested to inherit this status. If this forms the basis of Joseph's derision, then by implication he must believe his own maternal line to confirm his superiority over his brothers.[34] Moreover, R. Judah's remark is juxtaposed with two suggestions that Joseph's 'bad report' linked Bilhah and Zilpah's sons with immoral acts. This implies that accusations of maternal inferiority are as damning as accusations of immorality.[35]

God refutes Joseph's three accusations:

> R. Judah b. R. Simon said: With respect to all three, *A just balance and scale are the Lord's* (Prov. XVI, 11). The Holy One, blessed be He, rebuked him [Joseph]: 'Thou didst say, "They are to be suspected of eating a limb torn from a living animal": by your life, even in the very act of wrongdoing they

---

32. As noted above, the cur. edd. concur.

33. Cf. Steinberg, who argues that Ishmael's inferiority through his mother only becomes an issue in relation to Isaac. Prior to Isaac's birth, Ishmael's maternal roots do not seem to influence his right to inherit (Steinberg, 'Alliance or Descent?', 46–7).

34. Exum (*Fragmented Women*, 131) notes that the status of the mothers of the tribal ancestors does determine their sons' 'relative ranking'. Cf. Jeansonne, *Women of Genesis*, 135 n. 22; Epstein, *Marriage Laws*, 54, 60–1.

35. There is perhaps also a perceived connection between an individual's background and their behaviour.

will slaughter ritually', as it says, *And they killed a he-goat* (Gen. XXXVII, 31). 'Thou didst say, "They insult the sons of the bondmaids and call them slaves"'—*Joseph was sold for a slave* (Ps. CV, 17). 'Thou didst say, "They cast their eyes upon the daughters of the land": I will incite a bear against thee'—*His master's wife cast her eye upon Joseph*, etc. (Gen. XXXIX, 7).[36]

Joseph's accusations are misguided, including his choice to deride his brothers for their mothers' status, and he will suffer the consequences of his actions.[37] Jacob's twelve sons become the founders of Israelite tribes, regardless of the status of their mothers.[38]

Earlier in Genesis, the mother's appropriateness is crucial, as only one son can inherit the covenant promises. As Abraham's firstborn, and for a time his only son, Ishmael looks set to inherit from the patriarch. Yet God intends for Sarah to become the first matriarch of Israel and the covenant son will descend from her (Gen 17:16).[39] Abraham attempts to promote Ishmael alone as his heir; God reiterates that it is Sarah who will bear the covenant son (Gen 17:18-19). *Genesis Rabbah* 47:5 discusses the juxtaposition of Sarah's promised motherhood (Gen 17:19) with the assurance that Ishmael too will become a great nation (Gen 17:20).

The midrash begins by studying the threefold blessing in Gen 17:20: 'I will bless him and make him fruitful and exceedingly numerous'. Rabbi Johanan in the name of R. Joshua b. Ḥananiah first argues that Isaac is the subject of these three blessings. The reference to Ishmael at the beginning of the verse confirms that God's blessings on him are still valid.[40] A second rabbi, R. Abba b. Kahana in R. Biryai's name, follows the most literal meaning of the text and argues that the blessings in Gen 17:20 refer to Ishmael. By the principle of *qal vahomer*, if Ishmael is blessed, the blessings on Isaac will be even greater, because God will establish his covenant with Sarah's son (Gen 17:21).[41] *Genesis Rabbah* 47:5 employs the distinction between 'the son of the bondmaid' (בן האמה)[42] and 'the son

36. 'Bear' has an allegorical meaning of 'temptation' (Jastrow, 282).

37. So also Neusner, 3:189.

38. Cf. Schneider, *Mothers of Promise*, 35, 102, 128–30; Exum, *Fragmented Women*, 131, 146.

39. Exum, *Fragmented Women*, 108.

40. See Gen 16:10, and Freedman, 401.

41. *Qal vahomer* is an '[a]rgument *a minori ad maius*, from the lighter (less significant) to the weightier (more significant) and vice versa' (Strack and Stemberger, *Introduction*, 18). See also ibid., 24.

42. Although using a different word for 'handmaid', the phrase בן האמה is a clear parallel to the בני השפחות from *Gen. Rab.* 84:7. Schneider (*Mothers of Promise*, 103–8, 127–34) discusses the terms אמה and שפחה, concluding that there is no obvious difference between them.

of the mistress' (בן הגבירה), identifying Isaac and Ishmael through their respective mothers. Isaac is thus shown to be the legitimate heir, whilst Ishmael's maternal background precludes his role as covenant son.[43] The mother plays a decisive role in determining the identity of the second patriarch.

The mother's significance is confirmed in the next part of the midrash, which portrays Sarah and Ishmael as the founding figures of their respective nations:

> R. Isaac said: It is written, *All these are the twelve tribes* (shibṭe) *of Israel* (Gen XLIX, 28). These were the descendants of the mistress [Sarah]. Yet did not Ishmael too produce twelve [princes]? In truth those were *nesi'im* (princes) in the same sense as you read, *As nesi'im* [E.V. *'vapours'*] *and wind*, etc (Prov. XXV, 14). But these were *maṭoth* (tribes) as you read, *Sworn are the* maṭoth [E.V. *'rods'*] *of the word. Selah* (Hab. III, 9).

Israel is identified through its founding mother and this nation's permanence is compared with the passing importance of Ishmael's descendants. Genesis 49:28 and Hab 3:9 contain the words שבט and מטה respectively. Both terms can mean either 'tribe' or 'rod', suggesting that 'these tribes (of Israel) would endure like rods that are planted'.[44] In comparison, Ishmael's descendants are identified as twelve 'princes' (נשיאים) in Gen 17:20. This word is linked with its homonym meaning 'mist' or 'vapour', a term which appears in Prov 25:14 and confirms the passing significance of Ishmael's offspring.[45] *Genesis Rabbah* 47:5 highlights the legitimacy of Sarah and Isaac's line. The identity of the mother, chosen by God to become the first matriarch of Israel, confirms that her son is worthy of inheriting the covenant promises from Abraham.

In Gen 21:10, Sarah declares to Abraham that: 'the son of this slave woman (בן האמה) shall not inherit along with my son Isaac'. Schneider remarks that in this chapter, 'the issue is not Hagar the person, or even the slave, but the mother. She (Sarah) refers to Ishmael as "the son of that slave", focusing on Hagar's status as it impacts her son (Gen 21:10).'[46] Sarah employs the phrase 'the son of the maidservant' and elevates her own son above Ishmael, just as the midrash distinguishes between 'the

---

43. Ibid., 118.

44. Freedman, n. 3 402. The language in Hab 3:9 is difficult, but implies the permanence of rods, a suggestion followed in the NRSV and JPS translations. See Francis I. Andersen, *Habakkuk: A New Translation with Intro and Commentary*, Anchor Bible 25 (New York: Doubleday, 2001), 320–5.

45. BDB, 672.

46. Schneider, *Mothers of Promise*, 118; cf. 34.

son of the maidservant' (בן האמה/שפחה) and 'the son of the mistress'
(בן הגבירה). In *Gen. Rab.* 53:11, R. Simeon discusses various interpretations of מצחק, 'playing'. This participle appears in Gen 21:10 as the cause
of Sarah's plea that Hagar and Ishmael be banished from her household.
He concludes:

> This term sport [mockery] refers to inheritance. For when our father Isaac
> was born all rejoiced, whereupon Ishmael said to them, 'You are fools, for
> I am the firstborn and I receive a double portion'. You may infer this from
> Sarah's protest to Abraham: FOR THE SON OF THIS BONDWOMAN
> SHALL NOT BE HEIR WITH MY SON, WITH ISAAC (XXI, 10). WITH
> MY SON, even if he were not Isaac; or WITH ISAAC, even if he were not
> my son: how much the more, WITH MY SON, WITH ISAAC!

In Gen 21:10, Sarah rejects Ishmael's claim to inheritance. Ishmael is 'the
son of the maidservant' and, as Sarah claims, 'my son, Isaac' is Abraham's
true heir. Ishmael believed that he was entitled to 'a double portion'; but
in actual fact, Isaac is doubly worthy to inherit from their father, both
because he is Isaac and because he is Sarah's son. Isaac's legitimacy as the
covenant son is connected to his mother's status as a matriarchal figure.[47]
Sarah highlights her own recognition of this and identity has wider consequences here as it determines correct inheritance.

One final passage should be mentioned, as it raises the notion of
identification through the mother to a national level. *Genesis Rabbah* 71:9
includes a rabbinic debate about Elijah's tribal affiliation. The culmination
of this passage reads:

> On one occasion our Rabbis were debating about him [Elijah], some main-
> taining that he belonged to the tribe of Gad, others, to the tribe of Benjamin.
> Whereupon he came and stood before them and said, 'Sirs, why do you
> debate about me? I am a descendant of Rachel (בני בניה שלרחל).'

The national significance of matriarchal motherhood is made clear, as
a central figure in Israel's history identifies himself through a founding
matriarch.

Maternal identity plays a central role in determining covenantal inheritance. The matriarchs are the legitimate mothers of Israel and their sons
are worthy of inheriting the covenant promises. This has implications
throughout history, as the matriarchs continue to influence Israel's identity.

---

47. Cf. Exum, *Fragmented Women*, 108; Trible, 'Ominous Beginnings', 45.

6.2.2. *Sons Are Identified through Their Mothers: By Traits*

Mothers define their sons in a number of different ways. For example, *Gen. Rab.* 84:6 draws numerous parallels between Jacob and Joseph. Three of these concern their mothers, Rebekah and Rachel, who were both initially barren, suffered during childbirth and bore two sons. The experiences of these mothers invite a comparison between their sons. Furthermore, *Gen. Rab.* 92:5 comments on Gen 43:30-33. Joseph, now an authoritative figure in Egypt, dines with his brothers, who do not recognise him. Joseph draws a connection between himself and Benjamin: 'Again, I have no mother and this youth [Benjamin] has no mother, for his mother died on giving birth to him: therefore he must come and sit near me'. Of course, the irony is that Joseph and Benjamin share a mother, Rachel. This will later be revealed to the brothers when Joseph explains that he is their lost brother (Gen 45). Events occurring in the matriarchs' lives provide a means for identifying and comparing their sons.

Beyond this, sons share physical and personality traits with their mothers. The last line of *Gen. Rab.* 91:6 paraphrases Gen 43:30, explaining that when Joseph's brothers brought Benjamin to Egypt, Joseph 'rejoiced, because he was like his mother (שהיה דומה לאמו)'.[48] The resemblance between Rachel and her children evokes strong emotion in Joseph, even when he has not seen Benjamin for many years. This is a physical indicator of identity and the correct lineage.

Genesis Rabbah 86:6 further explores the notion of family resemblance as it discusses the phrase: 'Joseph was beautiful of form (יפה־תאר)' (Gen 39:6):[49]

> R. Isaac commented: Throw a stick into the air and it falls back to its source.
> Thus, because it is written, *But Rachel was of beautiful form*, etc. (*ib.* XXIX, 17), therefore we read, AND JOSEPH WAS OF BEAUTIFUL FORM, etc.

The same phrase is used of Rachel and Joseph at different points in the biblical text and this is said to betray their relationship as mother and son. Joseph takes after his mother, inheriting her characteristics. The midrash highlights the repetition of יפה/ת־תאר in Gen 29:17 and 39:6. These verses contain an additional parallel phrase, describing both Rachel and Joseph as 'beautiful of appearance' (יפה/ת מראה). The rabbis assume their audience's familiarity with the biblical text and thus they do not list this

---

48. Cf. *Gen. Rab.* 53:6, Isaac looked like Abraham. The same root, דמי, is used there.

49. My translation.

second repetition. The midrash highlights that traits pass from mothers to sons. As beauty often signifies moral worthiness in biblical and midrashic texts, Rachel and Joseph's physical appearances may indicate their authoritative roles as founding figures of Israel.[50]

Genesis Rabbah 71:5 depicts Rachel and Leah at the head of their respective lineages, passing definitive characteristics to their descendants.[51] This midrash interprets Gen 29:35, where Leah praises (root ידה) God for providing her with another son, Judah. Developing this, the midrash claims that 'Leah made *hodiyah* her *métier* (lit. "seized the spindle of thanksgiving/confession", הודייה)' and biblical verses are provided to show Leah's descendants, Judah, David and Daniel, exhibiting the same characteristic.[52] *Genesis Rabbah* 71:5 then claims that 'Rachel made silence her *métier* (lit. "Rachel seized the spindle of silence")'. This is based on the midrashic tradition that Rachel did not divulge her father's plan to deceive Jacob, giving Leah to him in marriage instead of Rachel.[53] Biblical verses are then employed to show her descendants, Benjamin, Saul and Esther, exhibiting this trait.[54]

The matriarchs' roles as founding figures of Israel are emphasised as Leah and Rachel's central characteristics continue to be manifested among their descendants. The quotation of Job 36:7 at the beginning of this section: 'He does not withdraw his eyes from the righteous', suggests Leah and Rachel's own righteousness, but no further evaluation of these women, their descendants or their actions is offered. This midrash's presentation of familial identity and continuity throughout the generations may provide a basis for tribal, or even national, identities. Such issues continue to influence rabbinic understandings of Israelite and Jewish identity, as the rabbis themselves are descendants of the patriarchs and matriarchs.

---

50. Moses is depicted as beautiful in the Bible. See Exod 34:29-35; Acts 7:20, Heb 11:23. Williams comments: 'The words *yapeh* (fair, beautiful) and *yopi* (beauty) are never used to describe someone who is not favored by the God of Israel, no matter how desirable he or she may seem to be otherwise (e.g., Delilah, Jezebel, Saul; in general, the *zarâ* in Proverbs)'. James G. Williams, 'The Beautiful and the Barren: Conventions in Biblical Type-Scenes', *Journal for the Study of the Old Testament* 17 (1980): 116. See also Rabow, *Lost Matriarch*, 35.

51. Cf. §3.5, 'Excursus: The Matrilineal Principle'.

52. Gen 38:26 (this does not use the root ידי, but the verb there, נכר, suggests recognition or acknowledgement; BDB, 647–8); Ps 136:1; Dan 2:23. The verb ידה can mean thanksgiving or confession; the biblical verses cited employ both meanings.

53. See e.g. *Gen. Rab.* 73:4; *Lam. Rab.* Proem 24. On the latter, which expands on the wedding night, see Rabow, *Lost Matriarch*, 54–6.

54. Exod 28:20; 1 Sam 10:16; Est 2:10.

6.2.3. *Summary*

Genesis Rabbah demonstrates the importance of identity through the mother. Having the correct mother is essential because descendants inherit various attributes from her. Familial identity forms the basis of Israel's identity as the nation emerges from the matriarchs, patriarchs and their offspring. Sons may be identified through the names of their mothers and this can have implications for a child's position within the family, especially when deciding issues of inheritance. Most notably, *Genesis Rabbah* contains passages where a distinction is made between 'the son of the mistress' and 'the son of the maidservant' (*Gen. Rab.* 47:5; 53:11; 84:7). Physical features and personality traits are also inherited from mothers, a notion made clear, for example, in *Gen. Rab* 71:5, which draws connections between Leah and her descendants and Rachel and her descendants. Identity through the mother is therefore a significant issue in Genesis and in *Genesis Rabbah*.

6.3. *Family Dynamics*

6.3.1. *Husbands' Respect for Their Wives as Mothers*

Genesis 12–50 recounts the history of a particular family, whose members became the ancestors of Israel. The biblical text builds up a picture of life in the ancestral family, portraying the relationships between husbands and wives, parents and children, and between siblings.[55] The rabbinic interpreters interpreted and supplemented this material in their midrashic explorations of Genesis. Women were expected to bear children, and thus their role as mothers played a significant part in determining their position within the family.[56] Motherhood engenders respect and the midrash portrays husbands and sons responding positively to mothers.

---

55. Petersen ('Family Values', 5–23) argues that Gen is concerned with family. He describes a notable shift in Exod 1 from stories about the family to stories about the nation (pp. 7–11). See also Miriam Peskowitz, 'Family/ies in Antiquity: Evidence from Tannaitic Literature and Roman Galilean Architecture', in *The Jewish Family in Antiquity*, ed. Shaye J. D. Cohen, Brown Judaic Studies 289 (Atlanta: Scholars Press, 1993), 9–36.

56. Cf. Ruth 4:11, and §5.1, 'The Anguish of Barrenness'. In Gen 24:60, Rebekah's heathen family bless her, praying that she will become fruitful. This suggests that motherhood was a concern throughout the ancient world. Callaway (*Sing, O Barren One*, 13) notes that fertility is a repeated theme in ancient Near Eastern literature.

Genesis Rabbah offers several pericopae demonstrating the respect that husbands have for their wives as mothers. *Genesis Rabbah* 98:20 explores the meaning of Jacob's 'blessings of the breasts and of the womb', part of his deathbed blessing on Joseph (Gen 49:25). Rabbi Luliani b. Turin in the name of R. Isaac suggests this this phrase refers to cattle, whose breasts and wombs are found next to each other. Rabbi Abba b. Zutra offers an alternate explanation:

> R. Abba b. Zuṭra said: Go forth and see how much Jacob loved Rachel. Even when he came to bless her son, he treated him as secondary to her, saying: BLESSINGS OF THE BREASTS, AND OF THE WOMB, which means, Blessed be the breasts that suckled such and the womb whence issued such.

Jacob demonstrates his love and respect for Rachel, blessing the parts of her body that enabled her to bear and nurse Joseph. This blessing elevates the mother above her son, celebrating her maternal attributes.[57] Chapman argues that the phrase 'breasts and womb', appearing several times in the Bible, 'suggest[s] a two-stage maternally focused fashioning process of an infant that begins in the womb and is completed at the breast'.[58] This process of bearing and raising children, especially sons, is necessary in the Bible for securing lines of inheritance. Motherhood is to be valued and the midrash portrays a patriarchal husband's recognition of this. In Genesis, the emergence of Israel depends on women becoming mothers and this helps to explain the respect afforded the matriarchs in *Genesis Rabbah*.

Thus, it appears that 'a woman's primary (if not entire) significance lies in her role as wife, mother, and homemaker'; and the rabbis praised and respected women for this.[59] *Genesis Rabbah* 73:2 establishes Rachel's fulfilment of these roles. The midrash begins by citing Ps 98:3: 'He has remembered his steadfast love (חסד) and faithfulness (אמונתה) to the house of Israel. All the ends of the earth have seen the victory of our God'. This verse is said to refer to Abraham and Jacob, based on similar terminology found in Ps 98:3 and Mic 7:20: 'You shall show faithfulness (אמת)[60] to Jacob and unswerving loyalty (חסד) to Abraham'. The midrash clarifies that in Ps 98:3, Israel is the patriarch rather than the nation and this leads to the question: 'Who was the "*house*" (בית) of our ancestor

---

57. Cf. the positive rabbinic attitudes to their own mothers. See Eliezer Berkovits, *Jewish Women in Time and Torah* (Hoboken: Ktav, 1990), 44.

58. Chapman, 'Breast Milk', 25. Other occurrences of the phrase mentioned by Chapman are Ps 22:10-12; Isa 7:14-16; 28:9-10. Cf. Luke 11:27.

59. Bronner, *From Eve to Esther*, 33. Cf. Wegner, *Chattel or Person?*, 5–6.

60. BDB suggests this is a contracted version of אמנת (BDB, 54).

Jacob?' The answer is Rachel, as she alone is referred to as 'Jacob's wife' in the biblical text.[61]

Baskin and Bronner note that in rabbinic literature, the term 'house' is used to refer to a woman's domestic role as 'a vessel for the bearing and nurturing of children', who 'will, in marriage, build the home'.[62] Referring to Rachel as 'the house of Israel' draws together her roles as wife and mother. This coheres with Gen 46:19, where Rachel is designated 'Jacob's wife'. This verse appears in a genealogy detailing Jacob's descendants through each of his different wives (Gen 46:8-27). As such, the verse emphasises Rachel's role as wife in the context of her motherhood. This suggests Rachel's primacy as a wife, even whilst it provides no specific information about her relationship with her husband.

To finish, *Gen. Rab.* 73:2 offers 'another interpretation' (ד"א, דבר אחר) of Ps 98:3, citing it alongside Gen 30:22.[63] A linguistic connection is established between these two biblical verses, as God is the subject of the verb זכר, 'to remember', in each one. This connection is strengthened by drawing on the now-established notion of Rachel as 'the house of Israel': 'Another interpretation: *"He hath remembered His mercy and His faithfulness toward the house of Israel"* alludes to, AND GOD REMEMBERED RACHEL, AND GOD HEARKENED TO HER'. Psalm 98:3 is understood to be fulfilled by the reversal of Rachel's barrenness in Gen 30:22. This final interpretation supports the preceding argument, highlighting Rachel's significance for Israel.[64] Far from signalling a position of subordination, the reference to Rachel as 'the house of Israel' indicates her prominent position in the ancestral family and confirms God's choice of this woman as a matriarch.

Genesis Rabbah 71:2 demonstrates the possibility for a drastic change in a husband's attitude towards his wife once she has assumed a maternal role. This midrash deals with the biblical statement, 'Leah was hated'

61. Rachel is called אשת יעקב (Gen 46:19). This is the only time Jacob's name appears next to the word 'wife'. Berkovits comments: 'the phrase "the house of Jacob" is usually interpreted as referring to the women' (Berkovits, *Jewish Women*, 13). See also Charlotte Elisheva Fonrobert, *Menstrual Purity: Rabbinic and Christian Reconstructions of Biblical Gender*, Contraversions: Jews and Other Differences (Stanford: Stanford University Press, 2000), 40–67; Baskin, *Midrashic Women*, 190 n. 25.

62. E.g. *b. Šabb.* 118b. Baskin, *Midrashic Women*, 18; Bronner, *From Eve to Esther*, 30. See also Baskin, *Midrashic Women*, 88, 96; Jastrow, 167–8.

63. For דבר אחר, see Jastrow, 41; Strack and Stemberger, *Introduction*, 240.

64. Neusner argues that this second interpretation is a condensed version of the first (Neusner, 3:64).

(Gen 29:31). Leah posed a particular problem for the rabbis. She was one of the founding matriarchs of Israel, giving birth to several tribal ancestors and certainly a much greater number than her sister, Rachel. Yet she is shunned in the biblical text, neglected by her husband and forced into rivalry with her younger sister, competing for Jacob's love and the chance to bear his sons (Gen 29–33).[65] As Rabow comments: '[Leah's] life is defined by a seemingly unending sibling rivalry over love, power, and status'.[66] *Genesis Rabbah* 71:2 begins by citing Ps 145:14, 'The LORD upholds all who are falling, and raises up all who are bowed down', arguing that this applies to barren women, whose position in their household improves when they finally bear children. Leah is biblical proof of this: at first she was 'hated' (Gen 29:31), but ultimately motherhood offered her the respect and appreciation that she deserved, especially from Jacob.[67]

The following section of the midrash further explores this change in Leah's status. The midrash first offers various explanations of the statement: 'Leah was hated' (Gen 29:31):

> AND THE LORD SAW THAT LEAH WAS HATED. This means that she acted like those who are hated. [Another interpretation]: She was bespoken for an enemy, for such was the arrangement, that the elder son [Esau] should marry the elder daughter [Leah], and the younger son [Jacob] the younger daughter [Rachel], but she wept and prayed, 'May it be Thy will that I do not fall to the lot of the wicked Esau'. R. Huna said: Great is prayer, that it annulled the decree; moreover she took precedence of her sister.

The rabbis try to explain the use of such strongly emotive language in the biblical text; in so doing they simultaneously undermine negative attitudes towards this matriarch. In particular, Leah weeps concerning her betrothal to the wicked Esau and R. Huna argues that Leah's piety ensures that she becomes a mother before her sister.

The midrash lists groups of people who hated Leah and women are said to deride Leah:

65. Sarna argues that 'hated' actually refers to 'a relative degree of preference' compared with a wife who is 'beloved' (Sarna, *JPS: Genesis*, 206). Rabow offers various possible nuances of this term (Rabow, *Lost Matriarch*, 72–3).

66. Rabow, *Lost Matriarch*, 3; cf. 10. Rabow (p. 179) suggests that this rivalry continues beyond Leah and Rachel's deaths, e.g. Gen 37–50, where Joseph is largely at odds with his brothers.

67. See §5.2.2, 'God's Support of the Disadvantaged, Especially Barren Women'; §5.3.2, 'The Reversal of Barrenness and Its Consequences'.

All hated [i.e. abused] her: sea-travellers abused her, land-travellers abused her, and even the women behind the beams abused her, saying: 'This Leah leads a double life (lit. 'her secret life is not like her public life'): she pretends to be righteous, yet it is not so, for if she were righteous, would she have deceived her sister! (*Gen. Rab.* 71:2)

Some of the language is almost identical to that found in *Gen. Rab.* 45:4, where Hagar tries to discredit Sarah's righteousness on the basis of her continued barrenness. That accusation was immediately falsified, as it appears in the midrash after the worthiness of the matriarchs is affirmed.[68] Similarly, in *Gen. Rab.* 71:2, the rabbis record people's hatred of Leah and yet, these individuals are mistaken because Leah is a pious and righteous woman. In this way, Leah's matriarchy and motherhood are justified. This woman is a central figure in the early history of Israel, even if her contemporaries failed to notice.

As well as justifying Leah's character, highlighting her piety and her undeserved vilification, the presentation of people's hatred of Leah softens understandings of Jacob's relationship with his first wife. The biblical text suggests that whilst Jacob adored Rachel, he did not offer Leah the same love or respect (e.g. Gen 29:18-34). This could suggest Jacob to be a callous, coldhearted husband, but by listing all those who hated Leah, the rabbinic interpreters show that he mirrored the attitudes of the rest of society. Jacob's lack of affection for Leah in Genesis still made the rabbis uncomfortable. To them, it was inconceivable that the patriarch would undervalue his matriarchal wife when she plays such an important role in the history of Israel. Motherhood, the central characteristic of Israel's matriarchs, proves pivotal in Jacob and Leah's marital relationship. *Genesis Rabbah* 71:2 explains:

R. Judah b. R. Simon and R. Ḥanan said in the name of of R. Samuel b. R. Isaac: When the Patriarch (lit. 'our father') Jacob saw how Leah deceived him by pretending to be her sister, he determined to divorce her.[69] But as soon as the Holy One, blessed be He, visited her with children he exclaimed, 'Shall I divorce the mother of these children!' Eventually he

68. See §3.6.3.4, '"Why were the Matriarchs Made Barren?" (ולמה נתעקרו אמהות)'. *Gen. Rab.* 45:4 contains the phrase 'she appears righteous but she is not' (נראת צדקת ואינה); *Gen. Rab.* 71:2 has: 'she appears righteous but she is not righteous' (נראת צדקת ואינה צדקה).

69. This refers to the deception of Jacob on his wedding night, when Laban gave him Leah as a wife instead of Rachel (Gen 29:23-26). Midrash comments extensively. See Rabow, *Lost Matriarch*, 45–65.

gave thanks for her, as it says, *And Israel bowed down* [in thanksgiving] *for the bed's head* (Gen. XLVII, 31): who was the head of our father Jacob's bed? surely Leah.[70]

Leah's role as the mother of Jacob's children, and therefore as the mother of several Israelite tribes, ultimately guarantees her husband's respect for her.[71]

The midrash reinterprets the phrase from Gen 47:31 in relation to Leah's role as a mother. Jastrow notes that an extended meaning of the Hebrew term, מטה, 'bed', is 'family, offspring'.[72] As Jacob's most fruitful wife, Leah can legitimately be described as the 'head of his family'. Genesis 47:31 is said to contain reference to Leah and, most importantly, to record a dramatic change in Jacob's opinion of her. Furthermore, this demonstrates the midrash's opening claim, made in relation to Ps 145:14, that the situation of barren women drastically improves after they become mothers.[73] In the biblical text, 'Leah wants Jacob's love but never gains it';[74] the midrash ensures that Leah receives the respect she deserves as an ancestress of Israel.[75] Re-examining Jacob's relationship with Leah allows the rabbis to uncover her patriarchal husband's acknowledgement of her significance. Thus, whilst Rabow suggests that 'we might find such a resolution to be a too-convenient invention that seems wholly unsubstantiated in the text', this pericope reveals the rabbis' respect for Leah and the matriarchs.[76]

The pericopae addressed here all concern Jacob and his wives. In the third patriarchal generation, the tribal ancestors of Israel are born and the nation emerges. Yet this generation is marked by intense sibling rivalry and a husband's preference for one woman above his other wives.[77] In *Genesis Rabbah*, the rabbis demonstrate that women are most respected

---

70. A similar pericope appears in *Gen. Rab.* 96 (MSV) (Freedman, 931).

71. See Baskin, *Midrashic Women*, 147.

72. Jastrow, 765. Moreover, Schneider sees Leah as Jacob's 'primary wife' (Schneider, *Mothers of Promise*, 65–6, 76, 78). Cf. Rabow, *Lost Matriarch*, 14, 182.

73. See §5.3.2, 'The Reversal of Barrenness and Its Consequences'.

74. Schneider, *Mothers of Promise*, 99.

75. See Rabow, *Lost Matriarch*.

76. Ibid., 190; cf. 185.

77. See Callaway, *Sing, O Barren One*, 25–6; Westermann, *Genesis 12–36*, 236–7. Rabow notes that according to Lev 18:18, a man cannot marry two sisters. The rabbis try to explain why Jacob breaks this Torah law (Rabow, *Lost Matriarch*, 69–70).

by their husbands when they bear children, fulfilling both their physically and socially ordained roles.[78] Thus, in *Genesis Rabbah,* even Leah is redeemed in Jacob's eyes through her role as a mother.

6.3.2. *Sons' Respect for Their Mothers*

Although mothers protect and promote their sons in Genesis, little information is provided about sons' attitudes and behaviour towards their mothers.[79] The midrash addresses this gap in the biblical portrayal of family dynamics, highlighting the respect that sons have for the women who bore and nurtured them. In *Gen. Rab.* 84:10, the rabbis interpret Joseph's dream about the sheaves (Gen 37:7). R. Aḥa interprets Joseph's words:

> Ye will hide (*ha-'alim*) (lit. 'are destined to conceal', להעלים) the truth about me from our father and assert, *An evil beast hath devoured him* (Gen 37:33); yet what will stand me in good stead (lit. 'what is rising [קאים] for me')? My mother's silence.

In the dream recounted in Gen 37:7, 'my (Joseph's) sheaf rose (קמה אלמתי)' whilst his brothers' sheaves showed deference to it. In *Gen. Rab.* 84:10, the Hiphil of עלם, 'to conceal', is employed as a play on the word אלמה, 'sheaf'.[80] The sheaf that arises is said to be Rachel's silence, which will protect Joseph from the lies his brothers tell about his death. As *Gen. Rab.* 71:5 notes, silence becomes Rachel's defining characteristic after she allows Laban to deceive Jacob, giving him Leah in marriage instead of her sister (Gen 29:23-26).[81] In this pericope, Joseph recognises the value of Rachel's maternal protection. By this point in Genesis, Rachel has already died giving birth to Benjamin (Gen 35:18). Rabbi Aḥa's interpretation thus suggests the enduring power of matriarchal motherhood. *Genesis Rabbah* 84:10 develops the relationship between a mother and her son, showing Joseph's respect for his mother.

---

78. See e.g. Baskin, *Midrashic Women*, 1–2, 17. Baskin argues that the rabbis praised women for fulfilling social and domestic roles, but suggests that this contributes to the subjugation of women within rabbinic society (ibid., 118).

79. Rabow, *Lost Matriarch*, 79. Jacob and Rebekah collude in the deception of Isaac (Gen 27); Reuben brings mandrakes to Leah (Gen 30:14); Joseph displays emotion after seeing his mother's other son, Benjamin, for the first time in many years (Gen 43:29-30). Cf. §6.4, 'Maternal Protection of the Covenant Son'.

80. See BDB, 761; Jastrow, 1084.

81. See §6.2.2, 'Sons Are Identified Through Their Mothers: By Traits'.

Later in *Genesis Rabbah*, Joseph reciprocates the protection that his mother affords him. When Jacob and Esau reunite after many years, Joseph is said to protect Rachel from the wickedness of Esau. *Genesis Rabbah* 78:10 and 90:4 provide almost identical treatments of Gen 33:6-7.[82] These verses explain that when greeting Esau, each of Jacob's four wives steps forward in turn with her sons. Regarding the handmaids and Leah, the woman is mentioned before her children; but in Rachel's case, Joseph is mentioned first:

> In the case of all the others it states, THEN THE HANDMAIDS CAME NEAR, THEY AND THEIR CHILDREN CAME NEAR, etc. (Gen 33:7). But in the case of Joseph it is written, AND AFTER CAME JOSEPH NEAR AND RACHEL, AND THEY BOWED DOWN (*ib.*). The fact is that Joseph said: 'This wicked man has an aspiring eye: let him not look at my mother', whereupon he drew himself up to his full height and covered her.

Joseph's actions suggest respect for his mother, developing the mother–son relationship beyond the brief details offered in the biblical text.

Genesis Rabbah 78:10 and 90:4 both conclude with reference to Jacob's blessing on Joseph at the end of Genesis: 'Joseph is a fruitful bough, a fruitful bough by a spring' (Gen 49:22). Rabbi Berekiah in the name of R. Simon repoints the phrase עֲלֵי־עָיִן, 'beside a spring', as עָלַי־עַיִן, 'it is for Me (*'alay*) to reward thee for that eye'. Thus, Jacob's blessing is interpreted as containing a divine promise to recompense Joseph for his action in protecting Rachel from Esau's dangerous eyes. As such, the midrash affirms the praiseworthiness of Joseph's attitude towards his mother.

The popularity of this tradition is confirmed by a third reference to Joseph's protection of Rachel. *Genesis Rabbah* 98:18 provides a shortened version of the pericope as it interprets Gen 49:22:

> R. Abun said: BEN PORATH means, Thou didst wax great; BEN PORATH, thou didst wax great, O Joseph; BEN PORATH JOSEPH: thou didst enlarge [thy stature], O Joseph. Of all the others it is written, *Then the handmaids came near*, etc. (Gen. XXXIII, 17). It was that which he said to him: It is for me to reward thee for that eye.[83]

---

82. Differences between the two passages are negligible.

83. This interpretation reads עין of the biblical text as 'eye' rather than 'spring' (see BDB, 744–5). The latter is the more commonly accepted translation for this verse; see NRSV; JPS.

This pericope shares some of its language with *Gen. Rab.* 78:10 and 90:4; the same biblical texts (Gen 33:6 and 49:22) also appear in all three pericopae. *Genesis Rabbah* 98:18 does not make explicit reference to Rachel, but the rabbis assume their audience's familiarity with the fuller tradition. Joseph is the focus of these passages and in particular of *Gen. Rab.* 98:18, which does not even mention Rachel. However, the divine praise of Joseph's actions and the repetition of this pericope within *Genesis Rabbah* suggest that the rabbis believed it was right to protect mothers, the women who raise children through their earliest and most vulnerable years. Motherhood affects sons' attitudes towards their mothers as well as husbands' attitudes towards their wives.

Genesis Rabbah 48:16 may be compared to the above tradition regarding Joseph's protection of Rachel. The midrash attempts to explain the mysterious phrase in Gen 18:10, 'he was behind him':[84]

> AND HE SAID: I WILL CERTAINLY RETURN UNTO THEE WHEN THE SEASON COMETH ROUND...AND SARAH HEARD IN THE TENT DOOR, AND HE WAS BEHIND HIM (והוא אחריו) (XVIII, 10). This refers to Ishmael: AND HE WAS BEHIND HIM, so that they [the angel and Sarah] should not be alone (lit. 'on account of a private meeting' [ייחוד]).

The Hebrew masculine singular pronoun הוא, 'he', is probably interpreted here as referring to a feminine subject, 'she', meaning Sarah: '*she* was behind him'.[85] Ishmael is identified as the subject of the male pronoun and the reason for his presence is explained. The Hebrew noun, ייחוד, deriving from the verb יחד, 'to unite', indicates a private meeting, particularly between a man and a woman. Such a meeting is improper when these individuals are not married, so Ishmael's presence safeguards Sarah's reputation and dignity.[86]

84. My translation.

85. In the Pentateuch, the consonants of the masculine pronoun הוא, 'he', are sometimes written when a feminine subject is referred to. This is called *Q're perpetuum*. Gen 3:20 is one example, as הוא is pointed with the vowel of the feminine pronoun (הִיא), so it appears in the text as הִוא. See BDB, 214–16. The MT does not mark Gen 18:10 as a *Q're perpetuum* but this midrash clearly interprets it as such. See Freedman, n. 3 416. The antiquity of this interpretation is confirmed by its attestation also in Sam (see *BHS* apparatus to Gen 18:10).

86. For ייחוד, see Jastrow, 573; Bronner, *From Eve to Esther*, 6. Cf. Berkovits, *Jewish Women*, 16; Bar-Ilan, *Some Jewish Women*, 152–3; Miriam B. Peskowitz, *Spinning Fantasies: Rabbis, Gender, and History* (Berkeley: University of California Press, 1997), 55–6; Biale, *Women and Jewish Law*, 190.

As Abraham stands outside the tent, Ishmael is the remaining male family member and the responsibility falls to him to stay with Sarah. Neusner concludes that: 'Ishmael had stayed there to protect his mother'.[87] He assumes a mother–son bond between Sarah and Ishmael, which is not otherwise suggested anywhere in *Genesis Rabbah*. Perhaps Ishmael's presence in the tent shows that although Sarah is not his birth mother, he respects Sarah for her maternal role within the ancestral family and wishes to protect her honour. This establishes a kind of familial unity which is not necessarily present in the biblical text.[88]

In the mandrake incident, the barren Rachel acquires aphrodisiacal mandrakes in return for allowing Leah to have sex with Jacob that night (Gen 30:14-16). The episode begins when Reuben 'found mandrakes in the field, and brought them to his mother Leah' (Gen 30:14). Schneider suggests that Reuben's actions reveal a 'positive relationship' with Leah, as he takes the mandrakes straight to her. Furthermore, Reuben 'indicate[s] that he understands his mother's situation in the family, especially in relation to Rachel, and he is trying to help' by providing her with an aphrodisiac.[89] *Genesis Rabbah* 72:2 develops this relationship, explaining that Reuben's action 'shows you how greatly he respected (היה כבוד) his mother, for he would not taste of them until he brought them to his mother'.[90] Reuben's complete respect for his mother is indicated by the use of the root כבד in the Piel, meaning 'to honour' or 'glorify'.[91] This same verb appears in the commandment to: 'Honour your father and your mother' (Exod 20:12; Deut 5:16). Reuben demonstrates the respect for one's parents that the Torah explicitly commands.

Reuben's respect for Leah is explored elsewhere in *Genesis Rabbah*. In Gen 35:22, 'Reuben went and lay with Bilhah his father's concubine; and Israel (Jacob) heard of it'. This verse was highly problematic for the

---

87. Neusner, 2:191.

88. In *Gen. Rab.* 84:11, Bilhah is said to have raised Joseph as her own son following Rachel's death.

89. Schneider, *Mothers of Promise*, 73. On mandrakes, see Walter E. Brown, 'Mandrake', *EDB*, 853. For the mandrake incident, see Pardes, *Countertraditions*, 66–7; Fewell and Gunn, *Gender, Power, & Promise*, 78; Jeansonne, *Women of Genesis*, 77–8; Schneider, *Mothers of Promise*, 70–3; Havrelock, 'Heroic Barrenness', 169; Byron, 'Childlessness and Ambiguity', 30–1; Rabow, *Lost Matriarch*, 101–5; Baskin, *Midrashic Women*, 148–9.

90. See Jeansonne, *Women of Genesis*, 79.

91. See BDB, 457–59; Jastrow, 606–7.

rabbis, as the Torah forbids sexual relations with the wife of one's father.[92] The only other mention of the incident is in Jacob's blessing on Reuben at the end of Genesis, where Jacob states: 'you shall no longer excel because you went onto your father's bed; then you defiled it—you went up onto my couch!' (Gen 49:4).[93] As Schneider remarks, 'the political aspect of Reuben's action' becomes apparent here, as his descendants' flourishing is curbed.[94] *Genesis Rabbah* 98:4 discusses this blessing (Gen 49:3-4). The midrash offers both positive and negative interpretations of the verses, focusing in particular on their connection to Reuben's encounter with Bilhah. Part of the midrash is a debate concerning Reuben's worthiness to judge others for engaging in sexual relations with their father's spouse (Deut 27:20), when he is accused of committing this sin himself.

The midrash reads:

> R. Abbahu—others say, R. Jacob in the name of R. Ḥiyya the elder, and R. Joshua b. Levi in the name of R. Simeon b. Yoḥai—said: We learned: He who is suspected of any offence, cannot act as judge or witness in a similar case [*m. Bek.* 4:10]. Now is it possible that he [Reuben] was one day to be one of the six tribes who would stand on Mount Ebal and proclaim, *Cursed be he that lieth* (שכב)[95] *with his father's wife* (Deut. XXVII, 20), and yet perpetuate this crime himself? The truth, however, is that he vindicated his mother's humiliation. For as long as Rachel lived her bed stood near that of the Patriarch Jacob; when Rachel died, Jacob took Bilhah's bed and placed it at the side of his. 'Is it not enough for my mother to be jealous during her sister's lifetime', he exclaimed, 'but must she also be so after her death!' Thereupon he went up and disarranged the beds.

According to the Mishnah law cited, Reuben's sexual encounter with Bilhah would prevent him from condemning others for the same sin. Yet, in Deut 27:13, Reuben's tribe is listed as one of six that can judge the Israelites for this and other transgressions.

92. See Deut 27:20; Lev 18:8. Schneider discusses the episode between Reuben and Bilhah in some detail (Schneider, *Mothers of Promise*, 133–5). See also Satlow, *Tasting the Dish*, 70–2; Rabow, *Lost Matriarch*, 168–70. For a discussion of biblical incest, see Epstein, *Marriage Laws*, 222–32; Biale, *Women and Jewish Law*, 179–83.
93. The Hebrew text reads עלה, third person masculine singular verb form. This should probably be emended to the second person singular form, עלתה, 'you went up', to fit with the rest of the verse. *BHS* apparatus notes that the LXX, Syriac and two of the Targums suggest such a reading.
94. Schneider, *Mothers of Promise*, 134.
95. The verb שכב is used in Gen 35:22.

The rabbinic interpreters listed offer an alternate explanation of Reuben's actions in Gen 35:22, exonerating him from the charge of having sexual relations with one of his father's wives. Jacob's poor treatment of Leah during Rachel's lifetime continues after Rachel's death. Not only did Jacob love Rachel more than her sister; he now privileges one of the handmaids above his first wife. This leads Reuben to defend his mother, preventing her continued subordination.[96] This becomes a further midrashic example of sons respecting their mothers, and it highlights Reuben's devotion to Leah. *Genesis Rabbah* 98:4 provides largely negative interpretations of Reuben's actions, confirming his sin; however, this one interpretation seeks to clear Reuben's name. Its use of Leah as a motivation for Reuben's actions demonstrates rabbinic respect for mothers.

6.3.3. *Summary*

In *Genesis Rabbah*, the rabbinic interpreters develop familial relationships far beyond the information given in Genesis. Most significantly, Leah receives some of the respect that she is denied in the biblical text; the rabbis portray Jacob's eventual recognition of her significance (*Gen. Rab.* 71:2) and develop Reuben's relationship with his mother (*Gen. Rab.* 72:2 and 98:4). The rabbis are motivated by their understanding of the matriarchs as the ancestresses of Israel. Hence, they portray the patriarchs and tribal ancestors demonstrating respect for these significant women. As Judith Baskin summarises,

> Rabbinic literature affirms that individual women, who are indispensable to reproduction and are required to provide essential family support services were not only necessary for the smooth functioning of everyday life in the present and for Jewish continuity in the future, but could also be cherished beings who were loved and protected by specific men.[97]

6.4. *Maternal Protection of the Covenant Son*

6.4.1. *The Role of Motherhood in Each Matriarch's Story*

Fuchs argues that 'Woman's parenthood in the biblical narrative is largely restricted to reproductive and protective functions'.[98] After the matriarchs have given birth, the second part of 'the matriarchal cycle', motherhood itself, comes into play. The matriarchs 'protect their sons and

---

96. So also Wenham, *Genesis 16–50*, 327; Sarna, *JPS: Genesis*, 244–5.
97. Baskin, *Midrashic Women*, 8; cf. 15, 43.
98. Fuchs, 'Literary Characterisation', 163. Cf. Baskin, *Midrashic Women*, 54.

promote their interests', working to ensure that the correct son inherits the covenant promises.[99] In this way, the divine intention for the continuation of the covenant is first enacted *upon* and then *by* the matriarchs.[100] The matriarchs assert their individuality as they act, often creatively, to protect their sons. The circumstances in each matriarchal generation differ. Each woman promotes her own son, but Sarah must promote Isaac above Ishmael, Hagar and Abraham's son; Rebekah must choose to protect Jacob above her other son, Esau; and in the final generation, where all of Jacob's sons become tribal ancestors of Israel, the rivalry between Rachel and Leah dominates the narrative.[101]

Exum argues that, in Genesis, the matriarchs are prevented from becoming fully rounded characters because the only actions narrated about them directly concern their sons.[102] Yet, she admits that 'as the plot of Genesis unfolds, the promises to Abraham do not pass automatically from Abraham to Isaac to Jacob; rather it is the matriarchs who see to it that the promise is passed on to the "right son" (that is, the rightful heir)'.[103] It is exactly this role that confirms the matriarchs' significance for the history of Israel. As Camp states: 'the roles of wife and mother also gave certain advantages to women that allowed them to exercise a less explicit, informal, but nonetheless systematic influence on their lives and the lives of those around them... To dismiss this...is to miss the point.'[104] In *Genesis Rabbah*, the rabbis portray the matriarchs' awareness of the covenant and their determination to ensure its correct continuation in accordance with the divine plan. As such, the matriarchs develop into independent figures in *Genesis Rabbah*, worthy of respect for their role in protecting the covenant.

---

99. Exum, *Fragmented Women*, 133. Exum argues that this reflects male assumptions about motherhood.

100. Cf. Jeansonne, *Women of Genesis*, 107.

101. Callaway, *Sing, O Barren One*, 25–9. Schneider (*Mothers of Promise*, 13, 68–9) suggests that Jacob's twelve sons do not necessarily all receive the covenant promises. Forsyth ('Sibling Rivalry', 453–510) offers a psychoanalytic analysis of sibling rivalry in Genesis, but disappointingly, does not discuss Rachel and Leah's rivalry.

102. Exum, *Fragmented Women*, 130. Cf. Ramon, 'Torah of Hesed', 166.

103. Exum, *Fragmented Women*, 130. Cf. ibid., 110, 146–7; Fewell and Gunn, *Gender, Power, & Promise*, 71.

104. Camp, *Wisdom and the Feminine*, 80. Pardes (*Countertraditions*, 75) notes that the extent of the mother's influence on her son's life determines how long she remains in the narrative after she has given birth. Many biblical mothers simply give birth and are not heard of again. So also Fewell and Gunn, *Gender, Power, & Promise*, 70–1.

6.4.2. *Sarah and Isaac*

Maternal protection of the covenant son is most critical in the first patriarchal generation, where it is necessary for Abraham and Sarah's long-awaited son to inherit the covenant promises as God intends (Gen 17:19).[105] Having overcome many obstacles to become a mother, Sarah is determined that her son will inherit from Abraham, and not Ishmael. Genesis 21, the scene of Isaac's weaning, provides the climax of the opposition between Sarah and Isaac, and Hagar and Ishmael. In Gen 21:9-10, Sarah tells Abraham to send Hagar and Ishmael away, after she 'saw the son of Hagar the Egyptian, whom she had borne to Abraham, playing (מצחק)'. Sarna suggests that 'He was either amusing himself or playing with Isaac'; whilst Wenham argues that 'it is dubious whether the piel of צחק will bear such an innocent interpretation'.[106] Schneider notes that the timing of Sarah's outburst may be as important as Ishmael's actions. Weaning marked the end of the most vulnerable stage of a child's life, when death was most likely.[107] After years of barrenness, Sarah gave birth to a son and she will now do all within her power to ensure that he is recognised as Abraham's legitimate heir.[108]

Genesis Rabbah 53:11, interpreting Gen 21:9-10, functions as a diatribe, demonstrating that Ishmael is unworthy to inherit the covenant promises. The meaning of the participle מצחק, 'playing', used to describe Ishmael's behaviour in Gen 21:9, forms the major part of the rabbinic interpretation.[109] Three rabbis offer different interpretations of the verb צחק, based on its usage in various biblical verses:

> Thus R. Akiba lectured: AND SARAH SAW THE SON OF HAGAR THE EGYPTIAN, WHOM SHE HAD BORNE UNTO ABRAHAM, MAKING SPORT. Now MAKING SPORT refers to nought else but immorality, as in

---

105. Jeansonne, *Women of Genesis*, 28.

106. Sarna, *JPS: Genesis*, 146; Wenham, *Genesis 16–50*, 82. Wenham compares usage here to the negative use of the verb in Exod 32:6 and Judg 16:25. Teubal suggests that: 'Ishmael's mocking action must have had a religious connotation' or Sarah would not have banished him (Savina J. Teubal, 'Sarah and Hagar: Matriarchs and Visionaries', in Brenner, ed., *A Feminist Companion to Genesis*, 236). Cf. Trible, 'Ominous Beginnings', 44.

107. Schneider, *Mothers of Promise*, 33–4. Also Wenham, *Genesis 16–50*, 81; Sarna, *JPS: Genesis*, 146.

108. Schneider, *Mothers of Promise*, 40; Baskin, *Midrashic Women*, 150. On breastfeeding, see Chapman, 'Breast Milk'; Mayer I. Gruber, 'Breast-Feeding Practices in Ancient Israel and in Old Babylonian Mesopotamia', *Journal of the Near Eastern Society* 19 (1989): 61–83.

109. Cf. Wenham, *Genesis 16–50*, 82.

the verse, *The Hebrew servant, whom thou hast brought unto us, came in unto me to* make sport (לצחק) *of me* (Gen. XXIX, 17). Thus this teaches that Sarah saw Ishmael ravish maidens, seduce married women and dishonour them. R. Ishmael taught: This term SPORT refers to idolatry (עבודה זרע), as in the verse, *And rose up to* make sport (לצחק) (Ex. XXXII, 6).[110] This teaches that Sarah saw Ishmael build altars, catch locusts, and sacrifice them. R. Eleazar said: The term sport refers to bloodshed, as in the verse, *Let the young men, I pray thee, arise and* sport (ישחקו)[111] *before us* (II Sam. II, 14). R. 'Azariah said in R. Levi's name: Ishmael said to Isaac, 'Let us go and see our portions in the field; then Ishmael would take a bow and arrows and shoot them in Isaac's direction, whilst pretending to be playing. Thus it is written, *As a madman who casteth fire-brands, arrows, and death; so is the man that deceiveth his neighbour, and saith: Am not I in sport* (משחק) (Prov. XXII, 18 f.)?

The midrash thus employs the exegetical technique of *gezerah shawah*, as the occurrence of the root צחק, 'to laugh', in other contexts is used to elucidate its unclear usage here.[112]

The verb צחק is provided with several negative connotations and Ishmael is associated with wickedness and immorality. With no definitive interpretation given of Ishmael's action in Gen 21:9, the reader is inclined to associate him with all of these actions.[113] The midrash supports Sarah's expulsion of Hagar and Ishmael, as Abraham's eldest son proves his unworthiness. Sarah recognises Ishmael's inappropriate behaviour and as 'Abraham has shown no intention of carrying out the Deity's wish for Isaac to inherit', she must act to ensure that Ishmael loses the inheritance.[114]

To the non-rabbinical eye, this midrash paints a picture of an immoral Ishmael; however, for the rabbis, this list of sins was far more horrifying. As *b. Sanh.* 74a explains, a Jew may break almost any Torah command-ment to avoid death, but even then, idolatry, sexual sin and murder must never be committed. It is no coincidence that Ishmael is linked with exactly these sins in the midrash.[115] As Satlow remarks, this 'catalogue was utilised as a whole, a trope, whose force was to designate absolute evil'.[116] The rabbis depicted the ancestors obeying Torah law, even though they lived centuries before the revelation at Sinai. Ishmael's actions are

---

110. This is part of the Golden Calf episode (Exod 32).
111. שחק is cognate with צחק (BDB, 965–6; Jastrow, 1550).
112. See §2.3, 'Common Midrashic Exegetical Techniques'.
113. Cf. Wenham, *Genesis 16–50*, 82.
114. Schneider, *Mothers of Promise*, 34. Cf. Exum, *Fragmented Women*, 108.
115. See Satlow, *Tasting the Dish*, 147.
116. Ibid., 324.

unforgivable, flouting central Jewish laws. *Genesis Rabbah* 53:11 therefore explains and justifies Sarah's expulsion of Ishmael from Abraham's
household.[117]

Ishmael does not simply disobey the as yet unrevealed law of God; he
also commits sins similar to those living before him. There are several
allusions in this midrash to the primeval narratives from Gen 1–11.
Genesis Rabbah 53:11 suggests that Ishmael commits 'uncovering of
nakedness' (גלוי עריות). This language first appears in Gen 9, when Canaan
sees the drunken Noah lying naked in his tent. The suggestion that מצחק
in Gen 21:9 refers to 'pourings out of blood' (שפיכות דמים) recalls the
warning of Gen 9:6: 'Whoever sheds (שפך) the blood of a human, by
a human shall that person's blood be shed (ישפך)'. Lastly, there is an
allusion to the Cain and Abel narrative. Rabbi Azariah in the name of
R. Levi depicts Ishmael luring Isaac into the fields and attempting to kill
him. This is reminiscent of Cain killing Abel in Gen 4:8.

In this midrash, interpretations of the participle מצחק, 'playing', associate Ishmael with the sins of those who come both before and after him,
in the primeval age and in Israel's later history. He neither learns from
the mistakes of the past nor anticipates some of Israel's most significant
commandments. Sarah's rejection of Ishmael is therefore 'rationalised
by the rabbis', as she perceives the inappropriateness of his character.[118] Sarah's maternal protection and promotion of Isaac above Ishmael
ensures that the covenant pass on to the correct son.

In the final part of this midrash, R. Simeon b. Yoḥai offers an alternate
interpretation of the verb מצחק, 'playing'. He claims:

> This term sport [mockery] refers to inheritance. For when our father Isaac
> was born all rejoiced, whereupon Ishmael said to them, 'You are fools, for I
> am the firstborn and I receive a double portion'.

Ishmael is both arrogant and ignorant. He assumes that, as firstborn
son, he will inherit from Abraham; yet he does not understand that the
covenant promises must pass to the correct son. His brother, Isaac, is
a source of joy, a sentiment confirming Sarah's proclamation in Gen
21:6, that 'everyone who hears (about Isaac's birth) will laugh with
me'. Sarah immediately nullifies Ishmael's claims for a 'double portion'
by presenting Isaac as doubly worthy to inherit from Abraham: he is

both Isaac and Sarah's son.[119] Far from portraying Sarah as 'cold and unfeeling', the rabbis demonstrate the necessity of Hagar and Ishmael's expulsion from the household.[120]

Genesis Rabbah 53:13 presents a comprehensive case against Ishmael inheriting the covenant promises from Abraham. Whether this relates to his immoral behaviour as seen by Sarah, or to Ishmael's misunderstanding of his role within the ancient family, Ishmael is not the chosen covenant son. Sarah protects Isaac's claim to inheritance, demonstrating that matriarchal protection of the covenant son extends beyond nursing and raising the child. Sarah thus protects God's covenant with Abraham.

Genesis Rabbah 53:13 depicts Sarah's continued protection of Isaac against Ishmael, even when the latter has been removed from Abraham's household. The midrash interprets Gen 21:14, which explains that Abraham gave Hagar a waterskin that she set 'on her shoulder, along with the child'. According to rabbinic calculations, Ishmael was twenty-seven years old when these events took place.[121] The midrash explains:

> This, however, teaches that she (Sarah) cast (הכניסה, Hiphil of כנס) an evil eye on him, whereupon he was seized with feverish pains (חמה). The proof lies in the verse, AND THE WATER IN THE BOTTLE (חמת) WAS SPENT (XXI, 15), a sick person drinking frequently.

Although the female subject of the root כנס is not specified, it most likely refers to Sarah: she is the only character, let alone the only female, in the biblical narrative to take issue with Hagar and Ishmael.[122] The midrash employs wordplay between חמה, 'fever', and חמת, 'waterskin', suggesting that details of Ishmael's illness are concealed in the biblical text of Gen 21 itself. Sarah is a devoted mother, who ensures that Ishmael poses no continued threat to Isaac's inheritance.[123] The passage attributes a certain power to this matriarch, as she reduces the adult Ishmael to such weakness that he must be carried by his mother. The rabbis introduce

---

119. See §6.2.1, 'Sons Are Identified Though their Mothers: By Name'.

120. Exum, *Fragmented Women*, 132. Baskin suggests that 'the only blot on Sarah's exemplary life is her relationship with Hagar' (Baskin, *Midrashic Women*, 151).

121. As Freedman explains, 'Ishmael was fourteen years old at Isaac's birth (cf. [Gen] XVI, 16, with XXI, 5). This assumes that Isaac was now thirteen years old' (Freedman, n. 2 472).

122. Freedman (472) and Neusner (2:255) identify Sarah as subject.

123. Fuchs ('Literary Characterisation', 162) notes that biblical mothers are usually portrayed as 'devoted' to their sons.

Sarah into this scene from Genesis, which increases her action and influence in the narrative. In protecting Isaac from Ishmael, Sarah also protects the future of Israel. This again highlights the national dimension of matriarchal motherhood.

Having overcome so many obstacles to become a mother, Sarah is determined that her son will inherit from Abraham. She therefore acts to protect Isaac and, ultimately, 'after bearing him and securing his place in the inheritance structure of the Deity's promise (21:9-10), she dies (23:2)'.[124] For the rabbis, Sarah's primary role as a matriarch is to ensure that the covenant passes on to the correct son.

6.4.3. *Rebekah and Jacob*

Circumstances differ completely in the second patriarchal generation as Rebekah bears two sons, Jacob and Esau. As twins with both a matriarch and a patriarch as parents, there seems no obvious way to determine which son is the rightful heir to the covenant promises.[125] Once more, the mother plays a decisive role in determining who will become the third patriarch. Rebekah favours Jacob over Esau and, as with Sarah, *Genesis Rabbah* provides support for the matriarch's choice, showing that it coheres with God's plan for the development of the patriarchal line.[126]

Rebekah is introduced into the biblical narrative in Gen 24; even at this early stage the midrash suggests that of her two sons, Jacob will be righteous and Esau will be wicked. *Genesis Rabbah* 60:14 interprets Gen 24:61, where Rebekah rides a camel as she goes to meet Isaac: 'The Rabbis said: As a camel possesses one mark of uncleanness and one of cleanness (Lev 11:4), so did Rebekah give birth to one righteous and one wicked son'. The camel indicates the relative attributes of Rebekah's offspring, long before they are born. Although this statement reveals little about Rebekah herself, it offers initial support for her promotion of one son over another later in the narrative. The sons are not yet named, but the rabbinic audience is aware that Jacob, the ancestor of Israel, will prevail over Esau.

---

124. Schneider, *Mothers of Promise*, 97. Sarah's death immediately follows the Aqedah of Gen 22, where Abraham almost sacrifices Isaac on Mount Moriah. Various rabbinic sources, including the cur. edd. of *Gen. Rab.* 58:5 (Freedman, 511), suggest that Sarah died of grief or shock after hearing that her son had (almost) been killed. Such news would clearly have been devastating for Sarah: her maternal determination for him to succeed would have come to nothing.

125. Westermann, *Genesis 12–36*, 438.

126. Jeansonne, *Women of Genesis*, 53.

The first biblical indication of rivalry between Jacob and Esau is found in Gen 25:22-23. The biblical text explains that: 'the children struggled together (רצץ, Hithpolel) within her', causing Rebekah pain. She seeks help from the Lord, who offers her an oracle in Gen 25:23: 'Two nations are in your womb, and two peoples born of you shall be divided; the one shall be stronger than the other, the elder shall serve the younger'.[127] *Genesis Rabbah* 63:6 interprets the sons' struggle in the womb in light of the oracle that follows.[128] Rebekah's pregnancy is painful because Jacob and Esau have opposing personalities and their lifelong struggle against one another begins in the womb:

> R. Joḥanan said: Each ran (רץ, root רוץ)[129] to slay the other. Resh Laḳish said: Each annulled (*mattir*) the laws (*ẓiwwuyaw*) of the other. R. Berekiah observed in R. Levi's name: Do not think that only after issuing into the light of the world was he [Esau] antagonistic to him, but even while still in his mother's womb his fist was stretched out against him: thus it is written, *The wicked stretch out their fists* (zoru) *from the womb* (Ps. LVIII, 4).

The sons oppose each other from the earliest stage of their lives. The midrash goes on to explain that even in the womb, Jacob showed excitement when Rebekah passed synagogues and study houses (בתי כנסיות ובתי מדרשות), whilst Esau was drawn to idolatrous temples (בתי עבודה זרה). Although both Jacob and Esau have legitimate parentage, Jacob proves himself to be the more righteous. Sarah recognised Ishmael's inappropriate behaviour and thus prevented him inheriting from Abraham alongside Isaac. Now Rebekah takes note of Esau's unworthiness and promotes Jacob as the covenant heir over his brother. Rebekah could have treated both of her sons equally, or even favoured Esau, yet Rebekah protects Jacob and God's intention for Israel.

Genesis 25:23 reveals the divine intention for Jacob to inherit, providing a possible explanation for Rebekah's subsequent actions. In fact, Schneider suggests that Rebekah 'may be acting not out of love for Jacob but out of devotion to the Israelite Deity', who has revealed this information to her.[130] In Genesis, Rebekah is unique among the matriarchs, as she receives direct information about the covenant.[131] Sarah is not directly addressed regarding her role in the covenant: she discovers that she will

---

127. Fewell and Gunn, *Gender, Power, & Promise*, 89–90.
128. The biblical author undoubtedly intended this connection to be made.
129. A play on רצץ, used in Gen 25:22.
130. Schneider, *Mothers of Promise*, 61.
131. See ibid., 62; Fuchs, 'Literary Characterisation', 155.

bear the covenant son after eavesdropping on Abraham's conversation with the men from God (Gen 18). Similarly, Rachel and Leah are told nothing of the covenant promises; their concern lies chiefly with bearing sons for their husband in order to secure his love and their positions in the household.[132] *Genesis Rabbah* increases the matriarchs' awareness of the covenant and of the national implications of their actions.[133] The portrayal of Rebekah in Genesis provides a basic model for this, which the rabbinic interpreters could then develop in accordance with their view of the matriarchs' significance.[134]

After Rebekah gives birth to Jacob and Esau, the sons continue to develop drastically opposing personalities. *Genesis Rabbah* 63:10 comments on Gen 25:27-28, noting that as the boys mature, Jacob remains righteous but Esau acts immorally.[135] The midrash concludes with glosses on Gen 25:28:

> NOW ISAAC LOVED ESAU, BECAUSE HE DID EAT OF HIS VENISON (Gen 25:28): choice meat and choice wine was reserved for his [Isaac's] mouth. AND REBEKAH LOVED JACOB (*ib.*): the more she heard his voice [engaged in study] the stronger grew her love for him.[136]

Once more, the patriarch favours the immoral son and it falls to the matriarch to promote the legitimate covenant son. Isaac's reason for loving Esau is rather shallow: he enjoys quality meals. The divine oracle together with *Gen. Rab.* 63:10's comments on Jacob's superior moral character support Rebekah's promotion of Jacob over Esau.[137] Maternal protection of the covenant son is necessary to ensure that Jacob becomes the third patriarch of Israel against Isaac's own inclinations.

Exum comments: 'To have Isaac favour his younger son over Esau, the elder, would be damaging to the patriarchal status quo, where the oldest

---

132. See e.g. Schneider, *Mothers of Promise*, 75.

133. Cf. §3.4.1, 'The Book of *Jubilees*'.

134. On Rebekah's biblical characterisation, see Turner, 'Rebekah', 42–50.

135. According to *Gen. Rab.* 63:9 (63:10 in Freedman's translation), Jacob frequents study houses (בתי מדרשות), whilst Esau visits idolatrous temples (בתי עבודה זרה). Cf. *Gen. Rab.* 63:6. See also §6.1.1, 'The Physical Act of Childbearing'. *Gen. Rab.* 63:10 offers a national perspective on Esau as a representative of Edom (Rome).

136. 'Y.T. [Yefeh Toar, commentary by R. Samuel Jaffe Ashkenazi]: this comment is based on the use of the present part., lit. "she loves"—her love progressively growing' (Freedman, n. 6 566).

137. Schneider, *Mothers of Promise*, 55. Schneider notes (pp. 60–2) that each parent's preference for one son does not exclude their love for the other.

son is the primary recipient of his father's estate. Thus, the narrator makes the matriarch responsible for disrupting the natural lines of inheritance.'[138] For Exum, the matriarchs are portrayed negatively, scheming and acting deviously to ensure that their sons inherit. In turn, this means that the patriarchs do not have to undermine the societal structures that provide their power.[139] Modern interpreters, including Exum, must not fall into this trap, assuming that when women in ancient sources are portrayed as headstrong and determined, this must indicate patriarchal condemnation of those figures.[140] The matriarchs' determination for their sons to inherit ensures that the covenant passes to the correct heir. Time and again, Genesis trusts these women to fulfil God's covenantal intentions. In *Genesis Rabbah*, the rabbis praise the matriarchs for protecting their sons and 'the matriarchal cycle confirms their legitimacy as the ancestresses of Israel. Some of the matriarchs' actions, including Sarah's harsh treatment of Hagar and Ishmael, and Rebekah's deception of Isaac, are morally questionable. Yet, for the biblical author and the midrashic interpreters, such behaviour was justified because it secured Israel's future. This explains the rabbis' respect for the matriarchs.

Rebekah is determined that Jacob will inherit the covenant promises above his brother, Esau. When she overhears the elderly Isaac ask Esau to fetch some game and he will then bless him (Gen 27:4-5), she tells Jacob, persuading him to meet his father instead (Gen 27:6-10). Jacob voices his concerns about fooling Isaac: 'Perhaps I shall…bring a curse on myself and not a blessing'; and Rebekah exclaims: 'Let your curse be on me (עלי), my son!' (Gen 27:12-13). *Genesis Rabbah* 65:15 offers interpretations of Rebekah's zealous claim:

138. Exum, *Fragmented Women*, 132.

139. Ibid., 131–3. Schneider suggests that women stand 'outside the traditional circles of power'. Interpretation of their actions alters 'depending on whether one considers that working within the realms of power is always appropriate or possible' (Schneider, *Mothers of Promise*, 56). Women may be best placed to subvert patriarchal norms because they are not bound to protect a system that limits them. See also Fewell and Gunn, *Gender, Power, & Promise*, 75; Havrelock, 'Heroic Barrenness', 155; Camp, *Wisdom and the Feminine*, 124–5; Turner, 'Rebekah', 46; Esther Fuchs, 'Who Is Hiding the Truth? Deceptive Women and Biblical Androcentrism', in *Feminist Perspectives on Biblical Scholarship*, ed. Adela Yarbro Collins, SBL Centennial Publications; Biblical Scholarship in North America 10 (Chico: Scholars Press, 1985), 137–44.

140. Cf. Bronner, *From Eve to Esther*, 185.

Said R. Abba b. Kahana: [She exclaimed to him]: 'When a man sins, is it not his mother that is cursed, as it says, *Cursed is the ground for thy sake* (Gen. III, 17)?[141] So thou too—UPON ME BE THY CURSE'. R. Isaac said: [She answered him]: 'I undertake (lit. "it is upon me", עלי) to go in and tell thy father, Jacob is righteous and Esau is wicked'.

As Exum notes, 'In a society where curses bear serious weight, Rebekah's "upon me be the curse, my son" shows just how much the narrator expects a mother to risk for her son'.[142]

Rabbi Isaac focuses instead on the particle עלי, 'upon me': Rebekah believes that it is her duty to prevent Jacob from being cursed by revealing to Isaac his sons' true nature. This interpretation highlights Rebekah's perceptiveness compared with her husband's ignorance of Esau's immorality. Rebekah takes both the 'reproductive and protective functions' of motherhood seriously, recognising that bearing a covenant son is only the first step in securing his inheritance.[143] Inheritance is an issue of national significance, and at least on some level, Rebekah seems to recognise this as she promotes Jacob.

Rebekah will let nothing deter her. Wenham notes that she even 'commands' (root צוה) Jacob to obey her, an action rarely attributed to female characters in the Hebrew Bible.[144] The rabbis repeatedly note Rebekah's devotion to her son and this theme continues in *Gen. Rab.* 65:15. The end of this midrash claims: 'AND HE WENT, AND FETCHED, AND BROUGHT THEM TO HIS MOTHER (Gen XXVII, 14); under constraint, bowed down, and weeping'. This suggests that Jacob unwillingly executed his mother's plan.[145] It may indicate recognition of Rebekah's actions as morally dubious and an attempt to maintain Jacob's righteous persona.[146] Yet Wenham suggests that, 'Probably, Jacob realised curses could not be transferred either and his submission to his mother's will again underlines his complicity in the scheme'. He thus concludes that 'it seems likely that he did inwardly support his mother's aims here, even though he had doubts about their success'.[147] Even if the rabbis question

141. The ground (אדמה) is seen as man's (אדם) 'mother' here, from which he was produced. See Gen 2:7; 3:19; Freedman, n. 4 591.

142. Exum, *Fragmented Women*, 140. Cf. Turner, 'Rebekah', 46.

143. Fuchs, 'Literary Characterisation', 162–4 (quote p. 163).

144. Cf. Est 4:5. Wenham, *Genesis 16–50*, 206–7. Cf. Jeansonne, *Women of Genesis*, 66.

145. Exum, *Fragmented Women*, 132.

146. Ibid.; Neusner 2:392.

147. Wenham, *Genesis 16–50*, 207, 216. Also Westermann, *Genesis 12–36*, 438.

the means of securing the covenant for Jacob, the outcome of Rebekah's intervention secures her role in Israel's memory. Rebekah is a mother of Israel the nation, but she is also the mother of Israel the person, as Jacob later receives this name in Gen 32:28. Rebekah is remembered for ensuring that the Deity's plan for Jacob comes to fruition.[148]

'Rebekah sets up the scenario whereby Jacob receives the blessing', dressing Jacob in animal skins and preparing meat to Isaac's taste, to deceive her aged, partially sighted husband into thinking that Esau stands before him.[149] *Genesis Rabbah* 65:14 and 65:17 reflect on some of the practical measures undertaken by Rebekah to ensure that her plan succeeds. *Genesis Rabbah* 65:14 expands upon Rebekah's instruction to Jacob to 'Go to the flock, and get me two choice kids, so that I may prepare from them savoury food for your father, such as he likes' (Gen 27:9). The midrash continues:

> R. Ḥelbo said: [She said thus to him]: 'If thou findest [of thy father's], 'tis well; if not, bring them to me out of my dowry (פראפורנון)'. For R. Ḥelbo said that he [Isaac] had engaged to provide her with two kids daily.

Rebekah offers her own resources to ensure Jacob's inheritance. The midrash explains that Isaac provides this 'additional dowry' (פראפורנון);[150] thus, ironically, the patriarch could aid his own deception. In *Gen. Rab.* 65:17 we read: 'R. Joḥanan said: The two arms of our father Jacob were like two pillars', and so Rebekah must have sewn several goat skins together to ensure that Jacob's arms were covered (Gen 27:16). These midrashic pericopae demonstrate Rebekah's determination for Jacob to inherit the covenant blessings by deceiving Isaac into believing that he is Esau, Isaac's preferred son.

In Genesis, Isaac remains unaware of Rebekah's role in his deception. However, in *Gen. Rab.* 67:2, Isaac's desperate plea: 'Who then is he (הוא) who hunted game and brought to me and I ate...?' (Gen 27:33),[151] is interpreted as concealing reference to Rebekah: 'R. Ḥama b. R. Ḥanina interpreted the passage: WHO THEN IS HE (*ib.*) that became an intermediary between me and the Almighty that Jacob should receive the

---

148. Sarna argues that Gen 25:23 offsets any suggestion that Jacob and Rebekah's immoral scheme secured the patriarchate for Jacob: Jacob's ascendancy was God's expected plan (Sarna, *JPS: Genesis*, 179). Cf. Turner, 'Rebekah', 45–6.

149. Schneider, *Mothers of Promise*, 57; cf. 56; Wenham, *Genesis 16–50*, 207.

150. This is a Greek loan word (παράφερνον) referring to '*the wife's additional settlement above the usual one*' (Jastrow, 1213).

151. My translation.

blessings? He thereby hinted at Rebekah his mother.'[152] This recognises Rebekah's intervention. Moreover, Isaac believes that by mediating between the patriarch and God, Rebekah disrupts the transmission of the covenant. In truth, Rebekah acts in accordance with the divine intention for Jacob to become the third patriarch of Israel.[153] Maternal protection of the covenant son is a crucial part of 'the matriarchal cycle'. The matriarchs work to secure the divinely intended covenantal line. Genesis already portrays Rebekah as a woman of determination and independent action, but *Genesis Rabbah* develops Rebekah's characterisation, exploring further her actions and increasing her awareness of God's covenant with the patriarchs. The midrashic portrayal of the matriarchs emphasises how these women enable the emergence of Israel and thus suggests the great respect that the rabbis have for them.

Despite Rebekah's resourcefulness, the midrash emphasises that God maintains ultimate control over the covenant's development. In *Gen. Rab.* 65:17, Rebekah gives Jacob the food she has prepared for Isaac (Gen 27:17). 'She accompanied him as far as the door and then said to him: "Thus far I owed thee [my aid] (lit. 'I was bound [חייבת] to you'); from here onward thy Creator will assist thee".' Rebekah does not appear at this point in the biblical narrative, but the rabbis remind the audience of her central role in orchestrating the situation.[154] Most importantly, Rebekah acknowledges that her role is limited and God must act to secure Jacob's inheritance from Isaac. In the midrash, Rebekah demonstrates her piety and worthiness as a matriarch of Israel. The rabbis value the matriarchs not only for their actions, but also because of their respect for God.

Maternal protection of the covenant son plays an equally important role in the second patriarchal generation. Rebekah acts in accordance with the divine oracle concerning her sons in Gen 25:23. With the Deity's help, Rebekah secures the covenant for Jacob.[155] Rebekah provides a good example of how 'rabbinic literature praises the supportive, resourceful, and self-sacrificing wife and mother'.[156]

---

152. The midrash interprets this as an example of *Q're perpetuum*, where the third person masculine singular pronoun may be reinterpreted as feminine. See 'Sons' Respect for Their Mothers'.

153. Cf. Gen 25:23; Schneider, *Mothers of Promise*, 51, 62.

154. Turner argues that: 'She is the prompter and the motivator, but because of her subservient status, that is all that she can be. The plan must unfold without her' (Turner, 'Rebekah', 46).

155. Teugels, *'The Wooing of Rebekah' (Gen. 24)*, 127–8.

156. Baskin, *Midrashic Women*, 17.

6.4.4. *Leah, Rachel and the Tribal Ancestors*

The first two patriarchal generations required one of two sons, Isaac or Ishmael, Jacob or Esau, to inherit the covenant promises from their patriarchal father. Maternal protection of the covenant son was critical for ensuring that the covenant passed to the correct child. When Jacob assumes his role as patriarch, the dynamics of the ancestral family change dramatically. This is the generation that will produce the ancestors of Israel's twelve tribes; thus, all of Jacob's sons are set to inherit the covenant promises.[157] The mother's role changes in this generation. The focus of 'the matriarchal cycle' shifts from producing the one covenant son to bearing the greatest number of Israelite tribal ancestors.[158] Sarah and Rebekah offered protection to the covenant son and managed the rivalry between sons; in the final patriarchal generation, the roles are, for the most part, reversed. Sibling rivalry appears not among sons, but between the matriarchs, Leah and Rachel; and rather than acting as their sons' protectors, these women are protected by their sons.[159]

6.4.5. *Summary*

As Schneider notes: 'the key function of the women in Genesis surrounds who inherits the Deity's promise'.[160] Many of the actions undertaken by the patriarchs' wives concern their sons and *Genesis Rabbah*'s 'matriarchal cycle' accentuates the role that mothers play in advancing the covenant. At the end of her monograph, Schneider claims that: 'The mothers in Genesis are rarely evaluated by what they do for their children, since for most there are few to no depictions of the women acting as a mother… The physical act of bearing, not motherhood, is the issue.'[161] This seems somewhat at odds with Schneider's earlier claims and it is inaccurate. Whilst Genesis certainly focuses on the matriarchs' barrenness

---

157. Cf. Steinberg, 'Zilpah', 170; Schneider, *Mothers of Promise*, 63, 68–9.

158. Cf. Exum, *Fragmented Women*, 131.

159. E.g. Reuben defends Leah's honour (*Gen. Rab.* 72:2; 98:4); Joseph protects Rachel from Esau (*Gen. Rab.* 78:10; 90:4; 98:18). One exception to this reversal is *Gen. Rab.* 84:10, where Rachel's silence protects Joseph after she has died. See §6.3.2, 'Sons' Respect for their Mothers'. Rabow (*Lost Matriarch*, 15–16, 30, 34) notes that the rivalry between Leah and Rachel matches that between Jacob and Esau.

160. Schneider refers here to the promise that Abraham's offspring will inherit the land (Gen 12:7; 15:7-15; 17:8; 26:3-5, 23; 35:11). Schneider, *Mothers of Promise*, 12; cf. 16.

161. Schneider, *Mothers of Promise*, 218. Also Fewell and Gunn, *Gender, Power, & Promise*, 70.

and its reversal, motherhood and maternal action are represented and commended. Matriarchal motherhood is not limited to natural processes, such as childbirth and breastfeeding, but includes the significant actions that these women perform on behalf of their sons and the covenant. The matriarchs, especially Sarah and Rebekah, protect their sons and ensure that they inherit the covenant as God intends. The 'reproductive and protective functions' of motherhood characterise the biblical portrayal of the Genesis matriarchs and they are emphasised by 'the matriarchal cycle' in *Genesis Rabbah*.[162]

6.5. *National Motherhood*

6.5.1. *The National Dimensions of Matriarchal Motherhood*

Childbirth and motherhood become metaphors for the emergence of the nation in Genesis and *Genesis Rabbah*. As Israel descends from the matriarchs and their sons, the entire 'matriarchal cycle' assumes a national dimension. Every maternal action undertaken by the matriarchs, from their determination to become mothers to their overt protection of the covenant son, contributes to Israel's establishment as a nation. 'The matriarchal cycle' thus highlights these women's roles as the historical and present mothers of Israel.

The rabbis drew on various traditions depicting Zion as a barren woman and as a mother to highlight the barren matriarchs' roles as national representatives.[163] These begin with passages from Isaiah and continue in post-biblical texts, such as Baruch and *4 Ezra*.[164] For example, Isa 66 suggests that the people should: 'Rejoice with Jerusalem...that you may nurse and be satisfied from her consoling breast; that you may drink deeply with delight from her glorious bosom' (Isa 66:10-11).[165] Similar imagery is found in Baruch's (second-century BCE) presentation of Jerusalem mourning and comforting her exiled children (Bar 4:11-21).[166] *4 Ezra* (first century CE) portrays Jerusalem as a barren mother who bears a son, before that son dies. This is a metaphor for the inhabitation of Jerusalem, followed by its destruction in 70 CE. The woman

---

162. Fuchs, 'Literary Characterisation', 163.

163. See §4.1, 'The Biblical Barren Matriarch Tradition'; §5.4, 'The Matriarchs as Representatives of the National Identity'.

164. See Callaway, *Sing, O Barren One*, 73–90.

165. For Isaiah's portrayal of Zion/Jerusalem as woman and mother, see Chapman, 'Breast Milk', 11–14. Callaway explores breastfeeding in relation to Zion and ancient mythology (Callaway, *Sing, O Barren One*, 77–80).

166. This brings to mind Jer 31:15. Ibid., 81–3.

ultimately transforms into the city, which Callaway argues represents the indestructible, heavenly Jerusalem (*4 Ezra* 9:26–10:59).[167] By the rabbinic period, there was an accepted, even popular, association of Zion with motherhood. The midrashists were able to draw upon these traditions to accentuate the role of the matriarchs as national representatives.

The midrashim discussed below exemplify, but do not exhaust, *Genesis Rabbah*'s portrayal of the matriarchs' national motherhood. The Genesis matriarchs mothered Israel's ancestors and embodied Jewish identity. As such, the majority of their actions may be interpreted as having national significance.

6.5.2. *Sarah: The First Mother of Israel*

Baskin notes that 'Rabbinic portrayals of Sarah, the mother of the Jewish people, are extremely positive'.[168] The Bible and midrash demonstrate that Sarah is destined to become the first matriarch of Israel and they acknowledge the central role that she plays in the foundation of the nation.[169] In Gen 17:16, God tells Abraham that: 'I will bless her (Sarah), and moreover I will give you a son by her. I will bless her, and she shall give rise to nations; kings of peoples shall come from her.' Abraham protests that Sarah is too old to bear a child and he tries to promote Ishmael as his heir, yet God has chosen Sarah as the first mother of Israel and insists that she will bear the covenant son (Gen 17:17-21). Genesis 17 emphasises the national dimensions of Sarah's motherhood. She will bear a son, Isaac, but Sarah also stands at the head of a dynasty as nations and rulers will descend from her. In Gen 21, Sarah orders Abraham to expel Hagar and Ishmael from the household and God supports this action. He repeats his choice of Sarah, explaining that it is her child who will continue Abraham's line (Gen 21:12-13).[170] The mother's identity again determines the legitimacy of the child.[171] As the mother of Israel, all members of that people, including the rabbis, descend from her. Sarah's motherhood transcends the centuries and this ensures her continued significance.

Isaiah 51 explains that 'you that pursue righteousness, you that seek the LORD' should 'look to Abraham your father and to Sarah who bore you; for he was but one when I called him, but I blessed him and made him many' (Isa 51:1-2).[172] This prophetic passage transforms the first

167. Ibid., 83–9.
168. Baskin, *Midrashic Women*, 151.
169. Cf. Zucker, 'Sarah', 221, 251–2.
170. Cf. Exum, *Fragmented Women*, 108.
171. See §6.2, 'Identity'.
172. My translation.

matriarch and patriarch into national symbols and shows that already in the Bible, the importance of these figures was recognised.[173] Sarah's role as representative of the nation is further explored in *Genesis Rabbah*. *Genesis Rabbah* 47:5 portrays Sarah and Ishmael as the heads of their respective nations: 'R. Isaac sad: "It is written, *All these are the twelve tribes* (shibṭe) *of Israel* (Gen. XLIX, 28)—these were the descendants of the mistress [Sarah]. Yet did not Ishmael too produce twelve [princes]?"' This passage directly associates Sarah with the twelve tribes of Israel, portraying her as the progenitor of that nation. Prior to this, the midrash contrasts Isaac and Ishmael and one would perhaps expect that contrast to continue here. The use of the matriarch highlights the national dimensions of Sarah's motherhood and confirms Gen 17:16's promise that nations and kings would descend from her.

Genesis Rabbah 53:5 again portrays Sarah as a representative of Israel. The end of the midrash reads:

> R. Adda said: The Holy One, blessed be He, is a trustee (lit. 'master of deposits', בעל פקדונות): Amalek deposited (הפקיד, Hiphil of פקד) with Him bundles of thorns [punishment], as it says, *I remember* (פקד) *that which Amalek did to Israel* (I Sam. XV, 2). Sarah laid up (lit. 'deposited', הפקידה, Hiphil of פקד) with Him a store of pious acts (*mitsvot*) and good deeds; therefore the Lord returned to her [the reward for] these, as it says, AND THE LORD REMEMBERED (פקד) SARAH (Gen 21:1).

This explores Sarah and Amalek's relationships with the divine, based on the appearance of the verb פקד, 'to remember', in both of their narratives. The midrash connects this with פקדון, 'deposits', as the rabbis conclude that: 'because Amalek deserved the visitation he received, so Sarah must have also deserved the visitation she received'.[174] The righteous Sarah was rewarded by God with a child, and Amalek was punished for his deeds. In this way, both Sarah and Amalek represent conflicting ways of life and the divine response to each of these.[175]

Amalek becomes a biblical paradigm for Israel's enemies. The Amalekites fight the Israelites while they are wandering in the wilderness and God ensures that Israel wins the battle (Exod 17:8-16). The Lord then claims that he will 'utterly blot out the remembrance of Amalek' and

173. See Callaway, *Sing, O Barren One*, 60–2; Darr, *Far More Precious*, 115–16; Ramon, 'Torah of Hesed', 163; Westermann, *Isaiah 40–66*, 236. The context for Isa 51 is the exile.

174. Callaway, *Sing, O Barren One*, 134; cf. 133–4.

175. As Rabow (*Lost Matriarch*, 4–5) notes, 'measure for measure', being rewarded or punished according to previous deeds, is common in rabbinic literature.

Moses notes that battle will ensue between the Lord and Amalek forever-
more (Exod 17:14-16). In Deut 25:17, Israel is called to 'Remember
what Amalek did to you on your journey out of Egypt', and 1 Sam
15:2 uses this attack to justify Saul's destruction of the Amalekites.
Genesis Rabbah 53:5 draws on this biblical presentation of Amalek and
provides Sarah as a contrasting paradigm. As a mother of Israel to whom
God responded favourably (Gen 21:1), Sarah demonstrates how Israel
should behave and, like Amalek, she becomes a national representative.
As Neusner comments, this passage employs the common midrashic
technique of connecting the matriarchs and patriarchs to Israel's wider
history.[176] Thus, *Gen. Rab.* 53:5 highlights Sarah's continued relevance in
the life of the nation and justifies her designation as matriarch.

The most striking portrayal of Sarah as a national representative
appears in *Gen. Rab.* 53:9, where she is portrayed as the archetypal
mother of Israel.[177] This midrash interprets Sarah's joyous exclamation
following Isaac's birth: 'Who would ever have said to Abraham that
Sarah would nurse children?' (Gen 21:7). The rabbinic interpreters note
that whilst Sarah only bore one child, she here refers to בנים, 'children'.
This observation inspires a midrashic interpretation of Sarah's miraculous
motherhood:

> THAT SARAH SHOULD HAVE GIVEN CHILDREN (בנים) SUCK (Gen
> 21:7): she suckled builders (בנאין). Our mother Sarah was extremely modest
> (צנועה). Said ('our father', אבינו) Abraham to her: 'This is not a time for
> modesty, but uncover your breasts so that all may know that the Holy One,
> blessed be He, has begun to perform miracles'. She uncovered her breasts
> and the milk gushed forth as from two fountains...

Whilst female modesty is usually praised by the rabbis,[178] Abraham insists
that Sarah abandon this characteristic so that she may become a sign of
God's wondrous power and of his ability to work miracles. Furthermore,
the rabbinic reference to 'our Father' suggests that Abraham acts within
his patriarchal role, giving credence to his request.[179]

---

176. Neusner, 2:248.

177. On this passage and its parallel in *b. Baba Meṣiʿa* 87a, see Ramon, 'Torah
of Hesed', 166–7.

178. Bronner discusses female modesty in her monograph. See Bronner, *From
Eve to Esther*, esp. 5–6, 33, 80, 186. Baskin mentions the ills of immodesty e.g.
Baskin, *Midrashic Women*, 141, 160. Both Freedman (468) and Neusner (2:251)
translate צנועה as 'modest' here.

179. Cf. §3.6.2, 'Uses of the Noun אם as "Matriarch"'.

When she uncovers herself, Sarah's breasts 'were gushing milk like two springs'.[180] This once-barren woman is now able to nurse many children and this reminds the audience of God's intervention to enable this old, childless woman to become a mother. The image of milk flowing from Sarah's breasts builds on Isa 66:10-12, where Jerusalem nurses its people. In these verses, the nation is personified as a woman, as in Isa 54; however, motherhood now becomes the focus of interpretation. As Callaway summarises, 'Zion has changed from the desolate woman who is redeemed by Yahweh to the all-sufficient mother whose abundance provides comfort and nourishment'.[181] The depiction of Sarah in *Gen. Rab.* 53:9 bears obvious similarities with this prophetic imagery. This previously infertile woman is the subject of God's wondrous miracle. Sarah reflects God's relationship with his own people, suggesting Israel's superiority over other nations; and her abounding fecundity helps to protect the nation that will descend from her. In this way, Sarah's physical motherhood provides the basis for her national motherhood, and as Callaway notes: 'For the rabbis, the significance of Sarah's story is in its relation to Zion's story'.[182]

Having set up this powerful image of Sarah as the archetypal mother of Israel, the rabbis now consider the effects of this miracle:

> noble ladies (lit. 'matronas', מטרונות) came and had their children suckled by her, saying, 'We do not merit that our children should be suckled with the milk of that righteous woman'.[183] The Rabbis said: Whoever came for the sake of heaven became God-fearing (לשום שמים נעשה ירא שמים). R. Aḥa said: Even one who did not come for the sake of heaven was given dominion [i.e. greatness] in this world (ממשלה בעולם). Yet they did not continue to enjoy it, for when they stood aloof at Sinai and would not accept (קיבלו, Piel of קבל) the Torah, that dominion was taken from them. Thus it is written, *He looseth the bonds of kings, and bindeth their loins with a girdle* (Job XII, 18).

---

180. Cf. *L.A.B.* 51:3 where Hannah exclaims: 'Drip, my breasts, and relate your testimonies, because you have been commanded to give suck. For he who is milked from you will be established, and the people will be enlightened by his words, and he will show statutes to the nations, and his horn will be very much exalted'. See also Chapman, 'Breast Milk', 25 n. 117.

181. Callaway, *Sing, O Barren One*, 78.

182. Ibid., 137. On *Gen. Rab.* 53:9, see ibid., 134–5.

183. Some manuscripts have 'righteous man' here. See Levinson, 'Bodies and Bo(a)rders', 352.

For Judith Baskin, *Gen. Rab.* 53:9 demonstrates 'the vindication achieved in giving birth after many years of infertility' and 'goes on to describe how all doubters were put to naught' after seeing this once-barren woman's fecundity.[184] Baskin's observations are accurate, but she does not deal with the national or universal consequences of Sarah's motherhood, which form a central part of the pericope.

Genesis Rabbah 47:2 discusses God's promise that Sarah would bear a son (Gen 17:16): 'Rabbi Abbahu explained it thus in the name of R. Jose b. R. Ḥanina: I will inspire all peoples with awe of her, so that they should not call her, "barren woman"'. *Genesis Rabbah* 53:5 repeats this statement to show that Sarah earns this universal respect when 'the LORD dealt with Sarah as he had said' (Gen 21:1).[185] The matronas in *Gen. Rab.* 53:9 demonstrate the effect of Sarah's motherhood on those outside Israel. The title מטרונה, 'matrona', describes 'an important woman of the ruling class' in Roman society.[186] The rabbis depict these socially prominent women coming to have their children suckled by the 'righteous' Sarah and they openly declare their subordination to her.[187]

Interestingly, the term מטרונה, 'matrona', derives from the Latin *mater*, meaning 'mother'.[188] Sarah is one of the Jewish 'matriarchs', the mothers (אמהות) of Israel. There is a parallelism in the roles played by these women. Both are significant female figures in their respective communities (Israel or Rome) and motherhood is the source of their authority. The Roman 'mothers' bring their children to the Israelite 'mother', and even express their own inadequacies.[189]

The matronas play a further role in the midrash's portrayal of Sarah's motherhood. These figures form an *inclusio* around Sarah's transformation from barren woman to mother. They appear in *Gen. Rab.* 45:4,

---

184. Baskin, *Midrashic Women*, 137. Cf. Adelman, 'Laughter and Re-Membering', 231; Levinson, 'Bodies and Bo(a)rders', 352–6.

185. As discussed above (§6.5.2, 'Sarah: The First Mother of Israel'), *Gen. Rab.* 47:2 and 53:5 mirror one another: the first sets out God's promises to Sarah, the latter shows their fulfilment.

186. Bronner, *From Eve to Esther*, 6–7; Jastrow, 769. The appearance of the Roman matronas is anachronistic; yet their purpose is clear. They represent non-Israelites and Sarah's role as a mother of Israel allows her to transcend the centuries.

187. See Levinson, 'Bodies and Bo(a)rders', 343–72.

188. For the Latin 'mater', 'matron', see Charlton T. Lewis and Charles Short, *A Latin Dictionary Founded on Andrews' Edition of Freund's Latin Dictionary* (Oxford: Clarendon, 1975), 1118–120.

189. Cf. the matrilineal principle and its Roman connections. See Cohen, 'Origins of the Matrilineal Principle', 43, and §3.5, 'Excursus: The Matrilineal Principle'.

asking after Sarah's health. Here, her motherhood seems most in jeopardy as Hagar conceives a son for Abraham, whilst Sarah remains barren. The matronas are seen again in *Gen. Rab.* 53:9, where Sarah's motherhood is finally secure and visible to all. In neither instance is the matronas' appearance negative: they express interest in Sarah's well-being and then show her respect. Their appearance invites comparison between the two situations, reminding the audience of the truly miraculous nature of Sarah's motherhood.

In *Gen. Rab.* 53:9, breastfeeding has important consequences. Cynthia Chapman argues that 'Through breastfeeding, a mother or wet nurse was understood to confer upon an infant her own tribal identity and royal or priestly status', and 'breast milk is the substantive conduit through which specific traits of the mother or wet nurse are transferred to the infant'.[190] Breastfeeding provides more than physical nourishment as the mother's milk is said to convey attributes and authority to her child. In this midrash, the Rabbis argue that if those witnessing the miracle came for pious reasons, they became God-fearing (ירא שמים). This term appears in various texts from the first centuries CE, referring to Gentiles sympathetic to the Jewish religion. These individuals often obeyed some of Judaism's tenets but they did not convert.[191] For these individuals, Sarah's breast-milk provided spiritual nourishment, bringing these people to a better

190. Chapman, 'Breast Milk', 3, 7. Her entire article explores this and she discusses the portrayal of breastfeeding in several biblical narratives (Hannah and Samuel; Isaac and Sarah; Moses and his mother; Naomi and Obed). She suggests that the presentation of Sarah breastfeeding Isaac in Gen 21 dispels any suggestion that the younger, yet inferior, handmaid, Hagar, may have nursed Isaac. Furthermore, it suggests that as a legitimate Israelite woman, Sarah's breast milk passed significant traits to her son, preparing him for his patriarchal role (Chapman, 'Breast Milk', 26–30). For ancient breast-feeding practices, see Gruber, 'Breast-Feeding Practices', 61–83.

191. See Joshua Ezra Burns, 'God-Fearers', in *The Eerdmans Dictionary of Early Judaism*, ed. John J. Collins and Daniel C. Harlow (Grand Rapids: Eerdmans, 2010), 681–2; Levinson, 'Bodies and Bo(a)rders', 356–60. Burns comments: 'Later rabbinic texts refer to friendly Gentiles as *yîrê šāmayim* ("those who fear heaven"), juxtaposing this designation with the standard terms for Jews and proselytes (e.g., *Mekhilta* 18). The substitution of the denominative "heaven" for "God" should be attributed to the lack of an idiomatic Hebrew equivalent to the Greek term *theos*, which the rabbis would not have considered a violation of the third commandment. Although the rabbis were favourably disposed toward these individuals, they afforded them no special status for practical purposes, in contrast to proselytes, who were classified under the biblical law of the "alien…"' (Burns, 'God-Fearers', 681).

understanding of God. Sarah therefore functions as a testimony to God's power and authority.[192] Rabbi Aḥa notes that even those who did not come for pious reasons gained power or rulership when they were breastfed by Sarah. However, this power was ultimately reneged because at the crucial moment, 'they separated themselves at Sinai and did not accept (root קבל) the Torah'.[193]

The universal effects of Sarah's motherhood become clear in this midrash as she suckles many, passing attributes and authority even to those outside of Israel.[194] In short, 'Sarah's abundant and bountiful nursing is envisioned as a divine outpouring of goodness that brings bounty to all who come near'.[195] Sarah's motherhood and this miracle are linked with the revelation at Sinai, when God's law was given to his people, Israel. Sarah and her descendants receive and accept Torah, whilst those whom she suckled from other nations lost the privileges gained through associ-ation with this 'righteous woman'. The root קבל, meaning 'to accept, receive' in the Piel, is a central term in rabbinic thought, conveying the receiving and passing on of the Oral and Written Laws.[196] At Sinai, Israel is set apart from other nations as she agrees to live by God's Torah; Sarah provides an early example of how one ought to respond to God and she nurtures many.[197] Her motherhood has consequences for other nations, yet they will distance themselves from God's law, setting themselves outside of Israel and so rejecting the matriarch's example.

Joshua Levinson suggests that this narrative addresses problems of the relation between God-fearers and Judaism in the rabbis' own time.[198] He argues that because God-fearers did not fully commit to the Jewish

192. Cf. *Gen. Rab.* 39:14. See §8.1.2, 'Piety'.

193. Job 12:18 is cited to support this: God has ultimate authority and control over kings.

194. Levinson ('Bodies and Bo[a]rders', 365–71) notes the connections between Sarai in this pericope and traditions about the goddess, Isis. Non-Israelites of the period would have recognised such connections. On ancient Near Eastern, see breastfeeding by goddesses, see Chapman, 'Breast Milk', 8–11.

195. Ramon, 'Torah of Hesed', 167.

196. See *m. 'Abot*; Danby, 446–61; Anthony J. Saldarini, 'The End of the Rabbinic Chain of Tradition', *Journal of Biblical Literature* 93, no. 1 (1974): 97–106; Jastrow, 1308–9.

197. Cf. images of Jerusalem nursing Israel in Isa 60; 66. See Chapman, 'Breast Milk', 11–14.

198. Levinson, 'Bodies and Bo(a)rders', 343–72, esp. 352–72. See also Levinson, 'Literary Approaches', 221–2.

religion by converting, but simply adhered to some of its standards, they confused the clear boundaries between those inside and those outside the Jewish community.[199] *Genesis Rabbah* 53:9 explains the existence of this group as Sarah, the premier mother of Israel, breastfeeds heathen children: 'The matriarch's body is literally transgressive (*transgredi* = to step across) in that it enables the outsiders to come in', giving God-fearers access to Jewish culture.[200] In this way, 'the transgressive nursing mother challenges the purity of ethnic distinctions based upon either belief-systems or genealogy and becomes an ideological vehicle for the creation of a cultural biography of the Godfearers'.[201] Moreover, the matronas' insistence on their own unworthiness reinforces Jewish identity, as the contemporary ruling class acknowledges the superiority of Israel's matriarch.[202]

Levinson's analysis offers insights into the possible purpose of this narrative as a source of constructing and maintaining Jewish identity. He draws particular attention to the matronas and the God-fearers, categories that the rabbis' contemporaries would have recognised from their own society. Levinson's interpretation is certainly plausible. The narrative clearly demonstrates Israel's superiority over other nations and emphasises the importance of identity through, or at least by association with, the matriarch. However, Levinson's argument does not extend to Sarah's role as the enduring mother of Israel in this pericope, which draws an explicit link with the Sinai revelation, and, by implication, with the Jewish people who descend from Sarah and obey God's Torah. Whilst it is impossible to discern the specific historical situation addressed by the midrash (if any), there is no doubt that *Gen. Rab.* 53:9's portrayal of Sarah's abundant motherhood is concerned with Israel's national identity.

Sarah is wholly deserving of the title 'the mother of Israel': she bears the first covenant son and God declares that nations will descend from her. Sarah's actions never relate solely to her own life but have implications for the identity of the Jewish people.

---

199. Levinson, 'Bodies and Bo(a)rders', 360–2.

200. Ibid., 363.

201. Ibid., 365.

202. Ibid., 354, 365–6. As Levinson notes: 'Now, I seriously doubt if these noble women who represent the actual hegemonic culture, in opposition to the imagined hegemony offered by the text, saw themselves in such a servile and subservient position, just as I seriously doubt if the Godfearers saw themselves as liminal or marginal' (ibid., 366).

6.5.3. *Rebekah: The Mother of Two Nations*

Like Sarah, Rebekah is destined to become a mother of Israel. She enters the narrative in Gen 24, a chapter devoted to finding Isaac a suitable wife.[203] Abraham's servant asks God to reveal the correct woman to him and Rebekah behaves as the servant specified (Gen 24:14-27). Following this, Rebekah agrees to marry Isaac and when her family tries to delay her departure to Canaan, she responds determinedly with one Hebrew word, אלך, 'I will go' (Gen 24:58).[204] As a matriarch, Rebekah's motherhood also has implications for Israel.

In Gen 25:23, a divine oracle informs the pregnant Rebekah that, 'Two nations are in your womb, and two peoples born of you shall be divided; the one shall be stronger than the other, the elder shall serve the younger'. As with Sarah, the national consequences of Rebekah's matriarchal motherhood are clear from the beginning. Israel will descend from Jacob and his sons, whilst Esau will found Edom, a nation in conflict with Israel throughout the Bible and which eventually becomes a symbol for the tyranny of Rome in postbiblical sources.[205] When Rebekah departs Haran, her family offers her the blessing: 'May you, our sister, become thousands of myriads; may your offspring gain possession of the gates of their foes' (Gen 24:60).[206] In *Gen. Rab.* 60:13, R. Aibu explains that this is the only dowry given to Rebekah by her impoverished family. Whilst the blessing is fulfilled, R. Berekiah and R. Levi in the name of R. Ḥama b. R. Ḥaninah note that this only occurs after 'Isaac prayed to the LORD for his wife' (Gen 25:21). Rebekah gives birth not because of her heathen family's blessing, but because an Israelite patriarch prays for her.

---

203. This is the longest chapter in Genesis, with 67 verses. See Schneider, *Mothers of Promise*, 62. On Gen 24, see Teugels, *'The Wooing of Rebekah' (Gen. 24)*. Rebekah is mentioned in Gen 22:23, but she does not appear until Gen 24:15.

204. Cf. Schneider, *Mothers of Promise*, 50; Jeansonne, *Women of Genesis*, 61–2; Teugels, *'The Wooing of Rebekah' (Gen. 24)*, 95.

205. See Gerson D. Cohen, 'Esau as Symbol in Early Medieval Thought', in *Jewish Medieval and Renaissance Studies*, ed. Alexander Altmann (Cambridge, MA: Harvard University Press, 1967), 19–48; Wenham, *Genesis 16–50*, 180; Carol Bakhos, 'Figuring (Out) Esau: The Rabbis and Their Others', *Journal of Jewish Studies* 58, no. 2 (2007): 250–62; Mireille Hadas-Lebel, 'Jacob et Esaü, ou Israël et Rome dans le Talmud et le Midrash', *Revue de l'Histoire des Religions* 201, no. 4 (1984): 369–92.

206. According to Westermann, this kind of 'farewell blessing' was common in the ancient world when someone left the family or died (Westermann, *Genesis 12–36*, 390).

The content of the blessing in Gen 24:60 is then analysed:

> and chiefs of thousands (*alufim*) descended from her through Esau and ten
> thousands through Jacob. Chiefs of thousands through Esau, as it says, *The*
> *thousands* (aluf) ('chiliarch', אלוף)[207] *of Teman, the thousands* ('chiliarch',
> אלוף) *of Omar*, etc. (Gen. XXXVI, 15). Ten thousands from Jacob, as it
> says, *I made thee into ten thousands* (רבבה), *even as the growth of the field*
> (Ezek. XVI, 7). Some say: Both descended from Israel, as it says, *And when*
> *it rested, he said: Return, O Lord, unto the ten thousands of the thousands*
> (רבבות אלפי) *of Israel* (Num. X, 36).

Both of Rebekah's sons become progenitors of peoples. However, Israel's
superiority over other nations is emphasised by the rabbis. God responds
to Israel's prayers and he will make her more fruitful than her heathen
counterparts. Rebekah's national motherhood is twofold: she is a matriarch
of Israel, but another nation also descends from her.

Genesis Rabbah 63:6 explicitly links Rebekah with the twelve tribes of
Israel, confirming her legitimacy as a mother of Israel:

> R. Huna said: [She exclaimed]: 'If I am to produce the twelve tribes only
> with such suffering, would that I had not conceived!' It was taught[208] in R.
> Nehemiah's name: Rebekah merited (ראויה)[209] that the twelve tribes should
> spring directly from her. Thus it is written, AND THE LORD SAID UNTO
> HER: TWO NATIONS ARE IN THY WOMB, etc. TWO NATIONS—
> there you have two; AND TWO PEOPLES—that is four; AND THE ONE
> PEOPLE SHALL BE STRONGER THAN THE OTHER PEOPLE—
> six; AND THE ELDER SHALL SERVE THE YOUNGER—eight; AND
> WHEN HER DAYS TO BE DELIVERED WERE FULFILLED, BEHOLD,
> THERE WERE TWINS IN HER WOMB—ten; AND THE FIRST CAME
> FORTH RUDDY—eleven; AND AFTER THAT CAME FORTH HIS
> BROTHER (XXV, 23-6)—total, twelve. Others deduce it from this verse:
> AND SHE SAID: IF IT BE SO, WHEREFORE AM I THUS—ZEH: *zayyin*
> is seven, *heh* is five: this gives twelve.

Rebekah recognises her own significance as a matriarch, and in *Genesis*
Rabbah she demonstrates awareness of her role in Israel's history.[210]

---

207. This noun, usually translated as 'chief' (e.g. NRSV; JPS), is thought to
derive from אלף, 'thousand'. See Freedman, n. 4 536; BDB, 48–9.

208. The verb תני indicates tannaitic authority. See Jastrow, 1861; Strack and
Stemberger, *Introduction*, 60, 65–83, 109.

209. Qal passive participle of ראה, meaning: 'chosen, selected; designated,
predestined; fit, worthy' (Jastrow, 1435).

210. In *Jubilees*, females show similar awareness. See §3.4.1, 'The Book of
Jubilees'.

Rebekah is explicitly connected with Israel and Gen 25:23-26 is shown to contain twelve references to Rebekah's offspring, corresponding to the twelve tribes. Moreover, using *gematria*, where each letter of the Hebrew alphabet has a numerical value, the word זה, here translated 'thus', appearing in Rebekah's complaint (Gen 25:22), also represents twelve.[211] Hence *Gen. Rab.* 63:6 emphasises Rebekah's suitability as a matriarch and suggests that she was always destined for this role. Providing a link between Rebekah and the twelve tribes of Israel reminds the audience that the entire nation descends from this woman and thus she is as worthy of the title 'matriarch' as Leah and Rachel, who bore tribal ancestors.

Rebekah's increased awareness of her matriarchal role is further explored in *Gen. Rab.* 65:14. Commenting on the moment Rebekah sends Jacob to find kids that will deceive his father (Gen 27:9), 'R. Levi said: [She bade him], "Go and anticipate [the blessings on behalf of] the people that is compared to a flock", as you read, *And ye My sheep, the sheep of My pasture* (Ezek. XXXIV, 31)'. The term צאן, 'flock', is used in the Hebrew Bible to describe Israel as God's people and Rebekah's language foreshadows this.[212] Furthermore, the goats Jacob will fetch must be 'good' (טבים) (Gen 25:9) and this is expounded in the midrash:

> R. Berekiah commented in R. Ḥelbo's name: They are good for thee and good for thy descendants. Good for thee, since thou wilt receive the blessings through them; and good for thy descendants, who will be pardoned through them on the Day of Atonement, as it is written, *For on this day shall atonement be made for you*, etc. (Lev. XVI, 30).

Within the historical and narrative context of Genesis, the two kids prepared as Isaac's favourite meal will secure Jacob's inheritance. The wider history of Israel is affected by these actions as goats will be offered as sin offerings on Yom Kippur. In *Gen. Rab.* 65:14, Jacob becomes a representative of Israel. Rebekah acts not only as Jacob's mother, but also as the mother of Israel. She is aware of the wider implications of her actions and recognises connections between Israel and its founding figures. For the rabbis, such actions confirm Rebekah's status as a mother of Israel.

Rebekah is the most independent and most assertive of all the Genesis matriarchs.[213] Even in the biblical text, Rebekah appears to have some awareness of the covenant. Whilst uncertainty characterised Sarah's

211. See §2.3, 'Common Midrashic Exegetical Techniques'.
212. E.g. Ps 77:21; 2 Sam 24:17.
213. Schneider (*Mothers of Promise*, 49) remarks: 'Rebekah is one of the more active women in Genesis'.

narrative as she struggled with prolonged barrenness, Rebekah's position as a matriarch is more stable. The covenant promises have been set in motion and from her entry into the narrative in Gen 24, Rebekah's legitimacy is clear. In the midrash, Rebekah's role as a national mother is developed as she makes connections between her own family and Israel. In *Genesis Rabbah*, her recognition of her matriarchal status in Israel is more explicit. The rabbis had great respect for the ancestresses of the Jewish people and the biblical portrayal of the headstrong Rebekah provided one basis for their developed midrashic characterisation of the Genesis matriarchs.

6.5.4. *Leah and Rachel: The Mothers of Tribal Ancestors*

Two legitimate matriarchs, Leah and Rachel, co-exist in the third generation of the ancestral family. These sisters and their handmaidens, Bilhah and Zilpah, give birth to the progenitors of Israel's twelve tribes, enabling the nation at last to emerge.[214] Leah and Rachel's sibling rivalry dominates the narrative. Exum argues, 'Their rivalry results not so much in a victory for either of the women (both are unhappy) as a victory for patriarchy: numerous sons are born to Jacob, ensuring that Israel will increase'. For Exum, rivalry controls these women, ensuring that they fulfil the patriarchal agenda and secure the nation's future.[215] Yet rivalry, usually among brothers, drives much of the plot of Genesis and cannot be said to reflect a suppressive attitude towards women.[216] Rabbinic interpretations demonstrate respect for Leah and Rachel in their roles as the ancestresses of Israel. The two women's lives are intertwined and as Schneider notes: 'The narrator wants us to compare them: they are sisters, married to the same man, they are seldom depicted with anyone but each other, and their children become the focus of the Hebrew Bible'.[217] Although these women can never be considered in isolation from one another; it is fruitful, and perhaps even necessary, to examine Leah and Rachel individually as matriarchs of Israel.[218]

214. Schneider treats each of these women separately (ibid., 63–94, 126–37). Exum argues that 'Rachel and Leah accept the sons of Bilhah and Zilpah as their own, thereby "correcting" the irregularity of their descent from women who are not of the proper lineage, and enabling the sons of the servant women to share in the promises to Abraham' (Exum, *Fragmented Women*, 131). See also, Sarna, *JPS: Genesis*, 207–8; Jeansonne, *Women of Genesis*, 19–20.

215. Exum, *Fragmented Women*, 131. Cf. Baskin, *Midrashic Women*, 141–60, esp. 145–50.

216. See Petersen, 'Family Values', 14; Forsyth, 'Sibling Rivalry', 453–510.

217. Schneider, *Mothers of Promise*, 63.

218. See ibid., 63, 78–9, 94; Rabow, *Lost Matriarch*, 188.

6.5.4.1. *Leah*

Leah is Jacob's first wife and mother to several of his children yet Genesis provides little information about her. The audience learns that Leah is 'hated' (Gen 29:31) and that her husband prefers Rachel. Furthermore, the biblical text portrays Leah's constant struggles with Rachel, particularly regarding childbearing (Gen 29–33). Yet Leah plays a fundamental role in the life of Israel as she bears several of the nation's tribal ancestors. For the rabbis, Leah was a mother of Israel alongside Sarah, Rebekah and Rachel; the midrash makes this clear.

Like Rebekah, the rabbis suggest that Leah and Rachel's formal introduction into the Genesis narrative reveals their matriarchal destiny (Gen 29:16). *Genesis Rabbah* 70:15 interprets this verse in two parts. First:

> NOW LABAN HAD TWO DAUGHTERS (XXIX, 16)—like two beams running from end to end of the world. Each produced captains, each produced kings, from each arose slayers of lions, from each arose conquerors of countries, from each arose dividers of countries. The sacrifices brought by the son of each overrode the Sabbath. The wars waged by the descendants of both overrode the Sabbath. To each was given two nights: the night of Pharaoh and the night of Sennacherib to Leah, and the night of Gideon and the night of Mordecai to Rachel, as it says, *On that night could not the king sleep* (Est. VI, 1).

The rabbis discuss the two daughters as equals, noting parallel achievements by their descendants throughout Israel's history. Rabow notes that this 'comparative, perhaps competitive relationship with one another' will characterise Rachel and Leah's lives and their place in Israel's history.[219]

However, just as the biblical text goes on to differentiate between the sisters, so too do the rabbis:

> THE NAME OF THE GREAT ONE [E.V. 'ELDER'] WAS LEAH (XXIX, 16). She was great (גדולה) in her gifts, receiving the priesthood for all time and royalty for all time. AND THE NAME OF THE SMALL ONE [E.V. 'YOUNGER'] WAS RACHEL (*ib.*): small (קטנה) in her gifts, Joseph [bearing sway] for but a time, and Saul for but a time.

According to the rabbinic interpreters, Gen 29:16 reveals more than Leah and Rachel's ages—it also indicates their relative statuses within the history of Israel. Both women are equally worthy of the title 'matriarch' as their descendants achieve great things in Israel. However, Leah is ultimately greater, as the Israelite priesthood and royalty descend from her sons, Levi

---

219. Rabow, *Lost Matriarch*, 30–1 (quote p. 31).

and Judah. These institutions are enduring, whilst Rachel's descendants have only temporary authority as rulers.[220] This midrash contrasts with the appearance of the biblical verse, which 'abruptly provides Leah with neither background nor history. She is simply introduced as Laban's elder daughter—implying, perhaps that she is not worthy of more description.'[221] *Genesis Rabbah* 70:15 explores matriarchal motherhood and its national implications. Leah's role as a matriarch is confirmed and, in this instance, she is even elevated above Rachel.

In rabbinic texts, the matriarchs often demonstrate awareness of their own significance; Leah is no exception. In Genesis, Leah and Rachel name their children based on their personal experiences.[222] For example, Leah's second son is called Simeon (שִׁמְעוֹן): 'Because the LORD has heard (שָׁמַע) that I am hated, he has given me this son also' (Gen 29:33). In *Genesis Rabbah*, many of these naming verses are provided with extended meanings. Leah's naming of Simeon is appended with the comment: 'This son will one day produce an enemy (*sone*)—of God—and who will heal his wound? THIS SON ALSO—Phinehas, who will spring from Levi' (*Gen. Rab.* 71:4).[223] Leah's naming of Simeon is said to conceal reference to Israel's later history.[224] This becomes one key way in which Leah fulfils her matriarchal role, as she demonstrates awareness of the national consequences of her motherhood.

Genesis Rabbah 71:5 combines the naming process with Leah's recognition of her role as ancestress to the royal and priestly tribes. The midrash interprets Gen 29:35, after Leah bears Judah: 'This time I will praise (ידה, Hiphil) the LORD'. This Genesis verse is interpreted by means of another verse, Num 17:17 (ET 17:2): 'Speak to the Israelites, and get twelve staffs from them, one for each ancestral house, from all the leaders of their ancestral houses'. Numbers 17 describes the Israelites' rebellion against Moses and Aaron's authority following the incident with the company of Korah. Twelve staffs, representing Israel's tribes, are set up

220. Cf. ibid., 1, 10. Rabow notes that the adjectives used 'are words commonly used to denote greater and smaller size, not age' (p. 31).

221. Ibid., 9.

222. See Callaway, *Sing, O Barren One*, 25; Pardes, *Countertraditions*, 64; Havrelock, 'Heroic Barrenness', 176–7.

223. Freedman comments: '"Also" is generally regarded as an extension, and is actually understood here as an allusion to Levi, the third son, though the verse actually refers to Simeon' (Freedman, n. 1 655).

224. Cf. Rebekah's words in *Gen. Rab.* 65:14 (see §6.5.3, 'Rebekah: The Mother of Two Nations'). Rachel's naming of both Joseph and Benjamin is also connected with events that take place later in Israel's history (*Gen. Rab.* 73:5, 6).

and God causes the rod associated with Levi to flower, confirming Aaron's legitimate priesthood.[225] In *Gen. Rab.* 71:5, 'R. Levi said: Out of them [i.e. the tribes] two tribes were exalted, the tribe of priesthood and the tribe of royalty'. Freedman explains:

> The blossoming of Aaron's rod, representing the tribe of Levi, showed that the priesthood was its prerogative; further, this rod that blossomed was entrusted to Judah, to be the sceptre of its kings (E.J. [*EncJud*]). Thus with the birth of Judah Leah saw that both priesthood and royalty would belong to her descendants, and for this she exclaimed, THIS TIME WILL I PRAISE GOD.[226]

Leah recognises at Judah's birth that her offspring will form the royal and priestly tribes; thus she praises the Lord and names her son in joyful response. The midrash then explains that the royal and priestly tribes have an equal status because: 'You will find that whatever is written in connection with one [the priesthood] is written in connection with the other [royalty]'. This includes, for example, references to 'crown, conse-cration' (נזר) and 'anointing' (root משח), which appear in relation to both dynasties.[227] Leah's motherhood has a significant national dimension, and in *Genesis Rabbah* she demonstrates awareness of this.

The mandrake incident (Gen 30:14-21) is one of the most debasing episodes narrated about any of the matriarchs in Genesis. Reuben brings mandrake plants to his mother and the barren Rachel then tries to acquire some of these known aphrodisiacs from her sister.[228] Following 'crude bartering for Jacob's sexual services', Leah gives some mandrakes to Rachel and goes to claim her night with Jacob.[229] Sarna argues that 'The pathetic nature of this barter arrangement is underlined by the striking fact that the verb *sh-k-v* [Gen 30:15], when employed in Genesis with a sexual nuance, never connotes a relationship of marital love but is invariably

---

225. Through a play on the words 'rod' and 'to stumble', the midrash links this episode to Israel's wider failings.

226. Freedman, n. 1 656.

227. נזר: e.g. Exod 29:6 (priesthood); Ps 132:18 (royalty). משח: e.g. Exod 28:41 (priesthood); 1 Sam 16:13 (royalty).

228. See Schneider, *Mothers of Promise*, 73, 84. For the mandrake incident, see §6.3.2, 'Sons' Respect for their Mothers'.

229. Schneider, *Mothers of Promise*, 79. Westermann (*Genesis 12–36*, 475) suggests that: 'The rivalry between the two women expresses itself here in an exchange of words'. Cf. Havrelock, 'Heroic Barrenness', 159; Byron, 'Childlessness and Ambiguity', 31.

used in unsavoury circumstances'.[230] Leah informs Jacob that: 'You must come in to me (אלי תבוא); for I have hired (root שכר) you with my son's mandrakes' (Gen 30:16). The language is direct: אלי, 'into me', appears before the verb as Leah demands that Jacob spend the night with her. Moreover, the root שכר, 'to hire', was last used regarding Jacob's wages when working for Laban (Gen 29:15) and is unexpected language for describing sexual intimacy between husband and wife.[231] Leah and Jacob have sexual relations and this leads to the birth of two more sons and a daughter to Leah.

Genesis Rabbah 72:5 focuses on the outcome of the mandrake incident, namely the births of Issachar and Zebulun. This justifies the means by which the sons are born:

AND SAID: THOU MUST COME IN UNTO ME (*ib.*). R. Abbahu said: The Holy One, blessed be He, saw that her motive was none other than to produce tribes, therefore Scripture finds it necessary to state, THOU MUST COME IN UNTO ME.

R. Levi observed: Come and see how acceptable was the mediation of the mandrakes, for through these mandrakes there arose two great tribes in Israel, Issachar and Zebulun. Issachar studied the Torah, while Zebulun went out to sea and provided Issachar with sustenance, and so the Torah spread in Israel; thus it is written, '*The mandrakes give forth fragrance*' (Song VII, 14).

Leah's coarse language reflects her eagerness to produce more Israelite tribes, rather than her own sexual desires.[232] Leah's actions are justified by the rabbis and this also explains why 'God heeded Leah' (Gen 30:17) and enabled her to bear more children following the mandrake incident. *Genesis Rabbah* 72:3 further supports a national interpretation of the mandrake incident, as R. Eliezer and R. Samuel b. Naḥman note that although Rachel gained mandrakes, she lost tribes to Leah.[233] Leah and Rachel's lives have important consequences for the emergence of Israel and in *Genesis Rabbah*, the women themselves are shown to recognise this.

230. Sarna, *JPS: Genesis*, 209.

231. Schneider, *Mothers of Promise*, 69. See also Rabow, *Lost Matriarch*, 105–11.

232. Cf. Freedman, n. 9 664; Baskin, *Midrashic Women*, 108–9; *Gen. Rab.* 80:1. See §8.2.2, 'Beauty and Sexuality'.

233. See §8.2.2, 'Beauty and Sexuality'.

Leah receives little attention in the biblical text of Genesis, especially compared with Rachel. In spite of this, '[t]he role of Leah's children is a recurring beat indicating that Leah is at least as important as Rachel'.[234] In *Genesis Rabbah*, the rabbinic interpreters emphasise Leah's matriarchal legitimacy and the national consequences of her motherhood, even demonstrating Leah's own awareness of her national role.[235]

6.5.4.2. *Rachel*

Jacob meets Rachel as she tends her father's flocks in Haran; he then agrees to work seven years in return for her hand in marriage.[236] Although Jacob is initially given Leah as a wife, another seven years pass and he marries Rachel (Gen 29). Jacob's love for Rachel is mentioned three times in Gen 29 (vv. 18, 20, 30) and he is shown to favour Rachel above her sister (Gen 29:30). Eventually, the barren Rachel bears Joseph (Gen 30:22-24) and Benjamin, but she dies during childbirth and is buried 'on the way to Ephrath' (Gen 35:16-20). In *Genesis Rabbah*, the midrashists portray Rachel's national motherhood.

In *Genesis Rabbah*, sons may be identified through their mothers as well as their fathers.[237] One tradition, repeated several times in the midrash, suggests that Esau/Edom will be defeated by Rachel's descendants:

> For R. Phinehas said in the name of R. Samuel b. Naḥman: It is a tradition that Esau will fall at the hands of none other than Rachel's descendants (בני בניה שלרחל), as it is written, *Surely the youngest of the flock shall drag them away* (Jer. XLIX, 20). And why does he call them *'The youngest of the flock'?* Because they were of the youngest of the tribes.[238]

Jeremiah 49:20, part of Jeremiah's oracle against Edom (Jer 49:6-22), identifies the destroyers of Edom as 'the little ones of the flock'. The midrash then connects this with Rachel's descendants. The familiar phrase, 'the son of Rachel' (בנה שלרחל) is raised to a national level, as Israel's historical enemy will be defeated by this woman's offspring. International

---

234. Schneider, *Mothers of Promise*, 66.
235. Ramon, 'Torah of Hesed', 167–8.
236. See Westermann, *Genesis 12–36*, 466.
237. See §6.2, 'Identity'.
238. This tradition also appears in *Gen. Rab.* 75:5; 99:2 and 97 (NV). There are minor orthographic and verbal differences between passages; meaning is unaffected. The tradition is invariably associated with Joseph. *Gen. Rab.* 75:5 and 73:7 suggest that Jacob did not leave Laban's household until Rachel bore Joseph, 'the adversary of Esau' (שטנו שלעשו/ס). Only then was Jacob ready to meet his brother again.

conflict has its roots in the patriarchal family, and significantly, Edom's destroyers are identified by their ancestress, Rachel. She becomes a representative of Israel, standing as the authoritative head of the people who will descend from her.

Genesis Rabbah 99:2 extends the international and historical aspects of R. Phinehas's tradition. This midrash sets out a schema for the course of history, based on the traditional identification of the four kingdoms in Dan 7 with Babylonia, Media, Greece and Edom, the latter used as a rabbinic designation for Rome.[239] According to *Gen. Rab.* 99:2, each nation is to be defeated by a particular Israelite tribe and its member(s), which the midrash names in turn.[240] Rabbi Phinehas's tradition is used as evidence to support the defeat of Edom by Joseph's descendants. In repeating the tradition linking Rachel with the defeat of one of Israel's key enemies, the midrash further highlights her national motherhood. The identification of Edom with Rome brings the midrash into the rabbis' own day, as they were living under Roman rule.[241] Rachel's motherhood has enduring relevance.

Rachel is portrayed as the archetypal mother of Israel in Jer 31:15: 'Thus says the LORD: A voice is heard in Ramah, lamentation and bitter weeping. Rachel is weeping for her children; she refuses to be comforted for her children, because they are no more'.[242] The verse is part of Jeremiah's description of Israel's future restoration following the Babylonian exile (Jer 30–31). Rachel is depicted as the nation's mother, mourning as her children are exiled from the promised land. The language used is highly emotive, as Rachel stands in utter sorrow at the fate of her children.

239. See §6.5.3, 'Rebekah: The Mother of Two Nations'.

240. Judah (Daniel); Benjamin (Mordecai); Levi (Hasmoneans); Joseph ('the one anointed for war who came from Joseph').

241. See Cohen, 'Esau as Symbol', 19–48.

242. See Freedman, n. 1 654. On Jer 31:15-17, see Jack R. Lundbom, *Jeremiah 21–36: A New Translation with Introduction and Commentary*, Anchor Bible 21b (New York: Doubleday, 2004), 434–40; Bar-Ilan, *Some Jewish Women*, 87; Pardes, 'Rachel's Dream', 39–40; Zlotnick, *Dinah's Daughters*, 5–6, 8–9, 164; Barnabas Lindars, '"Rachel Weeping for Her Children"—Jeremiah 31:15-22', *Journal for the Study of the Old Testament* 12 (1979): 47–62, esp. 52–3; Phyllis Trible, 'The Gift of a Poem: A Rhetorical Study of Jeremiah 31:15-22', *Andover Newton Quarterly* 17, no. 4 (1977): 271–80. Ritter conducted a detailed study of traditions concerning Rachel, particularly focusing on Jer 31, and including passages dealt with in the present study: Christine Ritter, *Rachels Klage im antiken Judentum und frühen Christentum: Eine Auslegungsgeschichtliche Studie*, Geschichte des antiken Judentums und des Urchristentums 52 (Leiden: Brill, 2003).

Rachel's actions elicit a direct response from the Lord in Jer 31:16-17:

> Thus says the LORD: Keep your voice from weeping, and your eyes from
> tears; for there is a reward for your work, says the LORD: they shall come
> back from the land of the enemy; there is hope for your future, says the
> LORD: your children shall come back to their own country.

According to Lundbom, 'These verses contain a cluster of very brief
hope and comfort oracles that answer the weeping of Rachel in v 15'.[243]
Maternal imagery plays a central role in these verses: Rachel regards the
exiles as her children and it is her maternal protection that will enable
their return to Israel.[244] Rachel continues to influence the life, history and
identity of Israel, and the Lord's response to Rachel's mourning demonstrates divine affirmation of her matriarchal role. In fact, Trible argues that
these verses emphasise the mother above her children and God.[245] This
image of the mother Rachel crying for her Israelite children after the exile
was extremely popular in the Second Temple period and in rabbinic literature.[246] The image appears several times in *Genesis Rabbah* and influences
rabbinic understandings of Rachel as matriarch.

Genesis Rabbah 71:2 discusses the biblical statement: 'Rachel was
barren' (Gen 29:31). Rabbi Isaac and R. Abba b. Kahana re-vocalise
עֲקָר, 'barren', to read עִקָּר, 'chief', suggesting that Rachel's barrenness
indicates her authoritative position within the patriarchal household.[247]
Rabbi Samuel b. Naḥman then argues that:

> Because the incidents are related about Rachel, Israel was called by her
> name, as it says, *Rachel weeping for her children* (Jer. XXXI, 15); and not
> only by her name, but by her son's name: *It may be that the Lord, the God*

---

243. Lundbom, *Jeremiah 21–36*, 439; Trible, 'Gift of a Poem', 276.

244. Israel is identified with particular ancestors and with feminine imagery
elsewhere in Jer 30–31. Jacob and Ephraim are used as designations for Israel.
Moreover, in Jer 31:21-22, Israel is depicted as 'virgin Israel' (בתולת ישראל) and
'faithless daughter' (הבת השובבה). On Jer 31:15-22, particularly its use of feminine
and masculine terminology and imagery, see Trible, 'Gift of a Poem', 271–80.

245. Ibid., 273.

246. E.g. *Lam. Rab.* Proem 24. On this passage, see Galit Hasan-Rokem, *Web of
Life: Folklore and Midrash in Rabbinic Literature*, trans. Batya Stein, Contraversions:
Jews and Other Differences (Stanford: Stanford University Press, 2000), 126–9;
Ramon, 'Torah of Hesed', 164–5; Ramon, 'Torah of Hesed', 54–6. Cf. Callaway,
Sing, O Barren One, 81–90, 142, although as noted above, she does not adequately
deal with this image of Rachel or its use in the midrash.

247. See §5.4, 'Matriarchs as Representatives of the National Identity'.

> *of hosts, will be gracious unto the remnant of Joseph* (Amos V, 15); and not
> only by her son's name, but also by the name of her grandson, as it says, *Is
> Ephraim a darling son unto Me* (Jer. XXXI, 20)?[248]

In Jer 31:15, Rachel is the archetypal mother of Israel and a symbol of the
nation. The inclusion of this image within the midrash highlights rabbinic
appreciation for this woman and acknowledges her centrality for Israel's
identity, as the nation may be referred to purely through her name. Further
examples are given of authoritative figures from Israel's early history
being used to personify the nation. The figures named here, Joseph and
Ephraim, are Rachel's descendants and this is used as further proof of
Rachel's authority.

Jeremiah 31 and Amos 5 are cited to demonstrate Israel's identification
through key ancestral figures. Both passages are prophetic oracles
anticipating and hoping for the restoration of Israel and the repair of
her relationship with God. Rachel and her immediate descendants are
associated with the theme of Israel's salvation. This is perhaps because
they lived in the 'golden age' of the patriarchal era, when the covenant
was newly established and Israel was emerging from its great fathers and
mothers. The members of this family become the ancestors of a nation and,
thus, Israel may be referred to by their names. Jeremiah 31:16 even argues
that Rachel's mourning persuades God to restore his people following the
Babylonian exile. *Genesis Rabbah* 71:2 records Rachel's movement from
barrenness to motherhood and highlights the interconnectedness of these
different stages of 'the matriarchal cycle'. As a matriarch, Rachel bore
covenant sons but she also continues to offer protection to the nation.
She is afforded great respect in the midrash as a representative of Israel's
national identity.

Jeremiah 31:15 is again employed in *Gen. Rab.* 70:10, which interprets
Gen 29:4-6, where Jacob arrives in Haran. Rabbi Jose b. R. Ḥaninah
relates these verses to the Babylonian exile of 586 BCE, initially through
wordplay and then by evoking Jer 31:15-17. In the biblical text, Jacob
meets men tending sheep by a well. The midrash suggests that Jacob's
meeting the men of the town foreshadows the exile:

> AND JACOB SAID UNTO THEM: MY BRETHREN, WHENCE ARE
> YE? AND THEY SAID: OF HARAN ARE WE (XXIX, 4). R. Jose b. R.
> Ḥanina interpreted the passage in reference to the dispersion [of Israel].

---

248. Part of *Gen. Rab.* 71:2 is repeated in cur. edd. *Gen. Rab.* 82:10 (see
Freedman, 760–1).

AND JACOB SAID UNTO THEM…AND THEY SAID: OF HARAN
(חרן) ARE WE—we are fleeing from God's (Holy One Blessed be He's)
wrath (*haron*) (חרון). AND HE SAID UNTO THEM: KNOW YE LABAN
(לבן) THE SON OF NAHOR (*ib.* 5)?—know ye Him who will one day
make your iniquities white (*labben*) (lit. 'cleanse', root לבן) as snow? AND
HE SAID UNTO THEM: IS IT WELL WITH HIM? AND THEY SAID:
IT IS WELL (*ib.* 6): For whose sake?—AND BEHOLD, RACHEL HIS
DAUGHTER COMETH WITH THE SHEEP (*ib.*). Thus it is written, *Thus
saith the Lord: A voice is heard in Ramah…* (Jer. XXXI, 15 ff.).[249]

Rabbi Jose b. R. Ḥanina takes this as an indication that Israel will be
restored following the exile, and Rachel, who is introduced into Genesis
immediately following Jacob's enquiry, is used to prove this.[250] The
midrash cites Jer 31:15-16, where Rachel mourns her children's exile and,
in direct response, God promises that Israel shall return to her homeland.

Jeremiah's depiction of Rachel as the archetypal mother of Israel forms
the climax of the midrash. Scriptural quotations in rabbinic literature are
usually terse, as the rabbis assume their audience's familiarity with the
Hebrew text; yet here, Jer 31:15-16 is cited more extensively, suggesting
the importance of this biblical passage for the rabbis. In *Genesis Rabbah*,
Rachel's introduction into the biblical narrative is immediately associated
with her role as the mother of Israel during the exile. *Genesis Rabbah*
70:10 builds up to the connection between Rachel and the exile, suggesting
that this image of the matriarch drove the midrashic interpretation of Gen
29:4-6. Rachel's motherhood is of national import, helping to define and
protect Israelite identity through one of the nation's most challenging
historical periods.

Rachel is a matriarch and yet she is not buried with the patriarchs and
their wives. Instead she is buried 'on the road to Ephrath' (Gen 35:19)
after she dies giving birth to Benjamin.[251] *Genesis Rabbah* 82:10 offers a
positive reason for this: 'Jacob foresaw that the exiles would pass on from
thence, therefore he buried her there so that she might pray (lit. "ask") for
mercy for them'. The midrash ends by quoting a sizeable portion of Jer
31:15-17. Rachel's burial on the road to Ephrath 'separates Rachel in a
physical way from the rest of the matriarchs and the clan' and the rabbinic
interpreters attempt to explain this.[252] Here, Jacob recognises that Rachel

249. The addition of (*haron*) and (*labben*) is by Freedman.
250. See Freedman, n. 2 644.
251. See Sarna, *JPS: Genesis*, 244, 407–8; Lundbom, *Jeremiah 21–36*, 437;
Pardes, 'Rachel's Dream', 35.
252. Schneider, *Mothers of Promise*, 98. Cf. ibid., 90.

will safeguard Israel's future long after her death. The patriarch's respect for his matriarchal wife further highlights rabbinic views on the matriarchs' authority and the connection to Jer 31:15-17 again demonstrates Rachel's role as mother of a nation.[253]

Rachel's burial place becomes significant for another reason in *Gen. Rab.* 99:1, which discusses the position of the Jerusalem Temple. Psalm 132 speaks about the Temple and v. 6: 'We heard of it in Ephrath; we found it in the fields of Jaar (or: "the forest", יער)', is used in this midrash to locate the Temple in Benjamin's territory.[254] Rabbi Simeon argues that the Temple is:

> in the territory of the son of the woman who died in Ephrath. And who died in Ephrath? Rachel. You might then think that it is in the portion of Joseph, seeing that he too was her son: therefore it states, *'We found it in the field of the forest'*, which implies: In the portion of him who was likened to the beast of the forest. And who was so likened? Benjamin, as it is written, BENJAMIN IS A WOLF THAT RAVENETH (Gen 49:27).

The identity of the mother is central for establishing the location of the Jewish Temple, God's dwelling place on earth. This building is a key symbol of Israel's national identity and Rachel's burial place again has implications in Israel's later history.

Genesis Rabbah 99:1 suggests that Rachel's burial place is not haphazardly chosen but has meaning for the nation that descends from her. Although this passage does not explicitly use maternal imagery of Rachel, it builds on her role as a founding ancestress of Israel.

The biblical portrayal of Rachel focuses on Jacob's love for her and on her prolonged barrenness. When she eventually bears two of Israel's tribal ancestors, Joseph and Benjamin, she dies in childbirth and is buried by the roadside as Jacob's family journeys on. Rachel appears again in Jer 31:15-17 as the archetypal mother of Israel, who laments her children's

---

253. Freedman cites the cur. edd. for *Gen. Rab.* 82:10, which contain huge expansions prior to the text given in Theodor-Albeck. This additional material discusses 1 Sam 10:2 and the location of Rachel's burial, the pillar erected by Jacob at Rachel's grave, and repeats the pericope concerning Israel being named after Rachel, Joseph and Ephraim (Freedman, 759–61). On Rachel's enduring role, see Rabow, *Lost Matriarch*, 183.

254. Freedman notes that whilst Jerusalem lies in Judah, the Temple is built on part of Benjamin's portion found within Judah (Freedman, n. 1 973). Rabbi Judah uses 1 Sam 17:12 to locate the Temple in Judah. On the location of the Temple and Rachel's burial place, see Wenham, *Genesis 16–50*, 326–7; Sarna, *JPS: Genesis*, 244.

exile to Babylon and in return, she receives a divine promise that Israel will be restored to its homeland. This powerful image of Rachel's national motherhood heavily influences her portrayal in *Genesis Rabbah*. Rachel protects the nation long after her death and Israel is identified through her and her offspring. Rachel is afforded great respect by the rabbinic interpreters for her role as a matriarch of Israel.

Leah and Rachel are the final two Genesis matriarchs and this generation sees the emergence of Israel through Jacob and his twelve sons. Although these sisters compete for Jacob's attention and for children in the biblical text, their equal status as matriarchs of Israel is recognised by the rabbis in *Genesis Rabbah*.

6.5.5. *Summary*

National motherhood forms a central part of the rabbis' presentation of the Genesis matriarchs. They bear covenant sons who become the founding fathers of Israel; thus the nation directly descends from the matriarchs. In *Genesis Rabbah*, each matriarch is linked with the twelve tribes of Israel. Leah and Rachel bore tribal ancestors, but each of the matriarchs is equally worthy of the title 'the mother of Israel', as they ensure that the nation emerged and continued to flourish. Moreover, the matriarchs themselves demonstrate an awareness of their matriarchal roles. Rebekah compares Jacob's situation with the nation that will later bear his name (*Gen. Rab.* 65:14), whilst Leah names her sons in recognition of their national roles (e.g. *Gen. Rab.* 71:4). Sarah, the first matriarch of Israel, is even portrayed breastfeeding heathen children, showing that her motherhood has not only national, but universal, consequences (*Gen. Rab.* 53:9).

6.6. *Conclusions*

Motherhood is the defining characteristic of the figures known as 'the matriarchs' (האמהות). *Genesis Rabbah* builds on the biblical portrayal of Sarah, Rebekah, Leah and Rachel as mothers and notes that matriarchal motherhood is multifaceted. In *Genesis Rabbah*, the rabbinic interpreters present the physical experience of bearing children, discussing painful pregnancies and death during childbirth. Furthermore, traits are passed from mother to son and sons may be identified through their mothers, even on a national scale. The rabbis depict male members of the ancestral family respecting females within their maternal roles, meaning that even Leah was eventually appreciated by Jacob, and sons protected and defended their mothers. Maternal protection of the covenant son is an extremely important theme, ensuring that the correct son inherited.

Finally, the matriarchs' lives and actions have national implications and they may be viewed as representatives of Israel.[255] *Genesis Rabbah* also suggests that the matriarchs themselves understand the wider consequences of their maternity. Motherhood completes 'the matriarchal cycle' and the matriarchs secure their roles as the ancestresses of Israel. For this, the rabbis greatly respect them.[256]

255. Cf. Baskin, *Midrashic Women*, 3.
256. Cf. Jeansonne, *Women of Genesis*, 117.

Chapter 7

LEGITIMACY AND SUCCESSION

The transformation of each matriarch from a barren woman to a mother of covenant sons does not happen by chance. Each of the four major matriarchs is chosen to become a 'mother of Israel' and her legitimacy is demonstrated in *Genesis Rabbah*. Sarah, Rebekah, Leah and Rachel possess the attributes and characteristics necessary to become matriarchs. Each legitimate woman then enters into a legitimate marriage with a patriarch, from which legitimate offspring may be born. Finally, in order for 'the matriarchal cycle' to continue into the next generation, matriarchal succession must be achieved, allowing a new matriarch to take over from her predecessor. This chapter will explore these issues.

7.1. *Sarah as the 'Capable Wife' (אשת חיל)*

Proverbs 31:10-31 describes an exemplary woman, the 'capable wife' (אשת חיל). She is a good wife and mother, respected by her male family members. She is resourceful and efficient, runs her household effectively and fears the Lord—a hugely important characteristic in the Hebrew Bible.[1] Proverbs 31:10 sets the tone for the rest of the poem: 'A capable

---

1. E.g. Genesis 22:12; Job 28:28. See Michael V. Fox, *Proverbs 1–9: A New Translation with Introduction and Commentary*, The Anchor Bible 18a (New York: Doubleday, 2000), 69–71. On the 'capable wife', see Camp, *Wisdom and the Feminine*, esp. 85–92, 96–7, 101, 263–4; Michael V. Fox, *Proverbs 10–31: A New Translation with Introduction and Commentary*, The Anchor Yale Bible 18b (New Haven: Yale University Press, 2009), 547, 888–917; Peskowitz, *Spinning Fantasies*, 95–108. Female imagery is used extensively in Proverbs, e.g. in the female personification of Wisdom and Folly (e.g. Prov 1:20-33; 8–9). See Camp, *Wisdom and the Feminine*; Fox, *Proverbs 1–9*; Fox, *Proverbs 10–31*; Peter Schäfer, *Mirror of His Beauty: Feminine Images of God from the Bible to the Early Kabbalah* (Princeton: Princeton University Press, 2002), 19–38; Brenner-Idan, *The Israelite Woman*, 42–5.

wife (אשת חיל) who can find? She is far more precious than jewels
(פנינים)'.[2] As Camp comments: 'The poem on the woman of worth,
31.10-31, presents us with a portrait of a wise wife which is on the one
hand concrete and vivid while at the same time idealised'.[3] The phrase
'capable wife' appears once more in the book of Proverbs, in Prov 12:4:
'a good wife (אשת חיל) is the crown of her husband'. The term חיל
means 'strength', 'wealth', and specifically here, '*ability, efficiency, often
involving moral worth*'.[4] In the Hebrew Bible, only one woman, Ruth,
is specifically designated a 'capable wife' (אשת חיל, Ruth 3:11). Ruth's
behaviour is exemplary: after the death of her husband, she refuses to
leave her mother-in-law, Naomi, even when encouraged to return to her
heathen homeland. Moreover, Ruth is the great-grandmother of King
David, whose dynasty is promised perpetual rule over Israel. The phrase
'capable wife' reflects Ruth's authority as Israel's monarchical ancestress.[5] This title clearly refers to a woman of high esteem, whose positive
qualities are unsurpassable.

In *Genesis Rabbah*, both Prov 12:4 and 31:10 are applied to Sarah.
Genesis Rabbah 45:1 interprets Gen 16:1: 'Sarai, Abram's wife, bore
him no children'. Barrenness still defines Sarai, who has not appeared in
the biblical narrative since Gen 12, when she was given to Pharaoh by
Abram. *Genesis Rabbah* 45:1 explores various meanings of Prov 31:10,
connecting the 'capable wife' with Sarah:

> NOW SARAI ABRAM'S WIFE BORE HIM NO CHILDREN, etc. (XVI,
> 1). It is written, *A woman of valour who can find, for her price* (mikrah) *is
> far above* (רחק מן) *rubies* (Prov. XXXI, 10). What does '*mikrah*' mean? R.
> Abba b. Kahana said: Her pregnancy, as you read, *Thine origin* (mekuroth)
> *and thy nativity* (מכרתיך ומלדתיך) (Ezek. XVI, 3). Now Abram was a year
> older than Nahor, and Nahor was a year older than Haran; [hence Abram

---

2. This plural noun is usually translated as 'corals', 'pearls', 'rubies', or 'jewels',
though its exact meaning is unclear (BDB, 819).

3. Camp, *Wisdom and the Feminine*, 90.

4. BDB, 298. JPS and NRSV translate חיל as 'capable', 'worthy', or 'valour'.
The male form of the term (איש חיל) appears a number of times, e.g. Exod 18:21, 25,
where men of skill and trustworthiness, who fear God, are sought to lead the Israelite
community. See also Fox, *Proverbs 10–31*, 548, 891; Peskowitz, *Spinning Fantasies*,
195 n. 1.

5. Bronner, *From Eve to Esther*, 63. Bronner discusses Ruth in biblical and
rabbinic sources (ibid., 61–81). She also highlights similarities between Ruth and
Sarah's portrayals in the midrash (ibid., 75). On biblical Ruth, see also Pardes,
Countertraditions, 95–111.

was] two years older [than Haran; deduct] the year of pregnancy with Iscah, and you find that Haran begot children at six years of age, yet you say that Abram could not beget? Hence, NOW SARAI ABRAM'S WIFE BORE HIM NO CHILDREN.

Rabbi Abba b. Kahana argues for an alternate translation of the noun מכר, 'value',[6] as 'pregnancy'. This is based on wordplay between מכרה (Prov 31:10) and מכרתיך (Ezek 16:3),[7] nouns that are etymologically unrelated but contain the same consonants. Rabbi Abba b. Kahana's interpretation assumes both that Sarah is a 'capable wife' (אשת חיל) and that child-bearing is compatible with that role.

The midrash now relies on the ambiguity of רחק מן, which can mean either 'far above' or 'distant from'.[8] When read in conjunction with the interpretation of מכרה as 'her pregnancy', this yields two differing meanings of Prov 31:10. The translation 'her pregnancy is far above jewels' suggests the superior value of motherhood, which far surpasses jewels, whilst 'her pregnancy is more distant than rubies' reflects the matriarchs' problems in conceiving: precious jewels are easier to obtain.[9] This richly ambiguous language is perhaps used deliberately by the rabbis. It took the matriarchs years to conceive, but when they finally did, their motherhood was extremely valuable: they bore Israel's covenant sons and ensured that the correct son inherited those promises.[10]

For R. Abba b. Kahana, the second interpretation, indicating distance rather than superiority, is preferable. To illustrate this point, the midrash queries why Abraham had no offspring when his brother Nahor fathered children at a very early age. This observation is juxtaposed with Gen 16:1,

6. The segholate noun מכר, from the verb 'to sell', means 'merchandise', 'value', 'price' (BDB, 569; Num 20:19; Neh 13:16).

7. This noun, מכורה, has an uncertain meaning. Here, it is paralleled with מולדת, 'birth', 'kindred', and this is used to inform its meaning. BDB (468) argues that מכורה derives from the root of uncertain meaning, כור, which probably relates to digging or hewing. Cf. ארץ מכרה in Ezek 21:35; 29:14.

8. Cf. Fox, *Proverbs 10–31*, 892: '*greater than [rahoq mi-]*: Lit., "more distant", thus harder to obtain and more valuable'.

9. See Neusner, 2:146; Freedman, n. 1 379.

10. Camp (*Wisdom and the Feminine*, 101; cf. 262–3) remarks: 'The concluding poem about the woman of worth in ch. 31 allows the material benefits that flow from one's love of and success in finding Wisdom to be interpreted in terms of the benefits of human love and the marital relationship'. Fox notes that the second part of the verse emphasises not that such a woman is nearly impossible to find, but that she is extremely precious (Fox, *Proverbs 10–31*, 891).

where Genesis reaffirms Sarai's barrenness.[11] No judgment of Sarai's unfortunate condition is offered by the rabbis and the remainder of this midrash highlights the value of barrenness for Sarai's legitimacy as an Israelite matriarch.

The midrash explores Sarai's barrenness through the phrase, 'she did not bear for him' (Gen 16:1):[12]

> [DID NOT BEAR TO HIM.] R. Judah said: TO HIM teaches that she did not bear to Abram, but had she been married to another she would have borne children. R. Nehemiah said: Neither to him nor to anyone else. How then does R. Nehemiah interpret DID NOT BEAR TO HIM? Interpret TO HIM and TO HER, thus: She did not bear to herself—on Sarai's own account—nor TO HIM—on Abram's account.

Rabbi Judah suggests either that Abram is the problem or that, as a couple, Abram and Sarai would not bear children. Rabbi Nehemiah argues that Sarai would not have had children with any man. He interprets the verse as relating to the couple's inability to produce children together.[13] Both interpretations provide space for God to intervene and cause pregnancy.[14] Finally, the midrash turns to the alternate translation of רחק מן as indicating the superiority of matriarchal conception. Returning to the base verse of Gen 16:1, the introduction of Hagar at this point in the narrative is regarded as significant. The midrash provides Hagar with a backstory, which in turn comments upon Sarai's matriarchal status:

> R. Simeon b. Yoḥai said: Hagar was Pharaoh's daughter. When Pharaoh saw what was done on Sarah's behalf in his own house, he took his daughter and gave her to Sarah, saying, 'Better let my daughter be a handmaid in this house than a mistress in another house'; thus it is written, AND SHE HAD A HANDMAID, AN EGYPTIAN, WHOSE NAME WAS HAGAR, he (Pharaoh) saying, 'Here is thy reward (*agar*)'.[15]

---

11. According to this midrash, Nahor fathered children at the age of six. See §5.4.1, 'Use of the Biblical Barren Matriarch Tradition and its Development'.

12. My translation.

13. As Freedman notes (p. 379), this contradicts later Masoretic punctuation of the verse.

14. On this pericope, see Porton, 'How the Rabbis Imagined Sarah', 204–5. Cf. *Gen. Rab.* 44:10, where Abraham and Sarah's name changes change their destinies so they can bear children. See §5.2.3, 'God Ensures the Reversal of Barrenness by His Power'.

15. The brackets are Freedman's.

This explains Hagar's Egyptian background. When Pharaoh saw the miracles performed by God for Sarai (Gen 12), he sent away his own daughter (identified with Hagar), believing her to be better off serving in the patriarchal household than retaining status as an Egyptian princess.[16]

A parallel incident occurs in Gen 20, when the foreign king Abimelech takes Sarah into his household. When he releases her to Abraham on God's command, Abimelech rewards Abraham with many possessions, including maidservants (שפחות). The midrash argues that Abimelech also gave his daughter to become a slave in Israel's ancestral household. The midrash then concludes: 'as it is written, *Kings' daughters are among thy favourites* (Ps. XLV, 10): viz. [the daughters of [two] kings.] *At thy right hand doth stand the queen in gold of Ophir (ib.)*—this alludes to Sarai.' Psalm 45:10 is said to address Sarah and provides proof that she keeps company with royalty. This highlights the matriarch's superiority by comparing her with important female figures from other nations.

In Gen 12 and 20, foreign kings acknowledge God's power and Sarah's authority. Moreover, Gen 16 begins to demonstrate the archetypal national hostility between Egypt and Israel. The episode between Hagar and Sarah occurs immediately after God's warning that Egypt will one day enslave the Israelites and his promise that Israel will ultimately triumph (Gen 15:14). Although these promises relate to the distant future, Sarai, representing Israel, dominates the Egyptian Hagar.[17] *Genesis Rabbah* 45:1 comments on a number of biblical episodes and transforms a statement of Sarai's barrenness into firm proof of her legitimacy as the first matriarch. Sarah's motherhood is extremely valuable and her status is universally recognised. She can be given no better credentials by the rabbis.[18]

Genesis Rabbah 47:1 applies Prov 12:4 to Sarah, as it interprets her name change from Sarai to Sarah in Gen 17:15:

> Rabbi Aḥa said: Her husband was crowned through her, but she was not crowned through her husband. The Rabbis said: She was her husband's ruler. Usually, the husband gives orders, whereas here we read, *In all that Sarah saith unto thee, hearken unto her voice* (Gen. XXI, 12).

---

16. Levinson ('Bodies and Bo[a]rders', 348–52) offers detailed exposition of this tradition.

17. See §3.3.2, 'Marriages between Patriarchs and Handmaids'.

18. Zucker and Adelman note that in *Tanhuma*, Prov 31:10-31 was understood to be a eulogy written about Sarah. See Zucker, 'Sarah', 247; Adelman, 'Laughter and Re-Membering', 241–2.

On Prov 12:4, Fox comments: 'It is not a wife's beauty that reflects honour (or prestige) on her husband but her *ḥayil*-strength of mind and character. If one takes a wife who lacks this, he will suffer pain and shame to the core of his being.'[19] Rabbi Aḥa argues that Abraham benefitted from being married to Sarah, though she did not benefit likewise.[20] 'The Rabbis' then offer their authoritative viewpoint, suggesting that whilst husbands usually command their wives in marriage, Sarah has authority over Abraham. The Bible portrays God insisting that Abraham obey Sarah when she tells him to banish Hagar and Ishmael (Gen 21:12). The identification of Sarah as the 'capable wife' indicates her authority and here, she is elevated above Abraham.[21]

Sarai's name change is then explored in greater detail:

> R. Joshua b. Ḳarḥah said: The *yod* which the Lord took from Sarai soared aloft before God and protested: 'Sovereign of the Universe! Because I am the smallest of all letters, Thou hast withdrawn me from the name of that righteous woman!' Said the Holy One, blessed be He, to it: 'Hitherto thou wast in a woman's name and the last of its letters; now I will set thee in a man's name and at the beginning of its letters', as it says, *And Moses called Hoshea the son of Nun Joshua* (Num. XIII, 16). R. Mana said: Formerly she was a princess [Sarai] to her own people only, whereas now she is a princess [Sarah] to all mankind.

God dismisses the *yôd*'s complaint, as it was given a superior position in Joshua's name. Although Sarah is called a 'righteous woman' by the *yôd*, the midrash appears to undermine Sarah on the basis of her gender. At its completion, the midrash again refers to Sarah's authority. Drawing on the common meaning of the name Sarai/Sarah as 'princess', R. Mana suggests that 'Sarah' indicates a more universal authority than 'Sarai'.[22] The midrash thus concludes with a positive statement of Sarah's legitimacy.

19. Fox, *Proverbs 10–31*, 547. On Prov 12:4, see ibid., 547–8.

20. Freedman suggests that this argument relates to Sarai's name change from שרי to שרה through *gematria*. *Yôd* (י) has the numerical value of ten. Abraham and Sarah each have a *hê* (ה) added to their names. As *hê* has a value of five, the two identical letters add up to ten, the value of the letter removed from Sarai's name. Abraham gained from his wife because a value of five was added to his name, but Sarah lost out because ten was removed and replaced only with five. Freedman gives no further evidence to corroborate that this is what R. Aḥa has in mind, but the argument itself is sound (Freedman, n. 1 399).

21. This pericope also appears in *Gen. Rab.* 52:5.

22. Freedman, n. 1 400. On 'Sarah' as 'princess', see Sarna, *JPS: Genesis*, 87; Wenham, *Genesis 1–15*, 273.

Her gender may sometimes be regarded as limiting her authority; yet Sarah is also understood as a 'capable wife', an authoritative woman within her family, her people, and ultimately, all mankind.

7.1.1. *Summary*

The 'capable wife' (אשת חיל) described in Prov 12:4 and 31:10 is an exemplary Jewish woman. She is the perfect wife and mother, who fears God. In *Genesis Rabbah*, both verses are applied to Sarah, confirming her legitimacy and authority (*Gen. Rab.* 45:1 and 47:1). Fox comments: 'The Woman of Strength is not a particular woman, but an ideal... She is a paragon of feminine virtues, practical and ethical. She is the counterpart of the wise man portrayed throughout Proverbs and serves the same paradigmatic role.'[23] In Sarah, the rabbis found a woman who met all of these expectations. Sarah is greatly respected and she may therefore act as an exemplar for Jewish women.[24]

7.2. *Sarah and Rebekah as Exemplars of Sexual Purity and Rachel in Relationship with God*

For the rabbis, virginity, chastity and sexual purity were key female virtues. *Genesis Rabbah* 53:6 is entirely devoted to Sarah's purity and chastity. First, the *soṭah* ritual is applied to Sarah. The rabbis often portrayed Israel's ancestors adhering to Torah law, centuries before the revelation at Sinai.[25] Numbers 5:11-31 describes the ritual performed on a woman if her husband suspects that she has had sexual relations with another man. It involves an offering and subjecting the woman to a humiliating trial:

> if she has defiled herself and has been unfaithful to her husband, the water
> that brings the curse shall enter into her and cause bitter pain, and her womb
> shall discharge, her uterus drop, and the woman shall become an execration

---

23. Fox, *Proverbs 10–31*, 912.

24. Fuchs ('Literary Characterisation', 164–5) and Exum (*Fragmented Women*, 135–6) interpret the biblical praise of women as mothers as patriarchy's attempt to suppress them. Fox (*Prov 10–31*, 916) argues that the 'capable wife' is, in fact, a paradigm for all Jewish people, whether man or woman.

25. See e.g. Neusner, *Essential Guide*, 78; Gershon Hepner, *Legal Friction: Law, Narrative, and Identity Politics in Biblical Israel*, Studies in Biblical Literature 78 (New York: Peter Lang, 2010). This applies also to rabbinic law. Cf. *Gen. Rab.* 53:11; 60:16; 72:5.

among her people. But if the woman has not defiled herself and is clean, then she shall be immune and be able to conceive children. (Num 5:27-28; cf. 5:21-22)[26]

In *Gen. Rab.* 53:6, R. Isaac applies this trial to Sarah: 'Then this woman [Sarah] who had entered the houses of Pharaoh and Abimelech and yet emerged undefiled—surely it was but right that she should be remembered'. Sarah found herself in two situations where her sexual purity could have been compromised (Gen 12, 20) and yet she remained pure.[27] According to Num 5:28, Sarah is (doubly) worthy of bearing a child. The later Israelite ritual is shown to apply to Sarah and she passes its test. Against a background of suspicion, she twice remains sexually pure.[28]

Genesis Rabbah 53:6 continues: 'R. Judah said: Although R. Huna said that there is an angel appointed over desire, Sarah had not need for such, but He in His glory [made her conceive]; hence, AND THE LORD

26. Although the *soṭah* ritual was defunct by the rabbinic period, it was still discussed at great length by the rabbis. On the ritual in biblical and rabbinic literature, see Lisa Grushcow, *Writing the Wayward Wife: Rabbinic Interpretations of Sotah*, Ancient Judaism and Early Christianity 62 (Leiden: Brill, 2006); Judith Hauptman, 'Feminist Perspectives on Rabbinic Texts', in *Feminist Perspectives on Jewish Studies*, ed. Lynn Davidman and Shelly Tenenbaum (New Haven: Yale University Press, 1994), 48–9; Hauptman, *Rereading*, 15–29; Jacob Neusner, *How the Rabbis Liberated Women*, USF Studies in the History of Judaism; South Florida Studies in the History of Judaism 191 (Atlanta: Scholars Press, 1998), 65–92; Satlow, *Jewish Marriage*, 229–30; Swidler, *Women in Judaism*, 151–4; Satlow, *Tasting the Dish*, 156–8, 170–82; Zlotnick, *Dinah's Daughters*, 105–31; Tikva Frymer-Kensky, 'The Strange Case of the Suspected Sotah (Numbers V 11-31)', *Vetus Testamentum* 34, no. 1 (1984): 11–26; Bonna Devora Haberman, 'The Suspected Adulteress: A Study of Textual Embodiment', *Prooftexts* 20, no. 1–2 (2000): 12–42; Herbert Chanan Brichto, 'The Case of the Sota and a Reconsideration of Biblical Law', *Hebrew Union College Annual* 46, Centennial Issue (1975): 55–70; Biale, *Women and Jewish Law*, 33–5, 183–90; Wegner, *Chattel or Person?*, 50–4, 91–3.

27. Cf. Sarna, *JPS: Genesis*, 94. On female purity, see Lynn T. Scott, 'Not Merely Chattel: Women as Guardians of Holiness in the Mishnah's Society', in *Recovering the Role of Women: Power and Authority in Rabbinic Jewish Society*, ed. Peter J. Haas, South Florida Studies in the History of Judaism 59 (Atlanta: Scholars Press, 1992), 23–37.

28. Baskin (*Midrashic Women*, 124–5, 195 n. 12) notes that Num 5:28 became a source of concern for the rabbis. They envisaged barren women orchestrating situations in which they would be found innocent of adultery following the ritual in Num 5 and would expect to become pregnant. *B. Ber.* 31a-b and *b. Soṭah* 26a solve this problem: the innocent woman will conceive more easily and her children will have better features. Cf. Neusner, *How the Rabbis Liberated Women*, 65.

REMEMBERED SARAH'. Sarah is distanced from sexual activity and bodily urges. Sarah is worthy of becoming a mother of Israel, as demonstrated by her sexual purity and God therefore intervenes to ensure that she conceives.

Finally, *Gen. Rab.* 53:6 reads Gen 21:2 closely, interpreting each part as confirming that Sarah (and Abraham) produced Isaac: 'AND SARAH CONCEIVED, AND BORE ABRAHAM A SON (XXI, 2). This teaches that she did not steal seed from elsewhere. A SON IN HIS OLD AGE: this teaches that his [Isaac's] features were like his own'. To conclude, the midrash discusses the phrase: 'at the time (למועד) that God spoke to him' (Gen 21:2), relating this to the time it took for Isaac to be born. Rabbi Judan argues that Isaac was born after nine months to quash any speculation that he may be Abimelech's son, and R. Ḥunia argues that Isaac was born at seven months, indicating his special status.[29] Genesis 21, recording Isaac's birth, immediately follows Sarah's encounter with Abimelech (Gen 20). As they interpret Gen 21, the rabbis confirm Sarah's exemplary character.[30]

Rebekah also reflects purity. Genesis 24 highlights Rebekah's worthiness to assume the matriarchal role and midrashic exegesis accentuates her outstanding qualities. Genesis 24:16 asserts that Rebekah was: 'a virgin, whom no man had known'.[31] In *Gen. Rab.* 60:5, this forms the basis for a discussion about virginity; and then, more specifically, for proving Rebekah's chastity.[32] The midrash begins:

> We learned: The marriage settlement of a woman who lost her virginity through a physical injury (מוכת עץ) is two hundred [*zuz*]:[33] that is the ruling of R. Meir. But the Sages maintain: The settlement of such a one is one hundred [*zuz*]. R. Abbahu said in R. Eleazar's name: This is R. Meir's

29. This is a tradition found elsewhere in Jewish literature, concerning Isaac and other figures, like Moses. See e.g. Pieter W. van der Horst, 'Sex, Birth, Purity and Asceticism in *Protevangelium Jacobi*', *Neotestamentica* 28, no. 3 (1994): 206–10; Jacobson, 2:720. A final argument in this midrash links Isaac to the exodus of Egypt, as R. Huna argues in R. Hezekiah's name that Isaac was born at 'midnight/half of the day', based on the use of the word מועד in Gen 21:2 and in Deut 16:6, which discusses Israel leaving Egypt at night. This highlights Isaac's connection to the wider history of Israel.

30. Grushcow (*Writing the Wayward Wife*, 285–7) discusses rabbinic traditions confirming that Abraham and Sarah were Isaac's biological parents.

31. See Sarna, *JPS: Genesis*, 165.

32. On this midrash and a detailed comparison with *p. Ketub.* 1:3, see Teugels, 'The Wooing of Rebekah' (Gen. 24), 193–211; cf. 193–226.

33. For coin terminology/values mentioned in this passage, see Jastrow, 385, 797.

reason: NEITHER HAD ANY MAN KNOWN HER: hence if she had lost her virginity through a physical injury (lit: 'if she were entered into/had intercourse by wood', נבעלה מעץ), she would still be a virgin. While this is the Rabbi's (*sic*: plural: 'rabbis'', רבנן) reason: A VIRGIN: hence had she lost her virginity through an injury (lit: 'if she were entered into/had intercourse by wood', נבעלה מעץ), she would no longer be a virgin.

Mishnah Ketubbot 1:2 specifies that the marriage settlement (*ketubah*) paid for a virgin is two hundred *denars*, whilst a widow is only worth one hundred.[34] Using Gen 24:16, R. Meir and the Rabbis debate whether the loss of virginity, specifically the breaking of the hymen, through accidental injury reduces the *ketubah* to one hundred *denars*.[35] The designation מוכת עץ, literally 'being injured/struck by wood', is here used to refer to an accidental injury incurred by the woman.[36] At issue is the exact nature of virginity, a trait highly valued in an Israelite bride.[37]

For R. Meir, accidental injury maintains the woman's virginal status for marriage, as 'no man had known (her)' (Gen 24:16); yet the Rabbis argue that with the hymen broken, her virginity is lost.[38] As Lieve Teugels notes, Gen 24:16 is used here purely for halakhic reasons.[39] Following this, the midrash turns specifically to Rebekah:

> Rabbi Joḥanan said: No woman [hitherto] had been intimate for the first time with a man who had been circumcised at eight days save Rebekah.

---

34. See Teugels, *'The Wooing of Rebekah' (Gen. 24)*, 193; Hauptman, *Rereading*, 66; Wegner, *Chattel or Person?*, 21–3, 222 n. 37, 227 n. 84. On Jewish marriage in antiquity, especially the ketubah, see Neusner, *How the Rabbis Liberated Women*, 93–41; Satlow, *Jewish Marriage*, esp. 199–224; Léonie J. Archer, *Her Price Is Beyond Rubies: The Jewish Woman in Graeco-Roman Palestine*, JSOT Supplement Series 60 (Sheffield: JSOT Press, 1990), 171–206; Biale, *Women and Jewish Law*, 44–69, 80–1; Wegner, *Chattel or Person?*, 43–5, 80–5, 222 n. 38; Baskin, *Midrashic Women*, 88–118.

35. See Teugels, *'The Wooing of Rebekah' (Gen. 24)*, 195–7, 200–202.

36. Jastrow, 910; Teugels, *'The Wooing of Rebekah' (Gen. 24)*, 195.

37. See Teugels, *'The Wooing of Rebekah' (Gen. 24)*, 195; Adler, *Engendering Judaism*, 130; Bronner, *From Eve to Esther*, 112; Satlow, *Jewish Marriage*, 118–19; Fonrobert, *Menstrual Purity*, 60; Ilan, *Mine and Yours Are Hers*, 191–9; Archer, *Her Price Is Beyond Rubies*, 106–13.

38. Wegner suggests that the mishnaic rabbis 'perceive the girl not as a human being possessing or lacking sexual experience, but as a chattel whose owner pays bride-price for an intact hymen…' Using *m. Ket.* 1:2d, Wegner notes that a girl's hymen was thought to repair itself before the age of three (Wegner, *Chattel or Person?*, 22–3).

39. Teugels, *'The Wooing of Rebekah' (Gen. 24)*, 194, 200–203. Cf. ibid., 207–11.

Resh Laḳish said: The daughters of the heathens guarded their virginity, yet abandoned themselves to unnatural immorality; but this one [Rebekah] was A VIRGIN in respect of her hymen, while NEITHER HAD ANY MAN KNOWN HER—unnaturally.

Isaac is the first son born into the covenant between God and Israel, and thus Rebekah is the first woman whose worthiness to become a matriarch must be shown.[40] Rabbi Joḥanan's comment links the preceding halakhic argument with the particular implications of Gen 24:16 for Rebekah's character. According to Resh Laḳish, Rebekah is a virgin in every respect. The double designation of Rebekah's virginity proves that she is untainted by sexual activity of any kind;[41] unlike the 'daughters of gentiles' (בנות גוים), who preserved their hymenal virginity but engaged in other forms of sexual activity. Teugels notes that although the designations 'Jewish' and 'gentile' are anachronistic for the patriarchal period, Rebekah is shown as a perfect Jewish woman in contrast with the women around her.[42] She thus becomes a model for national identity.[43]

Rabbi Joḥanan re-enters the discussion:

Since it states, A VIRGIN, surely we know that NEITHER HAD ANY MAN KNOWN HER? It means that no man had even made improper advances to her, in accordance with the verse, *The rod of wickedness shall not rest upon the lot of the righteous* (Ps. CXXV, 3).[44]

Scripture does not repeat details unnecessarily, so the double designation of Rebekah's virginity distances her even further from others' impure intentions.[45] Her ultimate chastity confirms that Rebekah is the legitimate matriarchal successor.

Rebekah's sexual purity is matched by her virtuousness. Her drawing up water is interpreted as a miracle in *Gen. Rab.* 60:5:

40. Sarah is married to Abraham when he receives his call; her union with Abraham is not scrutinised in the same way as Rebekah's with Isaac.

41. Teugels, *'The Wooing of Rebekah' (Gen. 24)*, 203–6.

42. Through wordplay, *Gen. Rab.* 63:4 asserts that the ethnic designation Aramean (ארמי) reveals Laban and Bethuel, as well as 'the people of her [Rebekah's] town', to be 'deceivers' (sg. רמאי). In such circumstances, 'this righteous woman [Rebekah] who came forth from among them, might well be compared to *A lily among thorns* (S.S. II, 2)'. Rebekah stands out from the rest of her community. See ibid., 204–5.

43. Ibid., 205.

44. See ibid., 206–7.

45. Ibid., 201.

All women went down and drew water from the well, whereas for her the water ascended as soon as it saw her. Said the Holy One, blessed be He, to her: 'Thou has provided a token for your descendants: as the water ascended immediately it saw thee, so will it be for thy descendants: as soon as the well sees them, it will immediately rise'; thus it is written, *Then sang Israel this song: Spring up, O well—sing ye unto it* (Num. XXI, 17).

In Gen 24, the servant prays that the right partner for Isaac will be revealed as the local girls come to draw water from the nearby well. The partner designated for Isaac will offer the servant a drink, but also his camel (Gen 24:11-14, 17-20).[46] She will therefore demonstrate the Near Eastern virtue of hospitality.[47] The midrash intensifies the servant's request for a sign, arguing that a miracle occurred when Rebekah went down to the water. It sprung up to meet her, foreshadowing a similar event occurring when Israel are wandering in the desert en route to Moab. God promises to give the people water at Beer and the Israelites sing a song to the well (Num 21).[48] By the end of *Gen. Rab.* 60:5, there is no doubt that Rebekah is a legitimate matriarch. As Teugels notes, Rebekah 'is shown to be a role model of moral purity and her physical virginity is, rather, a sign of her moral virtue'.[49]

The matriarchs are revered and praised for their positive relationships with the deity. As God intervenes to allow Rachel to become pregnant (Gen 30:22), *Gen. Rab.* 73:3 offers theological reflection on his relationship with humans. The argument centres on God's two names יהוה and אלוהים, which are linked respectively with the divine 'Attribute of Mercy' (מידת רחמים) and the 'Attribute of Justice' (מידת הדין):[50]

[AND GOD REMEMBERED RACHEL]. R. Samuel b. Naḥman said: Woe to the wicked who turn the Attribute of Mercy into the Attribute of Judgment. Wherever the Tetragrammaton [Lord] is employed, it connotes

---

46. See Esther Fuchs, 'Structure and Patriarchal Functions in the Biblical Betrothal Type-Scene: Some Preliminary Notes', *Journal of Feminist Studies in Religion* 3, no. 1 (1987): 8–9; Zlotnick, *Dinah's Daughters*, 46; Sarna, *JPS: Genesis*, 164.

47. See John Koenig, 'Hospitality', *ABD*, 3:299–301.

48. This is paralleled in *Gen. Rab.* 54:5, where a well springs up when Abraham's flocks approach, confirming that he owns the well. Num 17:17 is cited (see Freedman, 480).

49. Teugels, *'The Wooing of Rebekah' (Gen. 24)*, 194.

50. מידה literally means 'measure' but came to mean 'nature', 'character' (Jastrow, 732). These attributes are well-known in rabbinic thought and God is said to possess these opposing characteristics in equal measure: this is what enables him to act as a fair but loving God. See Urbach, *The Sages*, 448–61.

the Attribute of Mercy: *The Lord, the Lord, God, merciful and gracious* (Ex. XXXIV, 6); yet it is written, *And* the Lord *saw that the wickedness of man was great...and it repented* the Lord *that He had made man...and* the Lord *said: I will blot out man* (Gen. VI, 5 ff.). Happy are the righteous who turn the Attribute of Judgment into the Attribute of Mercy. Wherever *Elohim* (God) is employed, it connotes the Attribute of Judgment. Thus: *Thou shalt not revile* Elohim—God (Ex. XXII, 27); *The cause of both parties shall come before* Elohim—God (*ib.* 8). Yet it is written, *And* Elohim (God) *heard their groaning* (*ib.* II, 24); *And* Elohim *remembered Noah* (Gen. VIII, I); AND ELOHIM (GOD) REMEMBERED RACHEL.[51]

The personal name of Israel's God, יהוה, connotes the Deity's compassionate nature; whilst אלהים, 'God', refers to his justice.[52] Even so, in the Flood Narrative, it is the normally compassionate 'Lord' (יהוה) who determines to rid the earth of wicked humanity. Those who subvert 'the Lord's' compassionate nature are chastised. Noah and Rachel are both remembered (זכר) by the justice-enacting 'God' (אלהים) and it is 'God' (אלהים) who responds to Israel's plight in Exod 2. These individuals make the just 'God' act with compassion.

A specific event in Rachel's personal life connects her with Israel's wider history. She is compared both with Noah, an exemplar of righteousness, who alone was worthy of surviving the Great Flood, and with Israel during the exodus, an event that shaped national identity. This passage also anticipates Rachel's role as intercessor for the Babylonian exiles in Jer 31:15.[53] Noah acted as a representative of humanity during the Flood and, like Babylon, Egypt was a place from which Israel needed to be liberated and returned to their own land. Rachel's conception reveals her positive characteristics and highlights this woman's worthiness to become a mother of Israel.

7.2.1. *Summary*

Genesis Rabbah emphasises the matriarchs' purity, chastity and morality. Sarah and Rebekah refrained from inappropriate sexual urges and activity; Rachel persuades the just God to act with compassion. These qualities indicate these women's moral superiority.[54]

---

51. The brackets are Freedman's.
52. For אלהים meaning 'judges', see BDB, 43.
53. See §6.5.4.2, 'Rachel'.
54. Although Leah is not dealt with specifically here, the rabbis emphasise Leah's legitimacy and positive qualities throughout *Genesis Rabbah*. They made a particular effort, wanting to prove that she too was a worthy matriarch. See Part II of this study.

7.3. *Marriages*

7.3.1. *Legitimate Unions*

For women in ancient Israel, legitimate marriage was a key concern. A woman had to find an appropriate match to ensure her security and wellbeing.[55] *Genesis Rabbah* emphasises the legitimacy of the marriages between Israel's great matriarchs and patriarchs, leaving no doubt that these couples were destined to marry and produce children together. In *Gen. Rab.* 68:4, a Roman noblewoman asks what God has been doing since he created the world in six days. Rabbi Jose explains that God 'sits and makes matches…assigning this man to that woman, and this woman to that man'.[56] The matrona scoffs at the ease of this task and sets about creating unions between her slaves.[57] When those marriages disintegrate as the couples cannot tolerate each other, R. Jose explains how difficult it is to create effective matches, whilst R. Berekiah describes God's control over all human beings.

The midrash concludes by commenting on the patriarchal marriages:

> 'Some go to their companion, while in the case of others it is the reverse'.
> In the case of Isaac, his companion came to him, as it says, *And Isaac went out to meditate in the field…and saw, and behold, there were camels coming* (Gen. XXIV, 63). Jacob, however, went out to his companion, as it says, AND JACOB WENT OUT. (Gen 28:10)

God has control over marriage, including patriarchal marriages. Though these two marriages are effected differently, as Rebekah travels with the servant to Isaac, whilst Jacob seeks out his own wife in a foreign land, God still has ultimate control.

Genesis Rabbah 57:1 twice explains that 'while he [Abraham] was yet on Mount Moriah he was informed (or: 'received good tidings', נתבשׂר) that his son's mate (זיווגו) [Rebekah] had been born, as it says, BEHOLD, MILCAH, SHE HAS ALSO BORNE, etc.' (Gen 22:20-24). The root בשׂר, 'to bear tidings', here in the Nithpael, indicates the announcement

---

55. Satlow, *Jewish Marriage*; Hauptman, *Rereading*, 60–76; Epstein, *Marriage Laws*.

56. On matchmaking, see Satlow, *Jewish Marriage*, 111–16.

57. On the matrona, and passages concerning the matrona and R. Jose, see 'Sarah: The First Mother of Israel'; Ilan, *Mine and Yours Are Hers*, 240–62; Tal Ilan, 'Matrona and Rabbi Jose: An Alternative Interpretation', *Journal for the Study of Judaism* 25, no. 1 (1994): 18–51; Rosalie Gershenzon and Elieser Slomovic, 'A Second-Century Jewish-Gnostic Debate: Rabbi Jose Ben Halafta and the Matrona', *Journal for the Study of Judaism* 16, no. 1 (1985): 1–41.

of 'good news', and is often used for proclamations by or about the divine.[58] The noun זיווג, deriving from זוג, 'to join, couple, match', means 'destined marriage partner'.[59] Combined, these terms emphasise that God chose Rebekah to become the next matriarch. According to the midrash, Abraham is calmed by this knowledge, as the future of the covenant is secured.[60] As the founding figures of Israel, the matriarchs and patriarchs are central to a nation whose identity relies upon genealogical descent.[61] The rabbis take particular care to demonstrate the worthiness of each set of ancestors and to formalise succession between them.[62]

Both Rebekah's marriage to Isaac and Jacob's marriage to Rachel begin with betrothal scenes at wells (Gen 24:1-58; 29:1-20).[63] Abraham sends his servant to find Isaac a wife. The servant's initial interaction with Rebekah (Gen 24:17-27) is described in *Gen. Rab.* 60:6. The servant ran towards Rebekah 'to welcome her good actions' (Gen 24:17). Rebekah's worthiness is clear from the moment she sets foot on the biblical stage. Moreover, Rebekah was presented with jewellery by the servant (Gen 24:22) and this is linked with Israel's wider history.[64] Rebekah was given two bracelets 'corresponding to the two tables of stone' and these bracelets have a weight of 'ten *shekels*', 'corresponding to the Ten Commandments'. This link to Israel's history confirms that Rebekah is a legitimate match for Isaac. Moreover, that 'the road contracted before' the servant as God led him to the right woman suggests again that divine will guided the events of Gen 24.[65]

58. See BDB, 142; Jastrow, 119; Isa 40:9; 2 Sam 18:19.

59. See Jastrow, 383–4, 392.

60. Prov 14:30 is cited as biblical proof. See Freedman, n. 1 504.

61. See Hayes, *Gentile Impurities*, esp. 8–9.

62. See §7.4, 'Matriarchal Succession'.

63. Cf. Exod 2:16-21. On the betrothal type-scene, see Esther Fuchs, 'Structure, Ideology and Politics in the Biblical Betrothal Scene', in Brenner, ed., *A Feminist Companion to Genesis*, 273–81; Fuchs, 'Structure and Patriarchal Functions', 7–13; Williams, 'Beautiful and the Barren', 107–19, esp. 109, 112–15; Robert Alter, *The Art of Biblical Narrative* (New York: Basic, 1981), 47–62; Zlotnick, *Dinah's Daughters*, 45–7; Teugels, *'The Wooing of Rebekah' (Gen. 24)*, 45–58.

64. The servant changes this part of the story when he recounts it to Rebekah's family. In Gen 24:47, he says that he asked Rebekah who she was before he gave her the jewellery. Abraham specified that Isaac's wife must come from his own brethren (Gen 24:4).

65. Sarna (*JPS: Genesis*, 161) comments on the biblical text: 'Although God does not intervene in a supernatural manner, the reader nevertheless is left with the absolute conviction that the guiding hand of Providence is present from first to last'. Cf. Ramon, 'Torah of Hesed', 155.

Jacob also meets Rachel by a well (Gen 29:9) in a situation reminiscent of Gen 24. *Genesis Rabbah* 70:12 links the two events:

> AND LIFTED UP HIS VOICE, AND WEPT (*ib.*) Why did he weep? He said thus: 'What is written about Eliezer, Abraham's servant, when he went to fetch Rebekah? *And the servant took ten camels*, etc. (Gen. XXIV, 10). While I have come down without a single ring or bracelet.'

Jacob is mortified that he has no fine jewellery to offer Rachel as they meet for the first time. The rabbis fill a gap in the biblical text, explaining why Jacob cries on this otherwise joyous occasion.[66] Although offering no comment on Rachel's character, the comparison between Gen 24 and 29 suggests that Rachel will be a worthy successor to Rebekah.

Following the betrothal scene at the well, Rebekah resolves to leave her homeland and become Isaac's wife (Gen 24:57-58; *Gen. Rab.* 60:12):

> AND THEY SAID: WE WILL CALL THE DAMSEL, AND INQUIRE AT HER MOUTH (*ib.* 57). From this we learn that a fatherless maiden may not be given in marriage without her consent. AND THEY CALLED REBEKAH, AND SAID UNTO HER: WILT THOU GO (*ib.* 58)? R. Ḥanina, the son of R. Adda, said in R. Isaac's name: They hinted to her, WILT THOU [ACTUALLY] GO? AND SHE SAID: I WILL GO (*ib.*): I go in spite of you, whether you wish it or not.

Genesis Rabbah 60:12 explains Bethuel's sudden disappearance from the biblical narrative after Gen 24:50: he died in the night after trying to disrupt the divine plan for his daughter.[67] Thus, Rebekah's family asks her to make the decision to marry. A generalised rule is derived from Rebekah's situation, affording the 'fatherless maiden' the right to consent to her own marriage. The extent to which this translated into reality is, of course, uncertain.[68] According to R. Ḥanina, Rebekah's family question whether she will marry Isaac; Rebekah confidently agrees to leave,

66. Other explanations for Jacob's crying are also offered here: he realises Rachel will not be buried with him; the local townsmen accuse him of sexual impropriety.

67. Satlow, *Jewish Marriage*, 123–4. Cf. Wenham, *Genesis 16–50*, 149.

68. Cf. Biale, *Women and Jewish Law*, 6–7; Wegner, *Chattel or Person?*, 170; Baskin, *Midrashic Women*, 4, 188 n. 5. Rabbinic law stated that upon reaching the age of maturity (twelve and a half), a father had to ask whether his daughter agreed to marry; *b. Ḥul.* 26b (Bronner, *From Eve to Esther*, 136 n. 5). Also *m. Yebam.* 13:2; Berkovits, *Jewish Women*, 34, 44; Satlow, *Jewish Marriage*, 122; J. B. Segal, 'The Jewish Attitude Towards Women', *Journal of Jewish Studies* 30, no. 2 (1979): 121; Ilan, *Mine and Yours Are Hers*, 176; Biale, *Women and Jewish Law*, 59–61; Wegner,

whatever her family's desire.[69] Rebekah places the covenant and the emergence of Israel above her own familial ties. Like Abram in Gen 12, she is prepared to leave her homeland, travel to a distant land and begin a family in accordance with God's plan.[70]

Genesis Rabbah 71:8 and 84:5 state that Jacob went to Laban specifically to meet and marry Rachel:

> Were not his adventures (*pitule*) mine? Did not Jacob go to Laban for my sake?[71] (*Gen. Rab.* 71:8)

> THESE ARE THE GENERATIONS OF JACOB: JOSEPH (XXXVII, 2). These generations came only for Joseph's sake. Did then Jacob go to Laban for the sake of aught but Rachel?[72] (*Gen. Rab.* 84:5)

Isaac warns Jacob not to marry a Canaanite woman and sends him to find a wife from Rebekah's family in Paddan-Aram (Gen 28:1-2).[73] The midrash legitimises Rachel as the object of Jacob's quest and highlights that the couple are supposed to marry. *Genesis Rabbah* 84:5 adds a further dimension relating to Israel's history, noting Jacob's choice to leave Laban only after Rachel has borne Joseph (Gen 30:25). The matriarch gains significance through her son, whose actions protect Israel in Egypt and after they leave.[74] Rachel's union with Jacob is part of the divine plan and is necessary for the emergence and prosperity of later Israel.

Chattel or Person?, 15, 33, 38, 117–18. Wegner explores the status of the minor daughter and emancipated woman (Wegner, *Chattel or Person?*, 20–39, 114–44).

69. Cf. Freedman, n. 4 535. Fuchs argues that Rebekah displays obedience in the betrothal scene, accepting her family and the servant's wishes that she travel away from her homeland to marry Isaac (Fuchs, 'Structure and Patriarchal Functions', 9). She raises an interesting point. Perhaps Rebekah agrees to leave immediately in Gen 24:58 because she really has no choice: as a woman, she was expected to join her husband's household and she need not delay the inevitable. Cf. Archer, *Her Price Is Beyond Rubies*, 196–7.

70. Sarna, *JPS: Genesis* 161; Wenham, *Genesis 16–50*, 150; Turner, 'Rebekah', 42–4. *Jubilees* develops the relationship between these figures, at Isaac's expense. See *Jub.* 19:15-31; Halpern-Amaru, *Women in the Book of Jubilees*, 19, 58, 82–4.

71. כלום means 'anything, something', and can 'introduc[e] a question to which a negative answer is expected' (Jastrow, 640).

72. כלום is used again in this question. In fact, the wording is identical, except *Gen. Rab.* 71:8 has Rachel speaking in the first person whilst *Gen. Rab.* 84:5 speaks about Rachel.

73. This situation is orchestrated somewhat by Rebekah (Gen 27:42-46).

74. With the splitting of the sea and Israel's prosperity in Egypt.

The marriage between Jacob and Leah is particularly fraught, as Jacob wished to marry Rachel and was deceived into marrying her sister. *Genesis Rabbah* emphasises the legitimacy of Jacob and Leah's marriage, as this union produces several of Israel's tribal ancestors.[75] In fact, Leah bears more sons than Rachel. The relationship between Leah and Rachel is portrayed more amicably than in Genesis.[76] For example, in *Gen. Rab.* 73:4, several explanations are offered for why Rachel was 'remembered' by God (Gen 30:22), including, 'Her silence on her sister's behalf'. No further comment is made, but this assumes that Rachel knew Jacob was to be deceived into marrying Leah and it praises her for allowing this to happen. This, in fact, becomes a reason for Rachel finally conceiving a child.[77]

Genesis Rabbah 71:8 develops this, as Rachel names Bilhah's son Naphtali (נפתלי), based on the 'mighty wrestlings I have wrestled (נפתלתי) with my sister' (Gen 30:8):

> I allowed myself to be persuaded, I exalted my sister above me. R. Johanan interpreted it: I should have been a bride before my sister. Now had I sent a warning to him, Beware, you are being deceived, would he not have refrained? But I thought, if I am not worthy that the world should be built up through me, let it be built up through my sister.

Rachel allows Leah to take her place as Jacob's bride, sacrificing her own interests and discerning Leah's role in 'building up the world'. This language connotes childbearing, such as when Sarah muses, 'Perhaps I shall be built up from her'[78] as she gives Hagar to Abraham in Gen 16:2. Rachel's words have a national dimension as they suggest that she accepts Leah's role as a mother of Israel, who will produce several Israelite ancestors. *Genesis Rabbah* 71:8 and 73:4 justify Leah's status as a matriarch, legitimising both of Jacob's marriages.

7.3.2. *Illegitimate Unions*

Alongside the foundational members of the patriarchal family are those who belong to that family but do not inherit the covenant promises. Esau and Dinah are the offspring of a matriarch and a patriarch, Rebekah and

---

75. Including Levi and Judah, representing priesthood and royalty. See Sarna, *JPS: Genesis*, 205–6.

76. Ramon, 'Torah of Hesed', 167–8.

77. On Jacob's marriage to Leah, especially his wedding night, see Rabow, *Lost Matriarch*, 45–65.

78. My translation.

Isaac, and Leah and Jacob, respectively.[79] The Bible and midrash comment on the unacceptable marriages and sexual relationships these figures form. This helps to inform deeper understandings of the matriarchs' and patriarchs' suitable unions.

In Genesis, Esau's Hittite wives aggrieve his parents, Isaac and Rebekah (Gen 26:34-35), and this forms part of Rebekah's justification for sending Jacob to Paddan-Aram (Gen 27:46–28:5): she wants to protect Jacob from Esau's wrath but also ensure that Jacob finds a suitable wife. In Gen 28:6-9, Esau takes an additional wife, one of the daughters of Ishmael, after seeing his father warn Jacob against marrying Canaanite women. Esau chooses the daughter of Ishmael, Abraham's son who did not inherit the covenant, so even this union highlights Esau's own status as the non-covenantal son.[80]

In Gen 27:46, Rebekah tells Isaac: 'I am weary of my life because of the Hittite women. If Jacob marries one of the Hittite women such as these, one of the women of the land, what good will my life be to me?' Rebekah uses this as an excuse to send Jacob away; she does not want to explain to Isaac that Esau wants to kill Jacob, after she has engineered the deception that allowed Jacob to receive his father's blessing. However, her reasoning also reflects the importance of correct marriage. Unlike Esau, Jacob, the soon-to-be eponymous ancestor of Israel, must marry worthy women, ones who have the credentials to become that nation's matriarchs.[81]

Genesis Rabbah 67:11 expands upon Rebekah's biblical claim: 'I AM WEARY OF MY LIFE (XXVII, 46). R. Huna said: She expressed herself with gestures of utter abhorrence. IF JACOB TAKE A WIFE OF THE DAUGHTERS OF HETH, SUCH AS THESE—she struck at each in turn.' Rebekah's physical actions demonstrate her determination that Jacob will not marry an illegitimate woman. Rebekah has transformed from a woman being judged worthy to marry a patriarch to a woman judging others' worthiness.[82] Details about Esau's marriages shed light on the dynamics of legitimacy and succession in this early period of Israel's history.

---

79. See Schneider, *Mothers of Promise*, 101, 138; Jeansonne, *Women of Genesis*, 87.

80. On Esau's wives, see Schneider, *Mothers of Promise*, 59–60, 120–5; Sarna, *JPS: Genesis*, 196.

81. Sarna, *JPS: Genesis*, 195.

82. Cf. Turner, 'Rebekah', 47.

Dinah's story is a sad one.[83] She is Jacob's only daughter, born to him from his unloved wife, Leah. She appears twice in genealogies (Gen 30:21; 46:15) and only acts in Gen 34.[84] Here, she 'went out' and is raped by Shechem (Gen 34:1-2).[85] This triggers brutal events, as Shechem wishes to marry Dinah and is told by Jacob's sons that his people must be circumcised first. Whilst recovering from their operations, Simeon and

83. On Dinah and Gen 34, see Biale, *Eros*, 23; Lyn M. Bechtel, 'What if Dinah Is Not Raped? (Genesis 34)', *Journal for the Study of the Old Testament* 62 (1994): 19–36; Carmichael, *Women, Law, and the Genesis Tradition*, 6, 25–30, 35–42; Graetz, 'Dinah the Daughter', 306–17; Fewell and Gunn, *Gender, Power, & Promise*, 80–5; Jeansonne, *Women of Genesis*, 87–97; Schneider, *Mothers of Promise*, 138–47; Zlotnick, *Dinah's Daughters*, esp. 33–48; Mary Anna Bader, *Tracing the Evidence: Dinah in Post-Hebrew Bible Literature*, Studies in Biblical Literature 102 (New York: Peter Lang, 2008); Sarna, *JPS: Genesis*, 233–8; Wenham, *Genesis 16–50*, 310–19; Laffey, *An Introduction to the Old Testament*, 43–4; Rabow, *Lost Matriarch*, 144–61; Bronner, *From Eve to Esther*, 111–41.

84. Schneider, *Mothers of Promise*, 140.

85. 'He took her and he lay with her and he humbled her' (Gen 34:2, my translation). By modern definitions, this is rape, but there is some debate about the appropriateness of the term for a biblical episode. Bechtel argues that Gen 34 offers no suggestion of rape: the act is shameful, because Dinah has sexual relations with a non-Israelite, but there is no indication of violence or forced intercourse (Bechtel, 'What if Dinah Is Not Raped?'). On the Shechemites' uncircumcision, see Cohen, *Why Aren't Jewish Women Circumcised?*, 14–15; on honour and shame, see Satlow, *Jewish Marriage*, 101–4, 126. Cf. Schneider: 'Two different prepositions meaning "with" may accompany the verb [שכב], and often when the preposition associated with the verb is *'et*, as it is here, the verb refers to a sexual encounter against the wishes of the person identified as the object of the verb, such as the case of Dinah (34:2) and Tamar (2 Sam. 13:14)' (Schneider, *Mothers of Promise*, 135). According to Wenham: '"Laid her" instead of the more usual "lay with her" implies forcible illegitimate intercourse... "Shamed her" is another term always used to describe intercourse without marriage... The duplication of very negative terms shows the author's strong disapproval of Shechem's behaviour' (Wenham, *Genesis 16–50*, 311). See also Bronner, *From Eve to Esther*, 118; Rabow, *Lost Matriarch*, 148–50. On rape in the Bible and ancient world, see Hauptman, *Rereading*, 77–101; Harold C. Washington, 'Violence and the Construction of Gender in the Hebrew Bible: A New Historicist Approach', *Biblical Interpretation* 5, no. 4 (1997): 352–60; Satlow, *Tasting the Dish*, 132–4. On the use of Gen 34 in *Jub.* 30 to ban intermarriage with foreigners, see Cana Werman, 'Jubilees 30: Building a Paradigm for the Ban on Intermarriage', *Harvard Theological Review* 90, no. 1 (1997): 1–22. On rape and halakhah, see Biale, *Women and Jewish Law*, 239–55; Wegner, *Chattel or Person?*, 23–8.

Levi slaughter the Shechemites in revenge for defiling their sister.[86] The last narrative glimpse of Dinah is in Gen 34:26, where they 'took Dinah out of Shechem's house, and went away'. Jacob is largely passive in this narrative, delaying news of Dinah's ordeal until his sons return from the field (Gen 34:5-7) and only appearing in Gen 34:30 to chastise Simeon and Levi for their actions, which could invoke retaliatory action against Israel by the more numerous Canaanites.[87]

Genesis Rabbah 76:9 blames Jacob for Dinah's rape.[88] Genesis 32:23 describes Jacob and his 'eleven children' going to meet Esau. The rabbis assume that these are Jacob's sons and so they question Dinah's absence. Jacob is said to have locked Dinah in a box because 'This wicked man has an aspiring eye; let him not take her away from me'.[89] Jacob protects Dinah from Esau, in 'one of the very few passages in which Jacob shows any concern for Dinah'.[90] In so doing, Jacob brings Dinah into comparison with two matriarchs: Sarah was placed in a box to hide her beauty from the Egyptians (*Gen. Rab.* 40:5) and the same phrase regarding Esau's wickedness describes Joseph protecting Rachel from Esau (*Gen. Rab.* 78:10; 90:4).[91] However, Dinah will not become a matriarch and the midrash criticises Jacob for his actions:

86. According to Fewell and Gunn (*Gender, Power, & Promise*, 84), 'The issue, for the brothers, is family honour. Their sense of injury is of injury to themselves, not to Dinah... The term represents a male point of view: "defile" is not, in this instance, a synonym for "rape". She is not defiled because she has been raped, but because she is no longer a virgin.' Wegner (*Chattel or Person?*, 23–8) argues that, according to rabbinic halakhah, the rapist must pay damages to the girl's father, because the asset of her virginity has been ruined. Wegner maintains: 'That it is the father rather than the girl who receives damages for the pain and suffering of the rape symbolises a total disregard of the daughter as a person' (p. 38). See also Rabow, *Lost Matriarch*, 154–60.

87. On Jacob's role, see Bechtel, 'What if Dinah Is Not Raped?', 34–5; Rabow, *Lost Matriarch*, 153–4. Biale suggests: 'To make Jacob's position more plausible, the rape is turned into romantic seduction' (Biale, *Eros*, 23).

88. Dinah is blamed for her rape in various sources. See Bronner, *From Eve to Esther*, 119–21; Graetz, 'Dinah the Daughter', 312; Zlotnick, *Dinah's Daughters*, 34; Baskin, *Midrashic Women*, 52. See §8.1.3, 'Negative Rabbinic Portrayals: Beauty and Sexuality'.

89. Cf. *Tanḥ.* 8:19.

90. Bader, *Tracing the Evidence*, 33.

91. See §6.3.2, 'Sons' Respect for their Mothers'; §8.1.3, 'Beauty and Sexuality'.

> R. Huna said in the name of R. Abba Bardela the Priest: The Holy One,
> blessed be He, said to him: *'To him that is ready to faint kindness is due from
> his neighbour* (Job VI, 14): thou hast withheld kindness from thy neighbour;
> when thou gavest her in marriage to Job, didst thou not convert him? (or
> simply: "you did not convert him") Thou wouldst not give her in marriage
> to a circumcised person [Esau]; lo! she is now married to an uncircumcised
> one! Thou wouldst not give her in legitimate wedlock; lo! she is now taken
> in illegitimate fashion'; thus it is written, *And Dinah the daughter of Leah...
> went out*, etc. (Gen. XXXIV, I).

The rabbi argues that it would have been better for Dinah to marry within
the family than outside of it. She would have entered into a legitimate
marriage, being married to a man circumcised according to Gen 17.
Jacob's action prevents this from happening.[92] Dinah is denied the opportunity for a legitimate marital union and this affects her status, both within
her own lifetime and within Israel's history.[93]

7.3.3. *Summary*

Legitimate marriages between the patriarchs and their wives are extremely
important for the genealogically determined identity of Israel.[94] As such,
Genesis Rabbah emphasises the unions' suitability and suggests that the
matriarchs are appropriate wives for the patriarchs.[95] The matriarchs and
patriarchs are destined to marry (see e.g. *Gen. Rab.* 68:4) and the matriarchs themselves recognise the importance of establishing correct unions,
such as when Rebekah, despite her family's wishes, confidently agrees to
marry Isaac (*Gen. Rab.* 60:12). Esau and Dinah's marriages shed further
light on this issue, as their unsuitable unions confirm that they will not
inherit the covenant promises. Ultimately, these traditions seem to confirm
that legitimacy is the most important aspect of rabbinic marriage.[96]

---

92. There is a postbiblical tradition that Job lived during the time of Abraham and
married Dinah. See *L.A.B.* 8:8; *Gen. Rab.* 80:4; Halpern-Amaru, 'Women in Pseudo-
Philo', 91; Bronner, *From Eve to Esther*, 139 n. 45; Bader, *Tracing the Evidence*, 25,
33, 85. Another tradition states that Dinah married Simeon and bore his child (see
Bader, *Tracing the Evidence*, 48). For a summary of Dinah marriage traditions, see
Bader, *Tracing the Evidence*, 168–9.

93. Cf. the biblical text: 'The brothers, according to Deuteronomy [22:28-29],
interfered with his [Shechem's] obligation to marry her and were wrong to cut off her
only chance of marriage' (Graetz, 'Dinah the Daughter', 308).

94. Cf. Satlow, *Jewish Marriage*, 133–4.

95. Cf. Zlotnick, *Dinah's Daughters*, 45; Porton, 'How the Rabbis Imagined
Sarah', 199.

96. Zlotnick, *Dinah's Daughters*, 170.

7.4. *Matriarchal Succession*

Matriarchal succession describes the transition between one legitimate matriarch and the next, a process which allows 'the matriarchal cycle' to begin afresh in each generation. By the end of Genesis, there is a chain of four legitimate matriarchs over three generations: Sarah, Rebekah, and Leah and Rachel, who live concurrently. The Hebrew Bible implies succession between matriarchs and this is accentuated in *Genesis Rabbah*. Rebekah and Isaac's marriage becomes official in Gen 24:67: 'Then Isaac brought her into his mother Sarah's tent. He took Rebekah, and she became his wife; and he loved her. So Isaac was comforted after his mother's death.' With this action, Isaac effects a transition between Sarah, the first matriarch, and Rebekah, her successor.[97] This is noteworthy also because the succession is enacted by the largely passive Isaac.[98] Isaac replaces his mother with his wife, securing the second patriarchal generation and enabling the continuing development of the nation. The correct male and female ancestors are once again in place.

Genesis 24:67 confirms that Rebekah is to become the next matriarch.[99] *Genesis Rabbah* 58:2, interpreting the announcement of Sarah's death in Gen 23:1, portrays the calculated nature of succession. From Eccl 1:5, 'The sun rises and the sun goes in', the rabbis derive the following principle: 'before the Holy One, blessed be He, causes the sun of one righteous man to set, he causes the sun of another righteous man to rise'. God ensures that the next righteous individual has been born before the preceding one dies. A number of examples follow, beginning with rabbinic figures, 'on the day that R. Akiba died our Teacher[100] was born, [and they applied the same verse to him]', and then moving to the biblical, 'Before the Holy One, blessed be He, caused Moses' sun to set, He caused Joshua's sun to rise, as it says, *And the Lord said unto Moses: Take thee Joshua the son of Nun*, etc. (Num. XXVII, 18)'.

97. Cf. Sarna, *JPS: Genesis*, 161, 170; Wenham, *Genesis 16–50*, 152.

98. Gen 22:20-24 and 24 have already emphasised Rebekah's legitimacy and her divine advocacy so Isaac's action is not unanticipated. On Isaac's lack of patriarchal action and its implications for understanding Rebekah, see Teugels, *'The Wooing of Rebekah' (Gen. 24)*, 119–29; Teugels, 'A Matriarchal Cycle?', 62. See also Williams, 'Beautiful and the Barren', 112; Wenham, *Genesis 16–50*, 174–5; Turner, 'Rebekah', 42–2, 47. Rabow suggests: 'Isaac's traumatic last-minute escape from sacrifice seems to transform him from a potentially heroic Patriarch like his father, Abraham, into a tragically passive character' (Rabow, *Lost Matriarch*, 6).

99. See Schneider, *Mothers of Promise*, 181; Teugels, *'The Wooing of Rebekah' (Gen. 24)*, 66–7. Cf. Schneider, *Mothers of Promise*, 42–4.

100. R. Judah the Prince.

The final example relates to Gen 23:1:

> Before the Holy One, blessed be He, allowed Sarah's sun to set, He caused
> that of Rebekah to rise. Thus we first read, *Behold, Milcah, she also hath
> borne children* (Gen. XXII, 20), and after that, AND THE LIFE OF SARAH
> WAS A HUNDRED YEARS, etc.

Scholars suggest that one function of the genealogy in Gen 22:20-24
is to anticipate Sarah's death in Gen 23 by introducing Rebekah, her
matriarchal replacement.[101] The midrash makes explicit the biblical text's
suggestion of matriarchal succession. There is a smooth transition from
one generation to the next, overseen by God himself.[102]

Sarah and Rebekah are the only women mentioned in this midrash,
which suggests rabbinic respect for them. *Genesis Rabbah* 58:2 demonstrates God's assurance of a continuous chain of righteous individuals
throughout Israel's history, beginning with biblical figures such as Sarah
and Moses and ending with contemporary rabbis. This informs the
principle of Oral Law, which argues that oral traditions interpreting Torah
were presented to Moses at Sinai and have passed from teacher to student
ever since.[103] Including Sarah and Rebekah in the list shows that correct
succession between female figures is as important as that between males.
Matriarchal succession confirms the legitimacy of the women and, consequently, of the nation descending from them.

In the midrash, Rachel makes the connection between herself and her
matriarchal predecessors as she argues with Jacob about her barrenness
(*Gen. Rab.* 71:7):

> AND HE SAID: AM I IN GOD'S STEAD, WHO HATH WITHHELD
> FROM THEE THE FRUIT OF THE WOMB? (Gen 30:2) From thee He
> withheld it, but not from me. Said she to him: 'Did then your father act so
> to your mother? Did he not gird up his loins by her?' 'He had no children',
> he retorted, 'whereas I have children'. 'And did not your grandfather
> [Abraham] have children', she pursued, 'yet he too girded up his loins by
> Sarah?' 'Can you then do what my grandmother did?' he asked her. 'And
> what did she do?' 'She brought her rival into her home', he replied. 'If that is
> the obstacle', she returned, 'BEHOLD MY MAID BILHAH, GO IN UNTO

---

101. On Gen 22:20-24, see Teugels, *'The Wooing of Rebekah' (Gen. 24)*, 59–90.

102. Neusner (2:296) comments: 'Israel is never left without an appropriate hero
or heroine'.

103. See §2.2, 'The Theory of Midrash: The Rabbinic Worldview'.

HER...AND I ALSO MAY BE BUILDED UP THROUGH HER' (Gen 30:3): as she [Sarah] was built up through her rival, so was she [Rachel] built up through her rival.

The midrash expands upon Jacob's argument that God 'withheld (children) *from you*'. He argues that because he already has children with Leah, Rachel must be solely responsible for her childlessness.[104]

Rachel draws Jacob's attention to the couple's designated role in Israelite history. Jacob is surprisingly hostile and is chastised by God because he fails to understand that barrenness is a precursor to Rachel's matriarchal motherhood.[105] Rachel parallels herself with the other matriarchs, but contrasts Jacob with the preceding patriarchs, whom she argues did not neglect their wives in their barrenness. Rachel's impassioned rhetoric intends to earn Jacob's sympathy, but it also highlights recognition of her matriarchal role.

Rachel and Sarah's narratives share many features.[106] Both women were barren and their husbands' other wives seemed set to usurp their roles as matriarchs if they did not bear children. Both Sarah and Rachel offered their maidservants to their husbands, hoping that: 'I shall be built up from her' (אבנה ממנה, Gen 16:2; 30:3).[107] Rachel exclaims: 'And I shall be built up, also I (גם־אנכי), from her'.[108] For the rabbis, גם, 'also', was a particle of addition, indicating that extra information can be gained from a particular verse.[109] The use of גם may inspire the rabbinic interpretation of Rachel mimicking the steps that Sarah takes to have a child. These women evince a common determination to become mothers and this in turn highlights their legitimacy as matriarchs. As the first and last matriarchs to bear, Sarah and Rachel form an inclusio for the theme of barrenness and its reversal, which makes up an important part of 'the matriarchal cycle'. Though barrenness is only a minor part of Rebekah's narrative (Gen 25:21), it maintains that continuity through the

104. On this pericope, see Rabow, *Lost Matriarch*, 80–92. See also §5.1, 'The Anguish of Barrenness'; §5.2.1, 'God's Control Over Childbirth'; §6.2.1, 'Sons Are Identified Through Their Mothers: By Name'.

105. '"And the anger of Jacob was kindled" (Gen 30:2). The Holy One Blessed Be He said to him, "[Are you] thus answering women in distress?"' (*Gen. Rab.* 71:7).

106. See Rabow, *Lost Matriarch*, 87–90; Callaway, *Sing, O Barren One*, 28–9.

107. My translation. Cf. Sarna, *JPS: Genesis*, 119.

108. My translation.

109. This is one of R. Eliezer's 32 *Middot*. See Strack and Stemberger, *Introduction*, 23. See also §2.3, 'Common Midrashic Exegetical Techniques'.

intervening generation. In *Gen. Rab.* 71:7, the rabbis emphasise that their shared barrenness connects the matriarchs to one another.[110] In this way, it confirms the importance of succession, ensuring that each matriarch is succeeded by the correct woman.

7.4.1. *Summary*

Matriarchal succession is the final stage of 'the matriarchal cycle', as it effects the transition from the matriarch in one generation to the barren woman who will become a matriarch in the next. The Bible suggests the importance of correct succession and specifically notes the transition between Sarah and Rebekah (Gen 24:67). The midrash expands on this biblical theme, emphasising that God ensures correct succession and that the matriarchs themselves are aware of their roles in Israel's history. Matriarchal succession confirms that the family line from which Israel descends is carefully regulated.

7.5. *Conclusions*

Legitimacy and succession are the final part of 'the matriarchal cycle', necessary for ensuring that the correct women become matriarchs. *Genesis Rabbah* emphasises that they are morally worthy figures, whom God has chosen to mother the covenant sons. *Genesis Rabbah* takes up and emphasises this theme, which is already present in the biblical text. Sarah, Rebekah, Leah and Rachel are each shown within the midrash to be wholly legitimate and worthy of taking on the matriarchal role. As the first mother of Israel, Sarah is portrayed as Proverbs' 'capable wife' and her sexual chastity highlights her merits. Rebekah is regarded as highly chaste and moral, as her perfect virginity by all definitions shows (*Gen. Rab.* 60:5); whilst Rachel causes the just God (אלוהים) to behave with compassion. In turn, these women form legitimate unions with the patriarchs, providing the context within which legitimate covenantal heirs may be born. These marriages are destined by God and are contrasted with the illegitimate unions formed by Esau and Dinah, which in turn prove that those individuals will not inherit the covenant promises. Finally, Genesis and *Genesis Rabbah* provide a model for matriarchal succession, based on Rebekah taking on Sarah's role in Gen 24:67. This is a crucial part of 'the matriarchal cycle', effecting a transition to the next generation and thus allowing Israel's covenantal history to continue.

---

110. Callaway, *Sing, O Barren One*, 30–1. Leah is not mentioned here: this midrash relies on details given in the biblical text to make its argument and Gen does not call Leah 'barren'.

Part III

THE RABBIS AND THE MATRIARCHS AS WOMEN

Chapter 8

The Rabbis and the Matriarchs as Women

The matriarchs became the focus of rabbinic stereotypes of women, both positive and negative.[1] The rabbis praised pure and chaste women, respecting those who fulfil their domestic role. However, women were also regarded as flirtatious, as enjoying gossip and as eavesdroppers, alongside other negative traits. As there are fewer female characters in the Bible than male, the same few women are used to exemplify the rabbis' positive and negative views on women.[2] As Zlotnick surmises, 'Through

---

1. Numerous studies explore women's status in rabbinic Judaism. See, amongst other works, Adler, *Engendering Judaism*; Bronner, *From Eve to Esther*; Ilan, *Mine and Yours Are Hers*; Hauptman, 'Feminist Perspectives on Rabbinic Texts'; Zlotnick, *Dinah's Daughters*; Hauptman, *Rereading*; Saul J. Berman, 'The Status of Women in Halakhic Judaism', *Tradition: A Journal of Orthodox Thought* 14, no. 2 (1973): 5–28; Adeline Fehribach, 'Between Text and Context: Scripture, Society and the Role of Women in Formative Judaism', in Haas, ed., *Recovering the Role of Women*, 39–60; Neusner, *How the Rabbis Liberated Women*; Gail Labovitz, 'Arguing for Women in Talmudic Literature', *Shofar: An Interdisciplinary Journal of Jewish Studies* 14, no. 1 (1995): 72–9; Judith Romney Wegner, 'Tragelaphos Revisited: The Anomaly of Woman in the Mishnah', *Judaism* 37, no. 2 (1988): 160–72; Wegner, *Chattel or Person?*; Wegner, 'Image and Status of Women'. Swidler (*Women in Judaism*) and Berkovits (*Jewish Women*) provide further examples; Hauptman ('Feminist Perspectives on Rabbinic Texts', 43) criticises these 'popular works'. Segal focuses on biblical and Second Temple attitudes to women in Israel and surrounding cultures. He argues that this is the basis for post-70 CE Jewish views of women (Segal, 'Jewish Attitude Towards Women'). Cf. Archer, *Her Price Is Beyond Rubies*. Brooten suggests that women played an important role in ancient Jewish communities. She discusses Greek and Latin inscriptions, some of which contain the title 'mother of the synagogue', where 'mother' is an authoritative title. See Bernadette J. Brooten, *Women Leaders in the Ancient Synagogue: Inscriptional Evidence and Background Issues*, Brown Judaic Studies 36 (Chico: Scholars Press, 1982).

2. Cf. Amalek, who embodies opposition to God. See Exod 17:14; Num 24:20; Deut 25:19; *Gen. Rab.* 53:5.

a series of episodic narratives the Hebrew Bible produces images of women that have become icons of the desirable or the unacceptable, each contributing to the limits of female identity'.[3] The rabbis developed these images to their own ends. This chapter will consider positive and negative portrayals of women in *Genesis Rabbah*. Whilst *Genesis Rabbah* mainly portrays the matriarchs in a positive light, a few traditions offer negative interpretations of their roles.

8.1. *Positive Rabbinic Portrayals of the Matriarchs as Women*

8.1.1. *Prayer and Praise*

After the Second Temple was destroyed, prayer replaced sacrifice as the chief mode of Jewish worship.[4] God was said to listen and respond to prayers, which individuals could make for themselves or on behalf of the community. Prayer itself is a biblical practice, but the rabbis specified that it was to be performed at set times within the day and the obligation to follow this, as well as study Torah, was incumbent upon male Jews. Jewish women were excluded from these obligations, but were still required to pray.[5] Judith Hauptmann posits that the rabbis obligated women to pray at least twice a day.[6]

3. Zlotnick, *Dinah's Daughters*, 3.

4. See e.g. *b. Ber.* 32b. On prayer and its replacement of Temple cult, see Kimelman, 'Rabbinic Prayer', 573–611; Bronner, *From Eve to Esther*, 89–91; Falk, 'Reflections', 98; Sorek, 'Mothers of Israel', 4.

5. On women's exclusion from public and cultic life, see Bronner, *From Eve to Esther*, 1–21, 29; Bar-Ilan, *Some Jewish Women*, 112–13; Baskin, 'Rabbinic Reflections', 3, 6, 76, 79–87, 112, 162; Ilan, *Mine and Yours Are Hers*, 166–9; Archer, *Her Price Is Beyond Rubies*, 85–103, 244–5; Wegner, 'Tragelaphos Revisited', 170–1; Biale, *Women and Jewish Law*, esp. 10–43; Wegner, *Chattel or Person?*, 4–6, 18, 77, 145–67, 173–5. Bronner suggests that biblical women had more freedom than talmudic women. The only woman in the Talmud to engage in serious Torah study is Beruriah; see e.g. *b. Pesaḥ.* 62b (Bronner, *From Eve to Esther*, 9–15; cf. Baskin, *Midrashic Women*, 82–3). On the change in women's status from biblical to Talmudic times, see Theodore Friedman, 'The Shifting Role of Women, from the Bible to Talmud', *Judaism* 36, no. 4 (1987): 479–87. Hauptman argues that whilst women were secondary citizens in rabbinic society, the rabbis gave them increasing ritual responsibilities (Hauptman, *Rereading*, 221–43). Cf. Daniel Boyarin, 'Reading Androcentrism Against the Grain: Women, Sex, and Torah-Study', *Poetics Today* 12, no. 1 (1991): 29–53.

6. Judith Hauptman, 'Women and Prayer: An Attempt to Dispel Some Fallacies', *Judaism* 42 (1993): 94–103. See also Hauptman, 'Some Thoughts on the Nature of Halakhic Adjudication: Women and Minyan', *Judaism* 42 (1993): 396–413; Hauptman, *Rereading*, 225–31. The rabbis usually portray women praying in private. See Bronner, *From Eve to Esther*, 105. Also Irwin H. Haut, 'Are Women Obligated

'The prayer of only one female character in the Bible is recorded—the personal prayer of Hannah.'[7] Hannah (1 Sam 1–2) is a barren woman, taunted by her rival co-wife, Peninnah. She prays to God that she may bear a son (1 Sam 1:9-13) and that prayer is answered when she gives birth to Samuel (1 Sam 1:20). Mary Callaway identifies several differences between this narrative and the biblical barrenness narratives preceding it in Genesis and Judg 13. Most strikingly, Hannah 'does what none of the matriarchs did; she simply asks Yahweh for a child', and '[t]he portrayal of Hannah's character focuses on her faithfulness and piety. She is pictured as praying, making a vow to Yahweh, and finally, as fulfilling the vow.' She is 'a worshipping pilgrim', attending the sanctuary at Shiloh; and after vowing to dedicate her son to the Lord, she does this in 1 Sam 1:28.[8] Hannah's psalm (1 Sam 2:1-10) is one of the Hebrew Bible's greatest expressions of God's greatness, and of an individual's response to his majesty. Hannah recognises God's control over life and human destiny and she appeals to him directly. Falk comments that, 'In this behaviour she follows no convention—and she becomes extraordinary'.[9] Her right relationship with God is rewarded when she bears a child.[10]

---

to Pray?', in *Daughters of the King: Women and the Synagogue: A Survey of History, Halakhah, and Contemporary Realities*, ed. Susan Grossman and Rivka Haut (Philadelphia: The Jewish Publication Society, 1992), 89–101; Bar-Ilan, *Some Jewish Women*, 78–113; Leila Leah Bronner, 'Hannah's Prayer: Rabbinic Ambivalence', *Shofar* 17, no. 2 (1999): 46–7; Baskin, *Midrashic Women*, 79–81, 113, 135; Biale, *Women and Jewish Law*, 17–24; Wegner, *Chattel or Person?*, 6.

7. Bronner, *From Eve to Esther*, 87. Cook discusses Hannah in biblical and postbiblical literature, exploring connections to the wider barren matriarch tradition (Cook, *Hannah's Desire, God's Design*). See also Bar-Ilan, *Some Jewish Women*, 81–3.

8. Callaway, *Sing, O Barren One*, 42. Callaway also notes that: 'This is the only birth narrative in which the mother actively determines the role of the child before birth' (ibid.). For Klein, 1 Sam 1–2 highlights Samuel's great importance (Klein, *1 Samuel*, 11, 19). Whilst this is correct, Hannah as pious individual must not be overlooked: her characterisation is as important. This may be seen by the rabbis' use of Hannah as a model for all Jewish prayer (Callaway, *Sing, O Barren One*, 40). Cf. Bronner, *From Eve to Esther*, 93; Bar-Ilan, *Some Jewish Women*, 30; Ozick, 'Hannah and Elkanah', 89–90. On the possible theological implications of 1 Sam 1–2, see Bailey, 'Redemption of YHWH', 213–31; James S. Ackerman, 'Who Can Stand Before YHWH, This Holy God? A Reading of 1 Samuel 1–15', *Prooftexts* 11 (1991): 1–24; Brueggemann, '1 Sam 1', 33–48. Cf. Laffey, *An Introduction to Old Testament*, 107. On wives and their vows, see Wegner, *Chattel or Person?*, 54–60, 93–5, 128–9.

9. Falk, 'Reflections', 98.

10. Cf. Isaac and Rebekah in Gen 25:21. See Sarna, *JPS: Genesis*, 179; Bar-Ilan, *Some Jewish Women*, 85.

The rabbis recognised Hannah's virtues and she became a 'paradigm of prayer' in rabbinic literature.[11] Bronner notes that: 'despite their marked gender consciousness, the rabbis never once comment on the fact that Hannah was female when discussing her brilliant aptitude for prayer'.[12] The Babylon Talmud, *Ber.* 31a-b, deduces four characteristics of prayer from Hannah's example:

> R. Hamnuna said: How many most important laws can be learnt from these verses relating to Hannah! Now Hannah, she spoke in her heart: from this we learn that one who prays must direct his heart. Only her lips moved: from this we learn that he who prays must frame the words distinctly with his lips. But her voice could not be heard: from this, it is forbidden to raise one's voice in the Tefillah. Therefore Eli thought she had been drunken: from this, that a drunken person is forbidden to say the Tefillah. And Eli said unto her, How long wilt thou be drunken, etc.

According to the rabbis, Hannah's prayer should be emulated by all Jews, male and female.[13]

Hannah's prayerfulness also influences rabbinic depictions of women, especially biblical women, praying. Hannah's narrative in 1 Sam 1–2 formed part of the biblical barrenness tradition and because Scripture was regarded as a unity, these developments could be read back onto the stories of the Genesis matriarchs.[14] Just as Hannah was a pious individual engaging in efficacious prayer, so too could the rabbis praise Sarah, Rebekah, Leah and Rachel for their piety. In *Genesis Rabbah*, these connections are at times explicit. *Genesis Rabbah* 73:1, interpreting Gen 30:22, has R. Eleazar explain: 'On New Year Sarah, Rachel, and Hannah were remembered'.[15] This midrash cites Ps 106:4, evoking God's remembrance of his people. The three women are connected by their barrenness and by God's intervention to enable them to give birth to sons.[16] Bronner

11. Bronner, *From Eve to Esther*, 93; cf. 87–110; Falk, 'Reflections', 98; Baskin, 'Rabbinic Reflections', 113, 136; Kimelman, 'Rabbinic Prayer', 597; Biale, *Women and Jewish Law*, 19.

12. Bronner, *From Eve to Esther*, 93. Also Bronner, 'Hannah's Prayer', 37.

13. On Hannah's prayer in rabbinic literature, see Bronner, *From Eve to Esther*, 94–8. Bronner discusses their ambivalent attitudes towards Hannah's prayer (Bronner, 'Hannah's Prayer', 36–48).

14. See Chapter 4, 'Preface to Part II: The Matriarchal Cycle'.

15. The verb is singular but must be translated as a plural. See Bronner, *From Eve to Esther*, 95–7.

16. The verbs are different, but have the same meaning. In Gen 21:1, 'the Lord remembered (פקד) Sarah'; the verb זכר, 'to remember', is used of Rachel (Gen 30:22) and Hannah (1 Sam 1:19).

notes that the designated reading from the Prophets (*haftarah*) for New Year is Hannah's narrative (1 Sam 1), whilst the Torah reading concerns Sarah (Gen 21). Rabbinic tradition thus regards these women's narratives as inherently related to one another.[17]

Genesis Rabbah 72:1 applies part of Hannah's psalm (1 Sam 2:5-6) to Leah and Rachel's situation, enabling one barren woman's experiences to shed light on those of two others:[18]

> *They that were full hired themselves for bread*, etc (I Sam. II, 5). *'They that were full hired themselves for bread'* applies to Leah, who was full with children, yet hired herself; *And they that were hungry have ceased (ib.)* applies to Rachel, who though hungry for children yet ceased. *While the 'aḳarah (barren) hath borne seven (ib.)*—Leah, who was barren…bore seven; *She that had many children hath languished (ib.)*—Rachel, from whom it was natural ('fit', 'destined', 'worthy', 'chosen', ראויה)[19] that most of the children should be born, yet languished. And who caused this? *The Lord,* [who] *killeth, and maketh alive, He bringeth down to the grave, and bringeth up (ib. 6).*

Removed from the original context in which they were uttered, Hannah's words provide insight into the meaning and significance of another biblical situation.[20] In Hannah's prayer, she acknowledges God as the source of life. Barrenness could only be reversed by God and Bronner notes: 'because Hannah is barren, her petition makes eminent sense to the rabbis. Its fervour is an appropriate response to a situation that they perceive as desperate and the fact that Hannah becomes pregnant confirms that God answers prayers.'[21] *Genesis Rabbah* models the matriarchs after Hannah several times, depicting those women displaying her piety and prayerfulness.[22] These traits often link back to barrenness, but also extend into other parts of the matriarchs' lives.

Bronner comments that: 'the Midrash creatively puts prayer into Sarah's mouth, although her barrenness was not made the reason for her prayer'.[23] The Bible twice depicts foreign kings taking the beautiful Sarah into their households (Gen 12; 20). Abraham allows this to happen, not

---

17. See *b. Meg.* 31a. Bronner, *From Eve to Esther*, 97.

18. Leah is again barren here.

19. Feminine singular passive participle of ראה, 'to see'. See Jastrow, 1435.

20. Hannah's words can be understood as prophetic. She is elsewhere named as one of seven biblical prophetesses See Bronner, *From Eve to Esther*, 97, 163–84.

21. Bronner, 'Hannah's Prayer', 40. Cf. Baskin, 'Rabbinic Reflections', 110–13.

22. On rabbinic traditions of God responding to prayer, especially those made by barren women, see Callaway, *Sing, O Barren One*, 123–30, 137–9.

23. Bronner, *From Eve to Esther*, 99.

wanting to be killed because he is Sarah's husband and subsequently accepting gifts from the kings because of the beauty of his 'sister'. In both cases, the kings are punished with physical maladies 'for the sake of Sarai/Sarah' (עַל־דְּבַר שָׂרַי/שָׂרָה, Gen 12:17; 20:18).[24] This Hebrew phrase literally means: 'concerning the word of Sarai/Sarah', and the midrash uses this to give Sarah more of a voice than she has in the biblical text.[25] *Genesis Rabbah* 41:2 and 53:13 contain almost identical pericopae, interpreting Sarah's encounter with Pharaoh, and then with Abimelech. *Genesis Rabbah* 41:2 reads:

> all exclaimed, 'It is BECAUSE OF SARAI ABRAM'S WIFE'. R. Berekiah said: Because he dared to approach the shoe of that lady. And the whole of that night Sarah lay prostrate on her face, crying, 'Sovereign of the Universe! Abraham went forth [from his land] on Thine assurance, and I went forth with faith; Abraham is without this prison while I am within!' Said the Holy One blessed be He, to her: 'Whatever I do, I do for thy sake, and all will say, "It is BECAUSE OF SARAI, ABRAM'S WIFE"'. R. Berekiah said: Because he dared to approach the shoe of that lady. R. Levi said: The whole of that night an angel stood with a whip in his hand; when she ordered, 'Strike', he struck, and when she ordered, 'Desist', he desisted. And why such severity? Because she told him [Pharaoh], 'I am a married woman', yet he would not leave her. R. Leazar said (the same was also taught in the name of R. Liezer b. Jacob):[26] We know that Pharaoh was smitten with leprosy and Abimelech with the closing up [of the orifices]: how do we know that what is said here is to be applied there, and vice versa? Because *'for the sake of'* occurs in both places, that an analogy may be drawn.[27]

At the end of the pericope, *gezerah shawah* is explicitly invoked to explain that the repeated use of the phrase 'for the sake of (עַל־דְּבַר) Sarah', allows parallels to be drawn between the situations narrated in Gen 12 and 20.

The midrash has a clear structure. Sarah is suggested to outrank the foreign kings who 'dared to come near to the shoe of the matrona'. Sarah is described as a matrona, a term for a Roman noblewoman, and the kings

---

24. My translation. Westermann (*Genesis 12–36*, 323) suggests that these are not 'punishments' but methods preventing adultery being committed.

25. Freedman, n. 4 333. On different translations of עַל־דְּבַר שָׂרַי/שָׂרָה, see Fokkelien van Dijk-Hemmes, 'Sarai's Exile: A Gender-Motivated Reading of Genesis 12.10-13.2', in Bronner, ed., *A Feminist Companion to Genesis*, 231–2.

26. The brackets are Freedman's.

27. *Gen. Rab.* 53:13 is almost identical.

are chastised for their proximity to this righteous woman.[28] This statement of Sarah's authority is suitable background for her efficacious prayer. Sarah is depicted lying fully prostrated and she acknowledges God's majesty with the highly reverential title, 'Sovereign of the Universe'.[29] She asserts her faithfulness to God and bemoans the fact that she has become entrapped in this harmful situation, when she demonstrated faith equal to that of her husband. Sarah's prayer has an immediate effect. The phrase 'because of Sarai/Sarah' (על־דבר שרי/שרה) is interpreted as God's response to the matriarch: her sincere prayer leads God to protect her from the foreign kings.[30] Sarah thus becomes a paradigm for the efficacy of prayer. Rabbi Levi gives Sarah ultimate control over the situation, adding that an angel responded directly to her commands to either strike or leave alone the foreign kings. Sarah's passivity in the biblical text is overturned by the rabbis. Lastly, Sarah is cleared of any deception; she is said to openly declare that she is married and the kings persist with their advances. *Genesis Rabbah* 41:3 and 53:13 portray Sarah as a pious and chaste woman, who appeals to God in her time of need. In this way, '[t]he rabbis use the story of Abraham's making Sarah available to Pharaoh again to underscore the special relationship between God and Sarah'.[31] Sarah is depicted as a worthy matriarch, but her prayer is also worthy of emulation.[32]

Leah also resorts to prayer when faced with an unfortunate situation beyond her control. *Genesis Rabbah* 70:16 explains what the Bible means when declaring that Leah's eyes 'were tender (רכות)' (Gen 29:17):[33]

---

28. Cf. §6.5.2, 'Sarah: The First Mother of Israel'.

29. This could also be translated as 'Master of the Worlds'. See Andrew Chester, *Divine Revelation and Divine Titles in the Pentateuchal Targumim*, Texte und Studien zum Antiken Judentum 14 (Tübingen: Mohr Siebeck, 1986), 352. The rabbis depict Hannah as first to call God 'the Lord of Hosts' (Bronner, 'Hannah's Prayer', 42). They clearly believed Sarah too was capable of using such language.

30. Porton, 'How the Rabbis Imagined Sarah', 200.

31. Ibid.

32. Ibid., 199, 201. Cf. Baskin, *Midrashic Women*, 134–6. Bar-Ilan (*Some Jewish Women*, 30) argues that female figures from the Second Temple period, such as Judith, became better role-models for ordinary Jewish women. These later women were heroic, rather than passive, and were pious and prayed. The rabbis may have incorporated features of these later female model characters into their portrayal of biblical women to emphasise their relevance.

33. My translation; NRSV has 'lovely'. See BDB, 939–40. Rabow (*Lost Matriarch*, 31) suggests that this verse can mean: 'either eyes that are soft and beautiful, or eyes that are weak, dull, poor sighted, or sensitive'.

AND LEAH'S EYES WERE WEAK—RAKKOTH (רכות) (XXIX, 17). R. Joḥanan's amora translated (תרגם)[34] this before him: And Leah's eyes were [naturally] weak (רכיכין). Said he to him: Your mother's eyes were weak (רכיכין)! But what does *'rakkoth'* (רכות) mean? That they had grown weak (רכות) through weeping, for [people used to say]: This was the arrangement; the elder daughter [Leah] is for the elder son [Esau], and the younger daughter [Rachel] is for the younger son [Jacob], while she used to weep and pray, 'May it be Thy will that I do not fall to the lot of that wicked man'. R. Huna said: Great is prayer, that it annulled the decree, and she even took precedence of her sister.

R. Joḥanan is dissatisfied with the Aramaic translation רכיכין for the Hebrew רכות and insists that the particular nuances of the Hebrew be considered.[35] This leads to an explanation of how Leah's eyes became 'weak'.[36]

According to the tradition presented, Laban's eldest daughter, Leah, was betrothed to Isaac's eldest son, Esau, and their younger siblings, Rachel and Jacob, were betrothed.[37] Leah cannot bear the thought of marrying such a 'wicked' man and she cried and prayed to God, pleading for a change in circumstance.[38] Her forceful weeping made her eyes 'weak'. Like Sarah, Leah uses appropriate language and recognises God's authority over her life, as she prays that his divine will (רצון) be changed. Her prayers are answered and she is married before Rachel. This midrash alters the way in which Leah and Jacob's marriage is usually understood by focusing on Leah's character. Like Hannah, Leah functions as a paradigm for Jewish prayer, suggesting that any situation can be reversed following right response to God. The rabbis interpret the ambiguous biblical statement about Leah's 'weak' eyes as an indicator of her piety

34. תרגם means 'translate into Aramaic'.

35. In fact, רכיכין derives from the same verbal root (רכך) as רכות and has roughly the same meaning, 'soft, tender, young'. BDB, 939-40; Jastrow, 1478–80.

36. For interpretations, see Rabow, *Lost Matriarch*, 31–5.

37. In Gen 28:2, Isaac sends Jacob to marry one of Laban's daughters. Jacob's immediate encounter with Rachel may indicate that they are destined to marry. This may also explain why Jacob insists upon marrying Rachel even after he has married her sister. In *Gen. Rab.* 71:2, one reason 'Leah was hated (שנואה)' (Gen 29:31) was because people associated her with the 'hater' (שונא) of Israel, whom she was set to marry. Those people had the wrong impression of Leah, who was horrified by the prospect of marrying Esau (see Freedman, 653).

38. Weeping and prayer are linked elsewhere in *Gen. Rab.* See e.g. *Gen. Rab.* 82:10; Bronner, *From Eve to Esther*, 99–101.

and morality. As Leah prays to God, she takes control of her future and this contrasts with her passivity in Genesis, where she is simply used by Laban to further his own ends.[39] *Genesis Rabbah* continues to demonstrate Leah's worthiness as a matriarch.

The matriarchs are depicted in prayer elsewhere in *Genesis Rabbah*. Rachel prays that she may bear Jacob's twelfth son and the other matriarchs support her (*Gen. Rab.* 72:6).[40] Jacob is also said to bury Rachel on the road to Ephrath because he 'foresaw that the exiles would pass on from thence, therefore he buried her there so that she might pray (lit. "ask") for mercy for them' (*Gen. Rab.* 82:10). Rachel weeps and implores God to change the situation that her descendants are facing. Her petition is successful and God promises Israel's redemption from exile (Jer 31:15-17).[41] Finally, *Gen. Rab.* 45:4 gave the valued prayers of the matriarchs as one reason for their continued barrenness.[42] These passages highlight the importance of prayer and confirm the matriarchs' piety. By implication, the rabbis suggest that ordinary Jews should also pray, as prayer is valued by God.[43]

Israel's matriarchs and patriarchs put their faith in God and do not falter even when their situations are desperate. In *Gen. Rab.* 53:3, Habakkuk's description of the land's barrenness (Hab 3:17-18) is applied to Abraham and Sarah's childlessness:

> *For though the fig-tree doth not blossom* etc. (Hab. III, 17). This alludes to Abraham, as in the verse, *I saw your fathers as the first-ripe in the fig-tree at her first season* (Hos. IX, 10). *Neither is there fruit in the vines* (Hab. *loc. cit.*), alludes to Sarah, as you read, *Thy wife shall be as a fruitful vine* (Ps. CXVIII, 3).

39. Namely, marrying off his elder daughter before the younger, and cheating Jacob into working for a longer period (Gen 29:15-30).

40. See §3.6.3.1, 'The Matriarchs (האימהות) Were Prophetesses'.

41. See §6.5.4.2, 'Rachel'.

42. See §3.6.3.4, '"Why Were the Matriarchs Made Barren?" (ולמה נתעקרו אמהות)'.

43. Although she is not a matriarch, *Gen. Rab.* 85:7 portrays Tamar praying: 'Let it be your will that I shall not go out from this house empty'. Tamar bears twins, Perez and Zerah, Davidic ancestors, following the episode with Judah in Gen 38. The rabbis attribute this, in part at least, to a prayer made by their mother. This interpretation also justifies Tamar's somewhat questionable actions in this chapter: she tricks Judah into believing she is a prostitute so he will have sexual relations with her as retribution for his neglect of her following the death of his eldest two sons.

Proof that Hab 3:17 applies to the matriarch and patriarch is found not in verses from Genesis, but rather in prophetic quotations from Hosea and the Psalms.[44] These prophetic texts have a timeless quality, referring here to events in Israel's past. Abraham and Sarah are represented in, even embody, Scripture as they fulfil the prophets' words. The midrash thus highlights Abraham and Sarah's significance.

In the second half of *Gen. Rab.* 53:3, Sarah assumes Habakkuk the prophet's words from Hab 3:18:

> Sarah exclaimed, 'What! am I to lose faith in my Creator, *For I will rejoice in the Lord, I will exult in the God of my salvation'* (Hab. III, 18). Said the Holy One, blessed be He, to her: 'Since thou didst not lose thy faith, I too will not give thee cause to lose faith'. But rather, AND THE LORD REMEMBERED SARAH, etc.

Sarah models true faith. Placing Habakkuk's words into Sarah's mouth imbues her with the authority of a prophet, one who is appointed by God to speak before, and on behalf of, his people. This is a great accolade for a woman and Sarah follows the few female prophets mentioned in the Bible, such as Deborah (Judg 4–5) and Huldah (2 Kgs 22:14-20; 2 Chr 34:22-28).[45] Sarah submits herself to God's power, continuing to offer praise even when she is struggling. God ultimately rewards Sarah by providing her with a child. Unlike halakhah, which provides direct and unambiguous instruction, aggadah insinuates how one should behave.[46] The divine reward for Sarah's proclamation is a clear sign that she exemplifies right relationship with God.

---

44. On the Psalms and prophecy, see e.g. John W. Hilber, *Cultic Prophecy in the Psalms*, Beihefte zur Zeitschrift für die alttestamentliche Wissenschaft 352 (Berlin: de Gruyter, 2005). This was a popular idea at Qumran. See Vermes, *Dead Sea Scrolls in English*, esp. 307–13, 519–23. Much of this connection rests on the notion of David as the psalmist; see 2 Sam 23:1-7; Vermes, *Dead Sea Scrolls in English*, 313. On Hab 3:17-18, see Andersen, *Habakkuk*, 342–8; Ralph L. Smith, *Micah–Malachi*, Word Biblical Commentary 32 (Waco: Word, 1984), 114–17.

45. See §3.6.3.1, 'The Matriarchs (האימהות) Were Prophetesses'. See also Bronner, *From Eve to Esther*, 97; Bar-Ilan, *Some Jewish Women*, 37; Brenner-Idan, *The Israelite Woman*, 58–67.

46. Ilan, *Mine and Yours Are Hers*, 238; Darr, *Far More Precious*, 29; Teugels, *'The Wooing of Rebekah' (Gen. 24)*, 205, 222, 226; Heinemann, 'Aggadah', 41–55; Baskin, *Midrashic Women*, 4; Strack and Stemberger, *Introduction*, 51–2. See §2.4, 'Rabbinic Texts'.

8.1.2. *Piety*

For women in rabbinic times, piety often centred on the domestic realm, as females were excluded from most public worship.[47] *Genesis Rabbah* 60:16 portrays Sarah and Rebekah as exemplary Jewish women, performing cultic ritual within the home.[48] Moreover, as Rebekah is said to resume actions once performed by Sarah, piety becomes the basis for succession between these matriarchs:[49]

AND ISAAC BROUGHT HER INTO HIS MOTHER SARAH'S TENT (XXIV, 67). You find that as long as Sarah lived, a cloud hung over her tent; when she died, that cloud disappeared; but when Rebekah came, it returned. As long as Sarah lived, her doors were wide open; at her death that liberality ceased; but when Rebekah came, that openhandedness returned. As long as Sarah lived, there was a blessing on her dough, and the lamp (נר)[50] used to burn from the evening of the Sabbath until the evening of the following Sabbath; when she died, these ceased, but when Rebekah came, they returned. And so when he saw her following in his mother's footsteps (lit. 'doing according to the work of his mother'), separating her *ḥallah* in cleanness and handling her dough in cleanness, straightway, AND ISAAC BROUGHT HER INTO THE TENT.

Alongside performing various ritual actions, Sarah and Rebekah attract the divine presence, represented by the cloud.[51] As Ramon comments: 'The midrashim express a profound admiration of the matriarchs' ability to render the divine presence immanent in the running of the home and the evolution of the family'.[52] Moreover, these two women enact hospitality, an important ancient Near Eastern virtue.[53]

---

47. Ilan, *Mine and Yours Are Hers*, 235–6; Archer, *Her Price Is Beyond Rubies*, 226–7; Biale, *Women and Jewish Law*, 10–43.

48. Teubal (*Sarah the Priestess*) argues that Genesis contains traditions about Sarah and the matriarchs as revered and influential priestesses.

49. See Porton, 'How the Rabbis Imagined Sarah', 208; Zucker, 'Sarah', 248.

50. נר is used biblically for lights in the tabernacle and Temple. See 1 Kgs 7:49; BDB, 632.

51. Following the exodus, God was with the people in the wilderness as a pillar of cloud during the day and fire at night. See Cheryl Lynn Hubbard, 'Pillar of Cloud, Pillar of Fire', *EDB*, 1059; Exod 13:21, 22, 14:19-22, 24; 24:15-16; Num 9:15-22; etc. Wegner (*Chattel or Person?*, 155–6) discusses *m. Šabb.* 2:6, its mention of the commandments relating to dough and Sabbath lights, as well as death during childbirth as punishment for disregarding them.

52. Ramon, 'Torah of Hesed', 155; cf. 165–6.

53. See Koenig, 'Hospitality', *ABD*, 3:299–301.

Rabbinic Judaism specified three religious obligations that women are required to perform:

> her observance of limitations on marital contact during the prescribed period of menstrual impurity (*niddah*); the separation and burning in the oven of a piece of the dough used in making Sabbath bread (*hallah*), a reminder of Temple sacrifice; and kindling of Sabbath lights (*hadlaqah*).[54]

Porton highlights the differences between mishnaic prescriptions and the actions performed by Sarah and Rebekah in *Gen. Rab.* 60:16. Although dealing with similar topics, the Mishnah, produced in the third century CE, suggests a different attitude to women's obligations than *Genesis Rabbah*, emerging in the fifth century CE.[55] Many of *Genesis Rabbah*'s traditions date much earlier than the fifth century.[56] It is impossible to say whether *Gen. Rab.* 60:16 has its origins earlier or later than the Mishnah. Even though the matriarchs do not match exactly the demands of the Mishnah, Sarah and Rebekah are praised for their comparable actions. Moreover, both the Mishnah and midrash portray domestic responsibilities as religious obligations that women must fulfil.

Baskin notes that the three obligations set out for women in the Mishnah are often interpreted negatively, either regarding their supposed origins as punishment or atonement for Eve's primeval disobedience (Gen 3), or their neglect, which is said to lead to death. She thus explains that there were 'at least some strands of rabbinic tradition that did not regard women's performance of these ordinances as *mitzvot*, that is, as divine commandments whose observance enhanced the religious life of the observer and assured divine favour'.[57] This highlights the ambiguity surrounding female piety in rabbinic times. Whilst *Gen. Rab.* 60:16 is wholly positive, portraying the pious matriarchs perfectly fulfilling their duties, elsewhere in rabbinic literature, much more negative interpretations of female piety were circulating. The rabbis may even have used the matriarchs to show ordinary women how they should behave. As Baskin notes, such negative traditions surrounding female ritual obligations may

---

54. See e.g. *m. Šabb.* 2:6. Baskin, *Midrashic Women*, 71. See also Porton, 'How the Rabbis Imagined Sarah', 208; Fonrobert, *Menstrual Purity*, 33.

55. Porton, 'How the Rabbis Imagined Sarah', 208.

56. Cf. Satlow, *Tasting the Dish*, 9. See also §2.4, 'Rabbinic Texts'.

57. Baskin, *Midrashic Women*, 65–73, 79 (quote p. 71). See *Gen. Rab.* 17:8; *m. Šabb.* 2:6; *b. Šabb.* 31b-34a; *'Abot R. Nat.* B 42. Cf. Bronner, *From Eve to Esther*, 24–6, 36.

have sought to control female action.[58] Overall, *Gen. Rab.* 60:16 presents two women acting in accordance with rabbinic expectations of female piety and through this, their roles as acceptable matriarchs are justified.

Further proof of Rebekah's piety is found in *Gen. Rab.* 63:6. When the biblical text claims that Rebekah 'went to inquire of the Lord', *Genesis Rabbah* explains that she travelled to the school of Eber: 'Hence this teaches you that to visit a Sage is like visiting the Divine Presence'. Rebekah lived before 'synagogues and houses of study' were established, thus the most common ways of communing with God in the rabbinic period were unavailable to her. She knew, however, that consulting with a Sage would have the same effect.[59] Like with Hannah, the rabbis praise Rebekah's action and derive a teaching from it. This is rather astonishing, given that Rebekah steps beyond the typically female domestic realm and into the more male public realm, and it shows just how greatly the rabbis revered this woman as a model for all Jews.[60]

As well as displaying correct relationship with God in their own religious actions, in *Genesis Rabbah* the matriarchs influence the beliefs and practices of others. Whilst Genesis does not explain why Rachel steals her father's household gods (Gen 31:19), *Gen. Rab.* 74:5 comments:

> her purpose was a noble one, for she said: 'What, shall we go and leave this old man [Laban] in his errors!' Therefore Scripture finds it necessary to inform us, AND RACHEL STOLE THE TERAPHIM THAT WERE HER FATHER'S.

Rachel stole the gods hoping that it would force her father to turn from idolatry. This puts a positive gloss on a biblical action that could seem dubious.[61] Rachel is devoted to Israel's deity and hopes to steer her heathen father towards correct belief.

58. Baskin, *Midrashic Women*, 72. Cf. Satlow, *Tasting the Dish*, 9. Yet, 'the biblical record was clear that women, together and as individuals, could be models of exemplary piety and personal transformation' (Baskin, *Midrashic Women*, 141).

59. See Turner, 'Rebekah', 44–5.

60. Laffey (*Introduction to the Old Testament*, 2) suggests that patriarchy accepts such transgressions when they are the exception.

61. Sarna suggests that this becomes an act of defiance against her father, who tricked Jacob into marrying Leah before her. Menstrual blood is defiling and she shows Laban's idols no respect by sitting on them (Sarna, *JPS: Genesis*, 219). On menstruation and niddah, see Hauptman, *Rereading*, 147–76; Fonrobert, *Menstrual Purity*; Biale, *Women and Jewish Law*, 147–74; Wegner, *Chattel or Person?*, 162–5; Baskin, *Midrashic Women*, 22–9. Pardes suggests that by stealing the teraphim,

Genesis Rabbah 74:9 confirms that Rachel is blameless, as the teraphim became 'drinking glasses' so that Laban could not find them.[62] Tragically, however, Jacob utters the following curse in Gen 31:32: 'with whomever you (Laban) shall find your gods, he shall not live'. The midrash explains that this is '*Like an error which proceedeth from a ruler*' (Eccl 10:5),[63] irreversible from the moment it is uttered by this authoritative figure. Though Rachel had good intentions when stealing the teraphim, her premature death in childbirth (Gen 35:16-19) is blamed on this episode.

Sarah takes more direct action to turn gentiles away from their erroneous ways. Genesis 12:5 describes Abraham leaving Haran to travel to Canaan: 'And Abram took Sarai his wife…and the souls[64] that they had acquired (lit. 'made', עשׂה) in Haran' (Gen 12:5). *Genesis Rabbah* 39:14 queries the exact meaning of the verb עשׂה, 'to make, do':

> AND THE SOULS THAT THEY HAD MADE! It refers, however, to the proselytes [which they had made]. Then let it say, 'That they had converted'; why THAT THEY HAD MADE? That is to teach you that he who brings a Gentile near [to God] is as though he created him. Now let it say, 'That *he* had made'; why THAT THEY HAD MADE? Said R. Ḥunia: Abraham converted the men and Sarah the women.

Rabbi Leazar in the name of R. Jose b. Zimra argues that the 'souls' Abram took with him refers to the people he converted in Haran. The verb עשׂה, 'to make', is used, instead of גייר, 'to convert', because the proselytes were effectively re-created when they abandoned their previous idolatrous ways. Rabbi Ḥunia explains that the verb appears in the plural because Abraham and Sarah each converted those of their own sex. These ancestors are portrayed as God's greatest advocates and Sarah is equal to Abraham in her ability to proselytise.[65] This tradition bears similarities

Rachel hoped to gain ascendancy over Leah; Rachel had not borne Jacob's firstborn. The teraphim have symbolic significance. Cf. Deut 21:15-16. See also Pardes, *Countertraditions*, 71. Pardes ('Rachel's Dream', 34) notes: 'If one bears in mind that possession of the household gods could serve as a symbolic token of leadership in a given estate (as is evident in the Nuzi documents), what Rachel is after in this case is analogous to what Jacob cunningly wrests from his blind old father'. Cf. Teubal, 'Matriarchs and Visionaries', 237; Jeansonne, *Women of Genesis*, 81–4; Fewell and Gunn, *Gender, Power, & Promise*, 79.

62. Freedman, n. 2 682.

63. Freedman's translation.

64. The noun נפשׁ, 'soul, person', is singular, but clearly understood as a collective.

65. Porton, 'How the Rabbis Imagined Sarah', 200. Cf. Ramon, 'Torah of Hesed', 163–4. This tradition comes in the name of one rabbi (R. Leazar in the name of R.

to *Gen. Rab.* 53:9, where Sarah suckles gentile children, enabling them to become 'fearers of God'.[66] This matriarch is faithful to God and has authority over gentiles.

8.1.2.1. *Summary*

Genesis Rabbah depicts the matriarchs praying, modelling their actions after Hannah, the only female whose prayer is recited in the Hebrew Bible. The rabbis greatly respected Hannah and, as another biblical barren woman, the rabbis applied her actions to the matriarchs, showing them mirroring her prayerful example, as well as her words, when her psalm (1 Sam 2:5-6) is applied to Leah and Rachel's situation (*Gen. Rab.* 72:1). The matriarchs pray, praise God and exemplify right relationship with God.[67] They demonstrate righteousness through the many pious actions that they perform. This is most clearly seen perhaps in *Gen. Rab.* 60:16, where Sarah and Rebekah are shown to perform the same cultic actions within the home. The rabbis had an ambiguous attitude towards female piety, yet the Genesis matriarchs were exemplars and could be emulated by ordinary Jews. Piety and prayer contribute to the matriarchs' positive characterisation in midrash and these qualities are closely related to their gender.

8.1.3. *Beauty and Sexuality*

The male rabbis display ambiguous attitudes towards female beauty and sexuality, which they saw as both appealing and dangerous.[68] On the

---

Jose b. Zimra) and is supported by one other (R. Ḥunia). Nevertheless, it conveys a sense of Sarah as an exemplary Jewish woman, whose faith is worthy of emulation by Jew or gentile. On Jewish converts and Jew–Gentile relations from biblical to rabbinic times, see Hayes, *Gentile Impurities*. On the status of converts, see Shaye J. D. Cohen, 'Can Converts to Judaism Say "God of Our Fathers"?', *Judaism* 40, no. 4 (1991): 419–28; Baskin, *Midrashic Women*, 154–60. Proselytisation was a contentious issue in ancient Judaism. See Martin Goodman, *Mission and Conversion: Proselytising in the Religious History of the Roman Empire* (Oxford: Clarendon, 1994).

66. See §6.5.2, 'Sarah: The First Mother of Israel'.

67. See Ramon, 'Torah of Hesed'.

68. On rabbinic views of the body and sexuality, see Boyarin, *Carnal Israel*; Charlotte Elisheva Fonrobert and Martin S. Jaffee, 'Introduction: The Talmud, Rabbinic Literature, and Jewish Culture', in *The Cambridge Companion to the Talmud and Rabbinic Literature*, ed. Charlotte Elisheva Fonrobert and Martin S. Jaffee, Cambridge Companions to Religion (New York: Cambridge University Press, 2007), 270–94; Satlow, *Jewish Marriage*, 116–20; Hauptman, *Rereading*, 30–59; Satlow, *Tasting the Dish*; Biale, *Eros*, 11–59, 175–97; Wegner, *Chattel or Person?*

positive side, beauty and chastity could indicate a woman's worthiness and a number of passages in *Genesis Rabbah* reflect this.[69] As the first matriarch, Sarah's beauty is emphasised and it becomes a further means of legitimising her character.[70] Genesis 23:1 announces Sarah's death and the age at which she died. This is highly unusual for women in the Bible, where such records are usually reserved for men.[71] In *Gen. Rab.* 58:1, this indicates Sarah's morality:

> AND THE LIFE OF SARAH WAS A HUNDRED YEARS AND SEVEN YEARS AND TWENTY YEARS; THESE WERE THE YEARS OF THE LIFE OF SARAH (XXIII, I). It is written, *The Lord knoweth the days of them that are without blemish* (תמימם)*; and their inheritance shall be for ever* (Ps. XXXVII, 18). As they are whole [unblemished], so are their years whole; at the age of twenty she was as at the age of seven in beauty, and at the age of a hundred she was as at the age of twenty in sin. Another interpretation: '*The Lord knoweth the days of them that are without blemish'* alludes to Sarah; '*And their inheritance shall be for ever*', as it says, THESE WERE THE YEARS OF THE LIFE OF SARAH, etc.

Psalm 37:18 is applied to Sarah. Sarah's beauty confirms that she is a worthy woman, as her physical characteristics are matched by moral integrity.[72] The final part of the midrash confirms that Ps 37:18 refers to Sarah by citing her death notice as proof that the righteous live long lives, which are recognised by God.[73]

Sarah's beauty proves problematic in Genesis. Abraham worries that foreigners will kill him so they can marry Sarah (Gen 12:11-13; cf. 20:11) and, later, foreign kings ply Abraham with gifts because of her beauty (Gen 12:16; 20:14-16).[74] *Genesis Rabbah* 40:4 explains why Abram only notices Sarai's beauty in Gen 12:11, when he has been married to her for years:

---

69. Cf. Rebekah in Gen 24 (Sarna, *JPS: Genesis*, 165).

70. Sarah's beauty is the subject of 1Qap Gen XX, 1-9. For translation and commentary, see Joseph A. Fitzmyer, *The Genesis Apocryphon of Qumran Cave 1 (1Q20): A Commentary*, Biblica and Orientalia; Sacra Scriptura Antiquitatibus Orientalibus Illustrata 18a (Rome: Editrice Pontificio Istituto Biblico, 2004).

71. Zucker, 'Sarah', 248.

72. See Satlow, *Jewish Marriage*, 116.

73. Cf. Neusner (2:295): 'No. 1 does not necessarily refer to Sarah. No. 2 links the intersecting verse to the base verse. The praise of Sarah derives from the intersecting verse, as proved by the fact that the years of Sarah are carefully enumerated.'

74. Pharaoh gives Abraham gifts as he takes Sarai; Abimelech gives Abraham gifts after he has returned Sarah.

She was with him all those years, yet *now* he says to her, BEHOLD, NOW I KNOW THAT THOU ART A FAIR WOMAN TO LOOK UPON! The reason, however, is because travelling takes toll of one's beauty. R. 'Azariah in the name of R. Judah b. Simon: [Abraham said to Sarah:] We have traversed Aram Naharaim and Aram Nahor and not found a woman as beautiful as you; now that we are entering a country whose inhabitants are swarthy and ugly, SAY, I PRAY THEE, THOU ART MY SISTER, THAT IT MAY BE WELL WITH ME FOR THY SAKE etc. (*ib.* 13).

Sarai remained beautiful in spite of the long journey, a point further highlighted by comparison with the 'ugly' Egyptians. Upon entering Egypt, Abram worries that Sarai's beauty will be particularly noticeable.[75] The rabbinic interpreters transform Abram's rather flippant biblical statement into an affirmation of the matriarch's superiority over other peoples. *Genesis Rabbah* 40:4 goes on to compare Abraham and Barak, two biblical men who subordinated themselves to women, Sarah and Deborah (Gen 12; Judg 4). Beauty again reflects Sarai's superior nature.

The following midrash (*Gen. Rab.* 40:5) deals with Sarai's beauty at greater length. After asking Sarai to play an active role in Egypt, 'Say you are my sister' (Gen 12:13), the biblical text only mentions Abram entering the land. The rabbis provide a creative explanation for Sarai's apparent absence:

He had put her in a box and locked her in it. When he came to the customs-house, he [the customs officer] demanded, 'Pay the custom dues'. 'I will pay', he replied. 'You carry garments in that box', said he. 'I will pay the dues on garments'. 'You are carrying silks', he asserted. 'I will pay on silks'. 'You are carrying precious stones'. 'I will pay on precious stones'. 'It is imperative that you open it and we see what it contains', he insisted. As soon as he opened it the land of Egypt was irradiated with her lustre [beauty] (lit.: 'the land of Egypt shone from her light/glory').

Abram here protects Sarai and her beauty from the Egyptians. The final reference to jewels is reminiscent of Prov 31:10: 'A capable wife who

75. Wenham comments: 'Stranger still is Abram's supposition that Sarai, aged about 65 (cf. 12:4; 17:17), should be regarded as outstandingly attractive... [T]he Egyptians heartily concurred (vv 14-15)... [I]t should be borne in mind that ideas of feminine beauty in traditional societies differ from ours: well-endowed matronly figures, not slim youthful ones, tend to represent their ideal of womanhood. By such criteria, Sarai might well count as beautiful even at her age' (Wenham, *Genesis 1–15*, 288). Cf. Wenham, *Genesis 16–50*, 75–6; Sarna, *JPS: Genesis*, 94, 141; Bronner, *From Eve to Esther*, 74–5, 85 n. 50.

can find? She is far more precious than jewels.' Abram demonstrates this principle in a literal sense: he values Sarai more than jewels, as he does not hesitate to pay the high customs duties required for jewels in order to conceal his wife. This comparison seems particularly apt, as Sarah is equated with the 'capable wife' elsewhere in *Genesis Rabbah*.[76] When the dissatisfied customs officer asks Abram to open the box, Sarai's 'light' (אור) shines brightly: she is so beautiful that she immediately penetrates this vast and powerful land. This functions as a metaphor for Sarah's influential status.

The next part of *Gen. Rab.* 40:5 emphasises Sarai's unparalleled beauty:

> R. 'Azariah and R. Jonathan in R. Isaac's name said: Eve's image (איקונין) was transmitted to the reigning beauties of each generation. Elsewhere it is written, *And the damsel was very fair—'ad me'od* (יפה עד־מאד) (1 Kings I, 4), which means that she attained to Eve's beauty; but here in truth it is written, THE EGYPTIANS BEHELD THE WOMAN THAT SHE WAS VERY FAIR (ME'OD) (יפה הוא מאד)—which means, even more beautiful than Eve's image.

This tradition envisages a successive line of women who inherit a fundamental characteristic from the first woman, Eve.[77] The term איקונין, 'image', bears important theological connotations. It is used, for example, to express man's creation in the image of God (cf. Gen 1:26-27; 5:1, 3; 9:6) and of cultic statues bearing the likeness of ancient Near Eastern deities.[78] In this midrash, the 'image' relates to beauty and Eve becomes a 'standard' against which other women may be judged.[79] An argument

---

76. See §7.1, 'Sarah as the "Capable Wife" (אשת חיל)'. This is probably coincidental, especially as different words are used for 'jewels' in *Gen. Rab.* 40:5 (מרגלוון) and Prov 31:10 (פנינים).

77. On views of Eve, see Bronner, *From Eve to Esther*, 22–41. Baskin discusses rabbinic interpretations of creation and how these reflect and contribute to the rabbis' understanding of women as secondary to men (Baskin, *Midrashic Women*, 44–64). On female creation and the paradigm of the ancestress, see Brenner-Idan, *The Israelite Woman*, 123–9.

78. This midrash suggests that an important characteristic passed down the female line, as well as from Adam to the male line. See Silviu Bunta, 'The Likeness of the Image: Adamic Motifs and צלם Anthropology in Rabbinic Traditions About Jacob's Image Enthroned in Heaven', *Journal for the Study of Judaism* 37, no. 1 (2006): 55–84.

79. Freedman, n. 3 329. On the term איקונין, see Jastrow, 60; Bunta, 'Likeness of the Image', 62–3. Bunta (ibid., 74–6) notes that the transmission of beauty down the generations is part of the connotations of איקונין in rabbinic literature. See e.g., *b. B. Bat.* 58a.

is deduced from the words מאד, 'very, exceedingly, much',[80] and יפה, 'beautiful'.[81]

Abishag (1 Kgs 1:4) and Sarai (Gen 12:14) are both said to be very beautiful. The rabbis note, however, that Abishag is described as יפה עד־מאד, 'very (BDB, "exceedingly") beautiful'.[82] The biblical text intends the particle עד to be used in its sense, 'Of *degree*, to indicate a higher or the highest'; however, the rabbis interpret it with its common meaning: 'up to, as far as'.[83] By contrast, Sarai is described as יפה מאד, 'very beautiful'. The particle עד allows the rabbis to compare Abishag to Eve: she reached, but did not exceed Eve's beauty.[84] Sarah, however, is described as beautiful without limitation (no עד) and the rabbis therefore assert that she surpassed Eve's beauty. As the first matriarch in Israel, and the first woman since Eve whose story Genesis tells in detail, the rabbis emphasise Sarah's importance.[85]

Lastly, the midrash argues that Egyptian officials entered a bidding war for the right to take Sarai into Pharaoh's household. The rabbis understand the root לקח, 'to take', to refer to bidding in Gen 12:5, but also in the events described in Jer 38:6 (historical) and Isa 14:2 (future). *Genesis Rabbah* 40:5 gives the events in Gen 12 a national dimension, linking Sarai's beauty to the wider history of Israel. This midrash demonstrates Sarai's worthiness and authority as it expands upon biblical references to her beauty.

Genesis Rabbah 52:12 provides an interesting catalogue of ideas relating to female beauty, modesty and chastity. In Gen 20:9-16, Abimelech returns Sarah to Abraham, providing him with many possessions and free choice over where to live in the land. He turns to Sarah and explains: 'Look, I have given your brother a thousand pieces of silver; it is your exoneration (lit. "covering of eyes") before all who are with you; you are completely vindicated' (Gen 20:16). The meaning of Abimelech's words, especially the 'covering of eyes' (כסות עינים), is debated.[86] The

---

80. See BDB, 547; Jastrow, 721.

81. Freedman suggests two passages as background to this tradition: *Gen. Rab.* 8:5, where מאד in Gen 1:31 is said to refer to Adam (אדם) because they share the same consonants, and *Gen. Rab.* 21:2, which suggests that Prov 24:30 and Isa 44:13 refer to Eve as 'Adam' (Freedman, n. 3 58; n. 4 329).

82. BDB, 547.

83. BDB, 723–5; Jastrow, 1042.

84. See Ps 147:15; BDB, 724; Freedman, n. 4 329.

85. Cf. Zucker, 'Sarah', 252.

86. On the phrase's biblical meaning, see Westermann, *Genesis 12–36*, 328; Wenham, *Genesis 16–50*, 74; Sarna, *JPS: Genesis*, 144.

Hebrew verb כסה can have a range of meanings related to 'covering', including concealment, clothing, being overwhelmed and spreading over something.[87] The derived noun כסות means 'covering, clothing'. It appears, for example, in Exod 21:10, where a husband is required to continue providing clothing, food and marital relations to his first wife after taking a second.[88] *Genesis Rabbah* 52:12 explores what the phrase 'covering of eyes' (כסות עינים) means in Gen 20:16.

Rabbi Judah b. R. Ilai depicts Abimelech chastising Abraham for having twice traded Sarah in foreign lands: 'You went to Egypt and made merchandise of her, and you came here and traded in her'. He then states: 'If you desire money, here is money and cover up [your] eyes from her (כסי מינה עינה)'. According to Freedman, Abimelech's words could mean one of two things. Either Abraham must not trade Sarah again, implying that he should cover his own eyes from seeing her as a tradable item, or that he must protect her from the gaze of others who may wish to take her, as Pharaoh and Abimelech did.[89] 'The covering of eyes' protects Sarah from further harm. Abimelech criticises Abraham's treatment of his wife and this coheres with his biblical portrayal: this foreign king does not have sexual relations with Sarah, protests his innocence before God and immediately returns Sarah to her husband when he discovers she is a married woman (Gen 20:3-7).

Next, 'R. Joḥanan explained it: [Abimelech said to Abraham:] "Make thee a garment that all may look at *it*, not at her beauty". A COVERING OF THE EYES meaning a garment which attracts the eyes.' This interprets the biblical phrase literally, suggesting that a garment be made to distract from Sarah's beauty. This would protect Sarah and prevent others from lusting after her or attempting to take her for themselves. Thirdly, R. Berekiah also argues for a physical interpretation of the phrase: 'He [Abimelech] made her a noble lady (מטרונה, "matrona")'. Completely covering Sarah in a garment conveys her superior social status and demonstrates her modesty.[90] Rabbi Simeon b. Lakish offers an alternative suggestion: Abimelech hoped to turn Sarah against her husband, who did not protect her after they had been married for so long, whereas

---

87. BDB, 491–2.

88. Cf. Exod 22:26; Deut 22:12; Job 24:7; Isa 50:3. See BDB, 492.

89. Freedman, n. 2 458.

90. Freedman, n. 3 458. See Bronner, *From Eve to Esther*, 6, 80; Satlow, *Jewish Marriage*, 228–9; Hauptman, *Rereading*, 55; Peskowitz, *Spinning Fantasies*, 208 n. 32; Porton, 'How the Rabbis Imagined Sarah', 198–9; Archer, *Her Price Is Beyond Rubies*, 246; Friedman, 'Shifting Role of Women', 481.

Abimelech did all of this for her after only one night. Freedman suggests that this may 'bear the subtle suggestion that now Sarah would cover her eyes from Abraham—not look at him but desire Abimelech'.[91]

The midrash's final interpretation criticises Abraham and Sarah for lying about Sarah's marital status: 'You covered my eyes; therefore the son that you will beget will be of covered eyes'. This suggests that Isaac's future blindness (Gen 27:1) is a repercussion of Abraham and Sarah's actions in Gerar. *Genesis Rabbah* 52:12 offers multiple interpretations of the phrase 'a covering of eyes' (כסות עינים). These reflect rabbinic understandings of gender roles and female sexuality. Men have a duty to protect beautiful women; but women's behaviour and their dress may also prevent untoward attention from males.[92]

As suggested by the pericopae above, modesty and chastity were female virtues encouraged by the rabbis. *Genesis Rabbah* 60:15 and 85:7 connect Rebekah and Tamar:

> Two covered themselves with a veil, and they gave birth to twins, Rebekah and Tamar. Rebekah: AND SHE TOOK HER VEIL, AND COVERED HERSELF (Gen 24:65); Tamar: *And she covered herself with a veil (ib.* XXXVIII, 14).[93]

Similarities in the details of these women's narratives allow the rabbis to connect them.[94] No further comment is offered, but it seems that Rebekah and Tamar are praised for their modesty.[95]

Finally, *Gen. Rab.* 70:12 justifies Jacob kissing Rachel when they meet (Gen 29:11). The initial tradition claims: 'All kissing is indecent save in three cases: the kiss of high office, the kiss of reunion, and the kiss of parting'. Rabbi Tanḥuma then adds: 'The kiss of kinship too, as it says, AND JACOB KISSED RACHEL—because she was his kinswoman'. This removes any connotations of indecent behaviour or sexual lust from the situation. The matriarch and patriarch, Rachel and Jacob, behave appropriately.[96]

---

91. Freedman, n. 4 458.

92. See Porton, 'How the Rabbis Imagined Sarah', 203; Bronner, *From Eve to Esther*, 32–3; Satlow, *Tasting the Dish*, esp. 132–82.

93. *Gen. Rab.* 60:15 and 85:7 are virtually identical.

94. Rebekah and Tamar are also compared in *Gen. Rab.* 63:8; 85:13.

95. On the veil, see Archer, *Her Price Is Beyond Rubies*, 206, 212; Baskin, *Midrashic Women*, 68.

96. Rabow, *Lost Matriarch*, 18.

8.1.3.1. *Summary*

Genesis Rabbah describes matriarchal figures as beautiful and chaste. Several passages in *Genesis Rabbah* emphasise Sarah's unparalleled beauty and the fact that this is recognised not only by her husband but also by outsiders. The rabbis interpret a beautiful physical appearance as proof of the matriarchs' worthiness.[97] Moreover, their modesty indicates moral superiority. The rabbis believed that women should guard their sexuality and behave chastely. They presented the matriarchs as exemplars of such behaviour in *Genesis Rabbah*.

8.2. *Negative Rabbinic Portrayals of the Matriarchs as Women*

8.2.1. *Stereotypical Negative Characteristics*

There are a few pericopae scattered throughout *Genesis Rabbah* that associate the matriarchs with stereotypical negative female characteristics. The rabbis sometimes make blanket assumptions about women, even the matriarchs whom they revere. One example is *Gen. Rab.* 70:11: 'if you are anxious for a gossip, AND, BEHOLD, RACHEL HIS DAUGHTER COMETH WITH THE SHEEP (Gen 29:6)—for women are fond of gossiping'. Rachel is indelibly linked with gossip and the only justification given for this attribution is that women are prone to gossip. Rachel simply exemplifies a trait associated with the female sex.[98]

Other passages in *Genesis Rabbah* expand upon negative traits believed to characterise women. Two near-identical pericopae, *Gen. Rab.* 18:2 and 80:5, discuss stereotypical female traits in relation to the creation of woman:

> R. Joshua of Siknin said in R. Levi's name: WAYYIBEN ('and he built'; Gen 2:22) is written, signifying that He considered well (*hithbonnen*) from what part to create her. Said He: 'I will not create her from [Adam's] head, lest she be swell-headed; nor from the eye, lest she be a coquette; nor from the ear, lest she be an eavesdropper; nor from the mouth, lest she be a gossip; nor from the heart, lest she be prone to jealousy; nor from the hand, lest she be light-fingered; nor from the foot, lest she be a gadabout; but from the modest part of man, for even when he stands naked, that part is covered'. And as He created each limb He ordered her, 'Be a modest woman'.[99]

---

97. Ibid., 35.
98. Cf. Ilan, *Mine and Yours Are Hers*, 238.
99. This quotation is *Gen. Rab.* 18:2. *Gen. Rab.* 80:5 is almost identical.

Consonantal similarity between the verbs בנה, 'to build', and בין, 'to reflect', suggest that when creating woman, God carefully considered which of Adam's body parts would provide a suitable starting point. Body parts become metonyms for negative personality traits, as God rejects various body parts based on the character flaws he envisages women inheriting from them. God finally settles on the rib. As the most modest part of man, creating woman from here should make her modest. To secure this virtue, God continually charges the woman to be chaste as he creates her.

However:

> *ye have set at nought My counsel, and would none of My reproof* (Prov. I, 25). I did not create her from the head, yet she is swelled-headed, as it is written, *They walk with stretched-forth necks* (Isa. III, 16); nor from the eye, yet she is a coquette: *And wanton eyes (ib.)*; nor from the ear, yet she is an eavesdropper: *Now Sarah listened in the tent door* (Gen. XVIII, 10); nor from the heart, yet she is prone to jealousy: *Rachel envied her sister (ib.* XXX, I); nor from the hand, yet she is light-fingered: *And Rachel stole the teraphim* (*ib.* XXXI, 19); nor from the foot, yet she is a gadabout: *And Dinah went out,* etc. (*ib.* XXXIV, I).

Women assume the very characteristics that God sought to avoid and biblical proof texts are provided that show women exhibiting those traits. Included among the examples are two of the matriarchs, Sarah and Rachel, as well as Dinah, the daughter of a matriarch and patriarch. In *Gen. Rab.* 18:2 and 80:5, women are chastised for displaying such negative characteristics, particularly after God called upon them to remain chaste. As Bronner notes, according to this midrash: 'all women are guilty of these failings and remain in need of rules and regulations to ensure their modest demeanour and conduct'.[100]

Genesis Rabbah 45:5 provides an alternative set of negative female traits:

> R. Menaḥema [Nehemiah] said in R. Abin's name: She scratched (חימסה) his face. The Rabbis said: Women are said to possess four traits: they are greedy, eavesdroppers, slothful, and envious. Greedy, as it says, *And she took of the fruit thereof, and did eat* (*ib.* III, 6); eavesdroppers: *And Sarah heard in the tent door* (*ib.* XVIII, 10); slothful: *Make ready* quickly *three measures of fine meal* (*ib.* 6); envious: *Rachel envied her sister* (*ib.* XXX, I). R. Joshua b. Nehemiah said: She is also a scratcher and talkative. A

---

100. Bronner, *From Eve to Esther*, 31–2.

scratcher: AND SARAI SAID UNTO ABRAM: MY SCRATCH BE UPON THEE. Talkative: *And Miriam spoke against Moses* (Num. XII, I). R. Levi said: She is also prone to steal and a gadabout. Prone to steal: *And Rachel stole the teraphim* (Gen. XXXI, 19). A gadabout: *And Dinah went out (ib.* XXXIV, I).

R. Menaḥema reinterprets Gen 16:5, 'May the wrong done to me (חמסי) be on you', as 'My scratch is upon you', deriving חמסי from the Piel of חמס, meaning 'to scratch with nails'.[101] By this interpretation, Sarah does not simply complain to Abraham, but lashes out.[102] This leads to further discussion of the negative traits possessed by women. Four traits are initially presented by the authoritative group, 'the Rabbis' and a further two are then added by R. Joshua b. Neḥemiah and R. Levi. Each negative trait is illustrated by a biblical quotation.

In all three midrashim (*Gen. Rab.* 80:5; 18:2; 45:5), matriarchs are used to exemplify negative traits. This 'simultaneously creates an ideal of female virtue and a stereotype of feminine shortcomings and culpability'.[103] It is impossible to say whether the rabbis found biblical quotations to match characteristics they associated with women, or if they derived a list of negative female characteristics from examples found in the Bible.[104] Either way, this seems to illustrate Baskin's suggestion that: 'The rabbis' justifications of the patriarchy they themselves maintained and fostered relied on establishing the secondary nature of females from the moment of their creation'.[105] What is clear, however, is that whilst the rabbis respected the matriarchs, they also used them as examples of their sex, both the good and the bad.

It is difficult to discern why the rabbis used their revered matriarchs as examples of negative female traits. It may relate to the paucity of female characters in the Hebrew Bible, meaning that the same few biblical women had to exemplify both the best and worst traits associated with their gender. It may also indicate that the rabbis did not hold the matriarchs in as high a regard as their male counterparts.[106] Following its enumeration of various negative female traits, *Gen. Rab.* 45:5 continues:

101. Jastrow, 478; Freedman, n. 1 383.

102. See Porton, 'How the Rabbis Imagined Sarah', 206.

103. Bronner, *From Eve to Esther*, 32.

104. Cf. Porton, 'How the Rabbis Imagined Sarah', 198–9.

105. Baskin, *Midrashic Women*, 2; cf. 52–3.

106. Cf. §3.6.1.1, 'The Title "the Matriarchs" (האימהות) Paralleled with a Male Equivalent'.

> R. Tanḥuma said in the name of R. Ḥiyya the Elder, and R. Berekiah said in
> R. Eleazar's name: Whoever plunges eagerly into litigation does not escape
> from it unscathed. Sarah should have reached Abraham's years, but because
> she said, THE LORD JUDGE BETWEEN ME AND THEE (Gen 16:5), her
> life was reduced by forty-eight years.

Perhaps if Sarah had not possessed the weaknesses inherent to being a woman, she would have achieved her full lifespan.[107]

These traditions suggest a more negative rabbinic attitude to women; even the matriarchs' reputations are sullied. Though the title 'matriarch' appears nowhere in these passages, it is difficult to divorce the Genesis women from that group identity.[108] It would be wrong to ignore these traditions or to whitewash them: there is no doubt that the (male) rabbis operated within a patriarchal framework, which viewed women as second-class citizens.[109] Bronner even suggests that the 'bipolarisation of rabbinic views of biblical women' is evidence of their struggle to reconcile their social views of women with the positive portrayal of numerous biblical women.[110] The multivocality of rabbinic texts also allows many different traditions, some of which disagree with one another, to be preserved. Given the large number of positive pericopae concerning the matriarchs, it would be wrong simply to argue that these few negative traditions represent the definitive rabbinic view of women.[111]

8.2.1.1. *Summary*
Genesis Rabbah shows the matriarchs embodying stereotypical negative characteristics that the rabbis associated with women, such as greed, gossiping, eavesdropping and coquettishness. This should not undermine the numerous positive attitudes displayed by the rabbis about these figures, but suggests that when viewed as women, the matriarchs can be understood more negatively.

---

107. On women as inherently flawed, see Baskin, *Midrashic Women*, 52. For women and litigation, see Wegner, *Chattel or Person?*, 119–20. According to Wegner, the Mishnah allows women to engage in lawsuits.

108. Just as Abraham, Isaac, and Jacob may appear without the title 'patriarch' (אב), but are still understood to be part of that group.

109. Adler, *Engendering Judaism*, xiv; Satlow, *Tasting the Dish*, 12–13, 332–3. Cf. Biale, *Women and Jewish Law*, 14, 28–9.

110. Bronner, *From Eve to Esther*, xiv. Wegner (*Chattel or Person?*, 219 n. 10) suggests that the rabbis' general view of women may stem from their wider cultural context, rather than being specifically devised by the rabbis.

111. Bronner, *From Eve to Esther*, 185; Hauptman, *Rereading*, 6–11; Porton, 'How the Rabbis Imagined Sarah', 195; Satlow, *Tasting the Dish*, xiii, 333.

8.2.2. *Beauty and Sexuality*

Although the rabbis demonstrate positive views of female beauty and sexuality, they also believed these attributes to be distracting and able to put women in danger.[112] *Genesis Rabbah* 72:3 chastises Rachel for her treatment of Jacob during the mandrake incident (Gen 30:14-15). When Reuben brings mandrakes to his mother, Leah, Rachel bargains for them, hoping that their aphrodisiacal qualities will finally end her barrenness.[113] In return, Leah has sexual relations with Jacob and bears Issachar and Zebulun (Gen 30:16-20): 'R. Simeon taught: Because she [Rachel] treated that righteous man [Jacob] so slightingly, she was not buried with him. Thus it says, THEREFORE HE SHALL LIE WITH THEE TO-NIGHT, hinting: With thee will he lie in death, but not with me.' Genesis 30:15 is understood as an 'unconscious prophecy': Leah will be buried with Jacob, Rachel will not.[114] Rachel disrespected Jacob, believing that she had the right to determine Jacob's sexual relations.

Genesis Rabbah 72:3 continues:

> R. Eleazar said: Each lost [by the transaction], and each gained. Leah lost the mandrakes and gained the tribes…, while Rachel gained the mandrakes and lost the tribes… R. Samuel b. Naḥman said: The one lost mandrakes and gained [two] tribes and the privilege of burial with him; [while Rachel gained mandrakes and lost the tribes and burial with him].

Both Leah and Rachel benefitted, but also suffered disadvantages because of their bargain. Rachel loses the chance to bear two tribal ancestors and to be buried with Jacob. Whilst Leah's gains were much greater, even she lost the mandrakes. *Genesis Rabbah* 72:3 criticises both sisters, but especially Rachel, for bargaining with their own and Jacob's sexuality.

Genesis Rabbah 80:1 also criticises female sexuality. The midrash connects Gen 34:1: 'And Dinah went out (תצא)', with Gen 30:16, where: 'Leah went out (תצא) to meet him (Jacob)' after the mandrake incident. The same verb (root יצא, 'to go out') is used of both Dinah and Leah in situations that lead to sexual encounters. This is connected with Ezek 16:44: 'See, everyone who uses proverbs will use this proverb about you, "Like mother, like daughter"':[115]

---

112. See e.g. Baskin, *Midrashic Women*, 29–36, 173 n. 45.
113. See §6.3.2, 'Sons' Respect for Their Mothers'.
114. Freedman, n. 5 663.
115. On Ezek 16:44, see Allen, *Ezekiel 1–19*, 244; William H. Brownlee, *Ezekiel 1–19*, Word Biblical Commentary 28 (Waco: Word, 1986), 243–53. This nationalised

Said he [Jose of Maon]: 'Like the daughter so is the mother, like the gener-ation so is its leader (*nasi*), like the altar so are its priests'. Kahana says: According to the garden so is its gardener. 'You have not yet completely appeased him for the first', Resh Lakish exclaimed, 'and you are already bringing him another! What is really the meaning of this verse?' 'A cow does not gore unless her calf kicks; a woman is not immoral (lit. "running about as a prostitute", root זנה) until her daughter is immoral (lit. "running about as a prostitute", root זנה)', he replied. 'If so', said he, 'then our mother Leah was a harlot (זונה)!' 'Even so', he replied; 'because it says, *And Leah went out to meet him* (Gen. XXX, 16), which means that she went out to meet him adorned like a harlot'; therefore AND DINAH THE DAUGHTER OF LEAH WENT OUT.

The first half of the passage suggests that people and objects represent the individual who leads them. The Ezekiel proverb confirms that mothers and daughters bear similar characteristics in a kind of family resemblance. This explains why Dinah's action is comparable to Leah's. The passage then implies that a parent's true characteristics are made known when their offspring behaves in a particular way.[116]

Genesis Rabbah 80:1 demonstrates the rabbis' belief that women could use their sexuality to behave in morally inappropriate ways. Dinah's action in Gen 34:1 is interpreted here as an act of harlotry.[117] In particular, having 'gone out' 'was regarded as incorrect, even wanton, behaviour—a defiance of the regime of modesty'.[118] In Gen 30:16, Leah acts in an overtly sexual manner, going out to inform Jacob that she will have sex with him that night. The rabbis interpret this as harlotry, especially as Leah has just paid Rachel in mandrakes to spend the night with Jacob.[119] Both Dinah and Leah are depicted contravening rabbinic expectations of female behaviour.[120] In fact, Wegner argues that 'a woman's sexuality lies

image of Jerusalem is interesting in relation to Leah's national status as a matriarch. For the verse in biblical and rabbinic contexts, see Walter Zimmerli, *A Commentary on the Book of Ezekiel, Chapters 1–24*, trans. Ronald E. Clements from the German 1969 published by Neukirchener Verlag (Philadelphia: Fortress, 1979), 349–50.

116. Freedman, n. 2 736.

117. Cf. *Gen. Rab.* 18:2; 80:5; Bronner, *From Eve to Esther*, 119. See also §7.3.2, 'Illegitimate Unions'.

118. Bronner, *From Eve to Esther*, 120. Cf. Zlotnick, *Dinah's Daughters*, 33–4; Ilan, *Mine and Yours Are Hers*, 171–3; Peskowitz, *Spinning Fantasies*, 141, 147–8; Baskin, *Midrashic Women*, 112–14, 149.

119. Cf. *Gen. Rab.* 72:5 views Gen 30:16 positively. See §6.5.4.1, 'Leah'.

120. Bronner, *From Eve to Esther*, 120. On this pericope, see Rabow, *Lost Matriarch*, 148–9.

at the root of limitations on her personhood in both the private and the public sphere of mishnaic culture'.[121] This midrash seemingly supports her suggestion.

In this pericope, the rabbis associate Leah with prostitution.[122] It is particularly surprising that the rabbis here refer to Leah as 'our mother' (אימנו), a title highlighting her matriarchal status.[123] Positive material about Leah cannot be dismissed on the basis of this pericope, but *Gen. Rab.* 80:1 cannot be ignored. This may simply represent a further example of biblical women being used as exemplars of both positive and negative traits; or perhaps Leah serves as a warning: if this revered matriarch could behave immodestly, ordinary women should regulate their behaviour carefully. Whatever the explanation, *Gen. Rab.* 80:1 does not portray Leah or Dinah in a positive light.

Women can abuse their own sexuality, but men may also endanger women's sexuality. For example, R. Simeon b. Lakish identifies Og, a biblical character appearing more frequently in aggadah,[124] as the messenger who informs Abram of Lot's capture (Gen 14:13; *Gen. Rab.* 42:8). Og reveals this information, hoping that Abram will be killed in battle and he will be free to take Sarai for himself. Lust can be a dangerous motive and *Gen. Rab.* 80:5 further highlights this:

AND DINAH THE DAUGHTER OF LEAH WENT OUT. R. Berekiah said in R. Levi's name: This may be compared to one who was holding a pound of meat in his hand, and as soon as he exposed it a bird swooped down and snatched it away. Similarly, AND DINAH THE DAUGHTER OF LEAH WENT OUT, and forthwith, AND SHECHEM THE SON OF HAMOR SAW HER. R. Samuel b. Naḥman said: Her arm became exposed.

AND HE TOOK HER AND LAY WITH HER—in a natural way; AND HUMBLED [i.e. VIOLATED] HER—unnaturally.

121. Wegner, *Chattel or Person?*, 19.
122. On the rabbis and harlotry, see Bronner, *From Eve to Esther*, 142–62; Bar-Ilan, *Some Jewish Women*, 132–55; Satlow, *Tasting the Dish*, 132–56; Biale, *Women and Jewish Law*, 190–2; Wegner, *Chattel or Person?*, 174. Wegner (*Chattel or Person?*, 16–17) suggests that: 'a woman's illicit union with a man not the owner of her sexual function will infect that man with cultic pollution'. On prostitution in the biblical text, see Brenner-Idan, *The Israelite Woman*, 79–84, 106–14.
123. See §3.6.2, 'Uses of the Noun אם as "Matriarch"'.
124. See Josef Segal, 'Og', *EncJud*, 15:391–2.

Dinah's exposed flesh is compared to a piece of meat, snatched by a bird when uncovered. This analogy highlights the animalistic side of human nature that may be witnessed in Gen 34. According to the rabbis, the biblical language describing Shechem's sexual intercourse with Dinah reveals his 'natural' and 'unnatural' actions towards her. Although not explained further in the midrash, Neusner argues that these terms refer respectively to vaginal and anal intercourse.[125] The midrash thus suggests that Dinah's beauty and sexuality are abused by Shechem. Some rabbis did not see Dinah as entirely innocent, though. In the first half of *Gen. Rab.* 80:5, Dinah's 'going out' is used to characterise her as a 'gadabout' in the midrashic discussion of negative female characteristics. *Genesis Rabbah* 80:5 suggests both that women may be at danger from men's sexual desires, but also that women should not behave unchastely.[126]

Dinah is abused by a foreign king, but the midrash also blames her father for events in Gen 34. In *Gen. Rab.* 76:9, Jacob is chastised for having hidden Dinah in a box when his family meet Esau in Gen 32. As Jacob did not allow Dinah to marry a circumcised man (Esau), she was open to abuse by Shechem and ultimately married Job, both uncircumcised men.[127] Jacob is again blamed for Dinah's situation in *Gen. Rab.* 79:8:

> AND HE ERECTED THERE AN ALTAR, AND CALLED IT EL-ELOHE-ISRAEL (XXXIII, 20). He [Jacob] declared to Him: 'Thou art God in the celestial spheres and I am a god in the terrestrial sphere'. R. Huna commented in the name of R. Simeon b. Lakish: [God reproved him]: 'Even the synagogue superintendent cannot assume authority of himself, yet thou didst take authority to thyself. Tomorrow thy daughter will go out and be dishonoured!' Hence it is written, *And Dinah the daughter of Leah went out,* etc. (Gen. XXXIV, I).

Jacob compares his authority in the world with God's ultimate authority in the heavens.[128] The comparison with the synagogue superintendent reminds the audience that people cannot bestow authority upon themselves

---

125. Neusner, 3:149.

126. Cf. Berkovits, *Jewish Women*, 16; Hauptman, 'Feminist Perspectives on Rabbinic Texts', 45; Hauptman, *Rereading*, 30–1; Archer, *Her Price Is Beyond Rubies*, 263; Biale, *Women and Jewish Law*, 64–5, 112–13; Wegner, *Chattel or Person?*, esp. 156–62, 173–5.

127. See §7.3.2, 'Illegitimate Unions'.

128. 'No. 1's statement recalls the claim that Jacob's face had a counterpart engraved in heaven' (Neusner, 3:144). Cf. Bunta, 'Likeness of the Image'.

but must be nominated into such roles. Jacob's arrogance leads to Dinah's rape and Dinah's sexuality becomes an object to be abused. Presumably Dinah was a virgin when she was raped by Shechem. Given the emphasis on virginity in rabbinic thought, it is clear that this action will taint Dinah's character and affect her marriage prospects, a fact confirmed by *Gen. Rab.* 76:9.[129]

The rabbis devised a causal connection between Gen 33:20 and Gen 34:1, which immediately follows it in the biblical text. This suggests their struggle to make sense of the scenes portrayed in Gen 34, which appear without warning, explanation or trigger. The interpretation of events offered in *Gen. Rab.* 79:8 does not justify Dinah's abuse, even as it attempts to explain it. The use of Jacob's arrogance to understand what happens to Dinah draws attention to female objectification in the ancient world. Women's sexuality was often controlled by men and by the rules and standards imposed upon them by men.[130] Dinah is a woman debilitated by patriarchy.[131]

Finally, in *Gen. Rab.* 52:4, Sarah is declared to be Abraham's sister and given to Abimelech 'without her will or consent'. *Genesis Rabbah* 52:4 confirms that Sarah is passive during these events, as suggested by her silence in Genesis 20.[132] Wenham argues: 'Abram explains his fears and puts his plan to Sarai. No comments of hers are recorded, implying her consent to his scheme.'[133] This seems unfair, as Sarai is rarely allowed to voice her opinions in the biblical narrative. Interestingly, however, *Gen. Rab.* 52:6 suggests that Sarah was, in fact, complicit in these events: 'SAID HE NOT HIMSELF UNTO ME: SHE IS MY SISTER? AND SHE, SHE TOO (GAM) HERSELF SAID: HE IS MY BROTHER (XX, 5): she, her ass-drivers, and her camel-drivers, her domestics, and all her household'.[134] Abraham, Sarah and all of Sarah's household servants confirm her story. The episode from Genesis 20 highlights how women's beauty and sexuality may be abused by men for their own ends. Abraham fears for his own safety and puts Sarah at risk with no apparent regard for her.

---

129. Cf. Adler, *Engendering Judaism*, 130.

130. See Wegner, *Chattel or Person?*; Hauptman, *Rereading*, 31; Biale, *Women and Jewish Law*, xi–xii.

131. Cf. Hauptman, *Rereading*, 54; Wegner, *Chattel or Person?*, 181.

132. Cf. Freedman, n. 3 453. For Jeansonne, Sarah's agreement demonstrates her 'powerlessness' (Jeansonne, *Women of Genesis*, 17).

133. He comments, in fact, on Gen 12. Wenham, *Genesis 1–15*, 287–8 (quote p. 287).

134. '"*Gam*" is an extension, hence all these are included' (Freedman, n. 5 455).

8.2.2.1. *Summary*

Female beauty and sexuality could be dangerous: women could misuse their sexuality, for example becoming promiscuous; men could be tempted by beautiful women; and women could be endangered and objectified because of their appeal to males. In particular, the biblical episodes of the mandrakes (Gen 30:14-20) and Dinah's going out (Gen 34) provide a biblical basis for the rabbis' discussions of these issues. Whilst sexuality can be positively portrayed in *Genesis Rabbah*, the passages mentioned in this section are a reminder that a certain negativity surrounds this aspect of female identity in rabbinic literature.

8.3. *Conclusions*

This chapter has considered in detail *Genesis Rabbah*'s portrayal of the matriarchs in relation to their female gender. There is some ambivalence in rabbinic attitudes towards the matriarchs when they are portrayed specifically as women, exemplifying characteristics that the rabbis believed to be typical of their gender. On the positive side, the matriarchs are portrayed as pious and prayerful women, who demonstrate correct relationship with God. Their physical beauty and modesty reflect their deeper moral nature. In these capacities, the matriarchs embody the rabbinic view of the ideal woman and they should be emulated by ordinary Jewish women, in some cases, even by Jewish men. On the other hand, the matriarchs are portrayed as embodying negative personality traits, which the rabbis presented as common among females. This includes, for example, gossiping and jealousy. Women from Genesis, including Leah and Rachel, also appear inappropriately flouting their sexuality.

These more negative portrayals of the matriarchs seem to relate more to the matriarchs' status as women than as ancestresses of Judaism. It is perhaps the case that the matriarchs had more obstacles to overcome than men when being portrayed as authoritative: even the rabbis, who revere the matriarchs, cannot completely reconcile this status with their status as women.

Chapter 9

CONCLUSIONS

The aim of this study has been to consider the role and status of the matriarchs in *Genesis Rabbah*. Regarded as authoritative by biblical exegetes from the ancient through to the modern period, 'the matriarchs' (האימהות) have rarely been studied as a group and the title has never been adequately defined and explored. Using *Genesis Rabbah*, the classical midrashic commentary on the book of Genesis, it has been possible to explore rabbinic views on the biblical women regarded as Israel's matriarchs. Most importantly, the great respect that these figures were offered by the ancient Jewish rabbis has become clear. In this concluding chapter, I will restate the main conclusions reached in this study, before addressing issues of the unity of *Genesis Rabbah* and the impact of my findings upon current scholarly understandings of the role of women in ancient rabbinic society. Finally, I will consider further research avenues that are opened up by the work done here.

9.1. *Main Findings*

Before considering the impact of this work on the current scholarly climate, it is necessary to restate the conclusions reached in each chapter of this monograph. These conclusions have largely been self-evident, as the focus of this study has been close study of the language and content of a number of pericopae from *Genesis Rabbah*. Nevertheless, in reiterating its main findings, the true impact of the work will be revealed.

Part I of the study explored in detail the main terms and concepts that would continue to feature in this work. Chapter 2 dealt with midrash (מדרש), the term used to describe rabbinic exegesis. Central to the rabbis' worldview was their understanding of Scripture as a unity and as divine language. This influenced the exegetical techniques used to interpret the Hebrew Bible, which draw connections between different scriptural passages and show the hidden meaning of scriptural language. Four exegetical techniques were explored in some detail—wordplay, *gezerah shawah*, *gematria* and proems—which highlighted the creativity and dexterity of rabbinic biblical interpretations. Finally, rabbinic texts were introduced and background to *Genesis Rabbah*, the major source for this study, was offered. This Palestinian exegetical midrash, dating in its final form to the fifth century CE, offers a comprehensive rabbinic interpretation of the biblical book of Genesis, including the stories of Israel's earliest ancestors. As this work deals with these central figures and contains the title 'matriarch' (אם) multiple times, its use as the basis of this study was thereby justified.

The second chapter discussed the title 'the matriarchs' (האימהות). Modern scholarship has failed to adequately define the term. Although most scholars seem to use the title to refer to Sarah, Rebekah, Leah and Rachel, other women were at times included within the category and there was no clear consensus on its meaning. This lack of clarity meant that ancient sources were turned to in a bid to trace the origins and development of 'the matriarchs'.

First, Genesis itself was considered. Whilst the biblical text does not contain the title 'the matriarchs', the portrayal of female figures hugely influenced the later development of this category. Sarah, Rebekah, Leah and Rachel are shown to be the legitimate wives of Israel's patriarchs, Abraham, Isaac and Jacob, as they have the correct genealogical heritage to bear Israel's covenant sons. Genesis 24:67 even establishes matriarchal succession, allowing the authority of one key female figure to pass onto the next generation, as Rebekah is seen to take over Sarah's roles in the patriarchal household. In contrast, the handmaidens, Hagar, Bilhah and Zilpah, are shown to be unsuitable to assume these same roles.

Postbiblical texts like *Jubilees* and *L.A.B.* proved vital in the emergence of the group known as 'the matriarchs', as they developed the biblical characterisation of Israel's key ancestresses. In fact, *L.A.B.* is perhaps the first Jewish exegetical text to use the title 'matriarch', as Deborah and Tamar are referred to authoritatively as 'our mother'. By the third century CE, when the first rabbinic texts were emerging, the title 'the matriarchs' (האמהות) was being used as a category that could parallel the male 'patriarchs' (אבות). The matrilineal principle and the prohibition on intermarriage provided socio-historical factors that contributed to the emergence of 'the matriarchs', as mothers became central for determining Jewish identity and legitimacy became a more significant issue. This affected the portrayal of Israel's earliest mothers, who were able to legitimise the nation.

The second half of this chapter then considered the use of the title 'the matriarchs' in *Genesis Rabbah*. Overall, two main definitions emerged: first, 'the matriarchs' are the legitimate wives of the patriarchs—Sarah, Rebekah, Leah and Rachel. Secondly, in certain situations, Jacob's four wives, Bilhah, Zilpah, Leah and Rachel, may be referred to using this title. The first option is the more common usage. The wives of the patriarchs are referred to individually as 'matriarch' and no further justification of this title is offered, suggesting that its meaning was known to the rabbinic audience. Four characteristics are shown to unite the wives of the patriarchs as matriarchs: prophetic abilities, roles as 'women in the tent', 'the merit of the matriarchs' and, finally, barrenness. Barrenness was the most significant shared characteristic as each woman was barren before she became the mother of covenant sons.

Part II considered 'the matriarchal cycle' in *Genesis Rabbah*.[1] The development of barrenness traditions in the Hebrew Bible, from Genesis through to Isaiah, was discussed. The tradition began with three of the wives of the patriarchs in Genesis (Sarah, Rebekah and Rachel), who were barren before conceiving covenant sons. From here, the tradition developed in Judg 13, before reappearing in a more extended form in 1 Sam 1–2, which recounts the story of Hannah. Although Hannah is not explicitly called 'barren' (עקרה), the term appears in her psalm recorded in 1 Sam 2, and the biblical narrative explains that Hannah 'had no children' (ולחנה אין ילדים, 1 Sam 1:2) 'because the LORD had closed her womb' (1 Sam 1:6). Unlike the barren women before her, Hannah prays to God, asking that he give her a son. This development of the tradition is significant, as Hannah plays a more active role and requests the reversal of her barrenness. Following another return to the motif in 2 Kgs 4:8-37, the final stage of the biblical barrenness tradition is found in Isa 54. Zion is here called a barren woman (עקרה) and this prophecy uses the image of a barren female eventually giving birth to offer the exiled Israel hope that it will be restored. At each stage of the biblical tradition, the barren woman takes on a more developed role, coming to represent the experiences of others, even up to a national scale. The rabbis had access to all layers of this biblical tradition and utilised it extensively in their portrayal of the Genesis matriarchs.

The idea of 'the matriarchal cycle' was then discussed. Borrowing language from Lieve Teugels, I used this term to refer to the transformation of each primary Genesis matriarch from a barren woman to a

---

1. Developing language used in Teugels, *'The Wooing of Rebekah' (Gen. 24)*, 124, 129.

mother of covenant sons. There are three stages to this 'matriarchal cycle': barrenness, motherhood, and matriarchal succession. First, the legitimate wife of the patriarch is barren. After God intervenes to reverse barrenness, the woman gives birth to a son, allowing the continuation of the patriarchal line. The mother protects her son, ensuring that the correct child inherits the covenant promises. Once this inheritance is secured, there is a transition to the next generation, where the process is repeated. In Genesis, the basis of this cycle is seen during the patriarchal narratives, particularly concerning Sarah, Rebekah and Rachel. In *Genesis Rabbah*, the rabbis ensure Leah also conforms to this cycle, showing its importance for their understanding of the matriarchs. For the rabbis, 'the matriarchal cycle' reflected their vital role in the emergence of Israel.

Barrenness is the first stage of 'the matriarchal cycle'. Whilst barrenness was a distressing state for ancient women to find themselves in, as society expected them to bear children, the rabbis offer more nuanced reflections on barrenness, including the need to be considerate to those women suffering from it. Barrenness reveals the worthiness of the matriarchal women; their seemingly hopeless situation is reversed so that they could bear the covenant sons. In Genesis, Sarah, Rebekah and Rachel are all declared barren (עקרה, Gen 11:30; 25:21; 29:31), and in *Genesis Rabbah* the rabbis ensure that Leah is also explicitly given this characteristic. Moreover, as God is in control of childbirth, the reversal of barrenness highlights God's control over the life of Israel. It is God who must reverse the matriarchs' barrenness and this demonstrates their legitimacy to bear the covenant sons. In their barrenness, the matriarchs represent the disad-vantaged, and its reversal offers hope that others' situations will also improve. The biblical barrenness tradition culminates in a portrayal of Zion as a barren woman who bears children (Isa 54) and *Genesis Rabbah* utilises such imagery to portray the Genesis matriarchs as representatives of the nation. The matriarchs have a relevance beyond their own lives and this first stage of the 'matriarchal cycle' lies right at the centre of matriarchs' identity.

The matriarchs eventually achieve motherhood and this forms the next part of the 'matriarchal cycle'. *Genesis Rabbah* records the pain of childbirth and acknowledges death as a potential consequence. The rabbis do not shy away from the realities of childbearing. Sons inherit characteristics, both physical and personality traits, from their mothers. Most significantly, having the correct mother determines inheritance. The 'son of the mistress' prevails over the 'son of the bondsmaid' when the covenant is at stake. The rabbis showed their family members' respect for their roles as mothers. This is most pertinent with Leah, where she receives the attention she deserves in *Genesis Rabbah*, finally being respected by her husband and her son. Matriarchal motherhood extends far beyond simply bearing children as these women work to protect their sons, ensuring that they inherit the covenant promises. The matriarchs are developed far beyond their biblical shadows, and through their maternal actions the matriarchs become fully rounded characters. As with barrenness, motherhood also allows the matriarchs to function as representatives of Israel. Israel directly descends from the matriarchs as their sons become the founding fathers of that nation. In this way, as with barrenness, motherhood allows the matriarchs to take on a national role during 'the matriarchal cycle'.

The final chapter in Part II looked at the closely related issues of legitimacy and succession. Throughout *Genesis Rabbah*, the matriarchal women are shown to be exemplars of modesty, chastity and right relationship with God. For example, Sarah is the 'capable wife' from Proverbs; Rebekah's virginity is perfect by all definitions; and Rachel demonstrates a positive relationship with Israel's God. Moreover, the marital unions formed between the patriarchs and their legitimate wives, the matriarchs, provide the context within which covenant sons may be born. This ultimately allows the nation Israel to emerge. Legitimate unions are contrasted with illegitimate unions formed by other members of Israel's founding family (Esau and Dinah).

To ensure that 'the matriarchal cycle' is successful, a legitimate woman must be chosen in each generation so that the covenant can continue along the right lines. *Genesis Rabbah* builds on biblical notions of succession to show each matriarch taking over from the last. The basis for this may be found in Gen 24:67, where Rebekah assumes the matriarchal role, taking on the position after the death of her mother-in-law, Sarah. 'The matriarchal cycle' is the means by which the rabbis demonstrate their respect for the matriarchs. Their life experiences allow them to develop as characters and the rabbis show the matriarchs acting as the historical mothers of Israel, but also as the present mothers of Israel, because their influence is enduring.

In Part III, other traditions about the matriarchs in *Genesis Rabbah* were considered. These traditions portray the matriarchs primarily as representatives of their gender: namely, as women. The matriarchs become the focus for both positive and negative rabbinic stereotypes of females. On the positive side, their beauty highlights their morality, and they are shown to be pious. The matriarchs follow Hannah's example (1 Sam 1–2) and pray to God, and Sarah and Rebekah are shown to perform cultic actions within the home (*Gen. Rab.* 60:16). Modesty, chastity and a beautiful appearance reflect the matriarchs' moral superiority and their worthiness as matriarchs. On the negative side, the matriarchs exemplify vices that the rabbis believed women in general possessed. These include vices such as greed and eavesdropping. Whilst beauty and sexuality could represent positive characteristics, various matriarchs, including Leah, abuse their sexuality and behave inappropriately, whilst sexuality could also endanger women, as in the case of Dinah (Gen 34). Female sexuality was thus treated with ambivalence by the rabbis. This chapter highlights that the rabbis' attitudes to the matriarchs were not entirely positive: they wrote within a patriarchal context and, hence, their views of these women were influenced by their more general understanding of the sexes. As there are fewer women in the Bible than men, the rabbis used the women in Genesis to represent both the positive and negative aspects of femininity.

Overall, this study has shown that the matriarchs were an authoritative group and that they played an important part in rabbinic thought. Until now, their presence has been neglected. This study has corrected this, focusing on a particular text, *Genesis Rabbah*, and uncovering the many traditions it contains about these women.

9.2. *The Unity of* Genesis Rabbah

In spite of its multivocality, *Genesis Rabbah* evinces a demonstrable unity in its approach to the matriarchs. Although rabbinic texts are made up of numerous individual traditions, some of which even contradict one another, *Genesis Rabbah* suggests that the rabbis saw the matriarchs as authoritative figures, worthy of their title and their central role in Israel's history. 'The matriarchal cycle' is particularly telling. Each of the matriarchs conforms to its various stages and its recurrence in each generation gives a certain structure to the midrash. As the reader becomes familiar with *Genesis Rabbah*, we expect this 'cycle' to reappear in the life of each matriarch. Respect for Israel's matriarchs permeates the midrash, suggesting that this was an accepted attitude towards them. Positive traditions about the matriarchs far outweigh the negative, but even here there is a certain unity. Negative traditions about the matriarchs focus on their status as women, where they function primarily as exemplars of their gender, rather than as members of an authoritative ancestral group.

Whilst Neusner's claim that each rabbinic text is structured by its redactors so as to provide a united, philosophical treatise of one form or another is rather far-fetched and seems unlikely,[2] it is clear that *Genesis*

---

2. E.g. Neusner, *Essential Guide*.

Rabbah as a whole puts forward a particular picture of the group known as 'the matriarchs', which presumably reflects wider rabbinic society's attitudes towards them.

9.3. *The Views of Modern Scholarship*

In the Introduction, the current state of scholarship surrounding rabbinic views of women was discussed through reference to various scholarly works. This study has directly contributed to the field by offering a much-needed study of aggadic traditions contained within a key rabbinic text about a key group of women.

As mentioned throughout this study, it has been the tendency of modern scholars to insist on an overall negative rabbinic view of women, even when they recognise positive traditions about women.[3] There is a difficult balance to strike here. As Adler notes, a degree of distance is required when studying such ancient material: it would not be fair to judge the rabbis by our own standards and worldview, which differ so vastly from their own; equally, 'just because they themselves saw them as just, we cannot very well condone their brutalities or injustices'.[4] The misogynistic views held by the rabbis should not be excused or ignored. However, this study demonstrates that the rabbis had many positive things to say about women; in fact, positive traditions concerning the matriarchs in *Genesis Rabbah* far outweigh the negative.

9.4. *The Matriarchs: The Bible versus Midrash*

Comparing the biblical and rabbinic portrayals of the matriarchs, it is clear that the rabbis gave these women a greater voice and influence than

---

3. Judith Baskin has been the prime example of this; see her *Midrashic Women*. See also Zlotnick, *Dinah's Daughters*, 25, and Ilan, *Mine and Yours Are Hers*, esp. 1–2, 38. Notably, Baskin does not seem to view her work this way: '...I find that negative remarks and attitudes expressed towards women far outnumber positive statements' (Baskin, *Midrashic Women*, 175 n. 61, 179 n. 19).

4. Adler, *Engendering Judaism*, 4. Cf. Bronner, *From Eve to Esther*, 185–6; Berkovits, *Jewish Women*, 1; Boyarin, *Carnal Israel*, 242–5; Hauptman, *Rereading*, 3–5, 244–9; Porton, 'How the Rabbis Imagined Sarah', 195, 209; Wegner, *Chattel or Person?*, 4–9, 13. It may be useful to compare the approach of Greenspahn. He concludes that the Bible offers numerous positive portraits of women as well as the negative views that modern scholarship has mainly focused on. See Frederick E. Greenspahn, 'A Typology of Biblical Women', *Judaism* 32, no. 1 (1983): 43–50. Baskin is not unaware of these issues (e.g. Baskin, *Midrashic Women*, 6–8).

they had in the biblical text. The rabbinic interpreters recognised the significance of the women portrayed in Genesis, those who bore covenant sons and helped enable the emergence of Israel. The rabbis expanded and developed the characterisation of these women, making their significance more explicit in the midrash.

Between the Bible and midrash, a group identity emerged for the female ancestresses of Israel and they became known as 'the matriarchs'. There is a greater unity between characters, as they are shown to share various characteristics. This is made most clear in *Genesis Rabbah* through 'the matriarchal cycle'. As shown in Chapter 3, these women were even viewed, at least in some ways, as comparable to the great and well-established patriarchs of Israel. This study of the matriarchs in *Genesis Rabbah* has therefore highlighted some of the key developments in the characterisation of the matriarchs from biblical to rabbinic times.

9.5. *Further Research*

This work provides grounds for further research. This study has largely been text-focused, allowing a particular rabbinic text to speak on its own terms. This has shown how important the matriarchs, a group of female figures, were for the male rabbis in antiquity. It will now be necessary to consider the full implications of this study for our understanding of the role of women in ancient and rabbinic society. Although I touched on these themes in the final chapter, I did not move beyond the evidence provided by *Genesis Rabbah*. It is now important to bring both the positive and negative views found there back into the society from which they origi-nated, asking how what I have discovered may alter our current views about this period. It will therefore be important to compare and consider at length how these findings relate to the conclusions reached by studies about women's status in halakhah, such as Biale's *Women and Jewish Law* or Wegner's *Chattel or Person?*[5] This will also help to uncover any differ-ences between the rabbis' attitudes towards biblical women compared to ordinary Jewish women of their own time. This in turn will open up the question of the extent to which rabbinic texts accurately reflect the society in which they were produced.[6]

Finally, this study should also act as encouragement for further study of the portrayal of biblical characters, both male and female, in rabbinic literature. Studying the matriarchs in *Genesis Rabbah* has revealed the

---

5. Biale, *Women and Jewish Law*, esp. xi–xiii, 3–9; Wegner, *Chattel or Person?*
6. Cf. Wegner, *Chattel or Person?*, 170.

many different interpretations that arose from the Bible's portrayal of these figures and it would be interesting to see how the rabbis portrayed other biblical heroes and heroines, and why.[7]

Genesis Rabbah gave the biblical matriarchs a far greater voice than they had in the biblical text. I hope that in this study, I too have given the matriarchs the voice they deserve.

7. Cf. Schneider, *Mothers of Promise*, 218–19.

BIBLIOGRAPHY

Primary Texts and Translations

Baumgarten, Joseph M. on the basis of transcriptions by Józef T. Milik, and with contributions by Stephen Pfann and Ada Yardeni. *Qumran Cave 4 XIII The Damascus Document (4Q266-273.* Discoveries in the Judaean Desert XVIII. Oxford: Clarendon, 1996.

Danby, Herbert, trans. *The Mishnah Translated from the Hebrew with Introduction and Brief Explanatory Notes.* Oxford: Oxford University Press, 1964, repr. from 1933 ed.

Elliger, K., and W. Rudolph, eds. *Biblia Hebraica Stuttgartensia.* 5th rev. ed. Stuttgart: Deutsche Bibelgesellschaft, 1997.

Epstein, Isidore, ed. *The Babylonian Talmud Translated into English with Notes, Glossary and Indices under the Editorship of I. Epstein.* 18 vols. London: Soncino, 1936–52.

Freedman, H. trans. *Midrash Rabbah Genesis.* 2 vols. Vols. 1–2 of Midrash Rabbah translated into English with Notes, Glossary and Indices under the editorship of H. Freedman and Maurice Simon complete in 10 vols. London: Soncino, 1951.

Jacobson, Howard, trans. *A Commentary on Pseudo-Philo's Liber Antiquitatum Biblicarum with Latin Text and English Translation.* 2 vols. Arbeiten zur Geschichte des Antiken Judentums und des Urchristentums XXXI. Leiden: Brill, 1996.

Lauterbach, Jacob Z. *Mekilta de-Rabbi Ishmael: A Critical Edition on the Basis of the Manuscripts and Early Editions with an English Translation, Introduction and Notes.* 3 vols. The Schiff Library of Jewish Classics, Philadelphia: The Jewish Publication Society of America, 1933.

Neusner, Jacob, trans. *Genesis Rabbah: The Judaic Commentary to the Book of Genesis: A New American Translation.* 3 vols. Brown Judaic Studies 104–6. Atlanta: Scholars Press, 1985.

Theodor, J., and Chaim Albeck, eds. *Bereschit Rabba mit kritischem Apparat und Commentar.* 2 vols. Veröffentlichungen der Akademie für die Wissenschaft des Judentums, Berlin: Z. Hirsch Itzkowski, 1912–29. Repr. Pages in 3 vols. Jerusalem: Wahrman, 1965.

VanderKam, James C. *The Book of Jubilees: A Critical Text and Translation.* 2 vols. Corpus Scriptorum Christianorum Orientalum 510–11. Scriptores Aethiopici 87–88. Leuven: Peeters, 1989.

Reference Works

Berenbaum, Michael, and Fred Skolnik, eds. *Encyclopaedia Judaica*, 22 vols. 2nd ed. Detroit: Macmillan Reference USA, 2007.

Brown, F., S. Driver, and C. Briggs, *The Brown-Driver-Briggs Hebrew and English Lexicon with an appendix containing the Biblical Aramaic*. Peabody: Hendrickson, 2008. Repr. from 1906 ed.

Freedman, David Noel, ed. *Anchor Bible Dictionary.* 6 vols. New York: Doubleday, 1992.

Freedman, David Noel, ed. *Eerdmans Dictionary of the Bible*. Grand Rapids: Eerdmans, 2000.

Gesenius, Wilhelm. *Gesenius' Hebrew Grammar as Edited and Enlarged by the Late E. Kautzsch, Revised in Accordance with the Twenty-Eighth German Edition (1909) by A. E. Cowley With a Facsimile of the Siloam Inscription by J. Euting, and A Table of Alphabets by M. Lidzbarski*. 2d. Eng. ed. Oxford: Clarendon, 1910.

Jastrow, Marcus, *Dictionary of the Targumim, Talmud Bavli, Talmud Yerushalmi and Midrashic Literature*. 2nd ed. 1903. repr. New York: Judaica Treasury, 2004.

Other Works Cited

Ackerman, James S. 'Who Can Stand Before YHWH, This Holy God? A Reading of 1 Samuel 1-15'. *Prooftexts* 11 (1991): 1–24.

Adelman, Rachel. 'Laughter and Re-Membering'. *Nashim: A Journal of Jewish Women's Studies & Gender Issues* 8 (2004): 230–44.

Adler, Rachel. *Engendering Judaism: An Inclusive Theology and Ethics*. Philadelphia: The Jewish Publication Society, 1998.

Alexander, Philip S. 'The Rabbinic Hermeneutical Rules and the Problem of the Definition of Midrash'. *Proceedings of the Irish Biblical Association* 8 (1984): 97–125.

Alexander, Philip S. 'Midrash'. Pages 452–9 in *A Dictionary of Biblical Interpretation*. Edited by R. J. Coggins and J. L. Houlden. London: SCM. Trinity Press International, 1990.

Allen, Leslie C. *Ezekiel 1–19*. Word Biblical Commentary 28. Dallas: Word, 1994.

Alter, Robert. *The Art of Biblical Narrative*. New York: Basic, 1981.

Andersen, Francis I. *Habakkuk: A New Translation with Intro and Commentary*. Anchor Bible 25. New York: Doubleday, 2001.

Aptowitzer, Victor. 'Spuren des Matriarchats in jüdischen Schrifftum'. *Hebrew Union College Annual* 4 (1927): 207–40.

Aptowitzer, Victor. 'Spuren des Matriarchats im jüdischen Schrifftum (Schluss)'. *Hebrew Union College Annual* 5 (1928): 261–97.

Archer, Léonie J. *Her Price Is Beyond Rubies: The Jewish Woman in Graeco-Roman Palestine*. JSOT Supplement Series 60. Sheffield: Sheffield Academic, 1990.

Bader, Mary Anna. *Tracing the Evidence: Dinah in Post-Hebrew Bible Literature*. Studies in Biblical Literature 102. New York: Peter Lang, 2008.

Bailey, James L. 'Josephus' Portrayal of the Matriarchs'. Pages 154–79 in *Josephus, Judaism, and Christianity*. Edited by Louis H. Feldman and Gohei Hata. Detroit: Wayne State University Press, 1987.

Bailey, Randall C. 'The Redemption of YHWH: A Literary Critical Function of the Songs of Hannah and David'. *Biblical Interpretation* 3, no. 2 (1995): 213–31.

Bakhos, Carol, ed. *Current Trends in the Study of Midrash*. Supplements to the Journal for the Study of Judaism 106. Leiden: Brill, 2006.

Bakhos, Carol. 'Figuring (Out) Esau: The Rabbis and Their Others'. *Journal of Jewish Studies* 58, no. 2 (2007): 250–62.

Bal, Mieke. *Lethal Love: Feminist Literary Readings of Biblical Love Stories*. Bloomington: Indiana University Press, 1987.

Bar-Ilan, Meir. *Some Jewish Women in Antiquity*. Brown Judaic Studies 317. Atlanta: Scholars Press, 1998.

Baskin, Judith R. *Midrashic Women: Formations of the Feminine in Rabbinic Literature*. Brandeis Series on Jewish Women. Hanover: Brandeis University Press, 2002.

Baskin, Judith R. 'Rabbinic Reflections on the Barren Wife'. *The Harvard Theological Review* 82 (1989): 101–14.

Bechtel, Lyn M. 'What if Dinah Is Not Raped? (Genesis 34)'. *Journal for the Study of the Old Testament* 62 (1994): 19–36.

Ben-Eliyahu, Eyal, Yehudah Cohn, and Fergus Millar. *Handbook of Jewish Literature from Late Antiquity, 135–700 CE*. Oxford: Published for The British Academy by Oxford University Press, 2012.

Berkovits, Eliezer. *Jewish Women in Time and Torah*. Hoboken: Ktav, 1990.

Berman, Saul J. 'The Status of Women in Halakhic Judaism'. *Tradition: A Journal of Orthodox Thought* 14, no. 2 (1973): 5–28.

Bernstein, Moshe J. 'Women and Children in Legal and Liturgical Texts from Qumran'. *Dead Sea Discoveries* 11 (2004): 191–211.

Biale, David. *Eros and the Jews: From Biblical Israel to Contemporary America*. Berkeley: University of California Press, 1997. Repr. from 1984.

Biale, Rachel. *Women and Jewish Law: The Essential Texts, Their History, & Their Relevance for Today. With a New Foreword by the Author*. New York: Schocken, 1995.

Bird, Phyllis. 'The Place of Women in the Israelite Cultus'. Pages 397–419 in *Ancient Israelite Religion: Essays in Honour of Frank Moore Cross*. Edited by Paul D. Hanson Patrick D Miller, and S. Dean McBride. Philadelphia: Fortress, 1987.

Bird, Phyllis A. *Missing Persons and Mistaken Identities: Women and Gender in Ancient Israel*. Overtures to Biblical Theology. Minneapolis: Fortress, 1997.

Bodner, Keith. *1 Samuel: A Narrative Commentary*. Hebrew Bible Monographs 19. Sheffield: Sheffield Phoenix, 2009. Repr. from 2008.

Boling, Robert C. *Judges: Introduction, Translation, and Commentary*. Anchor Bible 6A. New York: Doubleday, 1975.

Boyarin, Daniel. *Intertextuality and the Reading of Midrash*. Bloomington: Indiana University Press, 1990.

Boyarin, Daniel. 'Reading Androcentrism Against the Grain: Women, Sex, and Torah-Study'. *Poetics Today* 12, no. 1 (1991): 29–53.

Boyarin, Daniel. *Carnal Israel: Reading Sex in Talmudic Culture*. Berkeley: University of California Press, 1993.

Brenner-Idan, Athalya. *The Israelite Woman: Social Role and Literary Type in Biblical Narrative*. 2nd ed. Cornerstones. London: Bloomsbury, 2015.

Brichto, Herbert Chanan. 'The Case of the Sota and a Reconsideration of Biblical Law'. *Hebrew Union College Annual* 46, Centennial Issue (1975): 55–70.

Bronner, Leila Leah. *From Eve to Esther: Rabbinic Reconstructions of Biblical Women*. Gender and the Biblical Tradition. Louisville: Westminster John Knox, 1994.

Bronner, Leila Leah. 'Hannah's Prayer: Rabbinic Ambivalence'. *Shofar* 17, no. 2 (1999): 36–48.

Brooten, Bernadette J. *Women Leaders in the Ancient Synagogue: Inscriptional Evidence and Background Issues*. Brown Judaic Studies 36. Chico: Scholars Press, 1982.

Brown, Cheryl Anne. *No Longer Be Silent: First Century Jewish Portraits of Biblical Women. Studies in Pseudo-Philo's* Biblical Antiquities *and Josephus's* Jewish Antiquities. Gender and the Biblical Tradition. Louisville: Westminster John Knox, 1992.

Brownlee, William H. *Ezekiel 1–19*. Word Biblical Commentary 28. Waco: Word, 1986.

Brueggemann, Walter. '1 Samuel 1: A Sense of a Beginning'. *Zeitschrift für die Alttestamentliche Wissenschaft* 102, no. 1 (1990): 33–48.

Bunta, Silviu. 'The Likeness of the Image: Adamic Motifs and צלם Anthropology in Rabbinic Traditions About Jacob's Image Enthroned in Heaven'. *Journal for the Study of Judaism* 37, no. 1 (2006): 55–84.

Burns, Joshua Ezra. 'God-Fearers'. Pages 681–2 in *The Eerdmans Dictionary of Early Judaism*. Edited by John J. Collins and Daniel C. Harlow. Grand Rapids: Eerdmans, 2010.

Byron, John. 'EGLBS Presidential Address Childlessness and Ambiguity in the Ancient World'. Proceedings *of the Eastern Great Lakes Biblical Society and Midwest Region of the Society of Biblical Literature* XXX (2010): 17–46.

Callaway, Mary. *Sing, O Barren One: A Study in Comparative Midrash*. SBL Dissertation Series 91. Atlanta: Scholars Press, 1986.

Camp, Claudia V. *Wisdom and the Feminine in the Book of Proverbs*. Bible and Literature Series 11. Sheffield: Almond, 1985.

Carmichael, Calum M. *Women, Law, and the Genesis Traditions*. Edinburgh: Edinburgh University Press, 1979.

Chapman, Cynthia R. '"Oh That You Were Like a Brother to Me, One Who Had Nursed at My Mother's Breasts": Breast Milk as a Kinship-Forging Substance'. *Journal of Hebrew Scriptures* 12 (2012): 1–41.

Charles, R. H. *The Book of Jubilees or The Little Genesis Translated from the Editor's Ethiopic Text and Edited, with Introduction, Notes, and Indices by R. H. Charles*. London: A. & C. Black, 1902.

Charles, R. H. *The Book of Jubilees or The Little Genesis Translated from the Ethiopic Text by R. H. Charles with an Introduction by G. H. Box*. Translations of Early Documents. London. Haymarket: Society for Promoting Christian Knowledge/Macmillan, 1917.

Chester, Andrew. *Divine Revelation and Divine Titles in the Pentateuchal Targumim*. Texte und Studien zum Antiken Judentum 14. Tübingen: Mohr Siebeck, 1986.

Chestnut, Randall D. 'Revelatory Experiences Attributed to Biblical Women in Early Jewish Literature'. Pages 107–25 in *'Women Like This': New Perspectives on Jewish Women in the Greco-Roman World*. Edited by Amy Jill Levine. SBL Early Judaism and Its Literature. Atlanta: Scholars Press, 1991.

Cohen, Gerson D. 'Esau as Symbol in Early Medieval Thought'. Pages 19–48 in *Jewish Medieval and Renaissance Studies*. Edited by Alexander Altmann. Cambridge, MA: Harvard University Press, 1967.

Cohen, Shaye J. D. 'The Matrilineal Principle in Historical Perspective'. *Judaism* 34 (1985): 5–13.

Cohen, Shaye J. D. 'The Origins of the Matrilineal Principle in Jewish Law'. *AJS Review* 10 (1985): 19–53.

Cohen, Shaye J. D. 'Was Timothy Jewish (Acts 16:1-3)? Patristic Exegesis, Rabbinic Law, and Matrilineal Descent'. *Journal of Biblical Literature* 105, no. 2 (1986): 251–68.

Cohen, Shaye J. D. 'Can Converts to Judaism Say "God of Our Fathers"?'. *Judaism* 40, no. 4 (1991): 419–28.

Cohen, Shaye J. D. *The Beginnings of Jewishness: Boundaries, Varieties, Uncertainties.* Hellenistic Culture and Society XXXI. Berkeley: University of California Press, 1999.

Cohen, Shaye J. D. *Why Aren't Jewish Women Circumcised? Gender and Covenant in Judaism.* Berkeley: University of California Press, 2005.

Cook, Joan E. 'Pseudo-Philo's Song of Hannah: Testament of a Mother in Israel'. *Journal for the Study of the Pseudepigrapha* 9 (1991): 103–14.

Cook, Joan E. *Hannah's Desire, God's Design: Early Interpretations of the Story of Hannah.* Journal for the Study of the Old Testament Supplement Series 282. Sheffield: Sheffield Academic, 1999.

Dahood, Mitchell, *Psalms II: 51–100.* Anchor Bible 17. New York: Doubleday, 1970.

Darr, Katheryn Pfisterer, *Far More Precious Than Jewels: Perspectives on Biblical Women.* Gender and the Biblical Tradition. Louisville: Westminster John Knox, 1991.

Davidson, Jo Ann. 'Genesis Matriarchs Engage Feminism'. *Andrews University Seminary Studies* 40, no. 2 (2002): 169–78.

Dimant, Devorah. 'Abraham the Astrologer at Qumran? Observations on Pseudo-Jubilees (4Q225 2 I 3-8)'. Pages 71–82 in *Textual Criticism and Dead Sea Scroll Studies in Honour of Julio Trebolle Barrera.* Edited by Andrés Piquer Otero and Pablo A. Torijano Morales. Supplements to the Journal for the Study of Judaism 157. Leiden: Brill, 2012.

Elbogen, Ismar, *Der jüdische Gottesdienst in seiner geschichtlichen Entwicklung.* 3rd ed. Schriften / hrsg. von der Gesellschaft zur Förderung der Wissenschaft des Judentums Grundriss der Gesamtwissenschaft des Judentums. Frankfurt: Kaufmann, 1931.

Epstein, Louis M. *Marriage Laws in the Bible and the Talmud.* Harvard Semitic Series XII. Cambridge, MA: Harvard University Press, 1942.

Eskenazi, Tamara C. 'Out from the Shadows: Biblical Women in the Postexilic Era'. *Journal for the Study of the Old Testament* 54 (1992): 25–43.

Exum, J. Cheryl. 'Promise and Fulfilment: Narrative Art in Judges 13'. *Journal of Biblical Literature* 99, no. 1 (1980): 43–59.

Exum, J. Cheryl. *Fragmented Women: Feminist (Sub)versions of Biblical Narratives.* Journal for the Study of the Old Testament Supplement Series 163. Sheffield: Sheffield Academic, 1993.

Falk, Marcia. 'Reflections on Hannah's Prayer'. Pages 94–102 in *Out of the Garden: Women Writers on the Bible.* Edited by Christina Büchmann and Celina Spiegel. London: HarperCollins, 1994.

Fehribach, Adeline. 'Between Text and Context: Scripture, Society and the Role of Women in Formative Judaism'. Pages 39–60 in *Recovering the Role of Women: Power and Authority in Rabbinic Jewish Society.* Edited by Peter J. Haas. South Florida Studies in the History of Judaism 59. Atlanta: Scholars Press, 1992.

Fewell, Danna Nolan, and David M. Gunn. *Gender, Power, & Promise: The Subject of the Bible's First Story.* Nashville: Abingdon, 1993.

Finkelstein, Louis. *Sifre on Deuteronomy. Published originally by the Gesellschaft zur Foerderung der Wissenschaft des Judentums. And now re-published by The Jewish Theological Seminary of America. Through the Generosity of the Stroock Publication Fund.* New York: The Jewish Theological Seminary of America, 1969. Repr. from 1939.

Fishbane, Michael. *The Exegetical Imagination: On Jewish Thought and Theology.* Cambridge, MA: Harvard University Press, 1998.

Fitzmyer, Joseph A. *The Genesis Apocryphon of Qumran Cave 1 (1Q20): A Commentary*. 3rd rev. ed. Biblica and Orientalia. Sacra Scriptura Antiquitatibus Orientalibus Illustrata 18a. Rome: Editrice Pontificio Istituto Biblico, 2004.

Fonrobert, Charlotte Elisheva. *Menstrual Purity: Rabbinic and Christian Reconstructions of Biblical Gender*. Contraversions: Jews and Other Differences. Stanford: Stanford University Press, 2000.

Fonrobert, Charlotte Elisheva, and Martin S. Jaffee. 'Introduction: The Talmud, Rabbinic Literature, and Jewish Culture'. Pages 1–14 in *The Cambridge Companion to the Talmud and Rabbinic Literature*. Edited by Charlotte Elisheva Fonrobert and Martin S. Jaffee. Cambridge Companions to Religion. New York: Cambridge University Press, 2007.

Forsyth, Dan W. 'Sibling Rivalry, Aesthetic Sensibility, and Social Structure in Genesis'. *Ethos* 19, no. 4 (1991): 453–510.

Fox, Michael V. *Proverbs 1–9: A New Translation with Introduction and Commentary*. The Anchor Bible 18a. New York: Doubleday, 2000.

Fox, Michael V. *Proverbs 10–31: A New Translation With Introduction and Commentary*. The Anchor Yale Bible 18b. New Haven: Yale University Press, 2009.

Fraade, Steven. 'Rewritten Bible and Rabbinic Midrash as Commentary'. Pages 59–78 in *Current Trends in the Study of Midrash*. Edited by Carol Bakhos. Supplements to the Journal for the Study of Judaism 106. Leiden: Brill, 2006.

Friedman, Mordechai A. 'Tamar, a Symbol of Life: The "Killer Wife" Superstition in the Bible and Jewish Tradition'. *AJS Review* 15 (1990): 23–61.

Friedman, Theodore. 'The Shifting Role of Women, From the Bible to Talmud'. *Judaism* 36, no. 4 (1987): 479–87.

Frymer-Kensky, Tikva. 'The Strange Case of the Suspected Sotah (Numbers V 11-31)'. *Vetus Testamentum* 34, no. 1 (1984): 11–26.

Frymer-Kensky, Tikva. 'Bilhah'. Pages 61–2 in *Women in Scripture: A Dictionary of Named and Unnamed Women in the Hebrew Bible, the Apocryphal/Deuterocanonical Books, and the New Testament*. Edited by Carol Meyers. Grand Rapids: Eerdmans, 2001.

Frymer-Kensky, Tikva. 'Hagar'. Pages 86–7 in *Women in Scripture: A Dictionary of Named and Unnamed Women in the Hebrew Bible, the Apocryphal/Deuterocanonical Books, and the New Testament*. Edited by Carol Meyers. Grand Rapids: Eerdmans, 2001.

Fuchs, Esther. 'Who Is Hiding the Truth? Deceptive Women and Biblical Androcentrism'. Pages 137–44 in *Feminist Perspectives on Biblical Scholarship*. Edited by Adela Yarbro Collins. SBL Centennial Publications. Biblical Scholarship in North America 10. Chico: Scholars Press, 1985.

Fuchs, Esther. 'Structure and Patriarchal Functions in the Biblical Betrothal Type-Scene: Some Preliminary Notes'. *Journal of Feminist Studies in Religion* 3, no. 1 (1987): 7–13.

Fuchs, Esther. 'The Literary Characterisation of Mothers and Sexual Politics in the Hebrew Bible'. *Semeia* 46 (1989): 151–66; reprinted as pp. 127–39 in *Women in the Hebrew Bible: A Reader*. Edited by Alice Bach. New York: Routledge, 1999.

Fuchs, Esther. 'Structure, Ideology and Politics in the Biblical Betrothal Scene'. Pages 273–81 in *A Feminist Companion to Genesis*. Edited by Athalya Brenner. The Feminist Companion to the Bible 2. Sheffield: Sheffield Academic, 1993.

Furman, Nelly. 'His Story Versus Her Story: Male Genealogy and Female Strategy in the Jacob Cycle'. *Semeia* 46 (1989): 141–9.

Gafni, Isaiah M. 'The Political, Social, and Economic History of Babylonian Jewry, 224–638 CE'. Pages 792–820 in *The Late Roman-Rabbinic Period*. Edited by Steven T. Katz. Cambridge History of Judaism 4. Cambridge: Cambridge University Press, 2006.

Gershenzon, Rosalie, and Elieser Slomovic. 'A Second-Century Jewish-Gnostic Debate: Rabbi Jose Ben Halafta and the Matrona'. *Journal for the Study of Judaism* 16, no. 1 (1985): 1–41.

Goitein, S. D., and Michael Carasik. 'Women as Creators of Biblical Genres'. *Prooftexts* 8, no. 1 (1998): 1–33.

Goodblatt, David. 'The History of the Babylonian Academies'. Pages 821–39 in *The Late Roman-Rabbinic Period*. Edited by Steven T. Katz. Cambridge History of Judaism 4. Cambridge: Cambridge University Press, 2006.

Goodman, Martin. *Mission and Conversion: Proselytising in the Religious History of the Roman Empire*. Oxford: Clarendon, 1994.

Goodman, Martin, and Philip Alexander, eds. *Rabbinic Texts and the History of Late-Roman Palestine*. Proceedings of the British Academy 165. Oxford: Published for The British Academy by Oxford University Press, 2010.

Graetz, Naomi. 'Dinah the Daughter'. Pages 306–17 in *A Feminist Companion to Genesis*. Edited by Athalya Brenner. The Feminist Companion to the Bible 2. Sheffield: Sheffield Academic, 1993.

Greenspahn, Frederick E. 'A Typology of Biblical Women'. *Judaism* 32, no. 1 (1983): 43–50.

Grossman, Maxine. 'Reading for Gender in the Damascus Document'. *Dead Sea Discoveries* 11 (2004): 212–39.

Gruber, Mayer I. 'Breast-Feeding Practices in Ancient Israel and in Old Babylonian Mesopotamia'. *Journal of the Near Eastern Society* 19 (1989): 61–83.

Gruber, Mayer I. 'Matrilineal Determination of Jewishness: Biblical and Near Eastern Roots'. Pages 437–43 in *Pomegranates and Golden Bells: Studies in Biblical, Jewish, and Near Eastern Ritual, Law, and Literature in Honour of Jacob Milgrom*. Edited by David Noel Freedman, Avi Hurvitz and David P. Wright. Winona Lake: Eisenbrauns, 1995.

Grushcow, Lisa. *Writing the Wayward Wife: Rabbinic Interpretations of Sotah*. Ancient Judaism and Early Christianity 62. Leiden: Brill, 2006.

Grypeou, Emmanouela, and Helen Spurling. *The Book of Genesis in Late Antiquity: Encounters Between Jewish and Christian Exegesis*. Jewish and Christian Perspectives 24. Leiden: Brill, 2013.

Haberman, Bonna Devora. 'The Suspected Adulteress: A Study of Textual Embodiment'. *Prooftexts* 20, no. 1–2 (2000): 12–42.

Hadas-Lebel, Mireille. 'Jacob et Esaü, ou Israël et Rome dans le Talmud et le Midrash'. *Revue de l'Histoire des Religions* 201. no. 4 (1984): 369–92.

Halpern-Amaru, Betsy. 'Portraits of Women in Pseudo-Philo's *Biblical Antiquities*'. Pages 83–106 in *'Women Like This': New Perspectives on Jewish Women in the Greco-Roman World*. Edited by Amy Jill Levine. SBL Early Judaism and Its Literature. Atlanta: Scholars Press, 1991.

Halpern-Amaru, Betsy. 'The First Woman, Wives, and Mothers in *Jubilees*'. *Journal of Biblical Literature* 113, no. 4 (1994): 609–26.

Halpern-Amaru, Betsy. *The Empowerment of Women in the Book of Jubilees*. Supplements to the Journal for the Study of Judaism 60. Leiden: Brill, 1999.

Harrington, D. J. 'Pseudo-Philo (First Century A.D.)'. Pages 297–384 in *Expansions of the "Old Testament" and Legends, Wisdom and Philosophical Literature, Prayers, Psalms, and Odes, Fragments of Lost Judeo-Hellenistic Works, Volume 2*. Edited by James H. Charlesworth. The Old Testament Pseudepigrapha. London: Darton, Longman & Todd, 1985.

Harrington, D.J., J. Cazeaux, C. Perrot, and P.-M. Bogaert. *Pseudo-Philon, Les Antiquités Bibliques*. Sources chrétiennes 229–30. Paris, 1976.

Hartman, Geoffrey H., and Sanford Budick, eds. *Midrash and Literature*. Yale: Yale University Press, 1986.

Hasan-Rokem, Galit. *Web of Life: Folklore and Midrash in Rabbinic Literature*. Translated by Batya Stein. Contraversions: Jews and Other Differences. Stanford: Stanford University Press, 2000.

Hauptman, Judith. 'Some Thoughts on the Nature of Halakhic Adjudication: Women and Minyan'. *Judaism* 42 (1993): 396–413.

Hauptman, Judith. 'Women and Prayer: An Attempt to Dispel Some Fallacies'. *Judaism* 42 (1993): 94–103.

Hauptman, Judith. 'Feminist Perspectives on Rabbinic Texts'. Pages 40–61 in *Feminist Perspectives on Jewish Studies*. Edited by Lynn Davidman and Shelly Tenenbaum. New Haven: Yale University Press, 1994.

Hauptman, Judith. *Rereading the Rabbis*. Boulder: Westview, 1998.

Haut, Irwin H. 'Are Women Obligated to Pray?'. Pages 89–101 in *Daughters of the King: Women and the Synagogue: A Survey of History, Halakhah, and Contemporary Realities*. Edited by Susan Grossman and Rivka Haut. Philadelphia: The Jewish Publication Society, 1992.

Havrelock, Rachel. 'The Myth of Birthing the Hero: Heroic Barrenness in the Hebrew Bible'. *Biblical Interpretation* 16 (2008): 154–78.

Hayes, Christine E. *Gentile Impurities and Jewish Identities: Intermarriage and Conversion for the Bible to the Talmud*. New York: Oxford University Press, 2002.

Hayward, C. T. R. *Saint Jerome's Hebrew Questions on Genesis*. Oxford Early Christian Studies. Oxford: Clarendon, 1995.

Hayward, C. T. R. *Interpretations of the Name Israel in Ancient Judaism and Some Early Christian Writings: From Victorious Athlete to Heavenly Champion*. New York: Oxford University Press, 2005.

Heger, Paul. 'Patrilineal or Matrilineal Genealogy in Israel After Ezra'. *Journal for the Study of Judaism* 43 (2012): 215–48.

Heinemann, Joseph. 'The Proem in the Aggadic Midrashim—a Form-Critical Study'. Pages 100–122 in *Studies in Aggadah and Folk-Literature*. Edited by Joseph Heinemann and Dov Noy. *Scripta Hierosolymitana*. Jerusalem: Magnes, 1971.

Heinemann, Joseph. 'The Nature of the Aggadah'. Pages 41–55 in *Midrash and Literature*. Edited by Geoffrey H. Hartman and Sanford Budick. New Haven: Yale University Press, 1986. Trans. from Hebrew, 1974.

Hepner, Gershon. *Legal Friction: Law, Narrative, and Identity Politics in Biblical Israel*. Studies in Biblical Literature 78. New York: Peter Lang, 2010.

Hilber, John W. *Cultic Prophecy in the Psalms*. Beihefte zur Zeitschrift für die alttestamentliche Wissenschaft 352. Berlin: de Gruyter, 2005.

Hurowitz, Victor Avigdor. 'רוקמה in Damascus Document (4Q270) 7 i 14'. *Dead Sea Discoveries* 9 (2002): 34–7.

Ilan, Tal. 'Matrona and Rabbi Jose: An Alternative Interpretation'. *Journal for the Study of Judaism* 25, no. 1 (1994): 18–51.

Ilan, Tal. *Mine and Yours Are Hers: Retrieving Women's History from Rabbinic Literature*. Leiden: Brill, 1997.

Jacobs, Irving. *The Midrashic Process*. Cambridge: Cambridge University Press, 1995.

Jacobson, Howard. 'Biblical Quotation and Editorial Function in Pseudo-Philo's *Liber Antiquitatum Biblicarum*'. *Journal for the Study of the Pseudepigrapha* 5 (1989): 47–64.

Jaffee, Martin S. 'The "Midrashic" Proem: Towards the Description of Rabbinic Exegesis'. Pages 95–112 in *Studies in Liturgy, Exegesis, and Talmudic Narrative*. Edited by William Scott Green. Approaches to Ancient Judaism 4. Chico: Scholars Press, 1983.

James, M. R. *The Biblical Antiquities of Philo Now First Translated from the Old Latin Version by M. R. James. Prolegomenon by Louis H. Feldman*. The Library of Biblical Studies. New York: Ktav, 1971. Repr. from 1917.

Jeansonne, Sharon Pace. *The Women of Genesis: From Sarah to Potiphar's Wife*. Minneapolis: Fortress, 1990.

Kalmin, Richard. 'The Formation and Character of the Babylonian Talmud'. Pages 840–76 in *The Late Roman-Rabbinic Period*. Edited by Steven T. Katz. Cambridge History of Judaism 4. Cambridge: Cambridge University Press, 2006.

Kaunfer, Alvan. 'Who Knows Four? The "imahot" in Rabbinic Judaism'. *Judaism* 44 (1995): 94–103.

Kimelman, Reuven. 'Rabbinic Prayer in Late Antiquity'. Pages 573–611 in *The Late Roman-Rabbinic Period*. Edited by Steven T. Katz. Cambridge History of Judaism 4. Cambridge: Cambridge University Press, 2006.

Klein, Ralph W. *1 Samuel*. 2nd ed. Word Biblical Commentary 10. Nashville: Thomas Nelson, 2008.

Krauss, Stuart. 'The Word "*Ger*" in the Bible and Its Implications'. *Jewish Bible Quarterly* 34, no. 4 (2006): 264–70.

Kugel, James L. 'Two Introductions to Midrash'. Pages 77–103 in *Midrash and Literature*. Edited by Geoffrey H. Hartman and Sanford Budick. New Haven: Yale University Press, 1986.

Kugel, James L. *Traditions of the Bible: A Guide to the Bible as It Was at the Start of the Common Era*. Rev. ed. Cambridge, MA: Harvard University Press, 1998.

Labovitz, Gail. 'Arguing for Women in Talmudic Literature'. *Shofar: An Interdisciplinary Journal of Jewish Studies* 14, no. 1 (1995): 72–9.

Laffey, Alice L. *An Introduction to the Old Testament: A Feminist Perspective*. Philadelphia: Fortress, 1988.

Lavee, Moshe. 'Rabbinic Literature and the History of Judaism in Late Antiquity: Challenges, Methodologies and New Approaches'. Pages 319–51 in *Rabbinic Texts and the History of Late Roman Palestine*. Edited by Martin Goodman and Philip Alexander. Proceedings of the British Academy 165. Oxford: Published for the British Academy by Oxford University Press, 2010.

Levine, Amy Jill, ed. *'Women Like This': New Perspectives on Jewish Women in the Greco-Roman World*. SBL Early Judaism and Its Literature. Atlanta: Scholars Press, 1991.

Levinson, Joshua. 'Bodies and Bo(a)rders: Emerging Fictions of Identity in Late Antiquity'. *Harvard Theological Review* 93, no. 4 (2000): 343–72.

Levinson, Joshua. 'Literary Approaches to Midrash'. Pages 189–226 in *Current Trends in the Study of Midrash*. Edited by Carol Bakhos. Supplements to the Journal for the Study of Judaism 106. Leiden: Brill, 2006.

Lewis, Charlton T., and Charles Short. *A Latin Dictionary Founded on Andrews' Edition of Freund's Latin Dictionary*. Oxford: Clarendon, 1975. 1st ed. 1879.

Lewis, Theodore J. 'The Songs of Hannah and Deborah: ḤDL-II ("Growing Plump")'. *Journal of Biblical Literature* 104, no. 1 (1985): 105–8.

Lindars, Barnabas. '"Rachel Weeping for Her Children"—Jeremiah 31:15-22'. *Journal for the Study of the Old Testament* 12 (1979): 47–62.

Lundbom, Jack R. *Jeremiah 21–36: A New Translation with Introduction and Commentary*. Anchor Bible 21b. New York: Doubleday, 2004.

Marmorstein, A. *The Doctrine of Merits in Old Rabbinical Literature*. London: Jews' College Publications, 1920.

McNamara, Martin. *Targum Neofiti 1: Genesis Translated, with Apparatus and Notes by Martin McNamara*. The Aramaic Bible: The Targums 1A. Edinburgh: T. & T. Clark, 1992.

McNamara, Martin, Robert Hayward and Michael Maher. *Targum Neofiti 1: Exodus. Translated, with Introduction and Apparatus by Martin McNamara, and Notes by Robert Hayward. Targum Pseudo-Jonathan: Exodus. Translated, with Notes by Michael Maher*. The Aramaic Bible: The Targums 2. Edinburgh: T. & T. Clark, 1994.

Menn, Esther Marie. *Judah and Tamar (Genesis 38) in Ancient Jewish Exegesis*. Supplements to the Journal for the Study of Judaism. Leiden: Brill, 1997.

Milikowsky, Chaim. 'The *Status Quaestionis* of Research in Rabbinic Literature'. *Journal of Jewish Studies* 39, no. 2 (1989): 201–11.

Miller, John W. 'Depatriarchalizing God in Biblical Interpretation: A Critique'. *The Catholic Biblical Quarterly* 48 (1986): 609–16.

Neusner, Jacob. *Pesiqta Derab Kahana: An Analytical Translation*. Brown Judaic Studies. 2 vols. Atlanta: Scholars Press, 1987.

Neusner, Jacob. *Sifre to Deuteronomy: An Analytical Translation*. Brown Judaic Studies. 2 vols. Atlanta: Scholars Press, 1987.

Neusner, Jacob. *How the Rabbis Liberated Women*. USF Studies in the History of Judaism. South Florida Studies in the History of Judaism 191. Atlanta: Scholars Press, 1998.

Neusner, Jacob. *Rabbinic Literature: The Essential Guide*. Abingdon Essential Guides. Nashville: Abingdon, 2005.

Niditch, Susan. 'The Wronged Woman Righted: An Analysis of Genesis 38'. *Harvard Theological Review* 72, no. 1/2 (1979): 143–9.

Ozick, Cynthia. 'Hannah and Elkanah: Torah as the Matrix for Feminism'. Pages 88–93 in *Out of the Garden: Women Writers on the Bible*. Edited by Christina Büchmann and Celina Spiegel. London: HarperCollins, 1994.

Pardes, Ilana. *Countertraditions in the Bible: A Feminist Approach*. Cambridge, MA: Harvard University Press, 1992.

Pardes, Ilana. 'Rachel's Dream of Grandeur'. Pages 27–40 in *Out of the Garden: Women Writers on the Bible*. Edited by Christina Büchmann and Celina Spiegel. London: HarperCollins, 1994.

Peskowitz, Miriam. 'Family/ies in Antiquity: Evidence from Tannaitic Literature and Roman Galilean Architecture'. Pages 9–36 in *The Jewish Family in Antiquity*. Edited by Shaye J. D. Cohen. Brown Judaic Studies 289. Atlanta: Scholars Press, 1993.

Peskowitz, Miriam B. *Spinning Fantasies: Rabbis, Gender, and History*. Berkeley: University of California Press, 1997.

Petersen, David L. 'Genesis and Family Values'. *Journal of Biblical Literature* 124, no. 1 (2005): 5–23.

Plaskow, Judith. *Standing Again at Sinai: Judaism from a Feminist Perspective*. San Francisco: HarperCollins, 1991.

Polaski, Donald C. 'On Taming Tamar: Amram's Rhetoric and Women's Roles in Pseudo-Philo's Liber Antiquitatum Biblicarum 9'. *Journal for the Study of the Pseudepigrapha* 13 (1995): 79–99.

Porton, Gary G. 'How the Rabbis Imagined Sarah: A Preliminary Study of the Feminine in *Genesis Rabbah*'. Pages 192–209 in *A Legacy of Learning: Essays in Honour of Jacob Neusner*. Edited by Bruce Chilton Alan J. Avery-Peck, William Scott Green, and Gary G. Porton. The Brill Reference Library of Judaism 43. Leiden: Brill, 2014.

Rabow, Jerry. *The Lost Matriarch: Finding Leah in the Bible and Midrash*. Philadelphia: The Jewish Publication Society, 2014.

Ramon, Eina. 'The Matriarchs and the Torah of Hesed (Loving-Kindness)'. *Nashim: A Journal of Jewish Women's Studies & Gender Issues* 10, no. 2 (2005): 154–77.

Reif, Stefan C. *Judaism and Hebrew Prayer: New Perspectives on Jewish Liturgical History*. Cambridge: Cambridge University Press, 1995.

Reif, Stephen C. 'Early Rabbinic Exegesis of Genesis 38'. Pages 221–44 in *The Exegetical Encounter Between Jews and Christians in Late Antiquity*. Edited by E. Grypeou and H Spurling. Jewish and Christian Perspectives Series 18. Leiden: Brill, 2009.

Reiss, Moshe, and David J. Zucker. 'Co-opting the Secondary Matriarchs: Bilhah, Zilpah, Tamar, and Aseneth'. *Biblical Interpretation* 22 (2014): 307–24.

Ritter, Christine. *Rachels Klage im antiken Judentum und frühen Christentum: Eine Auslegungsgeschichtliche Studie*. Geschichte des antiken Judentums und des Urchristentums 52. Leiden: Brill, 2003.

Saldarini, Anthony J. 'The End of the Rabbinic Chain of Tradition'. *Journal of Biblical Literature* 93, no. 1 (1974): 97–106.

Samely, Alexander, in collaboration with Philip Alexander, Rocco Bernasconi, and Robert Hayward. *Profiling Jewish Literature in Antiquity: An Inventory from Second Temple Texts to the Talmuds*. Oxford: Oxford University Press, 2013.

Sarason, R. S. 'Midrash'. Pages 155–7 in *Dictionary of Biblical Interpretation K–Z*. Edited by John H. Hayes. Nashville: Abingdon, 1999.

Sarason, Richard S. 'The Peiḥtot in Leviticus Rabba: "Oral Homilies" or Redactional Constructions?'. *Journal of Jewish Studies* 33, no. 1–2 (1982): 557–67.

Sarna, Nahum M. *The JPS Torah Commentary: Genesis: The Traditional Hebrew Text with the New JPS Translation Commentary*. Philadelphia: The Jewish Publication Society, 1989.

Sasson, Jack M. *Judges 1–12*. Anchor Bible/Anchor Yale Bible 6D. New Haven: Yale University Press, 2014.

Satlow, Michael L. *Tasting the Dish: Rabbinic Rhetorics of Sexuality*. Brown Judaic Studies 303. Atlanta: Scholars Press, 1995.

Satlow, Michael L. *Jewish Marriage in Antiquity*. Princeton: Princeton University Press, 2001.

Schäfer, Peter. 'Research into Rabbinic Literature: An Attempt to Define the *Status Quaestionis*'. *Journal of Jewish Studies* 37, no. 2 (1986): 139–52.

Schäfer, Peter. *Mirror of His Beauty: Feminine Images of God from the Bible to the Early Kabbalah*. Princeton: Princeton University Press, 2002.

Schäfer, Peter, and Chaim Milikowsky. 'Current Views on the Editing of the Rabbinic Texts of Late Antiquity: Reflections of a Debate After Twenty Years'. Pages 79–88 in *Rabbinic Texts and the History of Late-Roman Palestine*. Edited by Martin Goodman and Philip Alexander. Proceedings of the British Academy 165. Oxford: Published for the British Academy by Oxford University Press, 2010.

Schechter, S., and Prolegomenon by Joseph A. Fitzmyer. *Documents of Jewish Sectaries*. Volume 1. *Fragments of a Zadokite Work. Edited from Hebrew Manuscripts in the Cairo Genizah Collection Now in Possession of the University Library, Cambridge and Provided with an English Translation, Introduction and Notes*. Repr. The Library of Biblical Studies. New York: Ktav, 1970.

Schechter, Solomon. *Aspects of Rabbinic Theology: Major Concepts of the Talmud*. International Journal for Philosophy and Theology. New York: Schocken, 1965.

Schiffman, Lawrence H. 'At the Crossroads: Tannaitic Perspectives on the Jewish-Christian Schism'. Pages 115–56 in *Jewish and Christian Self-Definition*. Vol. 2, *Aspects of Judaism in the Graeco-Roman Period*. Edited by E. P. Sanders, with A. I. Baumgarten and Alan Mendelson. London: SCM, 1981.

Schiffman, Lawrence H. 'Jewish Identity and Jewish Descent'. *Judaism* 34 (1985): 78–84.

Schneider, Tammi J. *Sarah: Mother of Nations*. New York: Continuum, 2004.

Schneider, Tammi J. *Mothers of Promise: Women in the Book of Genesis*. Grand Rapids: Baker Academic, 2008.

Scott, Lynn T. 'Not Merely Chattel: Women as Guardians of Holiness in the Mishnah's Society'. Pages 23–37 in *Recovering the Role of Women: Power and Authority in Rabbinic Jewish Society*. Edited by Peter J. Haas. South Florida Studies in the History of Judaism 59. Atlanta: Scholars Press, 1992.

Segal, J. B. 'The Jewish Attitude Towards Women'. *Journal of Jewish Studies* 30, no. 2 (1979): 121–37.

Smith, Ralph L. *Micah–Malachi*. Word Biblical Commentary 32. Waco: Word, 1984.

Sorek, Susan. 'Mothers of Israel: Why the Rabbis Adopted a Matrilineal Principle'. *Women in Judaism* 3, no. 1 (2002): 1–12.

Steinberg, Naomi. 'Alliance or Descent? The Function of Marriage in Genesis'. *Journal for the Study of the Old Testament* 51 (1991): 45–55.

Steinberg, Naomi. 'Zilpah'. Pages 169–70 in *Women in Scripture: A Dictionary of Named and Unnamed Women in the Hebrew Bible, the Apocryphal/Deuterocanonical Books, and the New Testament*. Edited by Carol Meyers. Grand Rapids: Eerdmans, 2001.

Steinmetz, Devora. 'A Portrait of Miriam in Rabbinic Midrash'. *Prooftexts* 8, no. 1 (1988): 35–65.

Stern, David. *Midrash and Theory: Ancient Jewish Exegesis and Contemporary Literary Studies*. Rethinking Theory. Evanston: Northwestern University Press, 1996.

Stone, Michael E. 'The Genealogy of Bilhah'. *Dead Sea Discoveries* 3, no. 1 (1996): 20–36.

Strack, H. L., and Günter Stemberger. *Introduction to the Talmud and Midrash*. Translated by Markus Bockmuehl. 2nd ed. Minneapolis: Fortress, 1996.

Swidler, Leonard. *Women in Judaism: The Status of Women in Formative Judaism*. Metuchen: Scarecrow, 1976.

Tate, Marvin E. *Psalms 51–100*. Word Biblical Commentary 20. Dallas: Word, Publisher, 1990.

Teubal, Savina J. 'Sarah and Hagar: Matriarchs and Visionaries'. Pages 235–50 in *A Feminist Companion to Genesis*. Edited by Athalya Brenner. The Feminist Companion to the Bible 2. Sheffield: Sheffield Academic, 1993.

Teubal, Savina J. *Sarah the Priestess: The First Matriarch of Genesis*. Athens: Swallow, 1984.

Teugels, Lieve. 'A Matriarchal Cycle?'. *Bijdragen: International Journal for Philosophy and Theology* 56 (1995): 61–72.

Teugels, Lieve M. *Bible and Midrash: The Story of 'the Wooing of Rebekah' (Gen. 24).* Contributions to Biblical Exegesis and Theology. Leuven: Peeters, 2004.

Trible, Phyllis. 'Depatriarchalizing in Biblical Interpretation'. *Journal of the American Academy of Religion* 41.1 (1973): 30-48.

Trible, Phyllis, 'The Gift of a Poem: A Rhetorical Study of Jeremiah 31:15-22'. *Andover Newton Quarterly* 17, no. 4 (1977): 271–80.

Trible, Phyllis. *Texts of Terror: Literary-Feminist Readings of Biblical Narratives*. SCM Classics. London: SCM, 2002.

Trible, Phyllis. 'Ominous Beginnings for a Promise of Blessings'. Pages 33–70 in *Hagar, Sarah, and Their Children: Jewish, Christian, and Muslim Perspectives*. Edited by Phyllis Trible and Letty M. Russell. Louisville: Westminster John Knox, 2006.

Turner, Mary Donovan. 'Rebekah: Ancestor of Faith'. *Lexington Theological Quarterly* 20 (1985): 42–50.

Urbach, Ephraim E. *The Sages: Their Concepts and Beliefs*. Translated by Israel Abrahams. Jerusalem: Magnes, The Hebrew University, 1975.

van der Horst, Pieter W. 'Sex, Birth, Purity and Asceticism in *Protevangelium Jacobi*'. *Neotestamentica* 28, no. 3 (1994): 205–18.

van der Horst, Pieter W. 'The Site of Adam's Tomb'. Pages 1–6 in *Studies in Ancient Judaism and Early Christianity*. Edited by Martin Hengel. Ancient Judaism and Early Christianity: Arbeiten zur Geschichte des antiken Judentums and des Urchristentums. Leiden: Brill, 2014. Repr. from 2007.

van der Horst, Pieter W. 'Portraits of Biblical Women in Pseudo-Philo's Liber Antiquitatum Biblicarum'. *Journal for the Study of the Pseudepigrapha* 5 (1989): 29–46.

van Dijk-Hemmes, Fokkelein. 'Tamar and the Limits of Patriarchy: Between Rape and Seduction'. Pages 135–56 in *Anti-Covenant: Counter-Reading Women's Lives in the Hebrew Bible*. Edited by Mieke Bal. JSOT Supplement Series 81. Bible and Literature Series 22. Sheffield: Almond, 1989.

van Dijk-Hemmes, Fokkelien. 'Sarai's Exile: A Gender-Motivated Reading of Genesis 12.10–13.2'. Pages 222–34 in *A Feminist Companion to Genesis*. Edited by Athalya Brenner. The Feminist Companion to the Bible 2. Sheffield: Sheffield Academic, 1993.

Van Seters, John. 'The Problem of Childlessness in Near Eastern Law and the Patriarchs of Israel'. *Journal of Biblical Literature* 87, no. 4 (1968): 401–8.

VanderKam, James C. *The Book of Jubilees*. Guides to Apocrypha and Pseudepigrapha. Sheffield: Sheffield Academic, 2001.

Vermes, Geza. *The Complete Dead Sea Scrolls in English*. Rev. ed. London: Penguin, 2004.

Walters, Stanley D. 'Hannah and Anna: The Greek and Hebrew Texts of 1 Samuel 1'. *Journal of Biblical Literature* 107, no. 3 (1988): 385–412.

Washington, Harold C. 'Violence and the Construction of Gender in the Hebrew Bible: A New Historicist Approach'. *Biblical Interpretation* 5.4 (1997): 324–63

Wassen, Cecilia. *Women in the Damascus Document*. Society of Biblical Literature: Academia Biblica 21. Leiden: Brill, 2005.

Watts, John D. W. *Isaiah 34–66*. Rev. ed. Word Biblical Commentary 25. Nashville: Thomas Nelson, 2005.

Wegner, Judith Romney. *Chattel or Person? The Status of Women in the Mishnah*. New York: Oxford University Press, 1988.

Wegner, Judith Romney. 'Tragelaphos Revisited: The Anomaly of Woman in the Mishnah'. *Judaism* 37, no. 2 (1988): 160–72.

Wegner, Judith Romney. 'The Image and Status of Women in Classical Rabbinic Judaism'. Pages 73–100 in *Jewish Women in Historical Perspective*. 2nd ed. Edited by Judith R Baskin. Detroit: Wayne State University Press, 1998.

Wenham, Gordon. *Genesis 16–50*. Word Biblical Commentary 2. Dallas: Word, 1994.

Wenham, Gordon J. *Genesis 1–15*. Word Biblical Commentary 1. Nashville: Nelson/ Nelson Reference and Electronic, 1987.

Werman, Cana. 'Jubilees 30: Building a Paradigm for the Ban on Intermarriage'. *Harvard Theological Review* 90, no. 1 (1997): 1–22.

Westermann, Claus. *Genesis 12–36: A Commentary*. Translated by John J. Scullion SJ from the German 1981 published by Neukirchener Verlag. Minneapolis: Augsburg, 1986.

Westermann, Claus. *Genesis 37–50: A Commentary*. Translated by John J. Scullion SJ from the German 1982 published by Neukirchener Verlag. Minneapolis: Augsburg, 1986.

Westermann, Claus. *Isaiah 40–66*. Translated by David M. G. Stalker from the German Das Buch Jesaia 40–66 (das Alte Testament Deutsch 19) first edition 1966 published by Göttingen: Vandenhoeck & Ruprecht. Old Testament Library. London: SCM, 1969.

Williams, James G. 'The Beautiful and the Barren: Conventions in Biblical Type-Scenes'. *Journal for the Study of the Old Testament* 17 (1980): 107–19.

Wintermute, O. S. 'Jubilees (Second Century B.C.)'. Pages 35–142 in *Old Testament Pseudepigrapha*. Vol. 2, *Expansions of the 'Old Testament' and Legends, Wisdom and Philosophical Literature, Prayers, Psalms, and Odes, Fragments of Lost Judeo-Hellenistic Works*. Edited by James H. Charlesworth. London: Darton, Longman & Todd, 1985.

Woolstenhulme, Katie J. 'Leah: The "Lost Matriarch" in *Genesis Rabbah*'. Pages 133–52 in *From Creation to Redemption: Progressive Approaches to Midrash. Proceedings of the Midrash Section, Society of Biblical Literature 7*. Edited by W. David Nelson and Rivka Ulmer. Judaism in Context 20. Piscataway, NJ: Gorgias Press, 2017.

Zimmerli, Walter. *A Commentary on the Book of Ezekiel, Chapters 1–24*. Translated by Ronald E. Clements from the German 1969 published by Neukirchener Verlag. Philadelphia: Fortress, 1979.

Zlotnick, Helena. *Dinah's Daughters: Gender and Judaism From the Hebrew Bible to Late Antiquity*. Philadelphia: University of Pennsylvania Press, 2002.

Zucker, David J. 'Sarah: The View of the Classical Rabbis'. Pages 221–52 in *'Perspectives on Our Father Abraham': Essays in Honour of Marvin R. Wilson*. Edited by Steven A. Hunt. Grand Rapids: Eerdmans, 2010.

Zucker, David J., and Rebecca Gates Brinton. '"The Other Woman": A Collaborative Jewish-Christian Study of Hagar'. Pages 339–83 in *'Perspectives on Our Father Abraham': Essays in Honour of Marvin R. Wilson*. Edited by Steven A. Hunt. Grand Rapids: Eerdmans, 2010a.

Index of References

Index of Authors

Lightning Source UK Ltd.
Milton Keynes UK
UKHW020614300622
405171UK00004B/204